DATE DUE

China and
the Christian Impact

This book is published as part of the joint publishing agreement established in 1977 between the Fondation de la Maison des Sciences de l'Homme and the Press Syndicate of the University of Cambridge. Titles published under this arrangement may appear in any European language or, in the case of volumes of collected essays, in several languages.

New books will appear either as individual titles or in one of the series which the Maison des Sciences de l'Homme and the Cambridge University Press have jointly agreed to publish. All books published jointly by the Maison des Sciences de l'Homme and the Cambridge University Press will be distributed by the Press throughout the world.

China and the Christian Impact

A Conflict of Cultures

Jacques Gernet
Professor of Chinese Intellectual and Social History,
Collège de France, Paris

Translated by Janet Lloyd

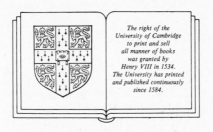

The right of the
University of Cambridge
to print and sell
all manner of books
was granted by
Henry VIII in 1534.
The University has printed
and published continuously
since 1584.

Cambridge University Press

Cambridge

London   New York   New Rochelle
Melbourne   Sydney

& Editions de la Maison des Sciences de l'Homme

Paris

Published by the Press Syndicate of the University of Cambridge
The Pitt Building, Trumpington Street, Cambridge CB2 1RP
32 East 57th Street, New York, NY 10022, USA
10 Stamford Road, Oakleigh, Melbourne, 3166, Australia
and Editions de la Maison des Sciences de l'Homme
54 Boulevard Raspail, 75270 Paris Cedex 06

Originally published in French as *Chine et christianisme*
by Editions Gallimard 1982
and © Editions Gallimard, Paris, 1982.
First published in English by Editions de la Maison des Sciences de l'Homme and
Cambridge University Press 1985 as *China and the Christian Impact*.
English translation © Maison des Sciences de l'Homme and Cambridge University Press
1985

Photoset and printed in Great Britain by
Redwood Burn Limited
Trowbridge, Wiltshire

British Library cataloguing in publication data
Gernet, Jacques
China and the Christian impact: a conflict of
cultures.
1. Missionaries – China – History
I. Title   II. Chine et christianisme. *English*
266′.0092′2   BV3417

Library of Congress cataloguing in publication data
Gernet, Jacques.
China and the Christian impact.
Translation of: Chine et christianisme.
Bibliography: p.
Includes index.
1. Christianity – China.   2. China – Religion.
I. Title.
BR1285.G4713   1986   275.1   85–7776

ISBN 0 521 26681 5 hard covers
ISBN 0 521 31319 8 paperback
ISBN 2 7351 0116 9 hard covers (France only)
ISBN 2 7351 0138 X paperback (France only)

Contents

The real miracle is not flying in the air or walking on the water: it is walking on the earth.

Entretiens de Lin-tsi (eleventh century)
by Paul Demiéville *Hermès*, VII, 1970, p. 12

Introduction

The subject of this book is China. Its theme is not the history of Christianity in that country, already the subject of countless other works, but rather Chinese reactions to this religion, which is a relatively new field. A fair amount is known of how the missionaries set about converting the Chinese but very little is known of what the Chinese themselves said about it. My aim is partly to satisfy a legitimate curiosity on this score and partly also to try to answer a very general question: to what extent do the reactions of the Chinese, at the time of their first contacts with the 'doctrine of the Master of Heaven' in the seventeenth century – before the debate was closed and stereotyped responses took over – reveal fundamental differences between Western and Chinese concepts of the world?

No doubt for many people the question does not arise: one implicit psychology – our own – valid for all periods and all societies is enough to explain everything. For the missionaries themselves, the Chinese were men just like any others, that is to say just like themselves, but corrupted by superstitions and false ideas and unfortunate enough to have remained in ignorance of the Revelation. All that was necessary was to undeceive them. And if Christianity found little success in China, if it was the object of violent attacks, it could only be for reasons that reflected poorly on the Chinese. Christianity was a religion that changed customs, called into question accepted ideas and, above all, threatened to undermine existing situations. Attention has been drawn to the jealousy of the Buddhist monks, who regarded the missionaries as dangerous competitors, the resentment of the employees and mandarins of the astronomical service at finding themselves supplanted by the Jesuit mathematicians introduced at Court, the rivalry between the missionaries and the Chinese men of letters[1] in respect of their authority over the common people and the connection established between the missionaries' evangelical efforts and threats to China from outside. There has been a tendency to see the enemies of Christianity as xenophobic conservatives, hostile to all new ideas, and to consider those who showed the missionaries sympathy or even went so far as to be baptised, as men more independent-minded towards Chinese traditions and more open to the world. Christianity has been associated with modernity. But

1

that thesis is contradicted by the facts: when the first contacts were made, from the last years of the sixteenth century to about 1630, the Jesuits provoked quite a large movement of interest and sympathy in China; but they won far fewer converts than might have been expected from such a warm welcome.

The milieu was not favourable and the best Christians were always those whom the missionaries had been able to raise since childhood in their own schools. The Rev. Father Vincent Shih observes:

the dependence of individuals on the group and the submission of the group to tradition ... rendered the individual members of a traditional society incapable of accepting anything new, the Gospel included. At any rate, the missionaries of the late nineteenth century found themselves caught in the following dilemma: to make Christianity accessible to the Chinese, they had either to suppress the novelty of its message or else modify the nature of Chinese society. As they could do neither, they set up 'Christian villages'.[2]

The action of the missionaries could thus only be truly effective within enclaves removed from the Chinese environment.

But it is a property of any society, not solely of so-called 'traditional' ones, to be founded upon a body of traditions accepted by all its members, who are, indeed, so little aware of the particular nature of these traditions that they consider them to be quite natural. These become rooted in history, are an inherent part of social behaviour, ways of thinking and feeling, and even languages. The missionaries, just like the Chinese literate elite, were the unconscious bearers of a whole civilisation. The reason why they so often came up against difficulties of translation is that different languages express, through different logics, different visions of the world and man.

There can be little doubt that, where the evangelical efforts of the missionaries were concerned, the Chinese reacted with a horror of anything new: it is even harder to imagine the reaction there would have been to missionaries coming from China to seventeenth-century Europe to preach a religion proclaimed to be universal. But we can do better than simply accept such evident facts; we can collect together and analyse what the Chinese themselves said and wrote, both favourably and critically, about the theses put forward by the missionaries and about their activities, noting their errors of interpretation and also the mistakes the missionaries made when examining the concepts of the Chinese. It is a subject of exceptional interest for it was around 1600 that, for the first time, real contacts were in fact made between two great civilisations that had developed entirely independently of each other.[3] The little that we know of the pre-Columbian civilisations cannot really be compared with the prodigious mass of information available on China, a country which developed book-printing as early as the tenth century.

China is part of the human and geographical *ensemble* situated on the other side of the great barrier of the Himalayan mountains. Compared with China, the civilisations that occupied the regions located between the valley of the Ganges and the Mediterranean share, as it were, a family resemblance that no doubt stems from the relative ease of exchanges and population movements. The extension of Indo-European languages and institutions within this vast area are proof of that.[4] A richness of mythology fulfilling important functions, an abundance of and precision in the representations connected with the gods, a development of ideas about the soul, individual salvation, defilement and religious sin are all characteristics to be found in the areas stretching from India to the shore of the Mediterranean. In these regions, man is *homo theologicus*. The same cannot be said of the Chinese: despite the importance of religious phenomena in China, as elsewhere, in China the place and functions of religion are different.

But it is clearly not simply a matter of religion, for it cannot be entirely dissociated from everything else. Consider the differences in languages, social forms and moral, political and philosophical, as well as religious traditions which necessarily separated Christian Europe from China, and it becomes clear that the questions posed by those first contacts cannot be limited to the narrow framework within which attempts have been made to contain them, namely that of an evangelical mission. Like it or not, it is the whole of the past that is called into question. Even if one accepts Roger Bastide's[5] thesis that Christianity is independent of its 'incarnation in Graeco-Roman culture', the fact remains that everything that goes to make up Christianity – the opposition in substance between an eternal soul and a perishable body, the kingdom of God and the earthly world, the concept of a God of truth, eternal and immutable, the dogma of the Incarnation – all this was more easily accessible to the inheritors of Greek thought than to the Chinese, who referred to quite different traditions. It is quite natural that such concepts should have seemed strange or incomprehensible to them.

The missionaries themselves were not unaware of this and the founder of the Jesuit mission, Matteo Ricci, who died in Peking in 1610, very well understood the necessity first to teach the Chinese to reason properly, that is, to distinguish between substance and accident, the spiritual soul and the material body, the creator and his creation, moral good and natural good. How else could the Christian truths be put across? Logic was inseparable from the religious dogma and the Chinese appeared to lack logic. It probably never crossed the minds of the missionaries that what seemed to them to be Chinese inaptitude was in fact a sign not only of different intellectual traditions but also of different mental categories and modes of thought. It no doubt never for an instant occurred to them that the differences in language might have something to do with all this.

The Chinese reactions to the writings and teachings of the missionaries make it easier to grasp something which does not in normal circumstances emerge so clearly: their virtue is that they illuminate what it is, precisely, that makes the Chinese traditions so different from our own. When analysed, they reveal a quite different conception of human agency, in which any opposition between reason and senses and any separation between the spiritual and the temporal are unknown. This accounts for their different concepts of man and the universe, their different moralities, the different relations for them between religion and politics, and their different modes of philosophising. All that we, from our Western point of view, regard as anomalous stems, on the contrary, from a faultless logic. In Chinese concepts, everything depends upon everything else, all things are connected, and this coherence makes the historical character of the mental schemata that have prevailed in the West stand out more clearly in contrast.

It is true that great civilisations are complex, incorporating many elements from different ages and that in each period one comes across a multiplicity of sometimes opposed currents. Who could claim to know all the answers where China is concerned, or to distinguish clearly all the effects of ancient religious and philosophical traditions, as well as those of Buddhism and of the concepts inherited from the great neo-Confucian synthesis of the eleventh and twelfth centuries and later syncretisms? And variations between different social milieux add further to the complexity. But the present work claims to be no more than a modest attempt. In it, it will almost always be the Chinese and the missionaries speaking and it is their dialogue that will enable us to pick out the fundamental differences in their inspiration.

Although this study does not set out to be a history of the missions, a word must be said about the policies of the missionaries. It will not otherwise be possible to understand certain of the reactions of the Chinese and the evolution of their relations with the foreign priests. Anxious to enter into relations with the literate and ruling circles, the Jesuits, who were the first to install themselves in China in a lasting fashion – from 1583 on – quite soon realised the necessity for them to make a great effort to adapt to a society and civilisation so different from their own. If they are virtually the only missionaries we shall be considering, that is because they were virtually the only ones who tried to learn about the Chinese traditions of learning and to engage in a dialogue with the educated classes. They were also the most numerous.[6] Other orders for the most part simply tried to convert the popular classes. Now, at that level, doctrines hardly ever came into it. It was the saintliness attributed to the priests and the efficacy ascribed to their religious actions that mattered.

The Jesuits tried to win over the Chinese with the scientific knowledge of Europe and to exploit any apparent analogies between Chinese and Christian traditions in morality and religion. Their early successes are to a large extent attributable to these methods. However, it was not long before the veracity of these resemblances began to be questioned on both sides. Just as there were, as we shall see, two kinds of men among the missionaries – the optimists, who put their trust in 'natural reason' and were ready to believe that the Chinese disposition was favourable to the Christian faith, and the pessimists, who could see nothing but superstition and atheism in China – similarly, on the Chinese side the missionaries found both sympathisers and enemies, the former marvelling at finding similarities between their own traditions and the teaching of these men from so far away, the latter condemning everything in the 'doctrine of the Master of Heaven' which stood in manifest contradiction to the social, political and moral order of China and also to the dominant concepts of China. The former favoured a syncretism based on the postulate of a universal human spirit, the latter pursued a sometimes vehement and passionate line that revealed fundamental differences between the two mental universes.

Sources

There is a mass of information of diverse origins on the first contacts and the first reactions on both the Chinese and the Western sides. It is provided by the missionaries themselves: letters,[1] memoirs and treatises written in Western languages, but also many works in Chinese composed with the help of Chinese men of letters. These missionaries were not always in agreement on the question of what the Chinese really thought, nor on what concessions should be made to their traditions. It is sometimes useful to compare their opinions. It was under the influence of their own educations as Europeans of the sixteenth and seventeenth centuries and their own prejudices and convictions that they made their judgements on China. Their accounts are usually inspired by their preoccupations with religious edification and apologetics. But if we bear in mind these inevitable emphases, their writings can provide us with often precious information which confirms or complements what we can learn from Chinese sources. Furthermore, their favourite themes of preaching reveal the principal difficulties that faced them and also the arguments which they learned from experience to be the most effective.

But the harvest is clearly richer on the Chinese side. Indeed, it would be impossible to take into account the vast body of seventeenth-century Chinese literature in its entirety. It is full of scattered remarks about the missionaries and their doctrines. But there are unlikely to be any arguments that are not incorporated or already expressed in the documents either translated or analysed in the present work. These documents are extremely varied: prefaces written by sympathisers or converts for works in Chinese by the missionaries, passages that appear in collections of miscellaneous observations, bibliographical notes, letters, short works and treatises composed by converts; but there are also pamphlets and works composed by the adversaries or declared enemies of the doctrine of the Master of Heaven. Considered as libellous, sometimes cited but never systematically studied, this anti-Christian literature, only a portion of which has – quite by chance – survived, reveals the confusions that arose over the clash between Chinese and Christian traditions and indicates the dangers to the social and political order of China that the missionaries and their doctrine represented.

It was through books that knowledge of the doctrine of the Master of Heaven and other new ideas introduced by the missionaries spread. Thanks to wood-block printing, books could be reproduced rapidly and cheaply and their predominant role as the chief means of diffusing ideas and knowledge[2] seems to have come as a surprise to the missionaries, who immediately endeavoured to turn it to their own advantage.[3] Ricci notes in his memoirs that, thanks to printed books, 'the name of Christian law is spreading faster and further'.[4] Elsewhere, he writes:

Literacy is so flourishing in this kingdom that there are few people among them who know nothing of books. And all their own sects have spread and developed more by means of books than through preaching and speeches made among the people. That is something that has been a great help to our people in the teaching of the prayers necessary for Christians, for they immediately learn them by heart, either by reading the printed *Christian Doctrine* themselves or by having it read to their relatives and friends, for there is never a shortage of people who know how to read.[5]

Father Alfonso Vagnone, who was in China from 1604 until his death in 1640, also recognises the great importance of the role of books: 'Among the Chinese, books are more persuasive and make the doctrine more easily understood than do disputations undertaken on the subject of our Law.'[6] It was thus through books that the Jesuit missionaries made their teaching known throughout China and also through books that they were attacked and resisted. That constitutes a great difference compared to the situation in India, which lacked any easy way of reproducing the written word and where all teaching was oral.[7]

There now follow a few notes on the principal works, written both in Western languages and in Chinese, which we have used in our analysis.

Nicolas Trigault, a Flemish Jesuit who arrived in China at the end of 1610, returned from Macao in 1613 with a manuscript work by Matteo Ricci entitled *Della entrata della Compagnia di Giesù e Christianità nella Cina*. It was divided into five books and comprised a compendium of general information on China (Book 1), followed by a history of the beginnings of the Jesuit mission there since the year 1582 down to the month before the author's death in Peking on 11 May 1610. The text, brought back to Rome in 1614, was completed by Trigault himself on the basis of the reports in Portuguese by Fathers Longobardo, Vagnone and Cattaneo of their own respective stays in China, and extracts from the annual letters in Latin for the years 1610 and 1611 by Father P. Sabatino de Ursis. Ricci's manuscript was not found again until 1909, and during the following years it was printed, together with the correspondence of the first two missionaries in China, Ruggieri and Ricci, under the direction of Tacchi Venturi with the title, *Opere storiche del P. Matteo Ricci*. In 1942–9, the same texts, without the correspondence but with fuller notes and identifications of people's names, appeared in another three-volume edition by Pasquale d'Elia with the title, *Fonti Ricciane*.

On his return to Europe, Trigault brought out, in Augsburg in 1615, a Latin translation of Ricci's work together with its additions in Portuguese and Latin. This translation, reworked to the taste of a European public, was in its turn the subject of numerous translations into many European languages between 1616 and 1625. Trigault's work, which is less exact than the original, was recently reprinted at last, in English, by Louis J. Gallagher (*China in the Sixteenth Century: The Journal of Matthew Ricci*, 1953) and in a French version, which had first appeared in Lyons in 1617 with the title, *Histoire de l'expédition chrétienne au royaume de Chine* (ed. Desclée de Brouwer, 1978). As a general rule, I have referred to the original text in Italian, which contains much information of exceptional interest.

Ten years after his arrival in China in 1583, Ricci, on the orders of Valignano, the Visitor of Japan and China, had set about studying the Chinese Classics with a view to producing a new catechism. The first one, entitled *A True Account of the Master of Heaven* (*Tianzhu shilu*) and composed after a preliminary version produced in Latin, the *Vera et brevis divinarum rerum expositio* (1581), was published in 1584. A first draft of the new work was completed in 1596 and a Latin translation of it was submitted to the Bishop of Japan, Luis Cerqueira, in the following year, but the definitive text, somewhat different from the early draft, dates only from 1601. The style had been revised by a talented member of the literate elite by the name of Feng Yingjing (1555–1606). Ricci had benefited from his discussions both with members of the literate elite and with Buddhist monks in Nanking and Peking over the years 1599–1601. The work failed to obtain the *imprimatur* from the Goa Inquisition and was printed by wood-block for the first time only in 1604 (or the December of 1603) with the title, *Tianxue shiyi* (*The True Meaning of the Heavenly Studies*). But numerous reprints followed under the more popular title of *Tianzhu shiyi* (*The True Meaning of [the Doctrine of] the Master of Heaven*).[8]

As Ricci explains, the work was not really a catechism. In effect, it was only concerned with those Christian beliefs which, he said, 'could be proved by natural reasons', such as God the creator of Heaven and Earth, the immortality of the soul, the existence of a paradise and a hell. The author also went to great pains openly to refute the ideas of the Buddhists and Taoists and, in a more veiled manner, also those of Confucianism itself, both ancient and modern.

Here is a general plan of the work:

Part I

(1) That the Master of Heaven first created Heaven, Earth and the Ten Thousand Beings; that he directs and succours them. Proofs of his existence.

(2) In which it is explained that people of the present time do not recognise the Master of Heaven. Ricci accuses Buddhism and Taoism of being founded upon the void and nothingness.

(3) That the soul of man, unlike that of animals, does not disappear.

(4) In which false notions concerning the spirits and the soul of man are refuted and it is explained that the Ten Thousand Beings of the world cannot all be of one substance as the Chinese thesis holds.

Part II

(5) In which the lies relating to the six ways of rebirth in Buddhism and the prohibition against the murder of animals are refuted, and the correct meaning of fasting is revealed.

(6) In which it is explained that intention must not be abolished (it is intention that qualifies an action as good or bad) and in which it is shown that, after death, there is retribution in paradise and in hell for all the good and bad things that men have done during their lifetimes.

(7) In which it is shown that human nature (when identified with reason) is fundamentally good.

(8) On Western moral concepts, the celibacy of priests and the coming of Jesus into the world.

A French translation of the *Tianzhu shiyi* by Father Charles Jacques (1688–1728) was published in *Choix de lettres édifiantes* (2nd edn, Brussels, 1838, vol. II, pp. 1–179) under the title, 'Entretiens d'un lettré chinois et d'un docteur européen, par le P. Ricci'. This translation, in which the two interlocutors speak like Europeans, gives a very inexact idea of how the work must have been read by the Chinese.

We owe one of the texts that is most interesting for the history of Chinese reactions to Christian theses to the disagreements between the Jesuits in China over the best methods to employ with regard to the Chinese. It was produced by Father Longobardo following an inquiry pursued over several years among a few members of the literate elite, and its title, in French, is *Traité sur quelques points de la religion des Chinois*. But the first version of this work was in Latin and entitled *De Confucio ejusque doctrina tractatus*. The treatise was written between 1622 and 1625. It refuted the idea that the Chinese had ever known anything 'that bore any relation to [ideas about] God, the angels or the rational soul', and it warned against the very real danger of confusion between Chinese and Christian ideas among the literate elite. It was condemned to be burned by the Vice-Provincial, Francisco Furtado, between 1635 and 1641, a time when the tendency towards compromise was prevailing in the Chinese mission. However, it was preserved in a Spanish version, which was published in Madrid by Domingo Navarette in 1676–9 in his *Tratados historicos, politicos, ethicos de la monarchia de China*. A French translation of the Spanish text was eventually published in Paris in 1701 by the Foreign Missions, a society created in Paris in 1658, under a misleadingly anodyne and less precise title than the original one: an infernal device to be launched against the Jesuits when the quarrel over religious rituals was raging. This treatise, which made a profound impression upon Leibniz, had the merit of setting out, for the first time in a Western language, the philosophical ideas that were the most widely diffused in China, and of reflecting relatively faithfully the opinions of the members of the literate elite of the period, both Christian and otherwise. Longobardo's work bears testimony to a remarkable critical mind: the author seeks to understand what is 'the doctrine of the literate elite, unadulterated and free from admixtures of the interpretations that we Christians provide'.[9] It was a recognition of the fact that the missionaries usually tended to delude themselves about Chinese ideas.

The *Traité sur quelques points importants de la mission de Chine* (1668) by Father Antoine de Sainte-Marie, published in Paris in 1701 in the wake of Longobardo's treatise, is a work probably inspired by a *Relatio Sinae sectarum* completed by the same author in 1662.

Antonio de Caballero, alias Sainte-Marie (April 1602–May 1669), was a Spaniard who had entered the Franciscan order in 1618. In 1628 he arrived in the Philippines, moving from there to Fu'an in Fujian province, which he reached in 1633 after stopping off in Danshui, close to what is nowadays known as Taibei, in Formosa. After being virtually imprisoned by the Jesuits during a voyage to Nanking, he installed himself in Fu'an and Dingtou, where he discovered that Chinese Christians were continuing to practise their own traditional cults, being authorised to do so on certain conditions by the Jesuit missionary, Giulio Aleni. This was the origin of the first controversy between the Jesuits and other orders. Taken prisoner on the western coast of Formosa by the Dutch as he was returning to Tainan, he was made to work as a convict in Batavia and Ternate. After eight months he was released and in June 1637 reached Manila, where he made his first report on the question of Chinese rituals and ceremonies. In 1640 he moved to Macao but was expelled in October 1644. In 1645 he was promoted by the Pope to the position of apostolic prefect and asked to return to China. He landed near Quanzhou in Fujian province in 1649 just at the time when the Manchus were installing themselves in that province. He wanted to found a mission in Korea but was obliged to give up the idea and in 1650 he settled in the region of Tianjin and Jinan in Shandong province. In 1659 he turned up in Hangzhou, where he questioned Martino Martini on the subject of the pontifical decree of 1656, which was favourable to the Chinese rituals. In September 1660 Caballero addressed a memorandum to the Cardinals of Propaganda on the subject of his interrogation of Martini and Martini's replies. He wrote another treatise on rituals in Jinan, dated 20 August 1661. But it was in October 1662 that he completed his *Relatio Sinae sectarum*. It comprises three parts:

(1) the school of ancient and modern Chinese philosophers
(2) the sects of spirits thriving among the common people
(3) the arrival of the Jesuits and the impact of their faith

Following a general order for the expulsion of all missionaries, Caballero was arrested and sent to Canton in 1665 and there he died in 1669.

The work published in Paris in 1701 purports to be a translation from the Spanish and carries the note, 'In China, in the province and town of Kham-tum [Canton], known in the Chinese language as Kham-cheu-fu [Guangzhou fu], 9 April 1668', with a postscript dated 9 December 1668. It no doubt incorporates passages from the *Relatio* and other earlier works. There is an excellent biography of Caballero in *DMB* which, however, does not mention the *Traité*, translated into French and published in 1701.

The second volume of the *TDXB* reproduces a work in Chinese by Caballero, the *Tianru yin*, or *On the Perfect Coincidence between the Doctrine of Heaven [Christianity] and Confucianism*, in which Caballero gives a Christian interpretation to certain phrases from the Four Books.

The *Poxie ji* (*PXJ*), or *Collection for the Destruction of Vicious Doctrines*, in eight volumes, is the richest collection of anti-Christian writings that we possess. It is relatively rare as the most easily accessible copies, in a late edition produced in Japan in 1855, are located in the Bibliothèque Nationale and the Library of Congress in Washington. It contains a general preface dated 28 December 1639, the work of one Xu Changzhi,[10] and three other earlier prefaces (volume III of the *PXJ*), one written in 1637 by the censor Yan Maoyou, another written in 1638 by Jiang Dejing, and a third written in the spring of 1639 by Huang Zhen. The presence of these four successive prefaces and the fact that the *PXJ* contains writings later than the two older prefaces indicates that it was compiled in a number of stages.

The first two volumes contain texts relating to the lawsuit against the missionaries of Nanking in 1616 and 1617. With the exception of the three most ancient polemical texts known (two by Yu Chunxi, a member of the literate elite with Buddhist sympathies, who died in 1621, and one by the Buddhist master, Zhuhong, dating from 1614), all the dated texts which appear in the *PXJ* belong to the period 1635–9. Many of the texts collected in the *PXJ* come from southern Fujian province and were produced for the purpose of countering the influence of the preaching of Father Giulio Aleni. They must all have been written after 1633, which, according to Huang Zhen's preface, was the date of Aleni's arrival in the region of Zhangzhou.

The most extensive work included in the *PXJ* is *The Aid to Refutation* (*Zuopi* (*ZP*)) in ten chapters, by Xu Dashou. It takes up one whole volume in the collection. Scarcely anything is known about the author except that he came from Deqing, in the prefecture of Huzhou to the south of Lake Taihu in Zhejiang province, and was the son of the civil servant and philosopher, Xu Fuyuan (1535–1604). Xu Dashou had clearly received a classical education but himself states in his work that he had studied Buddhism and Taoism. He gives an apparently accurate account of his discussions with Father Giulio Aleni during the period when Aleni was preaching in southern Fujian, between 1633 and 1639.

On the other hand, Xu Dashou's father, Xu Fuyun, is quite well known. After receiving his doctorate in 1562, at the beginning of the Longqing period (1567–73), he had been appointed to Guangdong province, where he had organised the capture of some Japanese pirates. He was prefect of Jianchang in Jiangxi province, then governor of Fujian province in 1592 and subsequently, from 1594 onwards, held a number of important posts in Nanking. He was promoted to be minister for war in Peking but was obliged to resign before ever assuming his duties because of an accusation lodged against him. Xu Fuyuan had won fame during his years in Fujian province through a project to confiscate one-sixth of the lands taken over by the Buddhist monasteries, and also through the fortification and agricultural exploitation of an island off the shores of Fujian province. There is a biographical note on Xu Fuyuan in the *Mingshi*, Chapter 283, and a note on his philosophical ideas in the *Mingru xue'an*, Chapter 41.[11]

Not much care to preserve the anti-Christian literature appears to have been taken among the literate elite. It is only by chance that the *PXJ* survived. Many of the authors whose works appear in this collection knew one another and appear to have been members of a quite limited circle. It is also quite by chance that other anti-Christian writings were discovered quite recently. One case in point is the *Pixie ji*, discovered in 1946 or 1947 by Monsignor Fang Hao, on the stall of a Peking street bookseller.[12] Despite being called a 'collection', it is quite a short work, containing a preface by the Buddhist monk, Gao'an; the correspondence exchanged between a member of the literate elite by the name of Zhong Zhengzhi, a native of Suzhou in Jiangsu province, and a *chan*[13] master called Jiming; and two polemical texts composed by Zhong Zhengzhi. The first, entitled *Tianxue chuzheng* (*TXCZ*), or *First Questions on the Heavenly Studies* (that is to say, on the teachings of the missionaries), includes an introduction which refers to the *Shengxiang lueshuo* (*Brief Explanations concerning Holy Images*), a work by João da Rocha, printed for the first time in 1619. The second text, entitled *Second Questions on the Heavenly Studies* (*Tianxue zaizheng*) (*TXZZ*), cites a work by Father Aleni, the *Sanshan lun xueji*, printed for the first time in 1627 or 1628, and the *Shengjiao yueyan* (*Brief Remarks on the Holy Doctrine*) by João Soerio, first printed in 1600. The cyclical indications that serve to date the preface must therefore correspond to the year 1643, and the collection as a whole cannot date from much earlier.

Another fortuitous find was that of a work in 16 chapters, the *Qingshu jingtan* by one Wang Qiyuan, with a preface dated 1623, which was also discovered, by Ch'en Shou-i, on a Peking street bookseller's stall, in 1930. Chapter 15 of this work contains a critical study of the 'doctrine of the Master of Heaven'.[14]

The most important work in the anti-Christian literature of the beginning of the Manchu period is the *Budeyi* (*I cannot contain myself* or *I must burst out at last*) by Yang Guangxian (1597–1669), the principal enemy of the missionaries at the time. It comprises works produced by the author at different dates. The first pamphlet is dated 1659, the later ones 1664. One of these is entitled the *Niejing* or the *Mirror of Monsters*[15] and is a critical study of the astronomical ideas introduced by the missionaries. The note on Yang Guangxian in the *Chouren zhuan* (vol. 36), a work on Chinese and Western astronomers and mathematicians by the great Ruan Yuan (1799), quotes Qian Daxin, who records a remark made by the philosopher Dai Zhen (1723–77) to the effect that the Europeans (*Ouluoba ren*) would buy all the copies of the *Budeyi* they could find, considering it worth paying their weight in gold, in order to burn them, so much did they abominate them. A modern edition of the *Budeyi* (a photocopy made in 1929) contains a final note by one Cheng Mian-zhuang, who claims that as soon as this book appeared it fetched sums of up to 200 ounces of silver from Westerners who were anxious to burn it, so that, he adds, 'the work has practically disappeared'. It had become extremely rare in the Yongzheng (1723–35) and Qianlong (1736–96) periods.[16]

The *Budeyi* is reprinted in volume III of the *TDXB*.

There is one Japanese work attacking Christianity which is the object of a painstaking study by George Elison.[17] It has a number of particularly original features and testifies to the fact that evangelical work in Japan followed a much more direct line than in China, where the missionaries were much more cautious, laying emphasis upon morality and the refutation of Confucian and Buddhist theses, and communicating Christian mysteries and sacraments only to initiates. However, this Japanese work of criticism also very often resorts to similar arguments to those of the Chinese.

Apart from the *Hai Yaso* or *Anti-Jesus* (1606),[18] the most remarkable work is by an apostate by the name of Fukan. Fukan, or Fucan as the missionaries spelled his name, a native of Kyôto and baptised Fabian, had entered the Society of Jesus at the age of 20, in 1586. In 1605, when he had become a subordinate brother, he wrote a dialogue between two Japanese ladies, expressing their satisfaction with the Christian truths and their disgust with the errors of Buddhism, Confucianism and Shinto. Later, however, Fucan abjured his faith, having reached the conclusion that Christianity was a perverse religion and that the teaching of the Bateren (the Fathers) was 'clever and apparently reasonable but in reality false'. Perhaps he had been disappointed by the humiliating, subordinate role which the missionaries assigned to the Japanese members of their Society. At all events, he became a redoubtable enemy of the Fathers. His *Hai Daiusu* (literally, *On the Destruction of the Deus*), published in 1620, is a methodical refutation of all Christian theses, using logical arguments or comparisons with Confucian or Buddhist ideas.

Together with the *Hai Yaso* and the *Hai Daiusu*, George Elison includes a number of texts which appeared after the proscription of Christianity and the closing of Japan. They are the *Kengiroku* (1636) by a Japanese apostate by the name of Ferreira, the *Kirishitan monogatari* (1639) and the *Ha Kirishitan* (1662), but they are of less interest.

Chapter 1

From sympathy to hostility

An enterprise of seduction

When the first Jesuit missionaries, the Italians Ruggieri and Ricci, installed themselves in what was to prove a definitive fashion in southern
China in 1583, the Chinese coasts were closely guarded on account of the
constant risks of piracy and abiding memories of the terrible Sino-
Japanese pirate raids of the mid-sixteenth century (the Wokou). The
Portuguese and the Castillians, highly combative individuals, were
viewed with particular distrust and the two priests had to persuade the
Chinese authorities that they had nothing, even remotely, to do with
such people. All previous attempts to gain a foothold in China, by
missionaries of other orders, had failed owing to insufficient prudence
or excessive zeal. It is understandable that, having managed to settle in
Zhaoqing, at that time the administrative capital of the provinces of
Guangdong and Guangxi, to the west of Canton, Ruggieri and Ricci took
great care not to provide any pretext for their expulsion.

In a letter to the General of the Jesuits dated 25 January 1584, Michele
Ruggieri wrote as follows:

In the early stages it is necessary to proceed very cautiously with this nation and
not to behave with indiscreet zeal, for we should very easily risk losing the advantages which we have gained and which we can imagine no way of recovering. I
say this because this nation is extremely hostile to foreigners and in particular
fears the Portuguese and Castillians, whom they regard as aggressive people.[1]

In another letter, dated 30 May of the same year, Ruggieri again stresses
the need to act 'cautiously and delicately' and is apprehensive at the pros-
pect of other missionaries entering China and compromising everything
with their clumsy impatience.[2]

The general policies of the Jesuit mission was laid down right from the
start: to avoid shocking people and to proceed unobtrusively, following
devious paths if need be. These precautions were all the more necessary
given that the objective was first to win the friendship of the most culti-
vated circles in order, eventually, to reach the Court: once the emperor
was converted, it was thought, the game would be won, since the whole

of Chinese society rested upon hierarchical relations. It was an opinion
that appeared to be borne out by the example of Japan, where the conversion of the daimyô of Kyûshû had been followed by that of all their
subjects.

Immediately following his arrival in Macao, Ruggieri wrote:

The greatest difficulty in converting this kingdom of China lies not in any will to
resist on their part – for they have no difficulty in understanding matters to do
with God and they understand that our law is holy and good[3] – but in the great
subordination that they observe in the obedience of some to others, depending
on their rank, all the way up to the king. That is why everything depends upon
the king's eventual desire and wish to summon the Fathers to his presence, for I
do not doubt that he would immediately grant them leave to preach and teach
their doctrine to all those who wished to receive it.[4]

Later on, Ricci came round to believing that the missionaries would one
day be in a position to exert a certain pressure upon the emperor and the
Chinese administration by facing them with a *fait accompli*. He wrote as
follows:

When there are already a fair number of Christians, it will not be impossible to
send a memorandum to the king, the result of which will at least be that the
Christians will be allowed to live according to their law, given that it does not run
contrary to the laws of China.[5]

This was, in effect, the procedure that was to be adopted once the Christian communities had been developed.

The first Jesuit missionaries had assumed the appearance and names
of Buddhist monks, hoping in this way to penetrate China and convert
the Chinese more easily. But they were surprised to find that in this
country priests had neither so much prestige nor so much authority as
they enjoyed in Europe. They therefore begged leave to assume the
costume of the literate elite instead of the robes of the Buddhist monks,
with whom up until then they had been more or less confused since they
were considered simply as another of their type. Ricci became initiated
in the Classics and he appeared in the costume of the literate elite for the
first time in May 1595, twelve years after his arrival in Zhaoqing. He had
learned that if he wished to be well received in Chinese high society,
what he should do was present himself not as a man of religion but as a
layman and a 'Western man of letters' (*xishi*).[6]

To gain acceptance in these circles where, as he himself observed, 'the
things of religion' were not greatly appreciated, Ricci was obliged to
present himself as a moralist, philosopher and scholar. And to start with,
it was with the words of a layman that he attempted to communicate with
the literate elite, adopting a form of discourse that was fashionable at the

end of the Ming period: that of the philosophical debate (*jiangxue*). He says so himself, in a letter written during 1596:

Since we have banished from our persons the name of monks, which for them is the equivalent of that of our friars (or monastic brothers), but with an extremely lowly and dishonourable connotation, we shall, in these early days, open neither church nor temple, *simply a preaching house, as do their own most famous preachers.*[7]

What Ricci calls a preaching house corresponds to the Chinese term *shuyuan*, which we should nowadays translate as 'academy'. Thus Ricci was anxious to be taken for a philosopher among the Chinese philosophers and did not wish to reveal himself as what he was: a priest who had come to preach the true God to pagans.

In another letter, he wrote:

I think that we shall open no more churches, but instead a preaching house and we will say mass in private in another chapel, although the hall where we receive visitors may serve this purpose for the moment: for one preaches better and more fruitfully through conversations than through sermons.[8]

Although one of Ruggieri's and Ricci's first concerns when they arrived in Zhaoqing in 1583 had been to open a church there, Ricci subsequently gave up the idea of founding any others. Although they had hurried as early as 1584 to print a catechism, which had received from the mandarins of China the polite reception due to all foreign curiosities, Ricci decided, once he acquired a better understanding of Chinese reactions, to reserve the revelation of Christian mysteries for those who already showed themselves to be favourably disposed towards the faith. And he made a study of the Four Books of the 'sect of Confucius' so that this might help him to prepare a new catechism 'of which we are in great need, for the one which was produced initially was not as well received as it should have been'.[9] But the new work, *The True Meaning [of the Doctrine] of the Master of Heaven*, was to bear scant resemblance to a catechism.

The prudence of this policy accounted for much of Ricci's success within literate circles. It also explains how it was that the Chinese took so long to understand the true intentions of the missionaries and the exclusive character of the Christian faith. They were impressed above all by the resemblances between the missionaries' preaching and their own tradition of private academies (*shuyuan*), in which certain masters would dispense their particular moral and philosophical interpretations of the Classics. As E. Zürcher points out, the atmosphere of the *shuyuan* did have something solemn and almost holy about it. Each meeting began with a ceremony in honour of the founder and Confucius. The rules of conduct were codified according to a convention (*huiyue*), which often included pious hymns sung by choirs of young boys. It was not unusual to come across numerous moral instructions strikingly expressed in the form of slogans such as 'the four essential things', 'the two illusions', 'the nine things to be avoided'.[10] As Zürcher comments, it is not surprising that the Jesuit Fathers felt quite at home in these surroundings.

In a letter dated 4 November 1595, written from Nanchang, the capital of Jiangxi province, Ricci lists the reasons for his fame as follows: the first is that, although a foreigner from so far away, he can speak and write Chinese relatively correctly; the second is that he possesses an astonishing memory and has learned by heart 'the Four Books of the sect of Confucius'; the third, his knowledge in the field of mathematics; the fourth, the curious objects that he carries with him (clocks, prisms of Venetian glass, religious paintings, Western books); the fifth, the talents as an alchemist with which he is credited; and the last of all, the doctrine that he teaches. And he goes on to add: 'those who come for the last reason are the least numerous'.[11]

With his great beard and his scholar's costume,[12] Matteo Ricci was much admired by all who met him. His modesty and discretion, his respect for Chinese customs, his use of the Chinese language both spoken and written, his knowledge of the Four Books and the Classics, his little moral works, his long treatise on foreign philosophy and his mathematical learning must all have contributed to his success among the literate and the authorities. He was called 'the extraordinary man' (*jiren*). Many people were anxious to see and entertain him and Ricci complains in one of his letters of no longer having a moment to himself – to the point where he would sometimes even forget to say mass.[13]

One of the first accounts of Ricci from the Chinese side comes from Li Zhi (1527–1602), a famous philosopher noted for his independence of mind and sensationalist works, who had met him several times in Nanking. In a letter to a friend, he wrote:

I have safely received your questions on the subject of Li Xitai [Ricci]. Xitai is a man from the regions of the great West who has travelled over 100,000 *li* to reach China. After a journey of more than 40,000 *li*,[14] he first arrived in south India, where he learned of the existence of Buddhism. It was only when he arrived in the southern seas, in Canton, that he learned that our kingdom of the great Ming had had first Yao and Shun, then the Duke of Zhou and Confucius.[15] He then stayed for about twenty years in Zhaoqing,[16] and there is not a single one of our books that he has not read. He asked an old man to write down for him the sounds and meanings [of the written characters]; he asked someone who was expert in the philosophy of the Four Books to explain their general meaning to him; he asked someone who was learned in the commentaries of the Six Classics to give him all the necessary explanations. Now he is perfectly capable of speaking our language, writing our characters and conforming to our conventions of good behaviour. He is an altogether remarkable man. Although personally he is extremely refined, his manner is as simple as can be. In a noisy and confused gathering of several dozen people, with everybody speaking at once, the arguments that he follows do not disturb him at all.[17] Among all the people I have ever seen, there is not his equal. [The fact is that] people err through an excess of either inflexibility or compliancy – either they make a show of their intelligence or their minds are limited. They are all inferior to him. But I do not really know what he has come to do here. I have now met him three times and I still do not know what he is here for. I think it would be much too stupid for him to want to substitute his own teaching for that of the Duke of Zhou and Confucius. So that is surely not the reason.[18]

That is a great Chinese scholar's account of Ricci around 1600. It expresses not only his great admiration for the man but also some perplexity as to his motives for being in China. The last remark shows that Li Zhi had sensed the missionary's strangely passionate conviction, but his bafflement is understandable: Ricci was taking good care not to reveal his true intentions. He contented himself with discussions and reference to the Classics, endeavouring to give them a meaning favourable to his own theses.

In 1596, he wrote:

To be sure, to this day, we cannot explain all the mysteries of our holy faith; nevertheless, we make progress by establishing its fundamental principles: God the creator of heaven and earth, the immortal soul, recompense for the good and punishment for the wicked – all things that are unknown to them and have not, until now, been believed; and they all listen to us with such contentment and so many tears that, very often, they burst into veritable paeons of praise, as if all our discourse consisted of discoveries made solely by us. It seems to us that, in these early days, there is a beginning of things that might well become confirmed.[19]

Ricci makes similar remarks in connection with his long treatise entitled *The True Meaning [of the Doctrine] of the Master of Heaven*, which is presented as a polemical work on the subject of Chinese and Buddhist beliefs. He writes:

This work did not touch upon all the mysteries of our holy faith, which should only be explained to catechumens and Christians; it considered only a few principles, in particular those which in some way can be proved by natural reason and understood through natural knowledge itself . . . such as the presence in the universe of a lord and creator of all things, which he maintains in perpetuity, the immortality of the soul and retribution through God for good and wicked actions in the next life, the falsity of the transmigration of the soul into the bodies of other men and also into those of animals – a belief to which many people here adhere – and other things of a similar nature.[20]

From the moment it appeared, this great treatise met with a remarkable success: it was written in good Chinese (Ricci's friends had made sure of that); it made many references to the Classics and sought to combat Buddhism with new arguments. Even if the 'Western man of letters' who is presented in it did put forward some curious and strange theses, its good points at least found favour among the literate elite who were hostile to Buddhist influences and preoccupied with questions of morality. Throughout, Ricci clearly makes a remarkable effort to adapt to the ideas of literate circles although, misled by his own traditions, he does sometimes interpret them incorrectly. Many men of letters praised the talent he showed in his skill in argumentation. For a foreigner it was in every respect regarded as a kind of *tour de force*.

However, other less important writings were even more successful: a number of short works on Stoic morality composed by Ricci[21] and a treatise by Father Sabatino de Ursis, which gave practical advice about overcoming one's passions, the *Qike*, or *The Seven Victories [over the Seven Deadly Sins]* (1604).

But Ricci was not content simply to appear as a philosopher and moralist; his map of the world and his teaching in mathematics and astronomy contributed just as much to his fame. And it was following his example that the seventeenth- and eighteenth-century Jesuits of China turned themselves into mathematicians, geographers, astronomers, engineers, doctors, painters and musicians.[22] It was by these means that they managed first to attract those interested in the sciences and technology and then to win the appreciation of the emperors, into whose service they entered. Furthermore, right from the start, Ricci and his companions were determined to make the most of the interest the Chinese showed in certain objects imported from Europe, and they would sometimes make presents of these to those whose sympathy it was advantageous to win. Clocks and paintings were even offered as tribute to the emperors. A description of Peking at the end of the Ming period[23] mentions, among other strange objects introduced by the Westerners: the hour-glass (the Chinese were using water clepsydras and incense clocks), the astrolabe, the suction pump and Galileo's telescope. The author describes the telescope as follows: 'it resembles tubes of bamboo fitting one into another. When folded up, it measures 30 cm but when stretched right out it reaches a length of about 1.50 m. When one applies one's eyes to it, one sees small things as large and the distance as close.' The same author also mentions the clavichord, the forerunner of our modern

piano. The list is by no means complete, for the missionaries also imported Venetian prisms made in Murano, where the glass industry continues
to flourish to this day (Ricci presented two of these prisms to the Court
eunuchs, for them to give to the emperor); religious paintings, which
much impressed the Chinese because they produced an illusion of relief
and were so lifelike;[24] bound and gilded European books with illustrations;[25] verge and folio clocks, the unique interest of which stemmed
from the fact that they chimed the hours, for which reason they were
dubbed 'the bells that chime of their own accord' (*ziming zhong*). They
were, in fact, much less exact than the clepsydras and frequently went
wrong.[26]

Ricci said that he owed much of his fame among the literate elite to his
map of the world and his scientific teaching (in mathematics and astronomy). The sciences (and technology, too) not only attracted quite a large
number of the literate elite to the missionaries, but also increased their
prestige and swelled their audience. That is a point upon which the
missionaries' friends and enemies alike were in agreement: the principal
success of the 'Western Barbarians' stemmed from their calendrical
methods,[27] from their being able – thanks to their astronomical instruments[28] – to reform the calendar, and from the fact that they helped to
make cannons. They were judged to be of use to the state and the
defence of the empire. That is why, despite the scandal provoked among
the missionaries of Macao and Goa by all these profane activities,
attempts to put an end to them were not successful, and the Fathers of
China continued to devote many of their energies to the teaching of the
sciences and to scientific research.[29]

In 1614 the Provincial for Japan and China, Valentim Carvalho, had
sent Manuel Dias to visit all the existing residences and forbid 'the teaching of mathematics or any other science, except that of the Gospel, to the
Chinese'.[30] It was, in effect, a condemnation of the policy that Ricci, with
his 15 years of experience, had realised to be effective. It had seemed to
him that the best way to win the interest and sympathy of the Chinese
was to present Christianity as a doctrine close to Confucianism and to
accompany it with scientific instruction.

Carvalho's intervention came at a time that saw a certain hardening in
missionary policies with regard to the Chinese. It was thought that too
many concessions had been made. However, the order was soon with-
drawn. Similarly, when in 1629 Palmeiro, the Visitor for China and
Japan, in his turn became alarmed at seeing certain missionaries neglecting religion in favour of the sciences and manifested his disapproval, the
affair remained without consequence.[31] It was hardly possible to prohibit
what had been the very cause of the missionaries' principal successes in
China.

Virtually all the literate converts of the early seventeenth century were attracted to the missionaries by their scientific teaching, and they then worked alongside them to translate into Chinese the manuals that were used in Jesuit colleges. The first of them, Qu Rukui, had studied mathematics with Ricci in Shaozhou in 1590 and 1591. Xu Guangqi (1562–1633), Ricci's most famous disciple, had helped him translate the first six chapters of *The Elements of Euclid* by Clavius, a work of trigonometry, and a little treatise on Western hydraulics. For Li Zhizao (1565–1630), who had been an enthusiast of geography ever since boyhood, it had been Ricci's map of the world that had clinched it. But he also studied mathematics under Ricci and collaborated with him in the translation of a work of geometry and a treatise on arithmetic. Sun Yuanhua (1581–1632) studied mathematics with Xu Guangqi, who then introduced him to the missionaries. He took a particular interest in Western firearms. Wang Zheng (1571–1644), who had inherited from an uncle a passion and genius for mechanics, was drawn to the missionaries when he discovered that they possessed illustrated works on mechanics and, in collaboration with Father Johann Schreck, he translated a treatise that he entitled *Illustrated Explanations concerning the Strange Machines of the Distant West*.[32]

Such, then, was the policy adopted by Ricci as early as the last years of the sixteenth century: to adapt to the milieu of the literate elite, to impress them with the sciences of Europe and thereby acquire among them the authority indispensable to men who had come to preach the true God in China, and to become initiated into their traditions of wisdom in order to be in a position to refute them or make use of them, depending upon whether they appeared to disagree with or support the truths of Christianity. It was a policy that was inspired both by the scant interest that the men of letters appeared to take in dogma and religious beliefs and also by his early recognition of the necessity of first establishing, as he puts it, 'the fundamental bases of faith': 'God, the creator of heaven and earth, the immortal soul, recompense for the good and punishment for the wicked – all things that are unknown to them and have not, until now, been believed'.[33]

That, no doubt, accounts for the mistakes made by most Chinese at the beginning of the seventeenth century: what Ricci, with a whole collection of arguments, had striven to prove in relation to the Master of Heaven and the spirits were his own ideas, not truths to which each and everybody was supposed to adhere. The literate elite, who knew nothing of the doctrine of the Master of Heaven except the general ideas that could be found in the works that were written for them, took some time to understand its true nature: namely, that it was a revealed religion, imperious and exclusive and founded upon mysteries beyond the powers of human reason. Thus, in the whole of Ricci's long treatise, there is only one brief allusion to Jesus.[34] Furthermore, even if the Jesuits of China were indulging in profane teaching and activities, with the sole aim of propagating and defending their faith, what was for them no more than accessory was by no means so for the Chinese: what the men of letters called 'Western' or 'heavenly' studies was an indivisible amalgamation of science, technology, philosophy and ethics.

At the beginning of the seventeenth century, circumstances must have favoured Ricci and his companions. There happened at that time to be a happy conjunction between the teaching of the Jesuits and the tendencies of the period. An orthodox reaction, hostile to the Buddhist influences which had deeply penetrated literate circles, had been developing ever since the last years of the sixteenth century. It was as much a political as a philosophical and moral reaction, for it soon became inseparable from the struggle between on the one hand the Palace and its all-powerful eunuchs and, on the other, a group of administrators and men of letters who were disturbed by the decline in political mores and the impotence of the state. The movement, which started in the private academy of the Donglin, in Jiangsu province, was to affect more and more members of the administration and literate circles.[35]

Along with Buddhism itself, the Buddhist-inspired deviations, originating in the school of Wang Yangming (Wang Shouren, 1472–1529), the great philosopher of the early sixteenth century, were being condemned. The egoistical quest for wisdom by the men of the fifteenth and sixteenth centuries was rejected as vain and immoral at the point when, faced with a general decline of society and its institutions, the elite circles were rediscovering the importance of their social responsibilities. The renewal of interest at the same time being shown in 'concrete studies' (*shixue*), that is to say the aspects of all practical knowledge which, on account of the scorn felt for utilitarian things, had been so long neglected in favour of vain speculation, was in harmony with these moral preoccupations.

Ricci's attacks against Buddhism, which he accused of corrupting the ancient traditions of China, the importance he attached to moral rigour, and his scientific teaching all appeared to answer the needs and aspirations of the age. The idea that the neo-Confucianism of the eleventh and twelfth centuries was not the true Confucianism of Antiquity[36] or, at least, that part of the neo-Confucian tradition had been corrupted by Buddhist influences, was one that was already in the air at the end of the Ming period and was to be developed and promoted by a number of philosophers and philologists of the Manchu period. Ricci's memoirs bring alive the favourable reactions elicited by his appreciation of Confucianism and criticism of Buddhism. In the course of one discussion, a certain Li Ruzhen, who had opposed Ricci with arguments drawn from the 'doctrine of the idols', that is to say Buddhism, found himself under attack for his inconsequentiality from another man of letters. The latter claimed that

it was shameful for Chinese people educated in the school of letters and of Confucius to have the audacity to refute Confucius and follow the doctrine of idols that were foreign, and it was something that astonished the great master Xitai [the name given to Ricci], who praised the doctrine of Confucius, declaring publicly that the doctrine of idols was false and followed by only a few people in the West, and even they were usually of low extraction.[37]

In his history of the Jesuit mission in China, which appeared in Rome in 1663, Daniello Bartoli remarked upon the large number of friends that the missionaries had won at the end of the Ming period among members of the literate elite who had rallied to the Donglin.[38] Their sympathy was not the result of mere chance and there are many testimonies to prove the hostility felt towards Buddhism by many members of the academy or of the Donglin party.[39]

The early years of the seventeenth century were thus quite exceptional ones for the missionaries. They had as yet attracted few critics, and many members of the literate elite were won over by the 'Western man of letters' and delighted by the analogies they thought they detected between his teachings and those of the Chinese tradition. It would indeed have been surprising if they had not admired his observation of the Chinese rules of politeness, his knowledge of the Classics and the written language, his astonishing memory,[40] his approval of Confucius, his condemnation of Buddhism, Taoism and Chinese superstitions, his ethics and his Stoic maxims,[41] the curiosities that he brought with him (paintings, books, clocks, astronomical instruments), his mathematical learning and his map of the world. His immediate successors were to add to this list methods of calculation that were more precise and reliable than the traditional Chinese ones and new ideas in the field of artillery and hydraulic machines – all things which could be of use to the general well-being and in the defence of the empire.

Recourse to the Classics

In order first to win over the literate elite, Ricci had to become familiar with their traditions and seek out anything that might be in accordance with the Christian faith and which might thus serve as a basis upon which to build. And the situation looked quite promising for him. He begins the chapter in his memoirs entitled 'On the various sects in China that are contrary to Religion' as follows:

Of all the pagan nations that are known to our Europe, I know of none which has made fewer errors contrary to the things of Religion than the nation of China in its early Antiquity. Indeed, in their books I find that they have always worshipped a supreme deity which they call the King of Heaven or of Heaven and Earth (for it perhaps seemed to them that heaven and earth were something animated, and together with this supreme deity which is, as it were, its soul, they imagined a living body) . . . They never believed such indecent things about the King of Heaven and other spirits, his ministers, as did our Romans, the Greeks, the Egyptians and other foreign nations. It may thus be hoped that, given the great goodness of the Lord, many of their ancients have been saved in accordance with natural law and with the special help that God is accustomed to provide for those who do all they can to receive it.[42]

This text is echoed by a passage from a letter written by Matteo Ricci in 1609, one year before his death:

To begin at the beginning, in ancient times, they followed a natural law as faithfully as in our own countries. For 1,500 years, this people practised the cult of idols hardly at all,[43] and those that they did worship were not so despicable as those of our Egyptians, Greeks and Romans; certain deities were even extremely virtuous and famed for their good actions. In fact, in the most ancient books of the men of letters – those that have some authority – they worship only heaven and earth *and the master of both*.[44] When we examine these books closely, we discover in them very few things which are contrary to the light of reason and many which are in conformity with it, and their natural philosophers are second to none.[45]

Note the expression 'and the master of both', which is Ricci's own addition and is symptomatic of the invincible tendency on the part of some of the missionaries to ascribe their own ideas to the Chinese – and particularly to the ancient Chinese.

The first missionaries were especially delighted to find in the Classics – the works venerated above all others among the literate elite – the term 'Sovereign on High' (*shangdi*), invocations to Heaven and expressions such as 'to serve Heaven' (*shi tian*), 'to respect' or 'fear Heaven' (*jing tian, wei tian*). For men so deeply convinced of the universal nature of their own religion, there was a strong temptation to suppose that the Chinese, who had unfortunately subsequently become atheists, had at one time had some knowledge of the true God or at least, as Ricci himself put it, that they had been enlightened by the 'light of natural reason'. These verbal analogies were at the heart of serious confusions on the parts of both the Chinese and the missionaries and were also at the heart of the disagreements that followed and grew until the time of the dispute over rituals. The missionaries' quotations from the Classics contributed to their early successes among literate circles. Passages in which the expressions 'Heaven' and 'Sovereign on High' appear were carefully noted down for their benefit; Ricci himself, in the second chapter of his great polemical work, *The True Meaning of the Master of Heaven*, quotes eleven passages that contain the phrase 'Sovereign on High'. It was his Chinese friends who recommended that he use this expression as an equivalent for 'Master of Heaven' (*tianzhu*), the Chinese translation of 'God', adopted as early as 1583.[46] Ricci thought that in it he had found a way of gradually leading the Chinese to Christianity. He had accordingly, without hesitation, declared in his work: 'When one reads the ancient books, one understands that the Sovereign on High and the Master of Heaven [of the Christians] differ in name alone.'[47] A conference held in Macao in 1603 pronounced approval of Ricci's point of view: the Chinese Classics could definitely provide elements useful for the introduction of Christianity in China. As early as 1595, Ricci was writing: 'During the last few years, whilst interpreting their works with good masters, I have found many passages which are favourable to the things of our Faith, such as the unity of God, the immortality of the soul, the glory of the elect, etc.'[48]

But it is often difficult to distinguish how much in the missionaries' attitudes should be ascribed to a desire for a provisional accommodation, and how much to an involuntary confusion or a sincere belief in the coincidence of the ancient Chinese ideas and those of the Bible. Attitudes appear to have varied from one individual to another. They range from a total rejection of any resemblance between Chinese and biblical traditions to a conviction that there was total agreement, which, among the figurists of the eighteenth century,[49] applied down to the last detail. For Ricci, at least, the idea that predominated was that of a 'natural religion' together with a practical desire to be effective. The existence of a single, creator God, and of a paradise and a hell, and the distinction between soul and body were, for him, truths that could be demonstrated by reason. It was therefore not at all surprising to him to find at least a trace of these ideas in the ancient Chinese: more purely inspired than the moderns, they had not yet been corrupted by the pernicious influences of Buddhism. However, Ricci, who was the first to refer to the formulae relating to Heaven and to the Sovereign on High in the Chinese Classics, was at the same time intending, as he says, 'to draw over to our opinion (*tirare alla nostra opinione*) Confucius, the principal of the sect of the men of letters, by interpreting in our favour certain doubtful writings left by him'.[50] Elsewhere, in a letter written in 1604 to the General of the Jesuits, he explains his methods of procedure with the Chinese texts more clearly: if he cites them, it is, after all, in order to make them say something other than what they really mean. This letter, composed in Latin, touches upon an important idea in neo-Confucian philosophy, that of Taiji, the first origin of the cosmos or the total mass of energy which is at the origin of the universe and contains within it a general principle of organisation. Ricci writes as follows:

This doctrine of the Taiji is new and was produced fifty years ago.[51] And for some, if you examine the matter attentively, it contradicts the ancient sages of China, who had a more exact idea of God. According to what they say, it is, in my opinion, nothing but what our philosophers call prime matter, for it is by no means an entity; they even say that it is not one thing and simultaneously that it is in all things as one of their constituent parts. They say that it is not a spirit and that it is not endowed with understanding. And although some people say that it is the reason for things, by reason they do not mean something substantial or intelligent, and it is a reason that is closer to reasoned reason than to reasoning reason.[52] In fact, it is not just their interpretations that differ for they make many absurd statements, too.[53] *Accordingly, we have judged it preferable in this* book [the *Tianzhu shiyi* or *The True Meaning of the Master of Heaven*], *rather than attack what they say, to turn it in such a way that it is in accordance with the idea of God,*[54] so that we appear not so much to be following Chinese ideas as interpreting Chinese authors in such a way that they follow our ideas. And because the men of letters who govern China are extremely offended if we attack this principle [of the Taiji], we have tried much harder to call in question their explanation of the principle than the principle itself. And if, in the end, they come to understand that the Taiji is the first substantial principle, intelligent and infinite, we should agree to say that it is none other than God.[55]

Ricci was in this way led to give the Chinese lessons on the interpretation of the Classics and the Four Books which, over the centuries, had been the subject of countless commentaries by eminent men of letters.

Thus, the phrase in the *Sayings of Confucius*, 'to respect the spirits and the gods while holding them at a distance', means, according to Ricci, 'not to sin against Heaven by addressing prayers to them'.[56] On the subject of filial piety, he puts forward a bizarre and curious thesis on the three duties that this comprises: towards the supreme father, who is the Master of Heaven; towards the sovereign, who is the father of the kingdom; and towards one's own natural father.[57] Elsewhere he criticises Mencius for having said that the greatest filial impiety is to have no descendants (the first of all obligations being, in effect, to perpetuate the family cult) and he adduces various reasons to explain the mistake, adding that the rituals contain many remarks which do not date from Antiquity but were added more recently.[58]

Interpreting the Classics was a procedure much favoured by the missionaries, even by those who rejected the idea that the Chinese had ever had any knowledge of the true God. Thus, Antonio de Caballero, a Franciscan, composed a work in which he gave a Christian meaning to a whole series of phrases taken from the Four Books,[59] his main object being to convince the Chinese that they had misunderstood their own traditions.

But the missionaries also often resort to another idea: namely that part of the ancient Chinese tradition had disappeared in the Burning of the Books ordered by the first of the Qin emperors in 213 BC and that it was precisely that part that set out the thesis of an all-powerful, creator God, the existence of heaven and hell and the immortality of the soul; the teaching of the missionaries fortunately made it possible to complete what had been lost in the classical traditions of China. This is, indeed, pretty well the thesis put forward by Ricci in *The True Meaning of the Master of Heaven*, where he explains to a Chinese man of letters why it is that the Classics make no mention of paradise and hell. The Chinese Saints were not able to transmit their doctrine in its entirety. Or, alternatively, not all their pronouncements were noted down. Or perhaps they were, but the recorded notes were subsequently lost. Or else, men of later generations, in their stupidity and not believing in those things, destroyed them. Then again, one should take into account the fact that such documents are liable to deteriorate. It could not be said that a thing had not existed just because no trace of it remained.[60]

The missionaries claimed that the ancient tradition not only suffered from lacunas such as these but had furthermore been deformed by the harmful influences of idolatry. Buddhism had corrupted the good doctrine of the ancients, introducing superstition and atheism into China. That is why the 'modern interpreters', or the neo-Confucian philosophers of the eleventh and twelfth centuries, who had propagated a materialistic interpretation, had betrayed the very spirit of the Classics. It was, indeed, just possible to explain that the allusions to Heaven in the ancient texts referred to an all-powerful, creator God, despite the fact that the texts never mentioned him at all; but the commentaries of the Sung period rendered such an interpretation quite impossible. The early missionaries therefore attacked the commentaries and took the course of stressing the literal meaning of the Classics. As Longobardo remarks, they judged that 'there was much advantage to be derived from following the text wherever it was favourable to them: they would in this way find it easy to unite with the sect of the men of letters and would thus win the hearts of the Chinese'.[61]

It therefore became customary in the Jesuit mission to oppose the true Confucianism of Antiquity, which accorded with 'natural religion' or – better still – with the Bible, to the modern ideas, which were considered to be a betrayal of the ancient traditions. Thus, in a short work entitled *On the Extreme Weight of the Sins of Man* (*Renzui zhizhong*), which appeared in Peking in 1698, Father Noël praises the teachings of the Classics and criticises the heresies that have developed since the Han period. He makes a distinction between the 'authentic Confucians' (*zhenru*) of Antiquity and the 'common Confucians' (*suru*) of contemporary times, who speak of a principle of order (*li*) and of Dao and Heaven, but for whom these are no more than empty words.[62]

All the same, despite their preoccupation with opportunism and tactics, many missionaries truly held the naive belief that the most ancient Chinese ideas were identical to those of the Bible. This coincidence was explicable to them quite naturally through their belief that, after the Flood, descendants of Noah had made their way to China, bringing with them knowledge of the true God. Given that the whole of human history is to be found in the Bible, the ancestors of the Chinese were bound to have come from Judaea. Despite increasingly bitter criticism and the scandal that broke in Europe over this assimilation of Chinese and biblical traditions, the Jesuits were for many years loth to abandon their policies, being convinced both of the viability of their thesis and also of the advantage they could derive from it in their dealings with many Chinese, not necessarily prominent men of letters or men of the people. As late as 1697 Father Joachim Bouvet believed that there was nothing 'in the world more likely to dispose the minds and hearts of the Chinese to embrace our holy Religion than showing them how closely it conforms with the principles of their own ancient and legitimate philosophy'.[63] Father Le Comte was to incur censure for writing, at the end of the seventeenth century: 'This people has, over practically two thousand years, preserved a knowledge of the true God and has honoured him in a manner that might serve as an example and instruction even to Christians.'[64] According to Father de Prémare, who was in China from 1698 to 1726 and was recalled by the Propaganda for having 'destroyed veneration for the Old Testament by praising the Chinese book, Y king (*Yijing*)',[65]

the religion of China resides entirely in the King (the Classics). There, so far as fundamental doctrine is concerned, one finds the principles of natural law that the ancient Chinese received from the children of Noah. They teach both knowledge of and reverence for a Superior Being.[66]

In 1753, after spending 24 years in China, Father Alexandre de la Charme published a *True Explanation of Human Nature and the Principle of Order* (*Xingli zhenquan*), an apparently neo-Confucian title. In the preface of this work, which was condemned in 1773, he praises the excellence of the Five Classics but at the same time explains that their profound meaning has escaped superficial minds. Furthermore, he adds, many texts were lost in the Burning of the Books by the Qin in 213 BC and subsequently, despite quite admirable efforts, it only proved possible to recover a small proportion of them, so that people have remained in ignorance of the complete and true meaning of the Five Classics. By dint of deep meditation, Father de la Charme himself managed to rediscover that complete and true meaning: it is that of the 'Five Classics of the Master of Heaven'; the true doctrine of the men of letters of Antiquity was none other than Christianity, which is, in effect, a doctrine that is universal.[67]

This work of Father de la Charme published at a time when, following the prohibiting of the Chinese rituals and ceremonies, it had become impossible to maintain that there had ever been anything good in the Chinese traditions, produced a general uproar. But it reveals the persistence of a tenacious idea the origins of which go right back to the earliest days of the mission: that of a probable, or even certain, agreement between the contents of the Chinese Classics and Christianity.

Errors and confusions

Up until Ricci's death in 1610, nobody had dared to question the wisdom of establishing an equivalence between the Sovereign on High of the Chinese Classics and the God of the Christians. The fact was that Ricci's entire policy had been founded upon the resemblance that existed between the precepts of the ethics of Antiquity and the teachings of Christianity, following the analogy between the Sovereign on High and the Master of Heaven. But after 1610, a number of missionaries came to the conclusion that too many concessions had been made to the idea of a natural religion and they began to question the validity of such policies. They might encourage deplorable confusions. Father Niccolò Longobardo was one of the first to become alarmed at the fact that the Chinese did not see their Sovereign on High as a personal, unique, all-powerful and creator God, but instead, and in conformity with traditional interpretations of the Classics, regarded him as an anonymous power of order and animation in the universe.[68]

Father Francesco Pasio, the Visitor of Japan, arriving in Macao in 1612, told him of 'errors similar to those of the Gentiles in the books composed in Chinese by the Fathers in China'. A number of missionaries in Japan, who were also informed about the Chinese doctrines, were convinced that the Fathers in China were making a mistake. In Peking, Longobardo noted that Father Sabatino de Ursis entertained the same scruples as he did on the subject of the Sovereign on High. They consulted three converted men of letters on the matter: Paul Xu (Guangqi), Michael Yang (Tingyun) and John,[69] who advised them to stick to the texts of the Classics when they were favourable and leave the commentaries aside. But Longobardo observed that 'the Chinese men of letters usually give the meaning of their own books to ours and imagine that it is possible to find in theirs explanations that tally with our own holy faith'.[70] Those who favoured deeper examination of the matter received the support of the Provincial, Valentim Carvalho, the Visitor, Francisco Vieira, and a missionary who had lived in Japan for many years but had recently been expelled, João Rodrigues.[71] The controversy came to a head around 1618 with Vieira's decision that two theses putting the opposite points of view should be composed on the themes of the dispute, namely God, the angels and the rational soul. Was there anything at all in the Chinese wisdom that related to these three things? Fathers Pantoja and Vagnone were of the opinion that the Chinese had indeed had some knowledge of them, whereas Father de Ursis maintained that 'the Chinese, according to the precepts of their philosophy, had had no knowledge of a spiritual substance quite distinct from the material ... and that consequently they had never known either God, the Angels or the Rational Soul'. Longobardo, for his part, undertook an inquiry among the men of letters, both Christian and pagan, the outcome of which, in 1623, was the publication of a work in Latin, the *De Confucio ejusque doctrina tractatus*. This was the first Western study to give a systematic idea of the concepts that were dominant in China. It was later translated into French with the title, *Traité sur quelques points de la religion des Chinois*, and printed in Paris in 1701 under the auspices of the Foreign Missions, who used it as a weapon against the Jesuits.

Longobardo had clearly recognised the danger of a policy that consisted in referring to the Classics but giving them an interpretation alien to literate traditions. He pointed out, quite rightly, that the text of the Classics was difficult and at times obscure. The commentaries were therefore indispensable. If the Chinese themselves were obliged to have recourse to the commentaries, foreigners surely had to do so all the more. If the texts were interpreted in a different sense from that of the commentaries, 'the Chinese will imagine that we have not read all their books or that we have not apprehended their true meaning'. That is indeed what happened in the case of Ricci's great book, *The True Meaning of the Master of Heaven*, which the Buddhist master, Zhuhong, criticised, suggesting that Ricci could be excused for not giving the Classics their true meaning since he was still in a state of ignorance. Similarly, Qu Rukui (Qu Taisu), baptised Ignatius in 1605,[72] produced a work in which he corrected what the Father had not properly understood. 'The Chinese had great confidence in and admiration for their commentaries. One could not go against them.'[73]

The discussions held on the subject of the Classics within the Jesuit mission in China led to a conference held in Jiading, near Shanghai, in

1628, by twenty-one missionaries and the four most famous converts of the age. It was decided that the use of the term Sovereign on High[74] as an equivalent for the God of the Christians should be proscribed, except in the works of Father Ricci, on account of their success among educated people. However, the Franciscan, Father Caballero, noted in 1668 that 'under the pretext that Ricci's opinions had not been condemned, the word Xamti (*shangdi*) has come back into use and is often to be found on men's lips and in the Chinese books which a number of Jesuit Fathers have reprinted'.[75] It is yet another proof that most Jesuits resisted abandoning one of their most effective arguments. Consequently, the terms Heaven (*tian*) and Sovereign on High had to be condemned all over again by Pope Clement XI in 1704 and 1715.[76]

In his treatise, Longobardo also draws attention to how little importance the literate converts attached to dogma and to the way that they considered everything to be reconcilable. He writes as follows:

Our Christian men of letters give us such advice [namely, to hold to the texts of the Classics, which are considered to be close to the Christian theses, rather than to the commentators, who are atheists] either because they do not understand how important it is that there should not be the slightest error in the subjects with which we deal or else because, in order to escape any reproaches that might be addressed to them for having embraced a foreign Law, they are overjoyed at finding in our Religion some conformity with their own sect. However, whenever these same men of letters produce works on the texts, they always conform to the commentators; if they did not, they would be regarded with scorn as being full of errors and contrary to the principles of the School of Confucius. Why do they seek to persuade us to do what they themselves fail to do?[77]

Although the translation of Longobardo's treatise aimed to damage the Jesuits, there is nothing in it to cast doubt upon its authenticity nor upon the sincerity with which Ricci's successor undertook his inquiry; the work contains too many precise details which agree perfectly with what we know from other sources. Now, Longobardo provides proof that the convert, the renowned man of letters Michael Yang Tingyun, who represented one of the mission's great successes, was Christian in no more than appearance. Longobardo records how he one day showed the Fathers in Peking a number of treatises that he had written, one of which was entitled *An Explanation of the Ten Commandments*.[78] Longobardo writes:

Now, although this explanation does contain some good things that he had heard our Fathers say, there are also several that are drawn straight from the precepts of the sect of the men of letters and that are quite clearly their ideas ... He states in his preface that all things are to such an extent one substance, which is the Li (the active principle of organisation inherent in the universal energy), that the only differences between them are those of expression and a few accidental qualities.[79]

According to Longobardo, Yang Tingyun was of the opinion not only that the three doctrines of China (Confucianism, Buddhism and Taoism) all shared the same purpose of 'establishing one and the same principle of the universe', but also that they were all in perfect agreement with the teaching of the missionaries.[80] Yang Tingyun, as we shall see, favoured a kind of syncretism in which Christian contributions were reinterpreted in traditional Chinese terms.

The religious instruction of this ardent defender of the doctrine of the Master of Heaven therefore left quite a lot to be desired.

Longobardo goes on to observe: 'In this explanation of the first Commandment, Doctor Michael says that one must honour Heaven *and Earth*,[81] and in relation to the third he says that one may offer sacrifices to our saints as one does in China to Heaven, Earth, doctors and the dead.'[82]

It is not hard to detect here the effects of a policy of accommodation based upon the idea of natural religion and a belief in the agreement between Christianity and ancient morality and religion of China.

In his *Treatise on a Number of Important Points relating to the Mission in China*, probably written a few years before his death in 1669, the Franciscan Father, Antonio de Caballero, expresses his opinion that all the discussions on the question of whether or not the Chinese knew of the true God in Antiquity are pointless:

What does it matter whether or not the ancient Chinese knew God? . . . We are here to proclaim the Holy Gospel, not to become apostles of Confucius. That is not where the difficulty lies. The difficulty is this: most Chinese graduates, once they have embraced the Christian Religion, are afraid that they will be reproached for having preferred a foreign Law . . . They have therefore adopted the idea that what they call Heaven or Shangdi (Sovereign on High) and *guishen* (spirits and gods) are really what we call God . . . and the guardian Angels.[83]

Caballero gives the same account of the behaviour of the converted men of letters as Longobardo does: they are afraid to show openly that they are Christian. But he immediately goes on to cast doubt upon whether they really are Christian, accusing them of mixing up Christian truths and Chinese errors indiscriminately:

all these accounts and combinations resemble the statue of Nebuchadnezzar: head of gold, body of silver and feet of clay . . . In the passages where they appear to speak of our God and his Angels, they are merely aping the Truth or, if you like, they resemble the peacock whose feet are a disgrace to its splendid rich plumage.[84]

There was, as it were, a general conspiracy, a tacit agreement between the men of letters who favoured the missionaries and certain of the missionaries themselves who placed an excessive confidence in the universality of human reason, a conspiracy which maintained the confusion between Chinese and Christian ideas.

When questioned by Longobardo, Xu Guangqi, who had for many years been in contact with Ricci and his companions, was the only one to admit that the God of the Christians had nothing in common with the Sovereign on High of the Classics, but he was of the opinion that it would be politic to proceed as if the Sovereign on High did possess all the characteristics that the missionaries attributed to the Master of Heaven. Longobardo writes:

Paul Xu confessed sincerely to me that he was convinced that the King on High could not be our God and that neither ancient nor modern men of letters had any knowledge of God; but that, given that our Fathers, for excellent reasons and principally so as not to alienate the men of letters, had seen fit to give the name of God to the King on High, they might just as well credit him with the attributes that are given to the true God.[85]

Similar advice came from other converted men of letters:

Doctor Leon [Li Zhizao] and the graduate, Ignatius [Sun Yuanhua], admit quite ingenuously that all the modern men of letters are atheists and follow only the explanations of the interpreters. They advise us, nevertheless, to hold fast to such texts as are favourable to us without bothering about what modern interpreters have said.[86]

From which it would appear that the Chinese men of letters were even more anxious than the Jesuits to effect a grand reconciliation. And, just as certain missionaries undertook to show that ancient Confucianism was nothing other than Christianity, converts and sympathisers composed books that set out to prove that the teachings of the missionaries were on every point in agreement with the traditional ideas of the Chinese.

As Longobardo observed, the Chinese men of letters of the early seventeenth century 'were delighted to find in our Religion a certain conformity with their own sect',[87] and the comments made by converts and sympathisers on the works composed by the missionaries testify to their delight. The theme that all minds are one and that of the profound analogy between Confucianism and the doctrine of the Master of Heaven are the ones that recur the most often.

A convert of the early seventeenth century writes:

The language and writing of the Westerners differ from those of China, but that does not stop us from understanding one another at all. The fact is that mind and reason are the same [amongst all men]. Furthermore, their teaching is at one with that of the Duke of Zhou and Confucius. That is why the great and people of standing daily seek out their company and respect them.[88]

One Chen Liangcai declared:

In the past, when I was a child, I heard of the doctrine of the Master of Heaven, Yesu... Twenty years later, when I was visiting Peking, I was able to enter into relations with Sire Pang [Pantoja] ... and that was how I came to learn all about his theories.

Chen Liangcai thought that Ricci's '*The True Meaning of the Master of Heaven* and the *Ten Chapters of an Uncommon Man* were in total agreement with the teachings of the Duke of Zhou and Confucius'.[89]

A certain Zhang Ruitu (1576–1641) sang Ricci's praises as follows:

Mencius spoke of 'serving Heaven' and our saintly Confucius of 'mastering oneself'. Who could believe that you are from a foreign country when your principles are so exactly in agreement with ours? What can the difference of places matter compared with the identity of minds and the universality of reason?[90]

For Michael Yang Tingyun, 'the doctrine of Confucius is perfect in every respect and identical to that of God'.[91]

The author of a preface writes:

Our countries entered into communication for the first time thanks to Ricci. Now, Ricci constantly exalts the good, respect for moral principles[92] and the service of Heaven. He is usually in agreement with the main ideas of Yao, Shun, Zhougong and Confucius ... Ah! There are not two reasons in the world; there are not two minds in man; there are not two ways of behaving rightly. And if one lifts one's head, there are not two Heavens and, in Heaven, there are not two Masters.[93]

It was because Ricci found his inspiration in Heaven, which, as we shall see, is to be found in each and every one of us, that he spontaneously found himself in agreement with the ancient Sages of China.

Another preface, composed around the mid-seventeenth century, runs as follows:

On hearing Ricci for the very first time, some people believed that he was setting out personal ideas of his own [which had no foundation], but upon examining what he was saying more closely, they perceived that his ideas were exactly those of our Confucianism, the essential one being that one must serve and fear Heaven ... The kingdoms of the West are scores of thousands of *li* distant from China. Since the beginning of the world, we have never communicated through interpreters. Our language and writing are different. But one fine day, these people, taking great care over what they brought with them, translated it into

Chinese, and there was then, as it were, the discovery of a perfect correspondence with the idea of our Saints and Sages when they declare that one must respect and fear Heaven. So where can they have found all this? It is just as our Confucianism says: 'there is nothing that is not included and covered by this marvel that is Heaven's work of creation–transformation'.[94]

The same author cites as authorities who 'have rejoiced to find that the teachings of these people were in accordance with those of our Saints and Sages' the minister of state, Ye (Xianggao) (1562–1627), the minister of rituals, Weng (Zhengchun) (1553–1626) and the minister of Public Works, Chen (Minzhi).[95]

When questioned as to the reasons for his adherence to Christianity, a convert from Fujian province declared: 'In the China since Confucius, it has no longer been possible to imitate Confucius. By coming to China [the doctrine of the] Master of Heaven teaches men to act rightly and thus causes each person to imitate Confucius.'[96]

The preface written in 1664 by the censor, Xu Zhijiang,[97] for the work of a convert, *A General View on the Transmission of the Doctrine of Heaven* (*Tianxue chuangai*) (1663) provides an excellent summary of the general attitude of converts and sympathisers towards the works and teaching of the missionaries. In it, Xu Zhijiang deplores the bad influence of Buddhism upon Confucian morality, the defenders of which he considers the missionaries, in contrast, to be. Echoing the words of the author of the *View* himself, he declares that 'the doctrine of the Master of Heaven consists in serving Heaven, overcoming one's egoistical inclinations, loving mankind, repenting of one's errors and proceeding in the path of goodness', and he concludes by saying that he has understood that 'their doctrine was in no way different from Confucianism'.[98]

In a little work entitled *Shangdi kao, An Examination concerning the Sovereign on High*, a Christian from Zhangzhou in Fujian province cites and comments in an altogether traditional fashion upon certain passages from the Classics in which the term 'Sovereign on High' appears.[99]

For Feng Yingjing (1555–1606), who was a fervent admirer of Ricci, the author of *The True Meaning of the Master of Heaven* simply wished to remind the Chinese of their ancient religious traditions. In his preface to Ricci's works, he wrote:

In Antiquity, sacrifices were made to Heaven, Earth, the god of the Soil, the god of the Harvests and the gods of the Mountains and Rivers, as well as to the ancestral tablets, whereas nowadays sacrifices are made only to the Buddhas.[100]

The missionaries made the most of the Chinese aspiration to rediscover the true doctrine of Antiquity, the lost secret of social and political harmony, claiming that under the title of 'the teachings of Heaven' (*tianxue*), they were bringing back the authentic teachings of the ancients. Some of them were even to claim that these teachings had come from Judaea at the time of one of the first sovereigns of China.[101] For most of the converts and sympathisers of the early seventeenth century, the doctrine of the Master of Heaven aimed to bring back to China the religious feeling that had inspired the ancients and informed all their actions. The difference from Chinese ideas was no more than a matter of emphasis. In the Chinese concept of Heaven, which means both nature and its organisational power, the Westerners made a clearer distinction between these two aspects. Chen Yi, the already cited author of a preface to a work by Father Aleni, put it as follows: 'Our Confucianism, when it considers things in a global fashion (*hun*), speaks of Heaven. These gentlemen from the West, when they lay particular emphasis upon one precise aspect of it (*di*), speak of the Master of Heaven.' And Chen Yi goes on to declare that he is convinced that there are things 'which depend upon the governor of Heaven' and that it is not enough to speak simply of the vast expanses of the blue Heaven.[102]

Even judging solely by the prefaces written by Christian men of letters for works by the missionaries, one is sometimes forced to the conclusion that they were converts in no more than appearance or else that, as the missionaries claimed, they did not dare to declare themselves openly. But in the latter case, they would certainly have been carrying the pretence quite far. In the preface composed by Li Zhizao (baptised in 1610) for a new edition in 1628 of Ricci's *The True Meaning of the Master of Heaven*,[103] this famous convert explains that Ricci's book contains an excellent moral teaching which 'in its essentials, requires that people repent their errors and rediscover the meaning of their duties (*yi*), that they repress their desires and retain intact within themselves the meaning of humanity (*ren*)'. Having come from a far-off land 'without any communication with China, however far back in the past, Ricci had never heard of the teachings of Fuxi, Wenwang, Zhougong and Confucius[104] nor of the explanations of Zhou Dunyi, Cheng Hao and Cheng Yi, Zhang Zai and Zhu Xi.[105] But on the sole basis of the great idea that it was necessary to "know and serve Heaven", he found himself in perfect agreement with what our Classics and commentaries have handed down.' The only difference is that he mentions paradise and hell. But the idea of retribution for good and evil can also be found in the Classics.

Having recognised that Ricci's ideas were in agreement with those of the neo-Confucian commentators from Zhou Dunyi to Zhu Xi, despite the fact that the missionaries had always tried to combat neo-Confucian theses, considering them to be atheistic and materialistic, Li Zhizao grants that, in his works, Ricci often expresses opinions that are different from those of 'recent Confucians'. On the other hand, he goes on, 'he is mysteriously in agreement with those books of Antiquity, the *Suwen* [a work of medicine], the *Zhoubei* [*suanjing*] [a work on mathematics], the *Kaogong* [*ji*] [a work on technology] and with Qiyuan [Zhuangzi, the Taoist philosopher] [!]'[106]

As will be seen, this surprising mixture of morality, religion, science and technology is quite common: the teachings of the missionaries made up a complex whole.

Considering the doctrine of the Master of Heaven to be a philosophical tendency similar to others familiar to them, the essential object of which was to strengthen individual morality, the Christian men of letters would, as was customary at the time, form congregations (*hui*) with their own particular statutes (*huiyue*). E. Zürcher, commenting upon this assimilation of Christianity to associations formed around academies, has drawn attention to a document preserved in the Bibliothèque Nationale: it is entitled 'Statutes of the Association [for the Promotion] of the Virtue of Humanity' (*Renhuiyue*), an association created by the convert, Wang Zheng, for purely philanthropic purposes, in the Chinese style.[107]

The reasons that led many men of letters at the beginning of the seventeenth century to show sympathy to the missionaries are clearly indicated through most of their reactions: as well as their science and technology, it was their moral rigour, control over the passions, good works and respect for Heaven – that is to say, as the Chinese saw it, for an order that exists simultaneously within nature, society and man himself – that were esteemed, the very things promoted by a literate tradition and all too much forgotten by the contemporary Chinese. Similarly, the missionaries deserved praise for combating superstitions, Buddhism and Taoism, all of which were hostile to the good doctrine.

But over the years, the situation evolved: by the end of the seventeenth century even men of letters who were the most favourably disposed towards the missionaries were expressing serious reservations about their doctrine.

In a pamphlet written towards the end of his life, one of the most famous men of letters of the seventeenth century, Huang Zongxi (1610–95), appears to be taking over the arguments of the missionaries: his compatriots have lost the true meaning of the word 'Heaven', and the religious sentiment which used to inspire the ancients has weakened. They have even reached a point where they have replaced Heaven with the abstract concept of a principle of universal order (*li*). He goes on:

Now, there truly is a mysterious power which presides over the order of the universe. Were there not, the four seasons would be upset and there would be no separation between men, animals and vegetables. Everything would be confused.

Then, following Ricci, whom he may have read, Huang Zongxi gives as a proof of the existence of a Sovereign on High the sacrifices to Heaven that took place in Antiquity and which had in fact remained customary down to contemporary times. But he goes on to say:

As for those who invented the doctrine of the Master of Heaven, they reject Buddhism and revere Heaven but, having done that, they set up an idol of the Master of Heaven and relate events in his life, which comes down to the same as substituting a ghost for Heaven and entirely doing away with even the idea of the Sovereign on High.[108]

The praises of Zhang Erqi (1612–78), a famous philologist of the early Manchu period, are accompanied by similar criticisms:

Compared with the contents of Buddhist books, what these people say is straightforward and full of substance (*pingshi*). The principal idea comes down to respecting the Master of Heaven, leading a life that conforms with morality, controlling one's desires and studying with zeal. They do not forbid the killing of animals and direct their attacks against Buddhism in particular. Whenever they come across Buddhist sûtra, statues or images of spirits or gods, they urge the people to destroy them. What they criticise in Buddhism is all that is uncouth and excessive about it.[109] They have produced two writings in response to Yu De[yuan] [Yu Chunxi] and the monk Lianchi [Zhuhong] and these are truly successful in shutting the mouths of their adversaries.[110] That is extraordinary. Nevertheless, their comments on the Master of Heaven are altogether inadequate as far as a true idea of Heaven is concerned... Furthermore, what they say about paradise and hell appears to differ barely at all from what the Buddhists maintain and they go even further than the latter when it comes to extravagance and nonsense.[111]

Similarly, in Zhang Chao, who compiled a collection of various works that was published in 1697, admiration of the most sincere kind does not rule out the expression of quite specific reservations. Here is what he wrote in the preface to a little work produced in collaboration with Fathers Buglio (1606–82), Magalhães (1610–77) and Verbiest (1623–88), entitled the *Xifang yaoji* or *Essential Ideas about the Countries of the West*, and completed in Peking in 1669:

These people are extremely intelligent. Their studies concern astronomy, the calendar, medicine and mathematics; their customs are compounded of loyalty, good faith, constancy and integrity; their skill is wonderful. They truly have the means to win minds. The kingdoms of India are also called Western lands (*xifang*) and Buddhist believers often vow that they will be reborn there, but for them it is a matter only of pure calm and extinction.[112] They know neither the joys experienced by husband and wife, nor the glory of honours and high positions, nor the pleasures of a succulent cuisine. How could one hesitate, faced with a choice between these two Western regions? Thus, the ideas of the distant West assuredly win out over those of other doctrines. The only trouble is that it is a pity that they speak of a Master of Heaven, an incorrect and distasteful term which leads them into nonsense which our men of letters have the greatest difficulty in accepting. If only they could leave [that idea] alone and not talk about it, they would be very close to our own Confucianism ... Our Confucianism has never held that Heaven had a mother or a bodily form, and it has never spoken of events that are supposed to have occurred before and after his birth. Is it not true that herein lies the difference between our Confucianism and their doctrine?[113]

Just as some missionaries thought that the Chinese men of letters possessed a suitable disposition to receive their faith, there were some men of letters who judged that, once rid of their false notions, such as the belief in a creator God, the missionaries might have made quite good Confucians.

The climate deteriorates

At the time of the maritime expansion of Europe, the only countries in the world where the missionaries made a real effort to adapt to alien civilisations were China and India. We should associate with the name of Ricci, for China, that of Roberto de Nobili, for India. Both of them took the trouble to initiate themselves into the traditions of wisdom of these countries with ancient civilisations. The situation was entirely different where the Portuguese and Spaniards had imposed themselves through conquest: in such circumstances the evangelical task could be carried out in a more authoritarian fashion. It was also different in Japan, where it was at the order of their daimyô, who had interests in the Portuguese trade with Macao, that many Japanese were baptised. The facilities from which the missionaries in Japan had benefited, where, it was said, there were as many as 300,000 converts in 1600, explain the severity with which they passed judgement upon the policies adopted in China. In the course of the first twenty-five years following Ruggieri's and Ricci's installation in Zhaoqing in 1583, progress had been very slow. According to Father Sabatino de Ursis, there were still barely one thousand baptised converts in 1605 despite the fact that there were, in China, sixteen Jesuit priests and four large residences – in Nanking, Peking, Nanchang and Shaozhou. Five years later, at the date of Ricci's death in 1610, the figures given are of around 2,500 baptised.[114] One can also understand the reactions of the missionaries in Macao, who, unaware of the obstacles Ricci had had to overcome in order to gain acceptance in literate circles and win their respect, were irritated at the slow progress of Christianisation and the circumspection with which the Chinese men of letters were treated.

Nobili, who had set out to convert the Brahmins of Madurai in southern India, had – like Ricci – been led to acquire a certain familiarity with the religious and philosophical traditions of the country: he was violently criticised for this by the hierarchy and also by the entire clergy in Goa who, living as they did in a colonial atmosphere, felt nothing but the deepest scorn for the Indian culture and were quick to condemn anything that smacked of concessions to paganism. In China itself, rivalry between the different religious orders, as well as national and political competitiveness, had arisen to poison the atmosphere. The question which had provoked internal dissension within the Jesuit mission to China following Ricci's death, was soon to become a matter of passionate interest to the entire Church; in Europe around 1700, it turned into the great religious, philosophical and political polemic over the Chinese rituals.

There had been many difficulties to overcome before acceptance could be gained in China, a country with an ancient and scholarly civilisation in which foreigners were normally regarded with suspicion and considered with a certain condescension. It was those difficulties that had dictated the policy adopted – namely, to proceed step by step without worrying overduly about making initial concessions. It was thought that, as evangelisation made progress, it would be possible to correct certain abuses or errors that were inevitable at the outset. Other orders, which clung more closely to principles and lacked relations with the Chinese men of letters and, above all, were jealous of the Jesuits, who intended to keep China as their own particular preserve, could not show such flexibility. It was more rare for them to take the trouble to acquaint themselves with the written traditions of China.

Around 1610, it nevertheless came about that a number of Jesuits in China who had become more conscious of the dangers of heresy that stemmed from an overhasty assimilation of Christianity to the ideas of the Chinese, began to criticise some of these accommodations. They judged that too many concessions had been made to the Chinese and that greater firmness should be shown. Curiously enough, it was at this same period that a similar reaction took place in the territories of America conquered by Spain. However, the conditions that obtained on the two sides of the Pacific were very different. Whereas, in China, a number of people were becoming disturbed by the mistakes made by the converted men of letters and were criticising what appeared to them to be a policy of excessive prudence, it seems that among the Indians of America, where the question of adapting to local cultures did not arise, too much had been expected from the miraculous effects of baptism. Jean Delumeau writes:

During the second half of the sixteenth century, the Church was not unduly alarmed by the vestiges of paganism that persisted. Once the Indians were baptised, they would progressively adopt the style of the Christian religion. However, at the beginning of the seventeenth century, in Peru in particular, it was noticed that ancestral cults still persisted in a more or less clandestine form. It was then, in 1610, that the campaigns of extirpation began.[115]

One year before his death, Ricci was still insisting upon the need for extreme prudence and upon the interest to be gained from first winning over figures of importance. He wrote that 'a few good Christians were worth more than a crowd' (*piuttosto boni cristiani che molta turba*) as were, if possible, 'a few high-ranking men of letters and mandarins who, with their authority, could reassure those who might be frightened by such novelties'.[116]

Nicolas Trigault, who arrived in China in 1610 and left again for Europe in 1613, entirely identified himself with Ricci's counsels of prudence. One of his letters runs as follows:

The point of capital importance is that the Chinese recognise that we have no revolutionary intentions, that we expect no material gain, but come to spread the one and only divine Law, which is in no way opposed to the well-being of the kingdom[117] ... That is why, quite deliberately but rejecting nobody, we do avoid great numbers – converts nevertheless have reached 5,000 within a few years[118] – and are wary of mass gatherings so as not to lose in a single day the fruit of so many years ... That is why, make no mistake about it, Christianity here will make progress as the divine Law and its messages acquire respect, and will lose ground proportionately as an overhasty zeal swells the numbers of converts.[119]

Nevertheless, even in Ricci's lifetime and despite his opposition to too hasty and too many conversions, a number of missionaries had already begun to preach among the people: Niccolò Longobardo in Shaozhou as early as 1597, Alfonso Vagnone in Nanking from 1605 on, and Lazzaro Cattaneo in Shanghai from 1608 on.[120] Their efforts resulted in quite a rapid increase in the number of baptisms.[121] The sympathy that Ricci had won in the literate and ruling circles quite misleadingly appeared to augur well for more efficacious action among the common people.

At the beginning of the seventeenth century, there had indeed been some celebrated conversions amongst eminent men of letters and high-ranking Chinese administrators. Most were the result of Ricci's own work but some were effected by his companions and his immediate successors. The most famous of the converts among the men of letters, some of whom held important administrative posts, were Xu Guangqi (1562–1633, baptised Paul in 1603), Li Zhizao (1565–1630, baptised Leon in 1610), Yang Tingyun (1557–1627, baptised Michael in 1612), Wang Zheng (1571–1644, baptised Philip in 1617 or 1618) and Sun Yuanhua (1581–1632, baptised Ignatius in 1621).[122] These influential figures, in particular the first three, who were known as the 'three pillars of evangel-isation', counted for a great deal in the early successes of the mission: they treated the missionaries favourably both in the provinces and in Peking, recommending them for being capable of reforming the calendar and protecting them when times were difficult. A number of other sym-pathisers, such as the grand imperial secretary, Ye Xianggao (1562–1627), also provided the missionaries with precious support.

Nevertheless, over the twenty years that followed Ricci's death, the general atmosphere gradually changed. The literate and ruling circles had initially regarded the missionaries as learned men of austere morals, enemies of Buddhism and great admirers of Confucius. Of their teach-ings they had retained in particular whatever appeared to be in agree-ment with the traditions of China. As they became better informed about the content of the doctrine of the Master of Heaven, and when they perceived more clearly the aims that the missionaries were pursu-ing, their attitude changed. The first thing to provoke their anxiety was the formation among the people of religious associations under the direc-tion of foreigners. From their point of view, these represented a threat of agitation and disturbance. They now realised at the very least that the missionaries had not come to China simply to discuss ethics and philos-ophy or to teach mathematics. The first measure of persecution, in 1617, which consisted in ordering the missionaries to be returned to Macao (some of them hid or subsequently returned clandestinely) was provoked entirely by the formation in Nanking of a popular association of the doc-trine of the Master of Heaven.

The fact is that after about 1620, the Jesuits made no more conversions among the important men of letters or high-ranking administrators. None of those whom they subsequently baptised possessed the renown or authority of Xu Guangqi or Li Zhizao, or even of the less important figures, such as Wang Zheng or Sun Yuanhua: the educated classes had, as a whole, become hostile to the missionaries and their doctrine, and the only famous conversions made under the Manchu were those of the princes of the imperial family.[123] The missionaries therefore quite nat-urally diverted their efforts towards the popular milieux: those of the peasantry and the lesser urban trades. Conditions in general underwent a further change when Jesuit Fathers were appointed to the 'Mathemati-cal Tribunal' in the Court in Peking. Although their hopes of converting the emperor, Kangxi (1661–1722), who considered it advantageous to have foreign scholars in his service, were dashed, they were at least in a position to take action to protect their companions in the provinces. It became less indispensable to take precautions where the men of letters were concerned.

During Ricci's lifetime, the only criticisms of his works worth mentioning had been those of the great Buddhist master, Zhuhong (1535–1615), and of a scholar who was a Buddhist sympathiser by the name of Yu Chunxi. Zhuhong had included at the end of a collection of notes, a brief refutation of Ricci's concept of Heaven, and Yu Chunxi had criticised the missionary for encouraging the murder of animals through his assurances that, unlike human beings, animals did not have immortal souls. According to the Christian, Yang Tingyun, at this time and throughout the years that immediately followed, the whole of Chinese high society respected Ricci and his companions, and its members competed to produce prefaces for them and other articles in their praise. It was not until later that the situation deteriorated.[124] Similarly, in his preface to a work in Chinese by Father Aleni, published in 1646, Chen Yi, a man of letters from Fujian province, observed that 'when Ricci came to the capital, he was joyfully welcomed there by the literate elite ... whereas, after his death, some of them began to criticise the differences between the Barbarians and the Chinese'.[125]

One Huang Zhen wrote as follows:

In the past, the only ones to refute their vicious ideas strongly were Yu Deyuan [Yu Chunxi] and the Buddhist monk Lianchi [Zhuhong] ... But alas, Lianchi died soon after [on 29 July 1615]. Besides, he had never even met Ricci in person and was not fully familiar with his vicious notions: his criticisms did not get to the bottom of the matter. Furthermore, the books of the doctrine of the Master of Heaven were not very numerous at the time and nobody knew that, in their opinion, King Wen [the patron saint of Confucianism] was in hell. Today, the books expounding this doctrine are much more numerous.[126]

Let us cite as evidence of the change of opinion that took place among many people, the case of a man of letters of Quanzhou in Fujian province, who notes in 1638 that he had sought out the company of the missionaries for as long as he had regarded them only as scholars occupied with the calendar and astronomical instruments, but that his opinion changed entirely when he discovered that 'they held Yesu, a man of the period of the emperor, Ai, of the Han dynasty, to be the Sovereign on High to whom the Chinese do homage'.[127]

Following Ricci's death, the number of missionaries had increased and, what is more surprising, did so particularly after the first attempt to expel them to Macao, in 1617.

Huang Zhen, once again, reports:

Shortly after the thunderbolt that the expulsion order of the vice-minister of the Board of Rites, Shen Zhongyu [Shen Que] represented, in the Wanli period, these Barbarians returned to China in even greater numbers than at any time previously [!].[128]

This increase in the number of missionaries is also noted by the authors of a collective letter to the academician, Jiang Dejing, written in the winter of 1638–9, which records that, after being expelled in 1617, they returned in force at the beginning of the Tianqi period (1621–7) and were, at the time of writing, even more active than during the Wanli period (1573–1620).[129] During these same years, the author of an anti-Christian pamphlet notes that 'at the time of the Nanking trial of 1616 and 1617, there were no more than 13 of these cunning Barbarians in China but now there are dozens of them'.[130]

The numbers of these foreigners and their activities among the literate elite and, even more, among the humbler people, appeared to present a threat to public order, for they possessed an art of insinuating themselves into people's minds and upsetting them which rendered them particularly redoubtable. It even appeared to some that there was a certain conscious allotment of roles among these foreigners, some of whom sought to win the adherence and support of important members of the literate elite and high-ranking functionaries who were interested by the ethics and sciences of Europe, while others concentrated upon seducing men of the people by holding out hope of eternal joys and inspiring a fear of hell. What they were therefore faced with was a multiform operation the purpose of which was to seduce and corrupt the mores and traditions of China. These Barbarians possessed a diabolical duplicity. The author of a report dated 1617 writes: 'In discussion with people of distinction, they speak of heavenly nature (*tianxing*), but when they are addressing the common people they speak of miraculous happenings.'[131] And it is quite true that, in their writings aimed at literate circles, the missionaries are chiefly concerned with philosophy and ethics, while anything that smacks of the sacred is to the fore in their evangelical efforts in popular milieux.

A native of Zhangzhou, in the south of Fujian province, writes as follows:

They conceal their scheming beneath an appearance of honesty. Helping to construct cannons, they delight people with their skill. Praying for rain, they persuade people that they possess magic powers, Their clocks, their clavichords and their magnifying glasses dazzle people by the skill to which they testify. They attract people thanks to the gold that they possess in great abundance and win them over with their extreme politeness.[132]

But, the same author goes on to explain, their secret intention is to destroy all the cults and all the moral and philosophical traditions of China. Xu Dashou writes:

They appear to be quite unpretentious, but their hearts are devious. Are we, fools and clever men, men and women alike, all to be contaminated by their poison and plunged, by them, into error? They are not only determined enemies of Confucianism but also diabolically committed enemies of Buddhism. Ah, alas![133]

With respect to prayers for rain, the *New Memoranda on the Present State of China* by Father Le Comte contains an amusing passage relating how, during a time of drought, missionaries from France, recently landed at Ningbo in 1678, had had the idea of praying for rain, offerings to the Chinese gods having proved ineffective. He tells how they were obliged to give up the project after the governor of the town had had the untimely idea of joining his prayers to theirs, having previously made sacrifices to a dragon. Despite their explanations – the God of the Christians is a jealous God – and their remonstrances – it would not be seemly for an educated man to lend credibility to the superstitions of the people – human dignity prevented the said governor from going back on his word 'despite the fact', says Father le Comte, 'that he was not very far from having the same sentiments as ourselves'. Some of the Reverend Fathers, following the example of Saint Francis Xavier, then suggested making a bargain over this victory for the devil: namely, that they should be allowed to erect a huge cross in the middle of the town, in exchange for which they would undertake to make it rain, while the mandarins would order that all idols be toppled and the God of the Christians recognised as the only God. But other Fathers judged the operation too risky. In the end,

they had to content themselves with lamenting in the privacy of their own hearts and beseeching God to unleash, in the place of rain, the heavenly fire that Jesus Christ had brought down to earth and in which he desired all people to be consumed.[134]

The author of one pamphlet writes as follows:

So great is men's taste for strange things that they become ecstatic when they see Ricci's map of the world[135] ... But all he did was delude men over what they could not see with their own eyes and over places which were beyond their reach.[136]

In a proclamation published in 1637, Shi Bangyao,[137] the maritime inspector for Fujian province, wrote:

Their clever talk and their great skill in argument were of a kind to renew the interest of amateurs in curious things. Their paltry talents in the field of the arts and technology were of a kind to stimulate the tastes of humble folk. Thus, in the most distant of villages and areas, they set up sanctuaries and residences, attracting to them the humbler men of letters, who came to pay homage to them and conceived an unshakeable faith in all their pronouncements.[138]

A certain Wang Chaoshi from Shaoxing in the province of Zhejiang analyses, from his own personal point of view, the missionaries' undertaking to seduce the Chinese, as follows. First he levels the usual accusation of financial corruption through which 'they bewitch the greedy and the fools'.[139] He then goes on to draw attention to:

- the extreme skill that they deploy in the arts and through which they attract the interest of those who have a taste for, and an interest in, those kinds of things (mathematics, astronomy and instruments of all kinds);
- the ethical works that they compose, such as *The Seven Victories* by Diego de Pantoja or the *Ten Commandments*, through which they win over those men of letters bent on moral improvement;
- their pronouncements on paradise and hell – an idea which they stole from Buddhism – by means of which they turn their followers into fanatics. In all these matters, the Barbarians know how to take into account the diversity of individual minds and aptitudes.[140]

The sole object of all these manoeuvres is to lure the Chinese in order the better to bring them to destruction by turning them away from their traditions.

And the monk, Purun, from Hangzhou, comments: 'From the outside they seem humble and respectful, but inside they are cunning cheats.'[141]

So it would seem that, in the years that followed Ricci's death, the early friendly relations gave way to a growing suspicion and hostility among the literate and ruling circles. This deterioration in the climate can no doubt be explained by a number of different causes: the increasing rigidity that took over in Jesuit policies, their desire for quicker results, the increase in the number of missionaries, the development of their activities among popular milieux, and the fact that the literate elite now knew more about them than just their moral teaching, their anti-Buddhist polemics and their scientific knowledge.

Apparent Confucians

A decisive reason had led Matteo Ricci to employ the highest style in his works in Chinese rather than forge new words and express himself in a barbarian fashion contrary to the spirit of the language: he had decided first of all to win over the people of high society. Being extremely sensitive to a writer's style, the latter would have rejected badly written works without even reading them through. Ricci, his Jesuit contemporaries and his successors were in contact with educated people and the latter played an essential part in the definitive presentation of their works.[142]

However, the use of a vocabulary which related to traditions and concepts very different from those of Christianity ran the risk of being misleading.

There is a passage in the great treatise on *The True Meaning of the Master of Heaven* where Ricci writes that:

those who followed their own desires (*yu*) had become daily more numerous while those who obeyed the principle of universal order (*li*) had daily become increasingly rare. So the Master of Heaven emitted a great thought of compassion and came in person to save the world so as to awaken beings everywhere.[143]

This passage alone provides a typical example of the danger inherent in all translation. The opposition of 'human desires' (*renyu*) – egoistical passions which develop in man as a result of his reactions to things and beings – to the 'principle of heavenly order' (*tianli*), of which all human nature is a reflection, had acquired great importance in neo-Confucianism since the eleventh and twelfth centuries. It is to that philosophy, which is quite contrary to Christian dogma, that Ricci seems here to be referring. As for the last sentence, one might believe it to be drawn from a Buddhist sûtra, what with its use of the term 'awaken' and the expression 'emitted a great thought of compassion' (*da fa cibei*), *cibei* being the translation of the Sanskrit *maîtrî-karuna*. In Buddhism, saving men meant bringing them to the Awakening (*bodhi*), which would reveal to them the illusory character of the phenomenal world and permit them to escape from the cycle of rebirth and death. Here, too, the implicit reference conflicts with the theses of Christianity. In order to express his own ideas, Ricci is led, without realising it, to use a neo-Confucian or Buddhist vocabulary, which evokes concepts quite incompatible with those of eternal salvation and redemption.

The Protestant pastor, C. W. Mateer, lamented the all too frequent mistakes made by the Chinese. As he put it, in 1908:

Is there any convenient method of stating the doctrine of the Trinity which does not imply the grossest materialism?[144] Who has been fortunate enough to discover a name for sin which does not dash us on to the Scylla of civil crime or engulph [*sic*] us in the Charybdis of retribution for the faults of a former life? Use whatever language you please to express the resurrection, and the uninitiated will understand it to mean transmigration.[145]

In *The True Meaning of the Master of Heaven*, Ricci had wanted to appeal not only 'to many reasons and arguments drawn (as he says) from our own holy doctors but also, and with much authority, to those drawn from their ancient books which the Father [Ricci himself] had noted when he read them, and this lent his book great authority and credence'.[146]

But by being so eager to cite the Chinese Classics, and in particular those passages in them that refer to the Sovereign on High (*shangdi*) and use the word Heaven (*tian*), he ran the risk of having the men of letters misunderstand the meaning that the missionaries gave these words. The same thing had already happened with the Jews of Kaifeng in Henan province, several centuries before the missionaries' arrival. By using the word 'Dao', which meant nature's mode of action, to translate 'God', they had 'passed on to later members of their community a term which, with its strong flavour of immanence, radically changed the character of their transcendental God'.[147] The Jews of China had similarly used the words 'Heaven' and 'Sovereign on High' to refer to Yahveh.

The language itself deforms the Christian message, giving it alien, Chinese resonances that are quite incompatible with it.

For Huang Wendao from Fuzhou, it is quite clear that it is Ricci's constant use of Chinese forms of expression and formulae culled from the Classics that has misled many of the literate elite into believing that the doctrine of the Master of Heaven is in conformity with Confucian traditions. He explains that, having been well treated by Emperor Wanli, who had done him the honour of accepting his gifts, Ricci

desired immediately to propagate his ideas on the Master of Heaven. Now, the words and sounds of his own language had nothing in common with those of Chinese and it was to be feared that his ideas might be in total contradiction to those of our Confucianism. He therefore invited some of the Chinese men of letters to instruct him in the Classics and, leaving aside the most elevated and difficult things in these texts,[148] he adapted his own discourse externally to them in such a fashion that there appeared to be not much difference between what he was saying and the writings of Yao, Shun, Zhougong and Confucius. But in reality he was secretly developing his own doctrine. Rejecting Buddhism, criticising Taoism and denigrating Confucianism, he meanwhile harnessed Yao, Shun, Zhougong and Confucius as a means of conveying his own teaching.[149]

And a little further on he adds: 'I used to think that they had come to China through love of our Dao [that is, our moral and philosophical ideas]. Now I know that they stole it only to betray it.'[150]

The analogies established by the missionaries between the Chinese and the Christian traditions caused many of the literate elite to misunderstand the true meaning of the doctrine of the Master of Heaven, so that some of them were subsequently obliged to make a very great effort to clarify the matter. Huang Zhen reports in his letter to the censor, Yan Maoyou, that it had been necessary for him to undertake a profound inquiry with Father Aleni in order to bring to light the elements in his doctrine which were threatening to the Chinese traditions. He writes as follows:

There recently arrived in our region of Zhang[zhou] [in southern Fujian province], a man of the doctrine of the Master of Heaven by the name of Ai Rulue [Giulio Aleni], a companion of Li Madou [Matteo Ricci]. Crowds of fools rushed to rally to him. It is all deeply deplorable. But what is worse is that intelligent people are constantly proclaiming that this man is remarkable; they are deeply moved by his speeches, guard him closely and stir up the minds of others. As soon as I saw him, I could see what it was about the man that was so pernicious. However, I did not yet know all the details, and it was by examining all that had happened since the Wanli period [1573–1620][151] that I understood for the first time to what extent the harmful action of this type of Barbarian could poison China. I could not do otherwise than go to listen to him for a few days. But [at first] I was not able to analyse what he was saying well enough to refute him. It almost made me ill. It was not until the fourth or fifth day that I clearly perceived wherein the harmful character of his teaching lay and so found myself in a position to expose those things in an orderly fashion. That made me feel cheerful again. Generally speaking, there are five reasons for which [their discourse] may be a great danger to society. As for the rest, there is hardly time to dwell on it. I simply beseech you, Master, to examine these reasons in detail and deign to hear me out. Allow me simply to explain [before you] the dangerous poisons of their doctrine. I shall then have some hope of convincing you.[152]

Huang Zhen's five reasons relate to the threats to the philosophical, moral and religious traditions of China, the increase in the number of missionaries, their implantation in virtually every province of the empire and the formation of communities devoted to them, which represent yet another threat to the independence of China.

The missionaries had tried to adapt, but by using a particular method of conversion and unconsciously borrowing from deeply rooted Chinese traditions, the meaning of which they failed to understand. All this was interpreted by many Chinese as duplicity. In the view of an author of the end of the Ming period, the missionaries

invented the doctrine of the Master of Heaven, first learning the language and writing of China, then reading the Chinese books relating to the three doctrines [Confucianism, Buddhism and Taoism]. By borrowing from Buddhism, adding to Confucianism, inventing on all sides and much manipulation, they created this vicious doctrine in order to use it to upset the world, deceive people and undermine the foundations of our empire.[153]

The doctrine of the Master of Heaven appeared, essentially, to be a mixture of misunderstood Buddhist and Confucian ideas.

At the end of the eighteenth century, the author of a bibliographical note on Ricci's pamphlet entitled *The Twenty-five Utterances* is of the opinion that the Westerners pillaged Buddhism in an extremely clumsy fashion. His remarks continue as follows:

In the traditions of the countries situated to the west [of China], the only books are, in effect, Buddhist ones. The Europeans therefore took ideas from these books, transforming them in a fantastic way but without managing to detach themselves very much from their model. Having subsequently entered China and become accustomed to the books of the men of letters, they also borrowed a great deal from them to ornament their theories.[154]

So it was not simply a matter of Confucianism. However, in the early days of their mission, it was the Jesuits' approval of Confucius and rejection of Buddhism that won them considerable sympathy in literate circles. As we have seen, the missionaries did deliberately encourage a certain confusion between the literal meaning of the Classics and the principles of their own religion. What they were saying appeared to echo what had been said in the most revered works in China, but the meaning they gave to their citations was fundamentally different. Their intention, in effect, was to inflect the Chinese traditions in a new way and transform them from within. The same treatment was applied to Chinese practices which they could not condemn outright, such as ancestor worship: these had to be given a new meaning that was compatible with the teaching of Christianity. But in the immediate instance, the missionaries' approval of Confucius was a powerful argument in their favour.

However, as Christian ideas became better known, more and more of the Chinese men of letters saw through their policies and denounced them. Many who initially looked favourably upon the missionaries, seeing them simply as austere scholars and defenders of the Chinese tradition, later, when they became better informed about their doctrines, turned against them.

The author of a pamphlet, the preface to which is dated 1643, relates that he was delighted to hear of men from the West who attacked Buddhism and respected Confucianism up until the day when he was shown a little work by Father João da Rocha,[155] printed in 1609 and entitled *Brief Explanations Concerning Holy Images*.[156] When he had read it, he exclaimed: 'These accursed Barbarians appear to reject Buddhism but without acknowledging the fact that they have stolen its cast-offs. They pretend to honour Confucianism, but in reality they have come to upset its traditions.'[157]

A report dated 1617 already contains the following remark: 'They seem to adhere to our Confucianism but in reality their teaching is different from the true doctrine.'[158]

Yang Guangxian writes:

Seeing Ricci attack Buddhism and Taoism, our respectable people believed him to be rather on the side of us Confucians. That is why they showered praises upon him, helped him and in the end forgot all about the detestable side to his ideas; they did not perceive what was so devilish about his doctrine.[159]

The Buddhist monk, Purun, was also of the opinion that the missionaries' approval of Confucianism was simply a ploy to ingratiate themselves among the literate elite:

They openly reject Buddhism and Taoism in order to encourage the belief that they are Confucians. But secretly they denigrate Confucianism and are feeling their way. They condemn the expression 'following nature',[160] criticise the Dao [the concept of immanent order] and censure the ancestor cult.[161]

So the reason for the missionaries not attacking Confucianism is merely tactical: it would be too risky to clash head on with the most revered traditions of China and imprudent to attract too many enemies all at once. In a letter written in 1609 to the Visitor, Francesco Pasio, Ricci himself acknowledges the fact:

in the books that I have written, I begin by singing their praises [i.e. those of the Confucian men of letters] and by using them to confound the others [the Buddhists and the Taoists], not refuting them directly but interpreting the points on which they are in disagreement with our faith ... A most distinguished person who belongs to the sect of idols has even called me an adulator of the literate elite ... And I am very keen that others should also regard me in that light, *for we should have much more to do if we were obliged to fight against all three sects*.[162]

Xu Dashou, the author of *The Aid to Refutation*, harbours very few illusions as to the missionaries' fundamental hostility to the morality and the religious and philosophical ideas of the Chinese:

Some people say: 'They attack Buddhism, but I do not think they would attack Confucianism.' To which I reply: 'They denigrate the Cosmic Origin,[163] the virtue of humanity (*ren*) and the sense of duty (*yi*).[164] That is to denigrate the principles. They denigrate Confucius, Yao and Shun. That is to denigrate men. If they have not yet dared to attack Confucianism as violently as they attack Buddhism, it is only because in every household in China we revere Confucius, because in every family we love Yao and Shun and because, seeing the obstacles that confront them, they seek for the time being to avoid them. If, as at the time of the Mongol Barbarians, society was divided into ten classes, with the Buddhists classified as the third while the literate elite, the prostitutes and the beggars occupied the eighth, ninth and tenth, they would be attacking Confucianism even more violently than they attack Buddhism.' Even now, their followers say: 'How could our master, Aleni, not be worth ten thousand such as Confucius?'[165]

In 1623, Wang Qiyuan, for his part, writes:

The Barbarians began by attacking Buddhism. Next, they attacked Taoism, next the later Confucianism [*houru*: i.e. neo-Confucianism]. If they have not yet attacked Confucius, that is because they wish to remain on good terms with the literate elite and the mandarins, in order to spread their doctrine. But they are simply chafing at the bit in secret, and have not yet declared themselves.[166]

One man of letters who had been friendly with Father Aleni, who had arrived in Zhangzhou in the south of Fujian province in 1635, states that he received several Christian works from him. However, he does not appear to have been convinced by them. He writes:

What one reads in them is extremely superficial and altogether absurd. They openly take issue with the vicious and false ideas of Buddhism and Taoism, but they criticise [what they take to be] the errors of Confucianism in a veiled fashion. Meanwhile, where they do take issue with Confucianism, they do not dare to open their mouths wide for they wish to use the cap and gown of the literate elite to introduce their doctrine even in Court, so as to spread their poison more effectively.[167]

So some people clearly were not duped by Ricci's tactics which consisted in 'interpreting, without refuting directly'.

Another man of letters from Fujian province, the author of *Humble Remarks on the Distinction between the Doctrines*, starts off by emphasising the worthy nature of the missionaries' teaching (Heaven should be respected), their skill in argument and the purity of their conduct. Furthermore, he continues, since these people reject Buddhism and Taoism while honouring Confucius, some people are delighted and believe them. But an attentive reading of their works reveals a whole series of profound differences between their teaching and that of Confucius:

Confucius speaks of serving men and reforming one's own daily conduct. They, on the other hand, speak of serving the Sovereign on High and filling one's mind with fantasies. Confucius speaks of understanding life and knowing how to stay in one's place. They, in contrast, speak of knowing death[168] and winning favours in the Beyond. Confucius makes the Taiji [the cosmic origin] the directing principle of the universe and considers it to be what is most truly venerable and noble. They, though, judge the Taiji to be dependent, low and despicable in the highest degree.[169] Believing the rewards and punishments of the sovereign to be of no importance, they reject the prince [they are quite without loyalty] and in that respect reveal themselves to be more guilty than Yangzi [the apostle of absolute egoism]; believing devotion to and care for one's parents to be of negligible importance, they reject the father [they are quite without filial piety] and in that respect reveal themselves to be more guilty than Mozi [the apostle of the uniformity of all affections]. Denying that the principle of universal order is a constitutive element of human nature, they think that moral sense is something external to man, and in this they are more guilty than Gaozi [who held that human nature is undifferentiated].[170] Consequently, their obedience and respect for Heaven and the Sovereign on High are only a pretext for advancing their own lying ideas. These people from the distant West, helping themselves by using Confucianism as an ally, come into our land with weapons in their hands. Alas, half of those who respect their teaching are prominent figures and educated people. And if humble men such as myself decide to stand up and fight them, there are many who spit upon us and insult us.[171]

A certain Jiang Dejing from Quanzhou in Fujian province tells of his relations with the missionaries. In the past he had helped Father Aleni publish a short work entitled *Questions and Answers about the Countries of the West* (*Xifang wenda*). At the time, he knew only of their talents with respect to the calendar and their skill with astronomical instruments. He was unaware that they had a doctrine of the Master of Heaven. He writes:

Recently, when I read their books, I thought that they had stolen from our Confucianism the idea of 'serving Heaven' (*shi tain*)[172] and I thought that their Master of Heaven was identical to our Sovereign on High. I did not know that, according to them, in the period of the emperor, Ai, of the Han dynasty [6 to 1 BC], Yesu was the Master of Heaven.

However, Jiang Dejing remained on friendly terms with the missionaries because he admired their irreproachable conduct. He writes: 'I realised that, being unmarried and not castrated either, they were far more admirable than our married Taoist priests (*huoju*) and that is why I did not break off all relations with them.' And he even interceded with a high-ranking civil servant to persuade him that the measures taken in 1637 against the missionaries and their followers should be moderated. It was at this point, however, that he became better acquainted with the doctrine of the Master of Heaven and the disastrous effects that it could have upon the traditions and the political and moral order of China. He writes:

Huang Tianxiang [Huang Zhen] of Zhangzhou then showed me the *Collection for the Destruction of Vicious Doctrines* (*Poxie ji*) and it became clear to me that their doctrine was inevitably bound to upset the world, that it was necessary to take immediate action to 'beat the drum' and that, in my way of proceeding, which consisted in condemning their doctrine but being in less of a hurry to chase them out, I was acting quite differently from Mencius, in the past, when dealing with Yang and Mo [the two enemies of Confucian morality].[173]

Huang Zhen, again, in his letter to the censor, Yan Maoyou, writes: 'Thanks to their fraudulent adherence to our Confucian axiom, "Serve the Sovereign on High with respect",[174] these people have been able to spread their poisons and develop their intrigues freely', and he continues: 'As my friend, Chen Shuishi, says: "with respect to our doctrine, they act like bandits who, having surreptitiously infiltrated the place, suddenly make a violent attack"'.[175]

A certain Zeng Shi, meanwhile, writes in his preface to a pamphlet entitled *I cannot bear to hold my tongue*:

How can it be claimed that their doctrine is in accordance with our Confucianism when, in *The True Meaning of the Master of Heaven* alone, Ricci explains that Confucius' idea of the cosmic origin is false,[176] the statement by Zisi [a disciple of

Confucius] to the effect that one should 'follow nature' is unfounded,[177] that Mencius' statement on the three filial impieties is erroneous,[178] that the commentaries by Zhu Xi on sacrifices to Heaven and Earth will not do[179] and that Cheng Hao's explanation on the double aspect of both substance and the regulating principle of Heaven is false?[180]

Zou Weilian agrees with Zeng Shi on the subject of Ricci:

Not content with insulting Buddhism and Taoism, he sets himself above the five sovereigns [of early Antiquity], the three kings [the founders of the most ancient dynasties], the Duke of Zhou and Confucius. Never has everything been turned so upside down. He criticises Confucius' teaching on the Taiji [the cosmic origin] and his writing on the Springs and Autumns;[181] he criticises Mencius' replies on the virtue of humanity and the sense of duty as well as his statement on filial impiety, which is constituted by the failure to produce any descendants.[182]

It cannot be denied that Ricci does attack both Confucianism as a whole and even its spirit when he says that what defines man is his faculty of reasoning, while Confucius' virtues (*ren*, humanity; *li*, sense of rituals or propriety; *yi*, sense of duty; and *zhi*, wisdom) are secondary;[183] when he dissociates moral good and natural good and, in opposition to the Chinese thesis of a natural source of morality and the superiority that this confers upon spontaneity over reflection, maintains that there is no good without the intention of doing good and no good without effort;[184] when he declares that perfecting oneself is not an aim in itself;[185] when he says that, compared with the Master of Heaven, our parents are alien to us;[186] when he denies the importance of maintaining lineages and perpetuity in the family cults;[187] and when he subordinates filial piety to one's duties towards God.[188]

As already noted, his ploy of twisting the meaning of the Classics or the texts of their principal interpreters did not escape detection by some of the Chinese men of letters, who saw in this a deliberate desire to falsify.

Li Can writes as follows:

They went so far as to borrow the following proposition from Zhu Xi [the great neo-Confucian master of the twelfth century]: 'The sovereign means the regulating power of Heaven', claiming that this proposition was in agreement with their own idea of the Master of Heaven. But they omitted part of the sentence and cut the text short.[189] That is perfectly ridiculous.

And elsewhere he writes:

Confucius said to Duke Ai: 'That is why man is absolutely obliged to perfect himself; desiring to perfect himself, he is absolutely obliged to serve his parents; desiring to serve his parents, he is absolutely obliged to understand other men; desiring to understand other men, he is absolutely obliged to know Heaven.'[190]

He did not, as Ricci suggests he did, quite simply say: 'In order to serve one's parents, it is absolutely necessary to know Heaven.' The fundamental idea in Confucius' whole paragraph is that it is important first and foremost to perfect oneself.[191]

The Christian thesis is that the principle of morality lies in God, the Chinese that it is impossible to rise to comprehension of the universal order without first fulfilling one's duties to one's parents. The Chinese morality consists in a continuous process of perfecting the self, the starting-point being one's most immediate relationships. So the meaning of the Classics had certainly been distorted.[192]

A similar type of accusation is levelled by Yang Guangxian, who, in his *Pixie lun* (1659), writes as follows:

They dissect and dismember the text of the Classics. Parrots, who know how to speak the language of men but are beasts none the less! Ricci claims to revere Yesu as the Master of Heaven. He places him above all the Saints of the ten thousand kingdoms. He cites all the passages in the Classics in which the words 'Sovereign on High' appear and, truncating the texts, he uses those passages to prove that our Sovereign on High is also his Master of Heaven.[193]

Ricci had been quick to understand the risks involved in revealing the mysteries of Christianity to the Chinese men of letters, unless they had first undergone a lengthy preparation. That is why his words aimed at the people of high society made no mention of those mysteries and, in the great treatise of the founder of the Jesuit mission in China, we find no more than a few lines on the Incarnation. Ricci himself explains his tactics: by alluding so briefly to Jesus, he hoped to intrigue the Chinese and provoke them into questioning the missionaries. He writes:

At the end of this work, there is a further explanation of the coming of Christ our Redeemer into the world to save and instruct it, with the aim of inciting the Chinese to ask the Fathers about their true doctrine, which is taught in a much more detailed fashion in other books.[194]

In view of the suspicions that might be aroused by the diffusion of doctrines considered threatening to the public order, it was to the missionaries' advantage to claim that they were teaching nothing new. Here, in effect, is what can be read in the *Proclamation following the Arrest of the Heterodox Association* at the time of the Nanking lawsuit of 1616–17:

In their plea and justificatory address, the Barbarians unanimously claim that their Master of Heaven is the same Heaven that the Chinese revere, and those who adhere to their doctrine also declare: 'Our China has always paid homage to Heaven.' Yet these Barbarians have published a *Short Version of the Doctrine of the Master of Heaven*,[195] in which it is clearly stated that the Master of Heaven was born in a particular year during the reign of Emperor Ai of the Han dynasty, that his name is Yesu and that his mother was called Yalima [Maliya]. So he is just a Barbarian of the western seas. They also say that he died nailed by evil administrators to a structure in the form of a character that denotes ten. So he is just a barbarian convict condemned to death. How could an executed barbarian convict be called the Master of Heaven? In their justificatory address they even go so far as to state clearly that the Master of Heaven descended to be born in a Western kingdom. And they have the audacity to abuse the ears of the emperor with such lying statements so contrary to propriety! Do they imagine that, in our China, nobody will notice their deception?[196]

Ricci's great treatise aimed only to establish 'the foundations of the faith', as the author put it. Apart from this work, the literate elite had at their disposal only ethical works through which to form an idea of the doctrine of the Master of Heaven. That is why Yang Guangxian, violently hostile to the missionaries, advised those who wished to be correctly informed of this doctrine to read the works reserved for the use of neophytes and catechumeni, in which it would be revealed in its true light, whereas, in the ethical and philosophical works, its principles remained hidden and dressed up so as to appear Chinese. He wrote:

The works circulated [by these Barbarians] most of the time pillage the language, style and even the propositions of our Classics, but every vicious theory in their books always stems from their doctrine. Possessing much gold, it is easy for them to persuade Chinese who are failures to edit and polish their writings for them, so that one subsequently sees only works in an ornate style and nothing remains of the vicious original. People thus eat the bloom knowing nothing of the fruit. They are trapped by the fog and fall into a perverted view of their duties. We must therefore have recourse to a complete critique in order to get to the very core [of their ideas].

So educated people should first peruse such and such a collection of pious pictures together with its commentary, such and such a catechism and collection of daily prayers, and they will need nothing more to be totally informed on the matter. Such was the advice that Yang Guangxian offered to his all too often duped compatriots.[197]

And Yang Guangxian also writes:

In his books, Ricci took very good care not to speak of the lawful execution of Yesu. Thus all the literate elite have been deceived and duped. That is what makes Ricci a great criminal. But his companion, Schall, who was less intelligent, set out everything concerning Yesu in his *Jincheng shuxiang*.[198]

Sciences and religion

For the literate elite at the end of the Ming period, the teachings of the missionaries – moral, philosophical, scientific and technological – were all part of a unified whole. Together they made up what the Chinese called 'the heavenly studies' (*tianxue*) or 'the Western studies' (*xixue*). In 1628, the famous convert, Li Zhizao, collected into a single series texts written by the missionaries which, from our point of view, belong to a number of quite different genres. His *First Collection of Heavenly Studies* (*Tianxue chuhan*) is, in effect, divided into works which relate to the principle of universal order (*li*) (i.e. those which concern ethics and philosophy) and works which relate to objects (*qi*) (i.e. those which concern the sciences and technology). Now, the two concepts of *li* and *qi*[199] were closely linked in the philosophy of the time. But there are plenty of other proofs of the way in which the Chinese saw the missionaries' teaching as a totality: for the important men of letters converted in the early seventeenth century, who were certainly inspired by the Chinese tradition of disciples displaying loyalty towards their master, the sciences and technology were inseparable from all the rest and, indeed, constituted one of the main reasons for their own adherence to the doctrine of the Master of Heaven.

To us, the way that the Chinese connected such different fields may seem surprising. But the Jesuits were themselves to some extent responsible for their doing so, since they used their scientific teaching as a kind of introduction to their religious instruction. Ricci had led the way and he was followed by many others. In 1735, Father Parennin was still writing:

In order to attract their attention, it is necessary to win credit in their minds and gain their respect through knowledge of natural things, about which they know very little and are curious to learn: there is nothing that better disposes them to listen to us when we speak of the holy truths of Christianity.[200]

The sciences did thus serve as a lure. But they were also supposed to provide supplementary proofs for the truths of religion: Christianity was founded upon reason. In their prefaces and even in the main body of their works on mathematics and astronomy, the Jesuits never failed to remind the reader of the existence of a creator God, responsible for the order which reigned in the universe.

As we have seen, at first the Jesuits' tactics served them well. If many of the men of letters expressed esteem and admiration for them, it was for a combination of reasons: because of the useful knowledge they brought to China, their moral rigour, and the care with which they appeared to be reminding the Chinese of their own religious traditions.[201] It was, as the Classics declared, necessary to 'serve', 'respect' and 'fear Heaven'. But distinctions were gradually made as, little by little, the general dogma and inspiration of the doctrine of the Master of

Heaven became better known and understood. The strange thing that then came about was that, whereas the Jesuits had sought to use the prestige of the sciences of Europe to reinforce the authority of religion, the Chinese rejected that religion, wishing to retain only the scientific knowledge.

Fang Yizhi (1611–71), almost all of whose works were written before the Manchu armies entered Peking in 1644, is one of the first to make this distinction. When he has occasion to cite scientific works dictated or composed by the missionaries, he systematically omits everything relating to their religious ideas. Thus, he pays no attention at all to an argument that frequently appears in their works, namely that the order of the world is proof of the existence of a creator God organising the world down to the last detail. Fang Yizhi was definitely of the opinion that the 'Westerners were clever at examining and fathoming things, but incapable of penetrating the innermost workings of the universe'.[202]

But during the Manchu period it became generally accepted practice to distinguish between the two parts of the missionaries' teaching: the scientific knowledge and technology that they had introduced to the Chinese were worth preserving; all their religious teaching was to be proscribed. Such was the position adopted by the author of the notes relating to works stemming from the missionaries, in the great bibliography of the late eighteenth century, the *Siku quanshu zongmu tiyao* (1782). One of these notes on the subject of the collection of works stemming from the missionaries and edited by Li Zhizao in 1628, contains the following remarks:

The superiority of the Western teaching (*xixue*)[203] lies in their calculations; their inferiority lies in their veneration of a Master of Heaven of a kind to upset men's minds. It is absurd to say, as they do, that 'from the immensity of Heaven and Earth down to the smallest creeping creature, there is not a single thing that has not been created by the hand of the Master of Heaven'. That does not even merit serious discussion. However, when they require people to consider the Master of Heaven as their closest relative and to abandon their fathers and mothers and place their sovereign in second place, giving the direction of the state to those who spread the doctrine of the Master of Heaven, this entails an unprecedented infringement of the most constant rules. How could their doctrine possibly be admissible in China?

By making known their methods of calculation, Li Zhizao and the others[204] have no doubt been successful in preserving the acceptable side of their teaching, but it was madness simultaneously to publish and spread their deceiving and misleading lies, which are manifestly in disagreement with the ideas of our Classics.[205]

The author of these notes then goes on to observe that the compilers of the great collection of printed and manuscript works put together at the end of the eighteenth century, the *Siku quanshu*, chose to preserve ten mathematical works from the scientific section of Li Zhizao's collection. As for the others, those in the *li* category (relating to the principle of universal order),[206] they preserved only the *Zhifang waiji*, a kind of cosmography produced by Father Aleni and Yang Tingyun in 1623. All the rest was censored. They also kept Li Zhizao's foreword so as to make known his crime: that of having encouraged heresy. In another note we read:

Assuredly, the Europeans are far superior to our own predecessors in respect of the accuracy of their astronomical calculations and the ingenuity of their instruments. But at the same time, no heterodox sect has ever gone so far where exaggeration, falsity, absurdity and improbability are concerned. By choosing to retain their technology and their talents and to prohibit the diffusion of their doctrine, our dynasty has shown its deep wisdom.[207]

And he comments upon an astronomical work printed in 1615 as follows:

The work opens with a preface by Manuel Dias in which, apart from his own speciality [astronomy], he exalts the work of the Master of Heaven. He even alludes to what he calls the twelfth immobile heaven, which he claims to be the dwelling-place of all the saints and the place that is paradise. Those who worship the Master of Heaven may ascend there. There is plenty here to delight fools and undermine them. The fact is that, attempting to refer to the exactitude of his calculations and deductions to prove the existence of a Master of Heaven, he takes a great deal of trouble to delude the world. But as for everything relating to astronomy, that is incontestably superior to our own ancient methods. Let us therefore disregard all his absurd and lying theories and only retain his precise methods, which are founded upon proofs. Let us do away with the preface in order to avoid having some people deluded. As for the absurdities which crop up in the main body of the work and which, if deleted, would make the text incomprehensible, we can leave them where they are but at the same time refute such vicious ideas as we have just done above.[208]

But the Western sciences themselves were not always entirely safe from criticism, for there are hardly any forms of science not founded upon particular *a priori* assumptions and particular representations of the world. Thus, it was the hypothesis that the world was created by a geometrician and clockmaker God that inspired the first developments of modern science in the West. What the missionaries taught about the celestial spheres and a universe created once and for all, limited both in space and in time, was in accordance with their theology; but it was in contradiction to the Chinese representations which, in comparison, may appear to us more modern. The Chinese imagined the heavens as an infinite space in which heavenly bodies floated and in which, over extremely long periods of evolution, universes formed and disintegrated as a result of the condensation or dissipation of an omnipresent, universal energy.[209]

The Church energetically opposed the heliocentric theory because it cast doubt upon an image of the world which it considered indissociable from its religious teaching. Similarly, in China, because the organisation of time and space had been one of the essential functions and privileges of royal power ever since Antiquity, anything that affected the calendar and astronomical questions – in short, anything that concerned the heavens – was part of, as it were, a reserved domain.

For the Chinese, the sky, or Heaven, was the guarantor and model for social and political order. In his act of accusation drawn up against Father Vagnone in 1616, Shen Que, the vice-minister of the Board of Rites in Nanking, refers to a traditional representation which identified the sun with the sovereign, the moon with his wife, the constellations near the pole with the administrators and the other stars with the common people.[210] Now, by introducing seven crystalline spheres corresponding to the orbits of the sun, the moon and the five planets, the missionaries upset the Chinese traditions relating to the heavens. It seemed like striking a blow against the order of nature, and Shen Que retaliated with the declaration that there is but one, single Heaven in which all the celestial bodies evolve, going on to say that to argue in favour of such things was to upset the world, delude people[211] and 'secretly harm the civilising influence of the sovereign'.[212] The last accusation clearly demonstrates the link that, in China, united the idea of Heaven with that of political order.[213]

The establishment of the calendar was a privilege of the sovereign, one of the clearest marks of his power to establish order in the world. By accepting their calendar from the emperor of China, vassal countries acknowledged their allegiance to him. The production of calendars by private individuals thus constituted an infringement of imperial prerogatives and, as it were, an attempt to usurp the supreme power. A law instituted by the founder of the Ming dynasty, at the end of the fourteenth century, forbade common individuals to occupy themselves with heavenly phenomena or to make astronomical instruments. Now, one of the charges preferred in the Nanking lawsuit of 1617 notes that the Barbarians from the West

privately possess and make astronomical instruments, thereby violating our laws. And they have pushed their audacity so far as to invent the theory of the seven heavens, thereby destroying the unity of Heaven. In view of all this, there is nothing in the world that they would feel the slightest hesitation in upsetting and disturbing with their lies. Furthermore, even at a distance of 100 *li*, things are no longer the same; at 1,000 *li*, the gnomon no longer casts the same shadow.

All the more reason then, for the measurements provided by the shadow of the gnomon 90,000 *li* away [the distance which, according to them, separates China from Europe] to be entirely different. What is suitable for them cannot be taken as the rule here.[214]

Another author also reminds the reader of the prohibition against the private pursuit of astronomy, but also adduces further reasons for his condemnation of the sciences. Like many other Chinese of his time, he imagined that the sciences held an important place in the doctrine of the Master of Heaven. He writes:

It is not the same as in our China where we choose our elite on the basis of their knowledge of the Classics. They do not know that the private study of astronomy and the unauthorised production of calendars were forbidden by the founder of our dynasty when he instituted the Code ... If we respect their teachings we shall inevitably come to destroy the Classics and the traditions of Confucius and Mencius, breaking with the moral heritage of Yao and Shun and thus sacrificing all care for public well-being in favour of observing the heavenly signs.[215]

In other words, the sciences – and here astronomy is seen as being very close to astrology – distract people from what is essential, namely the production and distribution of the necessities of life, and good behaviour. We are reminded of the Confucian precept: act well without bothering about things which are too far removed from us and which, like the future, are inaccessible to our knowledge.

Like the scientific knowledge brought by the missionaries, the innovations of their technology also provoked varied reactions. It was not simply a question of a greater or smaller degree of open-mindedness since those who praised and those who criticised did so in the name of the very same principles: the great criterion was that of utility. Those with the greatest interest in Western technology concentrated only upon those of its aspects that could encourage the production of wealth, make life easier for men, or reinforce the defences of the empire.[216] Meanwhile, pamphlets hostile to the missionaries saw in their scientific teaching no more than a vain display of cleverness. They reminded their readers that when it came to mechanical genius, the Chinese stood in no need of lessons from foreigners. They pointed out how contradictory it was, on the part of the Barbarians, to prohibit homicide and also to busy themselves with artillery.[217]

To arouse the admiration of the Chinese, the missionaries had, among other novelties, introduced into China clocks that chimed the hour. They must have enjoyed a measure of popularity since the Chinese wasted little time in setting about making their own. However, these verge and folio clocks registered the time in no more than a very approximate fashion. Real progress came only later, with the adoption of the Huygens pendulum right at the end of the seventeenth century. One thus comes across as many detractors in China as enthusiasts of these 'bells that ring of their own accord'. In a pamphlet published between 1630 and 1639 and entitled *Ricci Invented Fables in order to Delude the World*, a critic by the name of Wei Jun gives a detailed description of their mechanism and points out that, given that the force that moves them is gradually diminished, they cannot possibly run in accordance with the real time. It is therefore necessary to rewind them in order to accelerate their movement and reset them correctly every day by referring to a sundial. If the weather is cloudy several days in succession, it becomes impossible to set them correctly. All the same, the author acknowledges, it is a simpler method than that of the clepsydra.[218]

However, the most severe criticisms were of a moral order: it is wrong to waste one's time on futile things; the only things that matter are the well-being of men and good relations between them.

Xu Dashou spells it out: have people not heard that one should despise useless inventions, for 'however great the skill involved may be, it is of no profit to the human person or to the spirit'. Now, the inventions of the Westerners are, precisely, vain displays of skill:

Their clocks are not as good as our clepsydras. To produce them, scores of ounces of silver are used and all to no profit. It could be said of the balance for drawing water that it truly does economise on the efforts of men. But these clocks, which are so hard to make and so prone to go wrong, are they, on the contrary, not simply a waste?[219]

Chapter 2

Religious attitudes and the phenomena of assimilation

The literate elite

Accustomed as they were to rigorous dogma and firm beliefs, the missionaries were shocked to discover a certain indifference and absence of conviction in the religious sentiments of the Chinese men of letters. They also deplored their pronounced taste for all forms of syncretism. The fact was that it did indeed seem to the Chinese that everything was reconcilable and that, given that the truth was a matter of approximation, it was in one's interest to try to approach it from various different angles and to take inspiration from whatever was best in every doctrine. The means, basically, were of little importance.[1]

This attitude was in direct opposition to that of the missionaries, who were hoping to imbue the Chinese with an absolute faith and had come to China to preach a religion the dogmas of which were defined extremely precisely, as were its obligatory beliefs, its moral imperatives and its ways of worship. So Ricci was scandalised when he discovered the great popularity of syncretist tendencies in literate circles. He writes:

The most common opinion today amongst those who believe themselves to be the most wise is to say that these three sects [Confucianism, Buddhism and Taoism] are one and the same thing and can all be observed at once. By this they deceive themselves and others too, creating the greatest confusion, for it seems to them that, where religion is concerned, the more ways there are of putting things, the better for the kingdom.[2] And in the end, the result is just the opposite from what they hoped, for, desiring to follow all these laws, they find themselves without any and following none with all their hearts. Thus, what with some of them openly admitting their incredulity and others thinking that they believe but not truly believing most of them end up by remaining in the most profound atheism.[3]

Syncretism between the three doctrines and, more generally, between Buddhism and Confucianism, was indeed fashionable at the end of the Ming period. It was favoured not only by Buddhist masters such as Zhuhong (1535–1615), but also by important men of letters such as Jiao Hong (1541–1620), whom Ricci had met in Nanking at the beginning of 1599.[4] In Fujian province, a certain Lin Zhao'en (1517–98) had even

64

created a semi-popular religion which combined the 'three doctrines' (*sanjiao*) and had spread to the provinces of Jiangxi and Zhejiang and to the Nanking region. His temples contained statues of Confucius, Buddha and Laozi, all together.[5] Antonio de Caballero mentions these temples in a passage in his *Treatise*:

The statues of these three personages [Confucius, Buddha Sâkyamuni and Laozi], the authors of these three sects, are usually placed on the same altar, which is dedicated to them with the following inscription at the door of the temple: san kiao tank [*sanjiao tang*]. There is one of these temples built on a mountain from which one can see the capital town of the province of Xamtum [Shandong] [that is, Jinan].[6]

The absence of any system or dogmatic construction facilitated such borrowings and assimilations as did, above all, the absence of the idea with which we, in the West, are so familiar, namely that there is only one truth and only one religion can encompass it. Thus, the statistics relating to the membership of the various religious faiths in China have never held much significance because the very idea of belonging to one particular religion is inapplicable there. Quite apart from their classical education, which was sometimes profound, sometimes less so, most men of letters had tried out a bit of everything in the course of their lives – Buddhism, Taoism and techniques of longevity, divination and the science of the *yin* and the *yang* – moving from one to another with not the slightest compunction about mixing them up. Although orthodoxy might face some upsets, the barriers between the different doctrines were in no way insurmountable. And there were so many different currents, so many different aspects in the nebulae of Taoism and Buddhism that it was not possible to assimilate them to the Western type of religion with its clearly defined dogmas. For the Chinese, it was more a matter of different groupings of philosophical, moral, religious and – on occasion – technological teaching. And the Chinese of the seventeenth century considered the teaching of the missionaries from precisely that point of view, giving it the very general name of *tianxue* (heavenly studies), which applied to the sciences and technology just as much as to ethics and religion. Furthermore, for the Chinese, each and every doctrine had its political implications. European categories and, above all, European distinctions between the spiritual and the temporal as two completely distinct domains were inapplicable to the Chinese situation.

As for the common people, if beliefs, practices and cults were to be found among them, it could nevertheless not be said that they adhered to clearly defined religions, for the confusion between different currents and influences was even greater at that level. It was usually impossible to determine what any particular cult owed to the more ancient elements of peasant religion and what to the more or less scholarly contributions of Buddhism and Taoism.

The reason why the Chinese in general manifested such a pronounced inclination for compromises and syntheses was that, for them, there were no transcendent and eternal truths. The idea of a sacrosanct dogma was quite alien to them. Referring to his converts among the literate elite, Longobardo wrote: 'They do not understand how important it is that there should be not the slightest error in the subjects that we are dealing with.'[7] For most Chinese, it was the missionaries themselves – and Matteo Ricci first and foremost – who had invented the doctrine of the Master of Heaven. So, if necessary, a few improvements could be made to it. Thus, the emperor, Shunzhi (1644–61), whom Father Schall was attempting to convert, one day replied to the latter as follows: 'You are right but, really, how can you expect us to practise all these maxims? Cut out one or two of the more difficult ones and then perhaps we can get along with the rest.'[8]

What has hardly been emphasised at all by the historians of Christianity in China is that the converts among the literate elite were expecting to operate a kind of synthesis with Christianity itself. What the academician, Xu Guangqi, Ricci's most famous and best educated disciple, was advocating was not the pure Christian doctrine, but an amalgamation of Confucianism and Christianity similar to that which had emerged in the sixteenth century between Confucianism and Buddhism. In the preface to the treatise on Western hydraulics that he produced in collaboration with Father Sabatino de Ursis, namely the *Taxi shuifa* (1612), Xu Guangqi writes: 'One day I remarked that their teachings were altogether suitable for complementing Confucianism and replacing Buddhism (*buru yifo*).'[9] It was not, as the missionaries thought and hoped, a matter of a division of roles between a purely worldly doctrine and a doctrine that proclaimed transcendent truths, but rather that of a synthesis between on the one hand the Confucian system, in which no distinction was made between the secular and the religious, and, on the other, the moral, religious and scientific teachings of the missionaries. It is, after all, worth noting that this remark of Xu Guangqi appears in the preface to a treatise on hydraulics, not a discipline about which there is anything particularly Christian.

Even more striking, according to Longobardo, who had taken great pains to find out the truth about what both the pagan and the Christian men of letters really thought, Michael Yang Tingyun, one of the great converts of the early seventeenth century, had in mind a kind of syncretism between the 'four doctrines'. Longobardo writes:

As this maxim, that all things are of one and the same substance,[10] is held in common by the sect of the men of letters, the sorcerers[11] and the Buddhist monks, Dr Michael [Yang] speaks favourably of it in his treatises on these three sects, seeking to prove that their aim had been to establish a universal principle and that in this respect they are in agreement with our Holy Law and are essentially the same. To the objection that in those sects there are a number of things that are quite contrary to our religion, he replies that while the sects followed their doctrines in all their purity those errors did not arise and that the Interpreters [12] introduced them, not having correctly understood the meaning of the ancient authors. That is why he advised us to use, in our treatises and in the resolution of our controversies, ambiguous and equivocal terms which could please both parties[13] and, by these means, reconcile everybody. That is the fine advice and the fine manner of preaching the Gospel that we owe to Dr Michael.[14]

For a Christian, there is, on the contrary, only one true religion. That was what Ricci had tried to explain in *The True Meaning of the Master of Heaven*, by pointing out the logical absurdity of the syncretism of the 'three doctrines': either all three are true, he explained, and in that case one is enough; or one is true and the others are false, in which case the latter should be repudiated; or else all three are false, so all deserve to be repudiated. But, he went on to say, in reality Buddhism and Taoism were bad. Now, if one mixed the good (Confucianism) with the bad (Buddhism and Taoism), the result was bound to be disastrous. A true orthodoxy rejects any sharing and insists upon total commitment. How could one possibly reconcile doctrines as different as Confucianism and Buddhism which, over more than a thousand years, have developed quite independently the one from the other?[15]

In China, cults were a matter of custom: the question of deciding whether, from an absolute point of view, a religion was true or false, never arose. It was enough that it should be sanctioned by tradition, that its teachings strengthened public morality and its cults contributed, by their results, to the general order. In the ruling circles, the attitude to religion depended upon those criteria and upon political circumstances. Measures taken against religious movements considered to threaten public tranquillity could be particularly harsh, as in the case of the 'deviant religions' or 'vicious doctrines' (*xiejiao*) which developed beyond the control of the public authorities. Christianity itself, after the middle of the seventeenth century, was increasingly often compared to the irregular Chinese sects, and it too suffered from this type of persecution, particularly from the reigns of Yongzheng (1723–36) and Qianlong (1736–96) on. However, Chinese intolerance was much less inflexible than the kind that is fed by a certainty of the truth. It was not inspired by well-defined religious convictions. Seeking to show the intolerance of the Chinese in matters of religion, J. J. M. de Groot has provided an interpretation typical of the mental attitudes of the West.[16] It is an interpretation that was, needless to say, also that favoured by the missionaries. They considered their own apostolic mission as an unremitting struggle against false gods and Satan.

Father le Comte at some point expresses his amazement at the inconsequentiality of the literate elite. These atheists who criticise superstition in the name of the 'new philosophy' (neo-Confucianism), prostrate themselves before idols just as if they were men of the people.[17] The fact is they do sometimes allow themselves to believe in things that they would usually condemn. But their usual conduct can be explained by their respect for conventions and their uncertainty with respect to the existence of the gods and spirits. Perhaps there are none, but perhaps there are. When in doubt, it is better to be cautious and conform with the established customs.

In *The True Meaning of the Master of Heaven*, Ricci writes:

Those who today argue about the spirits and gods each have their own opinion. Some say that they definitely do not exist. Others say that they do exist if one believes in them and do not if one does not believe in them. Others say that it is just as false to say that they do exist as to say that they do not and that the truth is that they both do and at the same time do not exist.[18]

So, on Ricci's account, some totally denied that the spirits existed, others held that they only existed in men's minds, and others – no doubt the majority – held that the only suitable attitude to take where they were concerned was not to pronounce on the matter. All this could hardly have been to the missionaries' liking.

When questioned about the religion of the literate elite, Michael Yang Tingyun one day told Longobardo that they made sacrifices to universal Heaven, to Earth and to the Mountains, to give thanks for their favours. As for the spirits, 'they do not know with certainty that they exist, but on the simple enough grounds that they might, they honour them along with Heaven, Earth, the Mountains, etc. as being of one and the same substance as all these things'.[19]

The attitude of the literate elite to the traditional cults is marked by a respect that forbids all familiarity. Confucius said: 'Fulfilling one's duties as a man and respecting the spirits while holding them at a distance – that is what is called being wise.'[20]

What has been called the agnosticism of Confucius also finds expression in other forms, in his *Sayings*: 'The master spoke neither of miracles, nor of acts of violence, nor of disturbances, nor of spirits.'[21] And again: 'Whoever does not know how to fulfil his duties towards men, how could such a one possibly fulfil his duties towards the gods?'[22]

One of the greatest Chinese thinkers of the seventeenth century, Wang Fuzhi (1619–92), writes in one of his notes that one should maintain neither that there are spirits nor that there are not. To maintain that there are would be to open the door to all kinds of superstitions and encourage their development. But categorically to deny their existence would be to destroy the bases for the sacrifices of the classical tradition.[23] This position, which is inspired by Confucius' attitude towards discretion, may seem illogical to us, because from our point of view what counts is knowing truly whether there are or are not invisible spirits. But it is not illogical if one agrees with the Chinese that the problem of the existence of the gods is a secondary one, while the important thing is the behaviour of men.

Citing a commentary on one of the Classics, the Franciscan, Antonio de Caballero, declares that:

we are warned not to raise ourselves to what is above us and beyond our capabilities, such as wanting to discover the secrets of the spirits and understand very difficult things, while neglecting what befits us and is within our capabilities and can make us more perfect;[24] and holding this view, Confucius adds that we behave like weak men if we do not do what we know to be just and right.[25]

Serving Heaven (*shi tian*) consists in performing rituals which err neither through default (for that would show negligence) nor through excess (for that would show a lack of respect towards Heaven and a desire to obtain more than one's due, through flattery). Wang Fuzhi explains: 'The greatest errors begin in an undetectable and subterranean fashion ... Whoever forgets Heaven is a fool, but whoever makes it his master is a Barbarian.' And to give an example of the latter abuse, Wang Fuzhi cites

the mistakes made recently by Matteo Ricci with his expression 'Master of Heaven'. He has dared, showing not the slightest compunction, to turn his back upon the ancestors in favour of an unclean ghost. And, although he has dressed up his theories with speeches full of artifice, what they come down to in the end are the ideas of those we call Barbarians.[26]

Perhaps this should be taken as an allusion to Tengri, the god of Heaven of the nomadic herdsmen of the steppes. It is one of the rare passages in an extremely long work in which Wang Fuzhi indicates that he is informed about Christianity – which is a measure of his minimal interest in that religion.

While refuting Christianity, Xu Dashou refers to the discretion of Confucianism as far as things that are not knowable are concerned. Confucius said: 'Not knowing what life is, how is it possible to know what death is?'[27] The appendix to the *Book of Changes* states that it is the most subtle of energies which create beings and that errant souls are the causes of change. As for the master, Zhu Xi (1130–1200), he explains all things by transformations in the primordial energy. Why such prudence? It is because all that our Confucianism has wanted is that people should arrive at an understanding of the general order, starting from what is there before their eyes. It certainly does not permit people to think about what there might be before birth and after death. Thus, they do not come egoistically to seek to obtain good fortune from invisible powers and to avoid misfortune, but on the contrary employ all their efforts in practising the social virtues. As for Buddhism and Taoism, although the one does speak of reincarnation and the other of long life, they do produce good effects upon men, for they keep them from excess and bring them calm. Quite the reverse can be said of the doctrine of the Master of Heaven.[28]

The whole religion of the literate elite can be summed up as respect for the rituals and a perfect sincerity in performing them. Let each person, in the place that is his own, observe the duties that are his: such is the conduct that is required towards living people just as it is towards the dead and the invisible spirits.

Furthermore, what the educated converts of the early seventeenth century say in favour of the doctrine of the Master of Heaven shows up the differences between Chinese and Western attitudes:

- the doctrine of the missionaries is to be recommended for its references to the precepts of the Classics and seems to them to be a return to the Confucianism of Antiquity;
- they regard this doctrine as a recipe for good political order: if everybody observed its precepts – which are Chinese precepts anyway, namely to fear and respect Heaven – the golden age of the three ancient dynasties (Xia, Yin and Zhou) would return;
- they suggest giving this a try; the results will soon be evident;
- finally, they include in the same notion of 'heavenly studies' (*tianxue*) the moral, scientific and technological teaching of the missionaries: all this is useful to the empire.

As we have seen, in 1628 the great man of letters and convert, Li Zhizao, produced a collection of texts written by missionaries in collaboration with members of the literate elite: he called it the *First Collection of Heavenly Studies (Tianxue chuhan)*. On examination, the collection proves to contain no catechism nor, generally speaking, any text of religious instruction. Apart from the scientific and technical works which constitute the second part of this collection, we find an account of teaching and education in Europe, a treatise on the Nestorian stele of 781 discovered near Xi'an, three short ethical works by Ricci, his great treatise on *The True Meaning of the Master of Heaven*, which is a work more of philosophical controversy than of religion, a reply to the criticisms of the Buddhist master, Zhuhong, on the concept of Heaven and to those of the man of letters, Yu Chunxi, on the murder of animals, the famous work by Pantoja on the struggle against the seven deadly sins and, finally, the great cosmographical work by Father Giulio Aleni. What Li Zhizao by preference retained were the ethical, philosophical, geographical and historical works; religion, as such, has no place in his collection. Culti-vated circles would certainly hardly have looked with much favour upon what they would without doubt have interpreted as superstition and magic.

There would seem to have been nothing religious about the attitudes of the literate elite and yet, as we shall see, the idea of Heaven or of uni-versal order is, in fact, a religious one. It relates to morality, the rituals, and the social and political order. And it was in connection with Heaven that an agreement was reached between the literate elite and the missionaries – an agreement based upon a misunderstanding. Among the men of letters a cosmic mysticism of a sort did exist, more or less strongly marked from one individual to another and, together with it, went a profound mistrust of all fanaticism. They despised the beliefs of the common people and were alarmed at the success of certain deviant cults among them. To them, nothing seemed more threatening to social order than religious zeal. They were alarmed at whatever might harm the sense of a world order and the morality which was inseparable from it.

Although its bases and nature were quite different from those of Chris-tianity, the mysticism of the literate tradition was without doubt con-ducive to a number of conversions. But 'respect for and fear of Heaven', a precept from the Classics which the missionaries were only too pleased to cite frequently, did not necessarily imply among those who advocated them any particular sympathy for the doctrine of the Master of Heaven. A certain Wang Qiyuan, who uses such formulae, is violently hostile to the missionaries and invokes the Sovereign on High against them.[29] Simi-larly, another enemy of the doctrine of the Master of Heaven calls upon Heaven to witness his determination to oppose the pernicious influence of the Barbarians: Huang Zhen writes:

Ever since that time, I prostrate myself, before Heaven every day and silently invoke it saying: 'I, your little son, hereby vow to sacrifice my useless person to Confucius and Mencius in repayment to my sovereign and my ancestors, and to save all future generations in the world from the harm that could be done to them by the perverse doctrine of these Barbarians.[30]

Given that for the literate elite religion was identified with respect for the rituals which were an expression of social and natural order, they were ill-prepared to accept a religion which demanded total commitment and according to which eternal salvation was dependent upon faith.

Emperor Kangxi, who often took the opportunity to talk with the Jesuit Fathers who were in his service, was 'most astonished to see them so stubbornly devoted to the Christian religion' and one day had the following remarks conveyed to them:

Is it possible that you should be always preoccupied with a world which you have not yet reached, and count for nothing the one in which you live at present? Believe me, there is a time for everything; make better use of what Heaven places in your hands and defer until after life all these cares which are suitable only for the dead.

And he added, jokingly: 'For myself, I take hardly any interest in all these affairs of the other world and am not at all concerned to decide upon the activities of these invisible spirits.'[31]

The same Kangxi also found the missionaries too inflexible in their ideas:

Why do you not speak of God[32] as we do? People would rebel less against your religion. You call him Tien-tchu [Master of Heaven] and we call him Chamti [Sovereign on High]. Is it not the same thing? Need one abandon a word just because the people interpret it falsely?[33]

The missionaries concluded from the reactions of the literate elite that they were totally devoid of any feeling for religion. As Ricci put it as early as 1585: 'In China, matters of salvation are considered of very little account.'[34] At the same time, however, they often felt that they were nearing their goal: the conversion of these pagans who openly approved of what they said and wrote did not seem to pose any great difficulty. Yet conversions were rare: only those who had been in contact with the missionaries over an extended period had themselves baptised. Most of them were their disciples in mathematics or in other European sciences.

Buddhist monks

The missionaries had not arrived in virgin territory. On the contrary, the Chinese had already inherited an extremely rich complex of religious traditions dating from various periods and of more or less learned inspiration, which had produced a number of interacting influences. Buddhism, the most learned forms of which were Indian, had undergone a profound sinicisation at the levels of both practices and representations. In precisely the same way as the ancient Chinese altars of the god of the Soil, so monasteries, reliquary towers (*stûpa*) and Buddhist deities afforded protection to both territories and communities; the Buddhist rituals had even come to assume as their principal function that of ensuring the well-being of deceased ancestors, thereby responding to the needs of filial piety, which were so fundamental in China. With its temples and monks, its writings and its rituals, Buddhism remained the best organised and the most influential form of religion in China. Taoism, which had borrowed much from it while retaining a number of original characteristics, played only a secondary role. It was therefore Buddhism, both as a particular doctrine and as a representative expression of the religious traditions of China, that the missionaries set about attacking first and foremost.

The difficulties which the missionaries encountered in their evangelical work have often been ascribed to the jealousy of the Buddhist monks. But the hostility of the Buddhist monks and their supporters among the literate elite was prompted solely by the missionaries' own attitude towards them and their religion. The missionaries' attacks against the Buddhists were a response to the repugnance they felt for what they considered to be diabolical superstitions. This hostility furthermore had the advantage of adding lustre to their own image as orthodox and intransigent moralists in the eyes of some members of the literate elite. But at the time of the very first contacts, the Buddhist monks made it quite plain that they were only too willing to get along well with the foreign monks. Michele Ruggieri, Matteo Ricci and Antonio Almeida, tonsured and clad in Buddhist robes, had been received with open arms by those whom they were trying to resemble and who took them for co-religionaries of some kind.[35] In one of his letters, Antonio Almeida, who accompanied Ruggieri on his visit to Zhejiang province in 1585, describes as follows the enthusiastic welcome they received from Buddhist monks in the north of Guangdong province:

On 5 January, we arrived in the town of Gaoling, where our journey along this river came to an end, and there we said mass. So many people flocked to us that we could not defend ourselves. One idolater (that is to say, a Buddhist monk) came up to us with an invitation. He welcomed [us] with much festivity in his house which contained some large altars. And many Fathers, or rather Buddhist monks, who were reciting [prayers] and performing ceremonies, gave us a cordial welcome; and we ate with these Buddhist monks, who showed us a quite particular sympathy. We gave our host a book and certain prayers and they all allowed themselves to be convinced very easily.[36]

Elsewhere, he writes:

We are surrounded on all sides by monks who treat us in a friendly manner and every evening come to hear about the things of God; up until now – today is 8 February – there has been no way to protect ourselves from the multitude which gathers to see us; we show our altar to the most important of them and they do reverence to the image of the Saviour. All the high-ranking mandarins and men of letters have come along and are clearly pleased, saying that they will not let us leave. The most important of them have invited Father Ruggieri to their table and yesterday he even dined with a mandarin who is two grades higher than the ling-si-tau [the high-ranking provincial administrator of Guangdong province] and who, his mother having died, sent to invite us to the funeral; but the Father replied that our prayers were of no use to anyone who did not serve the Lord of Heaven.[37]

At this point the missionaries were regarded by laymen as a new kind of Buddhist monk. On his arrival at Zhaoqing, Ricci wrote:

Many also began to offer perfumes as incense for the altar and also alms to the Fathers for their food and for oil for the lamp that was lit before the altar. And it would have been easy to obtain from the mandarins income from the lands of their temples, but it seemed better to the Fathers not to accept such funds.[38]

Thus, in the days of the early contacts, the Chinese behaved towards the Christian missionaries in exactly the same manner as they were accustomed to behave towards the Buddhist monks: providing oil for the lamps, alms to feed the monks and granting an income from their land were, precisely, all things that laymen were expected to do for the Buddhist Church. Similarly, the men of letters and administrators made presents of sticks of incense, bowed as was customary before holy images[39] and asked the missionaries to come and officiate at their funeral ceremonies in the same way as the Buddhist and Taoist monks did. The assimilation was instantaneous. In the missionaries' questioners we can sense a mixture of politeness and curiosity, even a veritable sympathy. All the indications are that this foreign cult from the distant West would have been integrated quite easily into the religious practices of China if one had looked no further than appearances. Ruggieri wrote: 'Many wanted to receive holy baptism together with their relatives, who declared that our doctrine is very true.'[40] In his letter from Gaoling, he remarks: 'They allow themselves to be convinced very easily.'

Everything seemed to favour an alliance between the missionaries and the Buddhist monks. Ricci notes many resemblances in dogmas and rituals: the Buddhist monks recognised a kind of Trinity[41] and the existence of paradise and hell.[42] They practised penitence, observed celibacy and followed the custom of alms-giving. Their ceremonies were reminiscent of the masses of the Christians: 'When they recite, their chants seem just like our plainsong.'[43] Ricci also notes the pious images and lamps lit in the temples, and headgear similar to that of Christian priests.[44]

The five Buddhist prohibitions to be respected by lay believers are reminiscent of the Ten Commandments of Christianity: do not kill living creatures, do not steal, do not commit adultery, do not lie, do not get drunk.

But to Ricci and the missionaries, these resemblances were nothing but traps set by the devil. Almeida remarks: 'In this place [Gaoling], I have seen how the devil imitates the holy ceremonies of the Catholic Church.'[45] It is, as Jean Delumeau writes in connection with the Christian missions in America:

The devil, as described in the Bible, is above all a deceiver. For that reason, the missionaries did not allow themselves to be deceived by the analogies that they noted between the beliefs and rituals of the natives and those of Christianity: fasts and abstinences, female monasteries, ceremonies that appeared to resemble baptism and communion, certain forms of confession, a kind of Trinity in the Peruvian religion, etc. They spoke of devilish 'parodies' and 'usurpations' even though they considered that God, desiring to prepare the peoples of America for the true faith, had allowed the devil to imagine these analogies.[46]

It was, nevertheless, precisely those deceptive resemblances which proved the most effective aids to the missionaries in their task of conversion among the common people, who were for the most part quite incapable of seeing any difference between the various doctrines and were preoccupied above all with the effectiveness of the rituals.

The Buddhist monks and the missionaries exchanged accusations of fraudulent imitation. Each party reproached the other for having distorted what it had stolen from the rival religion, to the point where the thefts became quite unrecognisable. For many Chinese, Christianity, with its hell and paradise, was nothing but a crude counterfeit of Buddhism. Most of the ideas of the doctrine of the Master of Heaven were looted from the religion that had originated in India. But instead of recognising their debt in all honesty, the Barbarians criticised in the Buddhists precisely the things to which they gave full approval in themselves.

One author of an anti-Christian work writes:

They say that if, at the moment of death, one obeys the Master of Heaven and repents of one's crimes, one is saved. That is an idea they have stolen from the 'ten thoughts necessary at the approach of death' in Buddhism. If one of the two ideas is true, the other cannot be false. The same goes for the ten prohibitions [the Ten Commandments] and for acts of repentance: they have stolen everything from Buddhism and, having done so, they condemn those very same ideas among the Buddhist monks.[47]

The converse argument – that Buddhism is a degenerate form of Christianity – was used by Buddhist converts to the doctrine of the Master of Heaven to justify their devotion to Christianity. The Christian man of letters, Yang Tingyuan, who before his conversion had been a fervent Buddhist, explains in one of his works that, given that the Indian doctrine borrowed much from Christianity, twisting its meaning in the process, the true doctrine was that of the missionaries: through misinterpreting Christianity, the Indians had lost half of its true meaning and when the Chinese came to translate the Indian texts, they had lost the other half. The Buddhist miracles were nothing but extravagances and absurdities. In contrast, the Master of Heaven manifested his omnipotence through the alternation of day and night, the production and destruction of living creatures and the existence of the animal and vegetable kingdoms. Our five senses came to us from Heaven, not from Buddha. There were heavenly spirits which presided over all the transformations in the world and it was the Master of Heaven who gave them their orders. For Yang Tingyun, the Bodhisattva Guanyin (Avalokitesvara) is simply a distorted image of the Virgin. In the last analysis, Christianity is a kind of Buddhism, but more pure and closer to its origins.[48]

However, the solution that would have best satisfied the greatest number of those who were so willing to recognise the holiness of the religion from Europe, would have been to sacrifice nothing at all. Some, indeed, thought they had found a way to reconcile everything: it was by granting to this Master of Heaven the foremost place, that of the Sovereign on High of the Chinese, with whom he was so often confused, meanwhile retaining beneath him the whole heteroclite pantheon of China: Buddha, Bodhisattva, the gods and immortals of the Taoists, all the deified figures of the tradition of the literate elite and countless other deities too, each one being somehow delegated with a part of the universal power of the Master of Heaven. That is what is proposed by one of the interlocutors in an imaginary dialogue written by the convert, Wang Zheng.[49] If we are to believe Longobardo, it was also the solution that would have met with the approval of the masses. He writes:

For although it is very easy to persuade the Chinese to worship God, the Lord of Heaven, as the sovereign deity, conversely it is just as difficult to get them to tear down all their idols from their thrones and no longer honour them at all. For they cannot bear these images not even to be included among the ranks of the ministers of God or that they be refused the honour that we accord to our saints . . . thus, while in other respects accepting with reverence the truth of our religion and also its holiness, they notwithstanding wish to retain the memory of their own saints, which they have received from their ancestors.[50]

All religions can collaborate in the universal order.

In the opinion of another author of an anti-Christian work, the need for a delegation of powers on the part of the Master of Heaven seems equally indispensable: it is not normal for this Master of Heaven to settle everything on his own, without any appeal to intermediaries, as is customary in the administration of a kingdom. The missionaries say that the

Taoist immortals and the Buddhas are usurpers and refuse to allow them the right of receiving any delegation of powers from the Master of Heaven. That is something that it may just be possible to accept. But is it not strange that the Master of Heaven forbids men to render homage and sacrifices to Heaven, Earth and the spirits that he himself has created?[51] This author writes:

Imagine a man covered by the heavens, borne up by the Earth, given light by the sun and the moon, engendered by his father, raised by his mother, governed by his sovereign and inspired and protected by the gods and spirits. Yet he will grant them no recognition and will reserve all his gratitude for a vague Master of Heaven who has never been either seen or heard.[52]

Most Chinese would have liked to combine the Christian religion with the Chinese cults and regretted the fact that the missionaries forbade them to do so. A Buddhist–Christian syncretism would have found favour with many Chinese and there was at least one example of it taking place: the adventurer, pirate and trader, Zheng Zhilong (1601–61), baptised as a child in Macao, had devised in his stronghold of Anping in Fujian province a private chapel in which Christian and Buddhist images were placed side by side.[53]

The literate elite eventually decided that the Jesuits had only come out in favour of Confucianism for motives of prudence and a desire to be favourably regarded by people of influence, and that the doctrine of the Master of Heaven was in fact nothing but a bad copy of Buddhism. The author of a commentary on *The True Meaning of the Master of Heaven* writes:

Realising that he could not launch an attack against Confucianism, Ricci amalgamated his Master of Heaven with what is said about the Sovereign on High of our Six Classics, and he tried to win the day by attacking nothing but Buddhism. But his idea of a paradise and a hell is not so far removed from the Buddhist theory of transmigration. With some minor changes, his doctrine draws upon the same sources as Buddhism.[54]

Such a judgement may be found surprising but it has a basis in truth. The fact is that between the two religions there are more than the purely formal resemblances (which Ricci had noted in the setting and general atmosphere of their respective places of worship). Deeper analogies also exist. Buddhism and Christianity are both religions of individual salvation which speak of retributions to come. Both declare their scorn for the senses and the world as causes for attachments detrimental to salvation. Christianity probably had more affinity with the Buddhism from India than with the strictly Chinese and 'Confucian' ideas of religion seen as an activity of rituals within a hierarchical framework and as the expression of a universal and immanent order. It was for tactical reasons just as much as out of a natural antipathy felt for a rival religion that the Jesuits proclaimed themselves to be enemies of Buddhism and friends of Confucius.

At first well-disposed towards the missionaries, the Buddhist monks and their sympathisers among the literate elite later became upset at the attacks launched upon them by these foreigners who were so ready to pass judgement upon what they had not taken the trouble to understand. In his great treatise, Ricci poured ridicule upon the belief in transmigration as the fruit of one's actions and upon the prohibition against killing living creatures. Furthermore, giving an incorrect interpretation to the Buddhist thesis of the unreality of the self and the general phenomena, he advanced the claim that the only principle of Buddhism was nothingness. His attacks prompted Buddhists, in their turn, to criticise the doctrine of the Master of Heaven, and many of the writings hostile to the missionaries in the seventeenth century were in effect the work of Buddhist monks and members of the literate elite with Buddhist sympathies. However, it would be simplistic to oppose Buddhism and Confucianism, as is sometimes done, as two clearly distinct doctrines, the former opposed to Christianity and the latter in accord with it. On the whole, the reverse is closer to the truth, as we have just seen. Besides, Buddhism in China had become so thoroughly acclimatised that it had become more Taoist and Chinese than Indian. And just as many members of the literate elite had been deeply affected by the influence of Buddhism, by the end of the Ming and the beginning of the Qing periods the most eminent among the Buddhist monks had acquired a solid classical culture; their criticisms against the Christians were inspired by the defence of Confucian traditions as often as by that of their own religion.

Meanwhile, quite apart from questions of doctrine, one immediate cause for hostility was the behaviour of the foreigners. The Chinese were much struck at discovering in the missionaries an unexpected mixture of humility and arrogance. They were amazed to find that these people entirely lacked any Confucian sense of reciprocity.

The emperor, Yongzheng (1723–36), one day said to the Jesuit Fathers of Peking: 'If I were to send Buddhist monks into your European provinces, your princes would not permit it.'[55] And it is true that one can hardly imagine Chinese Buddhist monks coming to eighteenth-century Europe to preach of the unreality of the self and the phenomenal world and teach the way that leads to deliverance. From a Christian point of view, no reciprocity is conceivable: the truth cannot be balanced against error. As Saint Augustine put it, the traditional religions of the various nations are particular and therefore false. Only the true religion of Christ, founded upon universal reason and revealed by God, can be said to be universal.[56] Revealed truths are beyond dispute. However, the Chinese were not impressed by this argument of authority, and although some of them did come to adhere to the doctrine of the Master of Heaven, it was not for that reason.

The author of one short work is of the opinion that what the missionaries maintain with regard to the Master of Heaven and Jesus has no more reason to be believed than what could equally well be maintained with regard to Buddhism. Why should Sâkyamuni not equally well be the Master of Heaven who descended to be born on earth? Why should the Buddhist sûtra be lies and those of the Master of Heaven true? The missionaries claim that the Buddha appeared in the regions of the West but that nobody was there to bear witness to it. But then, the same could be said of Jesus in the distant West.[57]

The Buddhist monks and members of the literate elite would have liked to engage in discussion with the missionaries and their converts for, as a Buddhist monk put it: 'there are a thousand paths and ten thousand ways to arrive at the truth'. But they ran up against scorn and silence on the part of their opponents.

Two texts from the great collection devoted to the *Refutation of the heresy*, the *Poxie ji*, published in 1639, record the encounters between on the one hand the Buddhist master of Ningbo, Total Enlightenment, and a lay disciple of the Buddhist master, Zhuhong, and on the other the missionaries and converts of Hangzhou. The texts convey the atmosphere of these polemics and reveal the differences in the respective behaviour of the Buddhists and the Christians. The Buddhists reproach the Christians for their contemptuous attitude and their refusal to hold any discussion as equals. They furthermore accuse them of deliberately lying in order to further their cause.

Total Enlightenment relates how a certain Zhang Guangtian, a disciple of the great master, Zhuhong, went to Hangzhou to visit Father Francisco Furtado, who lived there from 1625 to 1630, in order to show him a short refutation of Christianity that the master had written. At first Furtado was delighted, thinking that he would be able to demolish the monk's arguments with ease, but he subsequently manifested the greatest embarrassment for he could not understand the text of Buddhist philosophy submitted to him by Zhang Guangtian at all. The famous convert, Li Zhizao, who happened to be presiding over the discussion, was called upon to help. But he too was, in turn, covered in confusion and asked why the monk could not be brought to discuss the matter in person. He was told that the master was in Ningbo (200 kilometres away) and it was suggested that he (Li Zhizao) should write a refutation. Some time later, the Christians spread a rumour to the effect that Total Enlightenment had come to Hangzhou and had been obliged to admit defeat in the face of the arguments of the missionaries and their friends. Whereupon Total Enlightenment pointed out that over the past five years he had never moved further afield than Dinghai, in the Zhoushan Islands (opposite Ningbo), and that whoever lied in this fashion on one point was also capable of lying on every other. And Total Enlightenment went on to say: 'That is why I maintain that your prohibitions [the Ten Commandments], your speeches and your books are all lies. If that were not the case, why so many precautions, why all the secrets? The way of the Saints, the Sages and the Six Classics of Confucius is not secret but open to everybody. The same is true of the way of the 5,418 volumes of the Buddhist canon. It is only in heterodox sects such as the Wenxiang and the White Lotus that only initiates are permitted to know the mysteries.'

Total Enlightenment provoked the Christians further by sending Zhang Guangtian back again to Hangzhou to make known the text written by the master, Zhuhong (1535–1615),[58] and carry the controversy right into the church of Hangzhou. This time the foreigners took good care to make no reply; instead, it was a convert by the name of Fan, a friend of the Christian, Yang Tingyun, who faced Zhang Guangtian. Putting Zhuhong's text away in his pocket without even glancing at it, he refused to enter into any discussion, on the pretext that the two doctrines were so different that no agreement could ever be reached. But Zhang Guangtian, for his part, could not see why they should be compared in order to discover which was the better. After all, why should the doctrine of the Master of Heaven reject Buddhism and destroy its images and statues? 'It must be so', replied Fan, 'since the two doctrines are different.' Total Enlightenment's comment was that the great resource of these people was not to reply and to refuse any discussion. Their favourite ploy was secrecy, as if they wished to show people a fortified place with imposing ramparts guarded by valiant soldiers, into which it was impossible to penetrate from any angle. But what kind of a procedure was this, that consisted in making initiates into one's own creatures and employing intimidation?

For my own part, I do not seek to triumph at any price in my discussions with the followers of the Master of Heaven nor to persuade people to follow me blindly. My only fear is that they should not discover the Dao [the Way] and should deprive themselves of knowledge ... Buddha means 'awakened' or 'correct awakening'. It is not an awakening that is for him alone. This awakening can be possessed by all beings equally. The Buddha is simply the first to have experienced it. Fish and dragons live in the water without knowing what water is. Living creatures find themselves permanently in this awakening, without realising what awakening is.

Total Enlightenment is of the opinion that learning a simple catechism does not prove that one has truly understood its meaning: there are a thousand paths and ten thousand ways of reaching the truth. The Westerners seek only to win out over others, not to reveal the universal truth, which is that all men possess truth and everyone can attain saintliness. Anyone can become a Yao or a Shun (Confucian Saints of Antiquity). 'They accuse others falsely in order to glorify themselves. They embellish and falsify things in order to frighten the foolish.'

The convert, Fan, declares the Buddhist master to have had the worst of it in his discussion with Ricci. Now, Zhuhong never in fact even met Ricci, who died in 1610, five years before him. Zhuhong wrote his critique of Ricci's ideas during the spring of 1615 and died in the autumn of the same year.[59] The *Bianxue yidu*, which is a reply from the missionaries to Zhuhong's critique, was falsely attributed to Ricci. How could Ricci possibly have written in advance a reply to a critique that he never had a chance of reading? Furthermore, in his postface to the *Bianxue yidu*, Mige (Michael Yang Tingyun) claims that on his death-bed Zhuhong repented and said: 'I was wrong and, worse still, I misled many people.' The truth was that Zhuhong never said any such thing. A whole crowd was present at that moment, one which Zhuhong had himself predicted exactly. And, says Zhang Guangtian, I, his disciple, was there. Besides, this postface only appears in the Fujian edition of the *Bianxue yidu* and is absent from the Zhejiang edition: that is because they thought they could deceive the people of Fujian province, who are more than a thousand *li* away, but not the countless eyewitnesses present at Zhuhong's death.[60]

Xu Dashou, the author of *The Aid to Refutation*, is also shocked that the missionaries wish to impose their views without justifying them. The Fathers say that the Master of Heaven is beyond conception and that it would be a crime to try to conceive him. But, the Chinese author retorts, there are only two kinds of thing that are inconceivable. One kind of inconceivable is in the world of living beings, namely the two forms of infinity that space and time represent. The other kind is in the world of the Buddhas, that is 'everything in which, for them, the path of the discursive is cut off and the way of the thinkable is interrupted'. But this is a kind of inconceivable which is within each one of us and which we can reach on our own. It is in no way 'something inconceivable that is supposed to consist of the fact that people are forbidden to conceive it'. And Xu Dashou goes on as follows, thereby testifying to the astonishment felt by the Chinese in the face of the – in their eyes – illogical attitude of the missionaries:

With regard to everything relating to what is beyond the world and the bases of the universe,[61] they always find obstructions to reasoning and points where they are at a loss for words. They then say: 'Our Master of Heaven never spoke of that.' What they detest above all is that people should think ... They forbid people to think about or to discuss questions which, notwithstanding, are perfectly thinkable and discussable ... They limit themselves to intimidating fools by saying to them: 'That is beyond conception.' It is like telling a child that there is a devil in the room but that he must not look or a great misfortune will befall him. If he has a modicum of common sense, he will strike a light and the phantom will immediately disappear.[62]

The common people

In the case of the literate elite, the missionaries were obliged to engage in long discussions in an attempt to combat well-established learned ideas, which were backed up by an abundant literature. They also had to persuade them to give up their concubines.[63] They were faced with no such difficulties when it came to the common people, as they themselves recognised: these people were easier to convince. In 1701, Father Foucquet writes from Nanchang:

Here, following our Saviour's example, we can point to the effectiveness of our mission, in that we are preaching to the poor. In China, as everywhere else, one finds among them fewer obstacles and more docility in the face of the truths of salvation than one does among the great and powerful of the age.[64]

In the early days, the missionaries believed that their task would be extremely easy: the Chinese declared themselves to be in agreement with them, applauded all they said and appeared to feel nothing but contempt for their own gods and priests, Buddhist and Taoist alike. In a letter dated 1581, Ricci writes:

They are not at all devoted to their sects: quite the contrary, they think that their fathers (that is to say the priests of their own sects) lie to them, and they whip them as if they were children. What am I saying – they even give their idols many lashes; they throw them into the sea to punish them, showing not the slightest scruple with regard to them. That is why there is not a single Chinese who does not desire to accept God's Law; but the rulers say that, to change sects and customs, an authorisation from the king is needed.[65]

In a letter written two years later, Ricci makes the same remarks and reaches the same conclusions:

As the Chinese have no faith in their idols, it will be easy to convince them of our truth if we can speak with them ... They do worship a few idols,[66] but when these do not grant them what they desire, they beat them hard and make peace again with them later on. They worship the devil as such so that he will do them no harm and thus they hardly observe any divine cult at all; their priests enjoy little respect and that makes the esteem in which they hold us all the more surprising.[67]

The conclusions reached by Ruggieri and Ricci, who took certain rituals
to be expressions of scorn for the gods, were somewhat overhasty; the
fact that the Chinese maltreated their 'idols' in no way implied that they
were not attached to them.

Longobardo also rejoices at the favourable disposition of the Chinese
in his report on the Shaozhou residence during the period of 1599–1603.
He judges them to be ready to worship the image of the true God and renounce their idols, reckoning that this may be 'either because of the fame
of our faith or as a result of the facility with which this nation will worship
any deity of any kind'.[68]

Writing at the end of the seventeenth century, Father Le Comte gives
an amusing description of the anger felt against their gods by the
common people when they have obtained nothing from them:

'What, you cur of a spirit (they sometimes say), we have housed you in a magnificent temple, you are well gilded, fed, perfumed with incense, and after all this
care that we lavish on you, you are so ungrateful that you refuse to give us what
we need' ... The idol is bound with ropes and dragged through the streets,
covered in mud and all kinds of filth.[69]

The same Father Le Comte cites the case of an inhabitant of Nanking
who brought a lawsuit against a god which had not cured his sick daughter. Despite conciliatory efforts on the part of the mandarins, the man
would not be dissuaded and the case was even referred to Peking. He
won his case, the idol was exiled, the temple torn down and its monks
punished.[70]

The caricature presented by this last example indicates the closeness
of the gods to men and the contractual nature of their relations: gifts
must, as a matter of obligation, be answered by other gifts. Each one
must acquit himself of the duties that fall within his own domain. Such
attitudes are relatively common and many other examples are to be
found outside China. A religion is evaluated according to its effects. The
common people had no reason to reject the new cults and rituals that the
missionaries proposed to them: perhaps they would turn out to be more
effective than the old ones.

The gods were constantly proliferating and being renewed; over the
years the names, attributes, functions and even personalities would
change. Many were former historical figures and Matteo Ricci himself,
who was the first to introduce clocks that chimed the hour into China,
was to be deified as the patron saint of clockmakers in Shanghai.[71] To be
transformed into a Buddhist deity was certainly a strange fate for a
missionary! But this illustrates the strength of the tendency to assimilate
the innovations introduced by the missionaries to the Chinese traditions.

The religious traditions and sensibility of an entire people and, in the case of the Chinese, a whole civilisation, were not to be transformed as easily as the missionaries imagined.

In his memoirs, Ricci wrote:

One thing that is hard to believe is the multitude of idols that exist in this kingdom, not only in the temples, which are full of them, for in some of them several thousand have been set up,[72] but also in private homes, where there are a great number, kept in a special place consecrated to them; in the squares, streets, mountains, ships and public palaces, one sees nothing but such abominations. But the truth is that few people believe what is told of these idols and only think that even if they do them no good, at least it does no harm to make a show of revering them.[73]

There are so many gods in China that there is perhaps no advantage in introducing still more: one author fears lest the 'hundred gods' of Christianity might crowd out the 'hundred gods' of China, who might then no longer be able to remain peacefully in their own places. In his view, there are already quite enough complications, what with the two doctrines of Buddhism and Taoism. If a third is added people will not know where they are.[74]

It is possible that when this author mentions the 'hundred gods' of Christianity he is thinking of the angels (*tianshen*) and saints. But it is more likely that he imagined Christianity on the model of the only religious systems with which he was familiar.

When the missionaries and – at their instigation – the most ardent of their converts set about destroying the religious statues, both Chinese and Buddhist, some Chinese, far from becoming upset at the ignominious treatment meted out to them,[75] reflected that it was, after all, up to the gods to take their own revenge for such sacrileges. However, one author of an anti-Christian work expresses indignation at such passivity. He writes as follows:

Some people, seeing these Barbarians destroying the statues of the Buddhas, the Taoist immortals and our Chinese deities, think that the gods mysteriously punish those who offend them, and so all that is necessary is to wait quietly for these people to fall when they bring themselves down. What's the point of troubling oneself? But they do not realise that, since the quintessence of Heaven and Earth has been distributed among men, it is only when people arise who are endowed with an ardent passion for their duties that the deities of good omen lend their silent aid to men. Man is occupied with the visible world, the gods with the invisible world. It is only when the visible and the invisible collaborate that devils and pestilences can be destroyed. How could one look on without doing anything while such things are done, leaving it all up to the gods?[76]

Although they insult and maltreat them, the Chinese are attached to their gods. These are somehow part of the family or the community and they only chastise them for their own good. As Longobardo observes, the Christian neophytes are averse to abandoning 'the little gods of their households and hearths in whose company they were born and brought up and whom they believe to be their guardians, only to treat them – as they see it – unworthily'. And the outrages inflicted upon them by the missionaries shocked those who witnessed them. Longobardo writes: 'All this appeared to the heathen not only unseemly but also entirely removed from all humanity.'[77]

The Chinese had given the missionaries the impression of being relatively unattached to their gods. But that was no more than an appearance resulting from the difference between their respective religious sensibilities. Prepared, as they were, to adopt new gods, they showed an interest in the religious rituals and images of Christianity. The missionaries were convinced that they were well inclined by disposition to receive the Christian faith: the attitude of profound respect and the exemplary modesty that they displayed in religious ceremonies was enough to persuade them of that. Father Le Comte makes the following judicious comment: 'The Chinese behave much better at mass than the people of Europe.'[78] The fact is that they enjoyed ritual and were accustomed to it from childhood. And in a letter written from Peking, where he lived from 1760 until his death in 1780,[79] Father Cibot described the Christian Chinese 'kneeling in the most respectful and profound silence', and added: 'Even the tiniest children, thanks to the good education they have received and the natural seriousness of their nation, behave there with admirable modesty.'[80]

Furthermore, the Chinese displayed a particular devotion to holy images. The religious paintings imported from Italy by the missionaries were the objects of a quite spontaneous veneration on the part of Chinese from all walks of life. It was a matter of custom: all things holy deserved respect. Thus, those who visited Ruggieri and Ricci in Zhaoqing quite naturally manifested their reverence to the Christian images just as they would before representations of Chinese or Buddhist deities. We are told as much by a passage in Ricci's memoirs relating to the last months of 1583:

That image of the Madonna and Child that we placed on the altar was worshipped by all the mandarins and other men of letters and the common people, as well as the ministers of the idols [the Buddhist monks] who came to visit the Jesuit Fathers – and they all made genuflexions, bowing right down to the ground with great respect, and at the same time they also admired the artistry of our painting.[81]

And Ricci adds:

It is true that, a little later on, the Fathers replaced the Madonna with a painting of the Saviour for, seeing the image of the Madonna on the altar without it being possible for us as yet to explain the mystery of the Incarnation, the Chinese were spreading the rumour that the God whom we worshipped was a woman.[82]

For converting the common people of the Shaozhou region – now Shaoguan – in the north of Guangdong province, Longobardo's tactics particularly and advisedly stressed the importance of holy images and involved the creation of a whole dramatic setting, which was apparently much appreciated by the Chinese. Having told the assembled people that

it was necessary to worship one sole God, the creator of Heaven and Earth and that, without this true religion, there could be no salvation ... he would recite the Ten Commandments of the Law and explain them as briefly as he could. After that, he would announce that he had an image of the one who first gave men this Law; whereupon he would place the image on the table or somewhere else which would do it honour, with lighted candles and perfumes;[83] and he would exhort them all henceforward to renounce their idols, which were the likenesses of false, not true, gods. The people seldom refused to do this, either on account of the fame of our faith or because of this nation's remarkable facility for worshipping any god there may happen to be.[84]

The eunuch, Ma Tang, who in 1660 was the first to see the paintings which Ricci intended for the emperor, Wanli, had spontaneously adopted an attitude of reverence at the sight of them. Ricci writes: 'He revered the altar paintings with great devotion, falling to his knees and promising the Madonna that he would give her a place in the king's palace.'[85]

Ricci's memoirs allow us to follow the subsequent history of these pictures and demonstrate how very realistic Italian painting, with its chiaroscuro and perspective, seemed in the eyes of the Chinese. He relates how struck the emperor was at the sight of the religious paintings that he had presented to the Court. He writes (no doubt following the report of a eunuch):

Upon seeing the pictures, the king was quite stupefied and exclaimed: 'There is a living Buddha!', thus speaking truer than he realised for all the other gods whom they worship are dead gods. The term that he used about our pictures has stuck to the present day and they refer to the Fathers as 'those who presented the living God'. But the king was so frightened of this living God that he sent the pictures of the Madonna to his mother, who was very devout towards idols (that is to say, a fervent Buddhist), and she was just as frightened at such a life-like impression; so she sent them to be put in her treasury where they have remained to the present day, and many of the mandarins go to look at them, with the permission of the eunuchs who are responsible for guarding this treasury. [The eunuchs] told the Fathers that the king revered them and made offerings of incense and perfumes to them, keeping in his room the little picture of the Saviour which our Father General had sent to the Fathers. But it is not possible to know anything very certain on this matter.[86]

This text, which shows how readily the Chinese welcomed foreign deities, is particularly interesting by reason of the confusion that it indicates between Buddhism and Christianity. According to Ricci, Emperor Wanli is supposed to have exclaimed, 'Questo è pagode vivo', that is, in all likelihood, *huo fo*, or 'living Buddha', by which the emperor meant both that the picture created an illusion of life and that it evoked an image of Buddha. But Ricci, who was unaware of the existence of the living Buddhas of Lamaism, gave the exclamation his own personal interpretation, translating the expression 'living Buddha' or avatar of Buddha as 'living God'. Meanwhile, it is quite clear that, so far as the Chinese were concerned, the assimilation with Buddhist traditions was both total and immediate.

The missionaries had noticed how important settings and ornaments were to the Chinese, accustomed as they were to the pomp of the Buddhist church. Father Le Comte writes:

What the Chinese need, even when it comes to an object of worship, is something that strikes their senses. Magnificent ornaments, singing, processions, the sound of bells and musical instruments and Church ceremonial – all this is to their taste and attracts them to the divine religion.[87]

Father Longobardo, who was living in Shaozhou, in the north of Guangdong province, at the beginning of the seventeenth century, also noted the great success among humble folk of what he calls 'the weapons of the spiritual militia': 'rosaries, little images of copper or medals, pieces of holy wax or the *Agnus Dei*'.[88]

Father Le Comte claims that he was always careful 'to draw attention to the elements that superstition usually in the long run suggests to the common people unless one is careful to guard against this'.[89] Being concerned about the dangers of a progressive corruption of Christian teaching, he is afraid that the respect granted to 'images, relics, medals and holy water' might degenerate into superstition. But he does not appear to acknowledge that right from the start there may have existed in the minds of the common people a confusion between what from the point of view of the missionaries was superstition and what was not. In other words, traditional Chinese ways of behaving may have been taken for striking proof of the effects of grace. Nevertheless, all the indications are that wherever Christianity enjoyed a measure of success, the foreign magi – the missionaries – and the objects of the Christian religion and rituals benefited from a transposition of Chinese attitudes and traditions relating to saintliness and the sacred. When they come from far away, saintliness and magic enjoy a greater prestige and are believed to be more efficacious. Here, all the accounts of the missionaries concur: the Chinese Christians manifested the most lively interest in any objects that might have some magic power. Le Comte writes: 'Their respect for the Eucharist also extended to images, relics, medals, holy water and in general all that in some way bears the mark of our Religion.'[90] Father Dentrecolles writes:

The Chinese would ask me for relics, medals, images and rosaries; and how eager they were to acquire holy water, which they would carry off in a well-sealed jar: they were enchanted to learn the secret of keeping it holy, which I told them. Generally speaking, our neophytes place the greatest confidence in holy water: this quite permissible devotion is encouraged among them by the often miraculous cures which it produces and with which God rewards the simplicity of their faith.[91]

The missionaries' letters do indeed provide numerous examples of the miraculous effects of holy water. It has the power to heal the sick, save the dying, exorcise those possessed and evict devils from haunted houses. Thus one Christian, when questioned, acknowledges that 'he went to the Hospital for children, where he pronounced magic words, pouring water on their heads to cure them'[92] and that baptism has the effect of chasing the devil out of the soul of an embryo inside its mother's body.[93] Of course, on this point the missionaries' psychology was at one with that of the milieux they were seeking to win over to them. They, too, believed in the reality of demonic possession and in the powers of sprinkling with holy water.

One of the first miracles effected by holy water is described by Michael Ruggieri. He writes:

I have also baptised the son of an important man of letters in this region [in Shaoguan, in the north of Guangdong province], because he was ailing and seriously ill. His father, seeing that human remedies were of no more avail than the prayers and superstitions of aged people, in order to save him from death, finally turned to me, asking me with great faith to give him some baptismal water. I could not refuse, seeing the danger in which the child lay; and after a few days, having received baptism, the child recovered. He is still alive and I have taken care that he be well instructed in matters of the faith.[94]

For the common people, baptism does indeed appear in many cases to have been regarded as a medication with magic powers. It fell into place in the tradition – well attested throughout history – of 'charmed waters' (*zhushui*), over which secret spells had been pronounced, or 'holy waters' (*shengshui*), and *shengshui* was in fact the name that was given to holy water. The tradition is to be found in both Buddhist and Taoist popular milieux. Thus, the biography of Li Deyu (787–849) records a famous case involving holy water held to produce miraculous effects on the sick, which was in great and lucrative demand. The chief minister of the Tang intervened to halt the trafficking in it, which was being organised by Buddhist monks.[95]

Like the Buddhist monks who, in the past, had come from central Asia or India, the missionaries possessed effective magic formulae which were, moreover, couched in a mysterious and incomprehensible language. The *dhâranî*, the magic formulae of Buddhism, reproduced an approximate rendering of the original Indian sounds into Chinese. The same happened to the Latin prayers of the missionaries from Europe. Thus, Longobardo had composed a number of short works with Chinese equivalents for Latin sounds, and writes:

These little works were first and foremost a prayer book arranged in such a way as to serve various purposes including the funeral service and the burial; it was printed in Chinese characters but without changing anything in the Latin terms – so far as the language allowed, at least. This delights the neophytes even though they understand nothing at all. We see the same happening in Europe with those who recite the divine service in Latin even though they do not understand it, for they often recite it with great devotion.[96]

As Louis Wei observes, in relation to the nineteenth century: 'since Latin was an unknown language, people believed liturgical prayers to be magic words or curses'.[97] That was certainly the opinion of the men of letters who were hostile to the missionaries, but in the history of religions it is a commonplace to find an ambiguity between the sacred and magic, the same things being considered good in the eyes of some, evil in the eyes of others.

Not only the language but also the holy texts themselves, as material objects, were charged with power. Possessing or touching them could produce miracles and conversions and no doubt this would have happened in the case of one particular young Chinese, had the devil not intervened. Father Longobardo tells the story of how this young man was seized with a fit of trembling as soon as he took hold of a catechism given him by one of his friends who was a neophyte. The missionary interprets the phenomenon as an attempt by the enemy of mankind to turn him away from religion.[98]

The missionaries often take on the role of exorcists, whether it be a matter of chasing away the ghosts which haunt certain houses or of curing fits of epilepsy or collective madness. Father Chavagnac tells the story of one entire family the members of which were all afflicted by fits of violent fury. Having tried everything else, they had recourse to the missionaries. The latter first insisted that they should destroy all the talis-

mans, Taoist books and statuettes that carried within them representations of intestines and physical organs and then effected the cure of
these possessed people by sprinkling holy water, making the sign of the
cross, hanging rosaries round their necks and making them repeat the
name of Jesus. The cure was so effective that it decided thirty people to
seek conversion.[99]

In a memoir dated 1703, Father François Noël notes that the sign of
the cross and holy water have proved to be all-powerful against the magic
and infections of the devil.[100] The missionaries' accounts are full of cases
in which the sick, the possessed and the mad are cured or women in childbirth are delivered thanks to sprinklings of holy water, the application of
holy relics, making the sign of the cross or pronouncing the words 'Ye-su'
and 'Ma-li-ya'. The scenario usually follows the same pattern: only after
having vainly tried medicine and Buddhist and Taoist ceremonies of
exorcism do the sick turn to the missionaries. In some cases, once satisfied by the results obtained by the Fathers, they revert to their former
paganism, as a result of which they suffer a relapse, which can only be
cured by appealing once again to the missionaries and renouncing the
false gods for ever.

Christian exorcisms may sometimes be more effective than the traditional ones, but they are of the same type. However much it delighted
the missionaries, the substitution of Christian ideas for Chinese ones was
not necessarily proof of a true change of mentality. Thus, the Virgin
could quite easily fill the role of a goddess of childbirth without the slightest change in concepts being necessary. At the beginning of the seventeenth century, Longobardo relates:

Another neophyte came one day to seek out our Father, complaining about his
wife, still at that time a pagan, on the grounds that she had removed an idol from
the collection of all those that were about to be burned[101] because she believed
that, through it, she would have an easier confinement. The Father ordered that
the idol, Choima,[102] which she had saved, should be replaced by an image of the
mother of God and that the woman should every day recite the Sunday orisons
and the salutation to the angels seven times, in memory of the seven joys of the
Virgin. Eventually, the woman obeyed her husband. When it came to the de-
livery, she gave birth to a son with admirable ease and, to make sure that there
could be no doubt about whose assistance had made this possible, the birth fell
upon the very day of the presentation of our Lady at the temple.[103]

The accounts of Christian miracles contain numerous themes common to
Chinese hagiography, exact counterparts to which are to be found in the
biographies of famous Buddhist monks between the sixth and the tenth
centuries or in the lives of the Taoist Saints. The missionaries were
clearly unaware of these antecedents and did not take much trouble to

discover whether, given the persistence and vigour of Chinese traditions, conversions were not more apparent than real. Even as they condemned the superstitions of the common people, they failed to see that these were perpetuating themselves before their very eyes. It is remarkable, however, that – to take an example that is famous – Father Faber, who preached in the south of Shenxi province from 1635 to 1657, should have been revered as god of the Soil after his death and more or less assimilated to a Bodhisattva, as indeed Matteo Ricci himself was subsequently revered as patron of the clockmakers of Shanghai.[104] Predicting the exact moment of one's death, dispersing tigers and natural calamities, leaving an incorruptible corpse, crossing rivers by flying – all are ancient folkloric themes on the manifestation of saintliness. And in the presence of a saint, Christians and non-Christians alike react in the same way: the villagers would *all come together* to revere the holy relics of a missionary.

In China, a Saint was recognisable from his body, which did not decompose even many years after his death. His face remained as fresh as in life and, sometimes, sweet smells would emanate from his corpse. It is a theme that is common to the accounts of the lives of both Buddhist and Taoist Saints. However, the fact that it was so ancient was not known to the missionaries. While they condemned the superstitions of the common people, they failed to perceive the indispensable role that these continued to play among the converted. According to Bartoli, writing at the end of the seventeenth century:

When the principal persecutor of religion, Chen K'io [Shen Que], had the coffin of Father Feliciano da Silva opened [in 1617], to the great amazement of the infidels his body was discovered to be free from all corruption and giving off a sweet smell. The sky, which had been clear, became covered by dark and stormy clouds as if, as the pagans themselves observed, they wished to make a protest against such irreverence.[105]

Here we have another traditional theme: it often happens that the sky becomes cloudy or suddenly clears on the occasion of some particularly moving event. In China a miracle is often conceived as being 'emotion and response' (*ganying*) on the part of nature in the face of exceptional acts of heroism or proofs of saintliness. Louis Pfister writes that the body of Father Martino Martini

was found untouched by corruption in 1679, eighteen years after its burial, according to the reports of Fathers Intorcetta, Couplet and Bouvet. When Father Intorcetta had the tomb opened to transfer it to the new cemetery that he had had constructed, it looked as though it had been buried only the day before: no smell, no lesions, no sign of corruption and the face coloured as though it were alive. Even the clothing was intact. At the news of this prodigious happening a great crowd assembled, not only Christians but pagans too, the latter out of curiosity to see something extraordinary, the former out of piety and respect for their Father in the faith ... Subsequently, and even until quite recently, the body remained in this same state. On festival days, the Christians had adopted the custom of going to the tomb, seating the body in an armchair, combing the hair and beard and reciting prayers in its presence. But when the pagans took to honouring it as if it were a deity and burning incense in front of the tomb, the body turned to dust.[106]

Whatever Pfister or his source may say, the attitude of the non-Christians was no doubt not fundamentally different from that of the converted: Father Martini was regarded by them all as a Saint whom it was profitable to revere. The doctrine that he had professed was of little importance.

All this attention paid to a corpse that resists corruption may seem strange, but there is ample testimony to the cult of the mummies of Buddhist monks in China from the third century down to the present day.[107]

The body and relics of a Saint retain a supernatural power and his tomb often becomes a centre of pilgrimage. That is what happened to Father Etienne Faber, who became the local god of the Soil (*fang tudi*) in a remote village in the upper valley of the Han. Father Faber was born in Avignon in 1597 and arrived in Macao in 1630. He was sent to this region of southern Shenxi province where, from about 1635 until his death in 1657, he preached in the villages. All the details of his biography testify to the total identification of the missionary with a Chinese, Buddhist or Taoist Saint, an ascetic healer and wonder-worker. It was said that he had been

transported in the air over rivers (a miracle that is ascribed in China to the more or less legendary Indian monk, Bodhidharma), that he had been seen in ecstasy, that he had predicted his own death and many other marvels of this kind (it is common for Chinese Buddhist monks to foresee the exact dates of their deaths).[108]

At the end of the seventeenth century, Father Le Comte describes Father Faber as 'walking ceremoniously along the roads in his stole and surplice' and dispersing locusts by prayers accompanied by the sprinkling of holy water. But having been successful in lifting the scourge, Father Faber had subsequently to perform the operation all over again as the Chinese had not followed his teaching and had thus provoked the return of the insects. It was the second miracle of the disappearance of the locusts that occasioned the founding of the village church.[109]

Probably the most remarkable of all, however, is the attraction that Father Faber's relics exerted after his death. The *Revue des missions catholiques* attests the fact that Father Faber's village remained a centre of the Christian faith right down to the nineteenth century.[110] In 1873, Christians and non-Christians alike were going to pray at his tomb, filing past in an uninterrupted line. And when the Han river flooded, the tomb was miraculously spared.[111] According to a relatively recent report:

the people still [in 1935] talked of the miracles worked by this holy apostle. In many pagodas along the paths and roads, you may find the statue of the Father, more or less transformed into a 'poussah', with a tiger at his feet.[112]

A story was indeed told of how, at the time of his early travels in the region, all the tigers miraculously disappeared. This, too, is a traditional theme: the Saint communicates with the wild beasts and has the power to make them go away.

With a few purely formal modifications, a number of transfers thus took place between the old and the new, leaving the modes of traditional thought unchanged: the missionaries may have been convinced that they had produced Christians, but we may remain sceptical as to whether the radical change in people's minds that true conversion implies did in fact take place.

In a text that originated in a Christian community in Quanzhou, in Fujian province,[113] there is an account of a Chinese Christian called before the 'Heavenly Court'. After remaining dead for a short while, he is returned to life by virtue of his merits. It is an amusing transposition of the edifying tales of Buddhist and Taoist inspiration about descents into hell. The angels of paradise appear in the role of infernal judges, assessors, ushers and their subordinates, and the bureaucratic atmosphere conveyed is similar to that found in traditional tales. The analogy holds good for many details: the messenger who accompanies the dead man in his visit to the infernal regions and, in this case, to the Court of Heaven and the Christian hell, the description of the court of justice, the existence of a register of merits and faults which determines the span of life granted to each man, the importance of pious actions such as adorning places of worship and reciting or copying sacred texts – all meritorious actions highly recommended in Buddhism which, if undertaken on behalf of the dead, made it possible to cut short their penances – and, finally, the errands entrusted by the inhabitants of hell to the one who has the quite exceptional chance of returning to the living. But here is a summary of this text.

A certain Yan Kuibin, a Christian from Quanzhou, recounts the vision that he had

being old and ill, on the fourteenth day of the seventh moon of the *gengchen* year in the Chongzhen period [1640]. In the afternoon of that day, he saw a heavenly spirit which came to him and announced that the Master of Heaven was summoning him. He declared himself ready to go. 'Why don't you tell your sons and grandsons?', asked the heavenly spirit. He replied: 'It is so long since I troubled to direct my household. The affairs of before birth and after death all depend upon the Master of Heaven. What good would it do to tell them of [my departure]?' – 'Very well, in that case, let us go.' So up they went and saw Yesu [Jesus], the Master of Heaven, on a high seat. He looked severe and imposing and was surrounded by a throng of heavenly spirits. There was also a great crowd of people, young and old, who were waiting to be judged: they were the thousands of people who had died on that day. Each one carried his own register on which were recorded his merits and his crimes. The director general of the heavenly spirits, Mi'e'er [Michael], was passing sentence in place of his master and on his orders, judging everything with great clearsightedness. Those who had committed abominable crimes were all sent to hell and devils at their side inflicted torments upon them. There was only one man of great virtue, who ascended to Heaven, and two people who were sent to the place where crimes are purified [purgatory]. At the sight of the great number of criminals, the Master of Heaven seemed full of compassion. When Kuibin's turn came, Michael raised his voice and said: 'You have been obeying the doctrine [of the Master of Heaven] for a long time. But the roots of three great crimes have not been eradicated [in you].'[114] And as Kuibin protested his innocence, Michael replied: 'It is simply that you are not aware of them. Your crimes are cupidity, avarice and anger.' Kuibin replied: 'All these crimes are caused by my poverty.' – 'That may well be in the case of cupidity and avarice, but anger cannot be caused by poverty. This root of evil may in the long run cause serious damage if one does not repent. You must correct yourself without delay. Nevertheless, last year you decorated the statues in the hall [of the Master of Heaven] in Quanzhou, working for forty days and forty nights and claiming no reward for all your trouble. You should therefore be sentenced to 24 days of calamities in the place where crimes are purified. But [I order] that you be sent back to the world so as to do a hundred times better there and serve as a guide to others, telling them of what you have seen [here] and exalting the omnipotence of the Master of Heaven.' – 'My words do not carry much weight', replied Kuibin, 'and I fear that people will not believe me. What is to be done?' – 'Ask advice from the *duode* [i.e. the missionary].'[115] The heavenly spirit [Michael] ordered the saint who was on duty that day to show him the way back and Kuibin thanked [Michael] for all his kindness.

Then there was a saint who came down the steps of the hall to meet him and said to him: 'Ever since you received the purification [baptism], the Master of Heaven has ordered me to protect you. Did you know that?' – 'What is your name?', asked Kuibin. – 'I am the second founding disciple.[116] You have won a chance in ten thousand of being allowed to return [to the world] and you owe it to the benevolence of the Master of Heaven and also to the aid of the Holy Mother. Now you will have to show great zeal and live up to my name. You must make as many gifts as possible round about you and you must control your fits of anger. I will see you later.'

Thereupon, the saint who was on duty[117] came up to him. He was very beautiful. Kuibin asked him his name. 'I am Zhang Mige [Michael Zhang]', he told him.[118]– 'I have long admired you', 'replied Kuibin, 'What luck to meet you today!' – 'I congratulate you upon returning to the world. Could I entrust you with a letter for my uncle? I am ordering him to eliminate three faults that he has – cupidity, pride and lying – and to strengthen the merits he already possesses and not allow himself to fall into lust. The whole family, men and women, young and old alike, has adhered to the doctrine. Unfortunately, the two mothers do not get along well together.' – 'How is your father?', asked Kuibin politely. Zhang Mige replied: 'My father is the most eminent figure in the province of Fujian, but he is wrong to continue to follow the profane.'[119]

Half-way along, to the east [they saw] a hell indicated by a door marked 'The door to eternal suffering', and a few paces away from it another hell indicated by a notice bearing the words 'Place of forging and purifying'. Reaching the door, Kuibin saw Zhang Ergu.[120] Ergu was delighted and wanted to open the door to let him in. 'Don't bother,' said Zhang Mige, 'the Master of Heaven has ordered me simply to accompany [Kuibin] on his return.' – 'You are returning?', exclaimed Ergu joyfully. '[In that case] I beg you to say a word from me to my son and daughter-in-law and to advise my nephew, Zhu Weidu, to make many new friends and to recite on my behalf 3,800 [Christian] sûtra to deliver me from the hell where one's crimes are purified.' Also present were those co-religionaries, Zhao Mo'ang and Bai Siduo.[121] They were dejected and said nothing. Mige said to Kuibin: 'Recently Wang Huwo and Nian, the doctor,[122] won the right to rest in the place of tranquillity [in paradise]. You must tell their sons and grandsons to show more application in their mourning.' Hardly had Mige finished speaking than Kuibin came back to life. It was the hour of cock-crow.

It was Kuibin's son, Yan Weisheng, who noted down this story in the thirteenth *chongzhen* year [1640].

This tale shows that, as the Franciscan missionary, Antonio de Caballero, feared, the Chinese probably did believe that 'offerings made in accordance with the fourth precept could deliver the dead from the sufferings of Purgatory and Hell'.[123] This is in effect an application of the Buddhist theory of the 'transfer of merit' (*parinâma*), according to which pious works could bring aid to the deceased and reduce the length of their stay amid the evil destinies of the infernal beings, ravenous devils or animals, or even, better still, deliver them definitively from the painful cycle of rebirths and deaths.

The story also testifies to the Chinese predilection for life: to be able to return among the living, even for just a short while, was considered a chance beyond one's wildest dreams. All that is borrowed from Christianity is totally within the traditional framework.

The missionaries usually refer to conversions in terms of numbers: they represented so many souls won over to God and saved from the everlasting flames. It was therefore necessary to save as many as possible. Hence the importance, in China, ascribed to the baptism of abandoned or dying children. With them, there was no fear of the apostasy that appears to have been so frequent. Father Foucquet, who was in China from 1699 to 1720, writes:

Those whom we convert as children may go back on their word and change when they become adult and there are all too many who are unfaithful to the grace they have received; whereas these abandoned children who die as soon as they have been baptised go infallibly to Heaven.[124]

There is a similar remark in a report on the state of the missions in China in 1703, written by Father François Noël. He remarks that the conversion of adults 'is exposed to plenty of backsliding into sin and idolatry', unlike that of dying children.[125]

There were no doubt missionaries, overconfident of the powers of baptism, who were somewhat hasty in administering it, just as was the case in Europe with forcibly converted Jews. Jean Delumeau writes:

There was ... one way of snatching the descendants of Judas from Satan's thrall. The most zealous churchmen have placed great hopes in the medication with magic powers that baptism is held to be. The holy water of baptism evicted the devil from the soul of the Jew, who forthwith ceased to be frightening and became quite harmless.[126]

From the point of view of the Christian faith, baptism constituted an important and decisive action since it washed away original sin, creating a new man. There was considered to be a radical distinction between a soul immersed in the darkness of paganism and one touched by grace. However, the historian for his part cannot help wondering about the content of these conversions. For him figures, on their own, are not enough. And when, for example, he finds that Father Etienne Faber in the course of a single year baptised 2,699 villagers in a remote little town in Shenxi province, he may well harbour some doubts about just how much these peasants really understood about a religion so profoundly alien to the Chinese traditions. We must therefore attempt to analyse how these conversions took place, despite the paucity of information on the subject: it was an aspect of the matter which did not interest the missionaries. For them, every conversion was a manifestation of divine grace and a proof of its omnipotence.

Father Le Comte writes:

What force, what attraction, could in a single moment capture rebellious wills beneath the yoke of a Religion as strict as ours, if Jesus Christ himself did not perform miracles and if the Holy Spirit, through the internal and invisible operation of grace, did not make up for the shortcomings of his ministers?

And the same Father Le Comte describes China as a country 'where despite the efforts of the devils, God is constantly glorified'.[127]

Where the common people were concerned, there could be no question of entering into all the details of dogma. A simple summary of the catechism sufficed and that, in itself, could give rise to plenty of confusions.

One convert from Hangzhou records that those who wished to be baptised had first to give clear explanations of the general sense of the doctrine, twice or three times over. 'So it is not easy to enter,' he proudly declared to the monk, Total Enlightenment, 'nor is it easy to leave.' This was quite different from Buddhism, which people could embrace and abandon as they pleased: 'With us, there are none who abandon the doctrine of Heaven and return to Buddhism.' However, these declarations, which contradict what we know of the frequency of apostasies, did not convince the monk, Total Enlightenment. He asked:

What proof is there that these people who have learned the rudiments of the Christian doctrine off by heart have really understood and have not blindly accepted statements that they do not understand?

Buddhism and Confucianism, for their parts, quite lacked any such formalism: 'A truth [a Dao] which may not be reached by a thousand different paths and through a thousand analogous arguments cannot be the truth.'[128] This absence of definitive dogma and formalism is one of the features that most clearly distinguish the Chinese traditions from the Christian.[129]

Thanks to the records of the lawsuit brought against the missionaries and their followers in Nanking in 1616 and 1617, we do know something of the conversions made in that town by Father Alfonso Vagnone between 1609 and 1616. The documents mention among the Christians converted by this missionary a cake-seller, a bookseller and occasional printer, a maker of straw hats, a gardener, a carpenter, a repairer of fishing nets, a gilder, a soldier and a water-carrier. Vagnone, who preferred not to attract too much attention, did not himself initially approach these people but used a Chinese from Macao as his propagandist. As soon as a candidate for baptism had indicated his agreement – and no doubt learned by heart a summary of the catechism – Vagnone would proceed to anoint him with oil and sprinkle him with holy water, except in the cases of women, who would be privately baptised by Zhong Minren, the convert from Macao.[130] We even know what was understood from the preaching of Zhong Minren by those whom he sought to convert. When arrested in 1616, a certain Xia Yu, a cake-seller by trade, declared in his statement that, having in the tenth moon of 1612 gone to visit the maker of straw hats, Cao Xiu, a follower of the doctrine of the Master of Heaven, the latter had said to him: 'The Master of Heaven produced the

Heavens, the Earth and the Ten Thousand Beings. Why do you not adhere [to the doctrine]?' Zhong Minren and others had then explained the principles of this doctrine to him. Xia Yu had said: 'But, since you call him the Master of Heaven, why does he have a statue?'[131] Zhong Minren is reported to have replied:

It is because, in the beginning, when the Master of Heaven produced the world by a magic transformation, there was only one man and one woman. Later on, people took to working at various professions. They no longer recognised the Master of Heaven. That is why he drowned them in a flood. After men had suffered this great disaster, the Master of Heaven took pity on them and descended to be born in a Western kingdom in order to convert the whole earth. That was 1,615 or 1,616 years ago.[132]

As can be seen, Zhong Minren's recollection of what he had been taught was not very good. And what he said must have been recorded with great accuracy, given the scrupulous care with which statements were taken down in China.

When visiting the bookseller, Zhou Yong, Vagnone slipped the following remarks into the conversation: 'You are old. Why do you not adhere to the doctrine of the Master of Heaven? Then your soul could go up to heaven.' That was enough to decide Zhou Yong.

Some of the converts among the common people knew more or less how to read. A case in point was the cake-seller, Xia Yu, who received from Zhong Minren 'fifteen books on the Barbarian doctrine'.[133] But most of the common people, and in particular those who lived in the countryside, can hardly have been taught other than orally and in an elementary fashion, and this explains how it was that certain Christian ideas were so readily assimilated to the popular traditions.

For a Christian, religion commits only the individual, for it affects his personal salvation. It is a dialogue between the soul and God. So it is strange that conversion, an essentially individual act which implies the commitment of soul and conscience, was, in China, often a group affair: an entire family, servants included, or a whole village would ask to be baptised. This would suggest that the consciences of individuals had very little to do with it and that motives other than deep personal conviction may have prompted these collective conversions.[134] The fact is that religious sensibilities vary from one society to another. There is no universal psychology valid for all civilisations and all periods of history. For the Chinese with whom the missionaries made contact from the end of the sixteenth century onwards, it went without saying that religious matters were a collective affair: they concerned a family, a lineage, a village. What mattered most was the saintliness of the men involved and the efficacy of the rituals and formulae. Now, the protection afforded by holy things was not usually limited to individuals. And it is noticeable that it was almost invariably happenings that were held to be miraculous which prompted the common people to ask for baptism.

For them, any cult, any religion had to demonstrate its efficacy, for they expected tangible advantages to accrue from it: good harvests, calamities averted, public peace, family good fortune, the well-being of deceased relatives. Even though Buddhism had introduced the theme of individual salvation into China, this never acquired such importance as the collective well-being of lineages or territories. The proof of the value of a religion lay in its supernatural effects. Hence the crucial importance of miracles.

Father Le Comte, who is such an excellent informer, tells us that the emperor, Kangxi (1662–1723), himself complained to the Peking Fathers that they were not showing them enough miracles:

The emperor, who has been told of the miracles that God has wrought among other nations, sometimes reproaches us on that account. He says: 'Are we of less account than the Barbarians who have so often seen their sick cured and their dead resuscitated? What have we done to God to make our conversion more difficult? You come from the other ends of the earth to preach a new Law that is contrary to nature and above reason; is it fair to expect us to believe you at your word? Perform some miracles which will assure us of the truth of your religion and I will assure you of the sincerity of our faith.[135]

But, Father Le Comte goes on, 'if miracles are in short supply in Peking, that is not the case in the provinces. They have occurred in several places and those of Father Faber[136] are so universally recognised that it is hard not to believe them.'[137] And, as examples of such miracles, he cites the following:
- the case of a house threatened by fire, which was spared thanks to the prayers of a Christian who, through them, made the wind veer and provoked the destruction of the house of an apostate;[138]
- a portrait of Jesus Christ, honoured by people prostrating themselves before it,[139] cured a whole family of idolaters whose recourse to doctors and Buddhist monks had met with no success. This miracle decided the entire family, and their neighbours too, to ask for baptism. Some of them, however, did raise objections, saying that the devil had nothing to do with the affair and that the cure could well be natural;[140]
- a girl possessed by the devil was persuaded by her mother to become a Christian. No sooner was she baptised than she was cured.[141]

The *Lettres édifiantes et curieuses* also record quite a number of miracles. The converts maintain that they are proof of the power of 'the jewel of the Barbarians' and of the advantages to be gained from becoming Christian. The immediate effect of miracles is to provoke conversions or, at any rate, to encourage people to ask for baptism.

Father de Fontaney relates how, in 1702, a fire spared the residence of the missionaries in Ningbo. Thanks to the prayers of the Fathers and Christians, the wind had in effect veered and neighbours swore that they had seen a big man in white on the roof, beating off the flames. Afterwards, visitors to the mission declared: 'the God of these Fathers from Europe must be extremely powerful'.[142]

Father Desrobert reports that after a similar miracle – when the house of a Christian fortunately escaped the flames – many conversions took place among the common people. Father Desrobert goes on to say: 'The Christian religion is now known throughout this area and all the neighbouring regions are ringing with the news of this event. People are now saying that "it is advantageous to be Christian".'[143]

Victory always goes to the strongest, however: a sick man declares himself ready to become converted if he is cured. But it is a drug prepared by the infidels that restores his health. He immediately gives up the idea of conversion: what works is all that counts.[144]

The same notion of utility appears in an edifying anecdote related by Father Le Comte: a dying man asks to be baptised because he reckons that, for him, there is more advantage in being Christian than Buddhist. The fact is that Buddhist monks have told him that he is to be reborn as a coaching-horse to pay for the advantages he has received from the emperor (he is a state pensioner). He tells Father Le Comte:

They exhort me to do my duty as soon as I am in this new state, not to stumble, not to bolt, not to bite, not to injure anybody. Run fast, they tell me, eat sparingly, be patient; in this way you will attract the compassion of the gods, who often eventually turn a good beast into a man of quality and an important mandarin... In my sleep it sometimes seems to me that I am already in harness, ready to gallop at the first stroke of the driver's whip. I wake up in a sweat and half out of my mind, not certain whether I am still a man or already a horse ... I have been told that those of your religion are not subject to such afflictions, that with you men are always men and remain the same in the other world as they are in this one. I entreat you to receive me amongst you. I know very well that your religion is difficult to observe, but even if it were harder I would be ready to embrace it; and whatever it may cost me, I would still prefer to be a Christian rather than a beast.[145]

Among the common people, the best argument in favour of any religion lies in its supernatural effects. If it is furthermore advantageous and easy to practise, it will win every vote. Efficacy is also the criterion of those who criticise this foreign religion. Xu Dashou writes:

Last year there was a fire in Hangzhou. Quite by chance the house of one of their followers was spared by the flames. Thereupon they falsely claimed that this was an effect of the jewel of the Barbarians. But can it be said that it is 'loving men' (*airen*) [one of the precepts most often proclaimed in the doctrine of the Master of Heaven] to spare only eight individuals and afford no protection to ten thousand? In my own village, there is a labourer by the name of Yan who was the first to adhere to their doctrine. Yet his house was totally destroyed by the fire, to such an extent that the flames even reached the third coffin.[146] So, in these cases, where is the efficacy of the jewel of the Barbarians? How can it be claimed that they are not lying?[147]

To judge from the reports of the missionaries, most of the common people who asked for baptism seem to have made up their minds on the strength of miracles ascribed to the efficacy of the ceremonies performed by the foreigners, or else on the strength of the missionaries' personal saintliness. These converts, no doubt hastily instructed in the truths of Christianity, did have a tendency to go back upon their commitment. But the missionaries managed to provide fuller instruction for some, although not many, neophytes and these individuals remained completely loyal to them, displaying an intransigence towards the traditional cults that testifies to a less superficial transformation. This limited number of the elect appear to have shared a common psychology. In the first place, it was a matter of pride at being distinguished from the common herd of their compatriots, who remained deep in the shadows of error while the converts alone could hope to ascend to heaven. They were even of the opinion that baptism should not be granted to all and sundry. The Christians of Shaoxing in Zhejiang province one day protested at Father Parennin baptising the Tumin, a sort of pariah group who lived in a separate street of their own in the town and of whom Father Parennin writes that 'they were only allowed to engage in the lowliest and most humble of trades, such as the sale of frogs or little sugar cakes for children, or playing the trumpet in front of the dead when they were carried to burial'.[148]

When one Chinese returned a money purse to its owner, a convert told him that 'it was fitting only for Christians to perform such actions' and that, in the state that he was in, however many virtues he possessed, these would not prevent him from being damned.[149]

But these converts also distinguished themselves through the ardour of their quest for austerity. The excesses to which they would go and in which the missionaries were often obliged to curb them were probably of a traditional nature. In China, as elsewhere, one sometimes comes across a kind of frenzy of asceticism. It finds expression in a number of heterodox movements. Grief at the death of relatives would also incite some people to manifest a desire for self-mortification – an urge which might be manifested in other circumstances too. Although Buddhism condemned self-mortification, some of the Buddhist monks and faithful occasionally practised it, believing that they were in this way making an offering of their bodies. Consider the testimony of a missionary of the late eighteenth century, on the austerity practised by certain Buddhist monks. He writes:

One comes across some who fasten heavy chains around their necks and drag them through the streets, going from door to door to beg, and declaring that it is impossible for people to wipe out their sins unless they often give alms to the monks. Others bang their heads against stones or lacerate their bodies with strokes of the whip. I have seen some who, as a result of their fasting and abstinence, seem so cadaverous that you would take them for walking ghosts.[150]

All this involved more than just a crude show designed to elicit alms, although that is all that the missionaries saw in it. It was also to do with setting an example in the virtue of giving and encouraging others to practise this cardinal virtue of Buddhism.

At the end of the seventeenth century, Father Le Comte, for his part, was also describing the acts of penitence that certain Buddhist monks imposed upon themselves in order to obtain alms: they wear chains around their necks and feet and strike their heads with bricks. One young monk is shut up in a sedan-chair studded inside with long pointed nails, closely massed together; those who give alms must buy off these nails, and there are more than two thousand of them.[151]

The most fervent of the converts seem to have shared this strong taste for self-mortification. Father Le Comte writes about the Chinese Christians: 'Their confessions were not only accompanied by tears (for the Chinese weep more easily than we do), but also by the harsh disciplines to which they submitted themselves in the sacristy, in the evenings.'[152] And elsewhere he describes 'their prostrations, with their faces glued to the ground, their cries and their tears'.[153] Elsewhere, he writes: 'Furthermore, they held the Holy Virgin in a devotion that would have gone altogether too far had we not taken care to control it.'[154]

At the beginning of the eighteenth century, Father Dentrecolles was writing: 'Many end each meditation with holy castigations which they inflict upon their flesh: I have sometimes been obliged to send them away from the church, to make them take a little rest.'[155]

The testimony of Father Jean de Neuvialle is more detailed:

Generally speaking, all our Christians display the greatest ardour in learning prayers by heart. There are some who, not knowing how to read, engage teachers to instruct them and, poor though they are, will cheerfully pay them the wages of an entire working day.[156] Austerities, iron belts and other instruments of penitence are in current use among them; their life could be regarded as a continual fasting . . . Furthermore, they do not regard all this self-mortification as in any sense going too far. After their confessions you often find them asking that fasts and disciplines be imposed upon them as acts of penitence.[157]

The son of Zhang Geng, the famous convert from Quanzhou in Fujian province, fell seriously ill at the age of 16 and was cured thanks to a miracle brought about through prayer: he saw Chinese characters inscribed in gold upon the curtains of his room (deities in China frequently manifest themselves in writing rather than orally). Father Aleni, being consulted, explained to him that the last phrase of the enigmatic text that appeared to him signified that he would ascend to heaven in three years' time and should therefore redouble his efforts. The young man then displayed an extreme ardour in exercising piety. Regardless of whether he was exhausted or starving, he never missed a single mass and ceaselessly mortified his flesh through flagellation, to such a degree that Father Aleni was compelled to intervene to preach moderation. The boy did indeed die a holy death at the time predicted and at that moment saw the holy face of the Master of Heaven. The date was 1622.[158]

These accounts of the extreme fervour of certain converts are confirmed by the missionaries' enemies. In a work dating from 1634, the monk, Purun, of Hangzhou describes the behaviour of the Chinese Christians as follows:

All those who adhere to the doctrine of the Master of Heaven cease altogether to make offerings to their ancestors, usurp the cult of the one true Master of Heaven and consign statues of the gods and Saints to the flames. They no longer make any sacrifices, except to the instrument of torture in the form of the cross, abolish the three-year period of mourning owed to parents and practise bandit rituals on the seventh day [Sunday mass]. There, they cry out: 'My Master, I am guilty', and as they do so they beat their breasts and tear their hair. In the darkness they anoint themselves with holy water and holy oil and fall to their knees, clicking their fingers and bowing their heads.[159]

Xu Dashou writes:

As for the way in which they manifest their respect for the Master of Heaven, it consists in beseeching him with groans in the darkness or in going to a solitary place, kneeling down there and crying out: 'True Master, deliver me!' The first invocation in the Barbarian sûtra runs: 'I wish your name to become holy' [Hallowed be thy name]. But why should a man free from all bonds ask to be delivered? And since this Master of Heaven is of a holiness that cannot be improved, I cannot see why he should be in any need of us men in order to be hallowed.[160]

Many Chinese were amazed at the passion that appeared to possess certain converts. Xu Dashou writes:

An old Buddhist monk has told me that, once someone was introduced to their vicious doctrine, it was like an evil seed in the field of the eight forms of knowledge,[161] like oil in flour, where it is impossible to get rid of it. So their crime is very serious and I do not know when a man will appear who is capable of bringing aid to the Buddhist Law.[162]

Le Comte relates the story of a converted doctor who defied the authorities of Hangzhou by distributing crosses and holy images. His nephew, also a Christian, wished to save him from a beating and undergo the punishment in his place. The situation was a classic one. More often it would be a son who, in order to show filial piety, would ask to be punished in the place of his father, but the relationship between nephew and uncle was similar to that between son and father. Father Le Comte interprets this generous action as being inspired by faith and he describes it as 'a combat which the Angels admired and which made even idolaters respect the Christian religion'. He notes the predilection of converts for martyrdom and the contagious effects of the behaviour of this doctor who, through his obstinacy, was successful in himself becoming the recipient of the beating.[163]

Such behaviour was not limited to the followers of the doctrine of the Master of Heaven: in deviant Chinese sects, scorn was poured upon those whose faith was not steadfast and who allowed themselves to be intimidated by the fear of punishment. In his *Appeal to those who have strayed* (1681) (that is to say, those who belonged to forbidden societies), Yan Yuan writes: 'The followers of deviant sects say about their fellows who are good people and afraid of punishments and who, therefore, leave the sect, that they are like rotten jujube which cannot withstand the wind.'[164]

In a little text of the early seventeenth century entitled *The Owl and the Phoenix do not Sing Together*, the convert, Yang Tingyun, contrasting the doctrine of the Master of Heaven with the heterodox Chinese sects, claimed that, unlike the Chinese sects, the missionaries did not seek to inspire people with wildly exaggerated hopes.[165] Nevertheless, in the Christian faith, the hope of gaining the infinite blessings of paradise and fear of the eternal fires were levers that were all the more powerful given that retribution was not automatic as it was conceived to be in Chinese and Buddhist thought.

Chapter 3

Religion and politics

God and Caesar

As the Chinese emperors held total power over the organisation of society and the universe, and space and time, it was not possible for religion in China to be an autonomous power. The various religious cults were therefore a political matter. The Chinese sovereigns reigned by mandate from Heaven (*tianming*). Heaven or, as the ancient texts sometimes put it, the Sovereign on High, would be informed of the advent of a new dynasty in the course of solemn sacrifices.[1] It, or he, was the guarantor of dynastic stability. It was through its close relations with the cosmic forces that the imperial power derived an essential part of its legitimacy and prestige. The emperor imposed order upon the world through inauguration ceremonies, the diffusion of the calendar, the bestowal of titles and names, the classification of the various cults and deities, the diplomas he granted them, and the general organisation of space. Consequently, whatever seems profane about these activities was not entirely so, and whatever seems religious incorporated purposes and meanings other than religious ones. The Chinese emperors combined, in their persons, functions and aspects in which the profane and the sacred were indistinguishable: the Chinese concept of universal order was a global one which tolerated no divisions.

These ideas derived their inspiration from the most ancient of traditions. Ever since Antiquity, kings, princes, holders of high office, barons and gentlemen had each, respectively, made sacrifices to the particular deities who corresponded to their own rank: religion, then, not only reflected the political order but actually cemented it together. To celebrate a cult reserved for a superior order was considered to be a political usurpation or, at the very least, proof of subversive intentions.

By placing itself outside and above the socio-political order instead of combining with it and reinforcing it as the established cults did, Christianity threatened to destroy that order. By remaining external and of a different nature, it was likely to ruin the very bases of a society and a state which depended upon respect for a total order and was oblivious to any opposition between the spiritual and the temporal.

105

One of the criticisms directed against Christianity was that it incited ordinary individuals to usurp an imperial privilege, namely that of making sacrifices to Heaven, the most eminent of the cosmic powers and the expression of social, political and natural order. Father Intorcetta, who arrived in China in 1659 and died in Hangzhou in 1696, writes:

It is not permitted for those of an inferior order to make sacrifices to spirits of a superior order; and if they do so, it is not with a pure heart nor according to ritual and the prescribed order but in the hope of obtaining some advantage and as though through flattery.[2]

Similarly, even in one of his earliest letters, Ricci wrote: 'But they believe that only the king should worship and make sacrifices to this King of Heaven (the Shangdi)[3] and that if others wished to do so they would be punished as the usurpers of a royal privilege.'[4] And Xu Dashou writes:

Recently, when I had set up a family temple to worship my ancestors, the Western men of letters [the missionaries] found fault with me, saying: 'These are your family masters.[5] But there must also be a greater master. Do you not recognise him?' To which I scoffingly replied: 'That greater master is the Sovereign on High (*shangdi*) and in our China only the son of Heaven may sacrifice to him. Nobody else would dare to do so.'[6]

And, if it was no business of ordinary individuals to worship a supreme deity, it was even more unthinkable that they should do so by associating him with the humble cult of their own ancestors. Now, the Jesuit missionaries had sometimes allowed themselves to tolerate ancestor worship by reason of the attachment of the Chinese to the family cult and the importance of filial piety in their social mores. They had advised their followers to worship God in their family temple or in the main room of their home, which served that purpose. One author is scandalised at such promiscuity between an all-powerful God, claimed by the missionaries to be the creator of Heaven and Earth, and ordinary family ancestors:

They say that the ancestors must be honoured in the self-same temple as the Master of Heaven. Now the rule established ever since Antiquity, which lays down that only the king has the right to sacrifice to all his ancestors, ought to apply even more in the case of the one they call the Master of Heaven, whom they place above both the round mound for sacrifices to Heaven and the square altar for sacrifices to Earth and whom they declare to have been forever superior to all other divine powers. And yet they dare to have him revered on an equal footing with the ancestors of ordinary individuals![7]

Such behaviour shows the Barbarians to be totally lacking in any sense of propriety. One author, bent on criticising the ideas of the missionaries, quotes the following passage from *The Ritual*, one of the Classics:

The son of Heaven sacrifices to Heaven and to Earth; princes sacrifice to the mountains and rivers within the domains; holders of high office sacrifice to the ancestral temple of the founder of their lineage; gentlemen and ordinary individuals sacrifice to the tablets of their own [immediate] ancestors.[8]

And he goes on:

In this way, *The Ritual* shows that [the cult of] that supreme majesty which is Heaven cannot be usurped and that there is an order in the sacrifices that cannot be upset. To suggest that each person should revere a single Master of Heaven and represent Heaven by means of statues before which one prays each day and each month, asking him to have mercy: is not this to usurp a cult for which one has no authorisation; is it not to profane Heaven by making unseemly requests?[9]

Another author expresses himself in similar fashion:

Our Confucianism says that every being contains the Taiji [that is, possesses in his nature a reflection of the universal order],[10] and it calls nature whatever is bestowed by Heaven. Thus, each individual has the capacity to fulfil his own role perfectly, and order reigns in the titles and ranks which fix the hierarchy of dignities. The son of Heaven sacrifices to Heaven, princes to the Mountains and Rivers, to the god of the Soil and the god of the Harvests, high officers sacrifice to the five domestic deities, gentlemen to their ancestors. But you speak of one single Master of Heaven. What difference is there between you and the Buddhists and Taoists?[11] That is why I maintain that you seem to criticise Buddhism but are secretly stealing its ideas. You pretend to respect Confucianism but in reality you are destroying it.[12]

In his act of accusation against the missionaries of Nanking in 1616, Shen Que was already expressing the same indignant astonishment:

In the glorious period of the three ancient dynasties, the one who governed all princes was called the King of Heaven (*tianwang*). He who is sovereign of everything beneath Heaven is called the son of Heaven. In its institutions, our dynasty [the Ming] has simply followed the ancient customs; in imperial decrees and proclamations the emperor is identified with Heaven. Now, these Barbarians speak of a Master of Heaven who, they say, governs Heaven and surpasses it in dignity.[13]

Xu Dashou writes:

According to the teaching of our Confucianism, the sovereign is equal to Heaven in dignity. That is why it is customary in the annals of the *Springs and Autumns* [eighth to fifth centuries BC] to call the sovereign 'King of Heaven' and his writings 'orders of Heaven' or 'punishments of Heaven'. Although Buddhism speaks of renouncing the world, in Buddhist temples there is always a prayer tablet wishing the emperor ten thousand years (*wansui pai*), and people do homage to that tablet with the utmost respect. If Buddhism entrusts the care of its sûtra and the Buddhist Law to the sovereign of the kingdom and his great ministers, how could this simply be flattery? It is assuredly prompted by a principle [of loyalty to the sovereign] that has existed for all time and which it would be impossible to disregard. Now, these Barbarians do not call themselves the subjects of their sovereign, but his friends.[14]

In 1659, Yang Guangxian explains that by saying that Heaven is subordinated to the Sovereign on High, the Barbarians show that they do not understand why the ancient Sages called the sovereign of men the son of Heaven. They thus turn the father of our sovereigns into a lowly servant of their Master of Heaven.[15]

The Western idea of a distinction between political and religious authority, each being vested respectively in the persons of kings and those of popes, was regarded in China as an aberration:

In their kingdoms they recognise two sovereigns. One is the political sovereign, the other the doctrinal sovereign. The former controls the government of a single kingdom, the latter holds a power that extends to all the kingdoms in the world. The former reigns by right of succession and passes on his responsibilities to his descendants. He nevertheless depends upon the doctrinal sovereign, to whom he must offer gifts and tokens of tribute. For the doctrinal sovereign, a man skilled in the doctrine of the Master of Heaven, is chosen when the question of succession arises. It comes down to having two suns in one sky, two masters in a single kingdom. Does this mean that if one can imagine the principles of Yao and Shun [the sovereign Saints of Antiquity] being suddenly replaced by those of their sûtra, our emperor himself would have to submit to this doctrinal sovereign and send him tribute? What audacity it is on the part of these calamitous Barbarians who would like to upset the [political and moral] unity of China by introducing the Barbarian custom of the two sovereigns.[16]

In China, then, religious matters are inseparable from the affairs of state. A cult is only authorised once it has been officially recognised and integrated into the hierarchy of cults, under the patronage of the emperor. Thus, in the past, the Buddhist and Taoist cults had to be associated with the official cults of the literate tradition. The emperor allots titles to the deities just as he allots them to the most eminent human personages.

Given that in China every political decision was based upon a study of precedent, Christianity was at a disadvantage since it had never been recognised by any previous dynasties. Xu Dashou writes: 'It has never been recognised by our emperors. It is upon their own initiative that the Barbarians have instituted the cult of the Master of Heaven. If that is not heterodox, whatever is it?'[17]

In such a situation it is easy to understand the importance, in the eyes of the missionaries and their followers, of the discovery in 1625 of a bilingual stele, bearing Chinese and Syrian inscriptions that traced the history of the Nestorian Church of Xi'an from 631 to the mid-eighth century.[18] Although the Nestorian heresy was condemned by the Council of Ephesus in 431, the Xi'an stele provided proof of the antiquity of Christian preaching in China and thereby strengthened the position of the new Chinese Christians. During the years that followed its discovery, a number of converts judged it wise to describe themselves as followers of Nestorianism (*jingjiao houxue*).[19]

But even before the discovery of the Xi'an stele, the missionaries were supporting Christianity with an argument based upon the new geographical knowledge that they brought with them to China: their doctrine was recognised throughout the entire world, they claimed; only China had never heard of it before. In the very opening lines of *The True Meaning of the Master of Heaven*, Ricci declares that:

from the west to the east, all the great countries practise and observe the Dao of the Master of Heaven... But the literate elite of your country [are unfamiliar with it because they] have seldom travelled to other kingdoms.[20]

China is an exception in a world in which it fills but a small place.

However, this argument ran counter to the ideas which were the basis for the entire socio-political system of China, where the emperor held an organisational power that extended to the religious domain.

Being unfamiliar with the idea of a clear-cut distinction between the spiritual and the temporal, the Chinese deemed it inadmissible that a religion should detach itself from the general order and dominate it instead of being integrated with it. From the point of view of the ruling and literate circles, religions were only acceptable if they reinforced the total order, which was at the same time cosmic, natural, political and religious; if they strengthened public morality through their teachings; and if they contributed towards the stability of the state and the collective prosperity by means of the supernatural blessings which they were believed to attract to the empire and all its regions. In such circumstances, they could be officially encouraged and recognised. Their cults could be integrated into the hierarchy of all cults patronised by the state. If, on the other hand, they threatened the general well-being[21] and public morality and tranquillity, they became the object of repressive legislation. Good clergy served the state and were under its control; bad clergy consisted of individuals with little to recommend them, who eluded that control.

Anxious to reassure the ruling groups, the missionaries were frequently at pains to insist that their religion did not threaten the public order. But they went even further when they adopted an argument more specifically intended to answer Chinese preoccupations: namely, that Christianity had political virtues and exerted a beneficial influence upon social mores. In effect, it preached submission. How could men who aspired only to heaven, scorning worldly possessions, possibly be rebellious against the civil power, the Christians argued.[22] They also sought to represent the Christian kingdoms as a world of peace and harmony, knowing that such an image would be likely to win over the Chinese. Replying to criticisms from a civil servant with Buddhist sympathies, Matteo Ricci[23] reminded him that ever since Buddhism entered China two thousand years previously,[24] things had been going from bad to worse. Were not the Buddhist men of letters always saying: 'Things are not what they used to be'?[25] And Ricci wrote:

In contrast, on the whole and so far as one can see – for I should not dare to exaggerate – ever since 1,600 years ago, when our countries became Christian, in the more than thirty kingdoms which adjoin one another, over more than 10,000 square *li*, there has not been a single change of dynasty, not a war, not the slightest dispute.[26]

Father Giulio Aleni's *Questions and Answers about the Countries of the West* (*Xifang wenda*), printed in 1637, also gives a most idyllic picture of Europe.[27]

And Xu Guangqi, the most famous of the converts of the early seventeenth century, in one of his works also insists upon the political advantages in adopting the doctrine of the Master of Heaven. He writes:

This doctrine can truly come to the aid of the moral influence of our sovereigns (*wanghua*), bolster up Confucianism and rectify Buddhism. The fact is that in the West of these people, there are more than thirty kingdoms neighbouring one another which all observe this doctrine. Now, over a whole millennium and several hundred years, right down to the present day, large and small kingdoms alike have helped one another, the superior and the inferior have lived in harmony without any armies to guard the frontiers or any changes of dynasty. In all these countries there are no cheats or liars. Ever since Antiquity, there has been no lasciviousness or thieving. People do not pick up objects lost on the roads,[28] the doors are not locked at night. And as for rebellions and disturbances, not only are they quite unknown, but there are not even any words or written characters to denote such things.[29]

Elsewhere, the same Xu Guangqi declares that if China adopted the doctrine of the Master of Heaven, it would enjoy endless peace and prosperity. He even goes so far as to propose that it be given a try locally: 'We could try it in one canton or little town', he suggests.[30]

Such an argument carried considerable weight in the eyes of the Chinese for, by virtue of their traditions, they tended to establish close links between morality, politics and religion. This is the line taken by the author of a preface to the work of one of his friends, a convert to the doctrine of the Master of Heaven: 'If people were capable of fearing and serving Heaven in all their actions, how could the [ideal] period of the three ancient dynasties [Xia, Yin and Zhou] possibly fail to return?'[31]

This idea, that Christianity, the doctrine of the Master of Heaven, could bring back a sort of golden age to China, appears to have been all the more acceptable to the converts among the literate elite given that they had taken over the thesis that some of the missionaries developed, namely that Christianity was, with a few additions, in fact the true doctrine of Confucius and Chinese Antiquity. Thus, in the preface to a Christian work dated 1711, a certain Ignatius Zhang Xingyao explains that the modern men of letters are heretics influenced by Buddhism and Taoism whereas he, Zhang, has rediscovered the authentic Confucianism which was the direct cause of the good order that reigned in Antiquity. He writes:

People of today do not realise that the doctrine of Heaven [Christianity] is precisely the same as [ancient] Confucianism, and they also do not know that the doctrine of Heaven complements Confucianism.[32] Therefore the doctrine of Heaven alone is capable of restoring to China the doctrinal cohesion and the unity of mores that are indispensable to political harmony. It can, in our own day and age, bring back to life the perfect order which used to reign in the times of Yao, Shun and the three dynasties of Antiquity.[33]

For Zhang Xingyao and Xu Guangqi, the ancient mental frameworks remain unchanged despite their conversions: orthodoxy must contribute towards the universal order and is recognisable by its beneficial moral and political effects. They make no separation between the domain of secular realities and that of religion.

Xu Guangqi's defence of the missionaries can be summed up as follows: all the things that they bring us are useful to the state, from their teaching on the obligation 'to serve Heaven and love others' to their calendar, their mathematics and their agricultural and hydraulic technology. Furthermore, their teaching conforms with Confucianism. Xu Guangqi suggests a confrontation with the Buddhist and Taoist monks: if the missionaries get the worst of it, let them be sent away.[34] The question of ultimate truths is not posed.

In attacking the Chinese cults of popular, Buddhist and Taoist origin and causing their statues to be destroyed, the missionaries appeared to be indicating their approval of a literate tradition which had always been hostile to what it considered as superstitions detrimental to morality and public order. Yet it was in the name of that very same tradition that many Chinese from the ruling classes opposed the 'doctrine of the Master of Heaven', once they realised how rapidly it was spreading among the common people.

Some texts reveal how it was that Christianity was able to adapt to the Chinese context. To one pro-Christian civil servant it appeared above all

as an encouragement to traditional morality. In a proclamation dated
1635, the prefect of Jiangzhou[35] adopts the arguments of the missionaries
with whom he had been in contact: Heaven or the Sovereign on High of
the Ancients was a true deity. How could this be confused with the
material heavens?

Do not even the most stupid men speak of the heavenly father, the heavenly
command, the principle of heavenly order? It is the Buddhists and the Taoists
who have upset people's minds and have persuaded them to revere themselves
rather than Heaven.

Christianity is useful against the heterodox sects which

deceive Heaven, contravene the [cosmic] order and in general attack the laws of
the empire. Fortunately Gao, the Confucian from the West [Vagnone],[36] considers that *the first thing of all is to teach loyalty to the sovereign and filial piety
with respect to one's parents*.[37]

This prefect, whose first and foremost concern is for public order, winds
up his proclamation with threats against the heterodox sects.

   Similarly, the author of the *Tianxue chuangai, A General View on the
Transmission of the Doctrine of Heaven*,[38] is of the opinion that Christianity makes it possible to fight effectively against the heterodox cults and
to 'set people's minds straight so that they observe the essential rules of
the principle of heavenly order'.

Christianity as a deviant sect

Among the ruling circles in China, there existed a long and ancient tradition of hostility towards religious movements that developed among the
people in an uncontrollable fashion. That was how all the great rebellions in history started. They were all inspired by religious doctrines and
messianic hopes of the coming of a society in which peace, equality and
justice would reign at last. That was the case from the great rebellion of
the Yellow Turbans at the end of the Han period right down to the formi-
dable insurrection of the Taiping in the mid-nineteenth century, and
from the Red Eyebrows at the beginning of the first century down to the
Boxer movement in 1900. The Chinese governors aimed to protect the
people, who were credulous and easily aroused, against all those who
sought to lead them away from the correct path. As soon as the missionaries, in defiance of the prudent advice so often proffered by Matteo
Ricci, began to try to set up Christian communities in popular milieux,
the same old reflexes came into play and a fear of sedition manifested
itself. That, and that alone, was the cause for the first measures taken
against the missionaries in 1617: an association of the doctrine of the

Master of Heaven had been set up in Nanking by Fathers Semedo and Vagnone. Furthermore, they had, on their own initiative, built a church there in 1611.

When Shen Que, the vice-minister of the Board of Rites in Nanking, drew up a report on the matter, dated the fifth moon of the year 1616, he was simply trying to impose police controls: an illicit association had been set up. This report, which was to earn its author a sinister reputation in the history of the Jesuit mission, was at the origin of what is known as the first persecution of Christianity in China. In it, Shen Que called for the missionaries in China to be sent back to Macao and for a ban on any further entry by these foreigners. But what did his memorandum actually say?

In it, he called for an inquiry into the origin of the missionaries' funds and how they had managed to enter China without official documents. He denounced Father Alfonso Vagnone for having, without authorisation, constructed a building to the west of the mausoleum of the emperor, Hongwu, setting up a 'barbarian statue' in it, and there leading the people astray with lies. He also accused him of having made a garden immediately alongside the mausoleum, which was a sacrilegious action in relation to the founder of the dynasty. But the memorandum was chiefly concerned with the constitution of a popular association. Vagnone was said to have given each member three ounces of silver and in each case to have made a full note of the names and dates of birth of all the members of each man's family.[39] He had organised both regular and special meetings, the smaller ones involving about fifty people, the larger as many as two hundred. He had stirred up the people to such a pitch that some of them, holding little flags in their hands, were declaring their desire to die for the Master of Heaven. The burden of Shen Que's remarks goes more or less as follows:

> We punish foreigners who enter China without authorisation even when they do not make trouble. We prevent them from spying. But if they also set themselves to stirring up the people day after day, as Vagnone does, that is inadmissible.

Finally, Shen Que expresses his surprise at the speed with which the Nanking missionaries learned of Peking's response to the proposals concerning them: the official post was reserved for the state. Leaks must therefore have occurred. The fact was that the matter would not have been so serious had not important figures been on good terms with them. But for the past twenty years, they had been establishing friendly relations with a large number of people, who protected them as soon as there was any attempt to implement the laws.[40]

Shen Que was probably one of the first to compare the Christian communities to the associations of the Chinese heterodox sects such as the

White Lotus (Bailian) and the Non-Action (Wuwei). This comparison was subsequently to become increasingly frequent as the missionaries increased their efforts to form Christian parishes in popular milieux, something quite unknown before Ricci's death in 1610. Thus, in two proclamations published against the Christians of Fujian province at the end of 1637, the followers of the doctrine of the Master of Heaven are cited alongside those of the Non-Action sect as belonging to associations detrimental to public morality.[41] In a short work written the following year, a certain Huang Yanshi, who had received his doctorate in 1619, accused the missionaries of being in league with the secret societies of Non-Action, the Grandmother (Nainai), the Heavenly Mother (Tianmu) and Complete and Sudden Awakening (Yuandun). Huang Yanshi explained that, of all these associations, the Non-Action was the most dangerous. In appearance, it seemed opposed to that of the Master of Heaven, but secretly it was in collusion with it.[42]

The missionaries were scandalised to see their religion brought down to the level of Chinese superstitions. Accustomed, as they were, to establishing a radical distinction between what related to God and what belonged to Caesar, and being not quite always aware of the extreme sensitivity of the Chinese to the political implications of any religious preaching in popular milieux, they saw this accusation that they upset people's minds and sought to subvert the state purely as an unfair pretext to bring about their own destruction.

To counter the attacks beginning to be launched against the missionaries, the convert, Yang Tingyun, produced a short work which aimed to show that the doctrine of the Master of Heaven had nothing at all in common with the popular sects, and he entitled this little piece *The Owl and the Phoenix do not Sing Together*. Yang Tingyun thinks that many of his compatriots make overhasty and superficial judgements when they compare the doctrines of the missionaries to the heterodox sects of China. In reality, the missionaries operate quite openly and do not organise nocturnal meetings.[43] The heterodox sects address themselves to the inferior classes whereas the missionaries maintain relations with people of good society, important members of the literate elite and civil servants, who write prefaces for them and in praise of them. The books of the heterodox sects are uncouth, vulgar, unworthy of attention. Those of the 'Western men of letters', in contrast, are scholarly works adorned by illustrations and explanations. The leaders of the Chinese sects are interested parties, they seek to make as many new recruits as possible and insist upon an oath and absolute secrecy. The missionaries are disinterested, do not accept supporters without discrimination, wanting only the most convinced of followers; they require no secrecy from them. The Chinese sects mingle the sexes together whereas the 'Western men of letters' are against all sexual laxity; their doctrine glorifies chastity. The sects give the people false hopes and flatter the vulgar masses. In contrast, the missionaries teach that only good conduct makes it possible to obtain happiness after this life. They teach men to despise worldly pleasures and to bear the misfortunes of the world with patience. They want people to struggle against the prevailing current. The sects frequently resort to magic. The missionaries speak only of morality and daily conduct, filial piety, and obedience and loyalty towards the sovereign and other superiors. Yang Tingyun concludes by declaring that the fundamental idea of the teaching of the Westerners is that all our Saints and Sages of Antiquity knew of and served Heaven. That is why good morality and good political order reigned in those days. But later, people began increasingly to respect Buddhism above our own Confucianism. Now, the doctrine of the Master of Heaven leads us back to the ancient Confucianism.[44]

Yang Tingyun's work was written during the period when the popular milieux still remained relatively unaffected by the preaching of the missionaries. As Ricci often emphasised, their first and foremost aim had been to win the sympathy of the upper classes, using the most diverse means. This the missionaries had essentially achieved by the beginning of the seventeenth century. However, in time, the atmosphere changed as the very content of the doctrine of the Master of Heaven came to be better known and the missionaries began to extend their evangelical efforts in the direction of the people.

The comparison of Christianity to the Chinese deviant sects (*xiejiao*), probably first introduced by Shen Que's memorandum of 1616,[45] continued to be a constant feature throughout the subsequent history of Christianity in China, right down to the twentieth century.[46] From a Chinese point of view, there appeared to be some justification for it. As soon as the missionaries took to concentrating above all on creating 'associations of the doctrine of the Master of Heaven' (*tianzhu jiao hui*) amongst the people, Christianity appears to have become the victim of a kind of mimetism: it fell quite naturally into a category which had existed in China long before it was ever introduced there, namely that of the *xiejiao*. The existence of cults with subversive tendencies was an inevitable consequence of a dominant tradition which integrated religion with political order. Given that there was a hierarchy of deities and cults fixed by the state, as well as gods who received their qualifications from the emperor, and authorised local cults in which the civil servants of the provinces participated, everything else – by the same token – fell outside the system and became the object of measures of repression. Now, Christianity was impossible to integrate within the system of Chinese religions: placing itself, as it did, above all temporal power and rejecting all pagan cults, it was bound to be classified among the subversive sects.

There were, furthermore, a number of features which established a connection between the associations of the Master of Heaven and the illegal and more or less secret religious societies: the fact that it was a cult which disregarded the hierarchy of religions, since only the emperor had the right to make sacrifices to Heaven; the links of brotherhood which united its members; the mystery which surrounded their meetings; the suspicion that it resorted to magic; the association of men and women gathering in the same places; the fanaticism of some of the converts; and a doctrine which preached of martyrdom and promised blessings beyond the grave. All this appeared to fall foul of the law since, as was pointed out in one of the documents in the Nanking lawsuit of 1617, the Code of the Ming dynasty forbade

ordinary individuals to address themselves directly to Heaven, [prohibited] the production of charmed water, the making of amulets bearing written characters, the secret possession of drawings and statues, assemblies of large numbers of people on the occasion of ceremonies in which incense is burned, and meetings which start at nightfall and break up at dawn.[47]

The missionaries' condemnation of the ancestor cult and the restrictions they placed upon it, together with their prohibition of the cult of the five household gods, constituted a further point of resemblance between Christianity and the heterodox sects: the members of certain prohibited sects also rejected the traditional cult of the household gods and ancestor worship.[48]

Like the secret societies, the Christian communities were organised. A Chinese text of the mid-eighteenth century accuses the missionaries of setting up some kind of responsible leader at the head of every group comprising fifty Christians and picking out the most determined of their converts to perform this function.[49] Elsewhere, an author at the end of the Ming period writes:

All those who have become their followers have as a sign of identification the design of a soft tortoise on the lintel of their doors. As soon as he joins the associ-ation, the new member must open 'a register of the three generations', to be pre-sented to the residence of the Barbarians. What is the difference between them and the sect of the White Lotus?[50]

At the interrogation of Father Vagnone in Nanking in 1616, the Chinese authorities noted that the converts stuck on to their doors characters cut out of paper as signs of identification.[51]

Descriptions of Christian gatherings unconsciously repeat the tradi-tional themes that are applied to the meetings of the forbidden cults. Xu Dashou writes:

They assemble their followers in the halls of the Master of Heaven and there discuss much ridiculous nonsense. At night, they proceed to perform their culpable actions, men and women together, letting down their hair and beating their breasts and [now] being let into the most secret explanations. Tradition deems sacrificing in the fields with one's hair let down to be evil. What should one think of these people who, both individually and family by family, act in such a manner with no valid motivation?[52]

Some missionaries brandish the threat of heavenly retribution. They say that 'if we do not make all haste to become their followers, in three years from now the Master of Heaven will become angry with us and will refuse to accept us'. These are the lengths to which they go in their seditious talk![53]

The same author writes:

They seduce good folk, men and women alike, without rhyme or reason, encouraging them to see spirits and devils,[54] thus corrupting their innate intelligence and ruining the moral sense that they have possessed ever since Antiquity. Such a crime deserves worse than death. They are [hypocrites like] Wang Mang,[55] initially full of humility, then, once they have acquired power, glorying in their success and virtues.[56]

And elsewhere, on the subject of the destruction of Chinese religious statues, he writes:

There is no end to the ignorance of the common people. If somebody comes and tells them that by flattering the hundred gods, they will obtain a hundred blessings, a heterodox cult immediately develops. If these people now come and tell them that by destroying the hundred gods [of the Chinese cults] and thereby flattering the Master of Heaven, they will acquire the greatest good fortune possible, the hundred gods will be abolished on the spot.[57]

In China, the co-members of a secret society were sworn brothers and had, in many cases, sealed that fraternity with blood on the occasion of their swearing an oath. This egalitarian tradition persisted right down to contemporary times. In the mid-nineteenth century, one of the favourite themes of the Taiping, who were influenced by the propaganda of the Protestant missionaries, was the equality of all mankind. But the Jesuit missionaries of the seventeenth century were also proclaiming the equality of all men, in the sight of God. Ricci wrote:

My sovereign and I are prince and subject; my father and I are father and son. But if one compares these relationships with those that exist between our Father in common – the Master of Heaven – and the whole of mankind, all differences are abolished, even between sovereign and subject, father and son, and all men are brothers . . . However close to us our relatives may be, as are, for example, our father and mother, they still are further away from us than the Master of Heaven.[58]

From the point of view of Chinese morality, these were scandalous propositions. The Christian thesis of the equality of men threatened their entire system since behaviour, morality and social and family hierarchies – all things which ultimately depended upon the public order – were tied in with the distribution of roles between those who were set above and those who were set below. Chen Houguang observes: 'The fact that they serve one single Master of Heaven means that they place on the same level son and father, subjects and sovereign.'[59] Another author writes:

These people say quite simply: 'If we consider that the Master of Heaven is our Father and that all peoples are, as it were, his sons, the virtues of humanity and filial piety can do nothing but prosper. In this world, our prince and our father are our brothers. How could they deserve to be served as much as the Master of Heaven?' Is not this the height of a spirit of rebellion?[60]

The author of *The Aid to Refutation* explains that relationships between sovereign and subject are founded upon respect, those between father and son upon good will, those between the elder and the younger upon the order of birth, those between husband and wife upon the distinction between the sexes, those between friends upon good faith. All these relationships imply a general order which cannot be turned upside down and which posits the hierarchical inferiority of subjects, sons, women and younger siblings. However, 'these Barbarians say that, in their kingdoms, the relationships between princes and subjects are regulated by friendship'.[61] Regardless of the importance attributed in China to social status and age-ranks, the missionaries tell the people: 'The moment you follow our doctrine, whatever the age and quality of whoever you are addressing, you must call him "brother in the doctrine" (*jiaoxiong*).'[62]

In one passage of his great treatise, *The True Meaning of the Master of Heaven*, Ricci explains to the Chinese that they have three fathers: one is the Father of all mankind who is the Master of Heaven, the creator of Heaven, Earth and the Ten Thousand Beings; the next, their sovereign; the third, finally, the one who 'gave birth to' them. And Ricci goes on to write: 'When a son obeys the orders of a superior father, and by so doing violates the orders of an inferior father, that constitutes no assault on filial piety.'[63] That was a strange interpretation of what was, for the Chinese, the first and foremost cardinal virtue, namely filial piety. From a traditional point of view, it amounted to an encouragement to political revolt and filial disobedience, crimes which the law condemned most severely.

That was certainly the understanding of some Chinese: the converts no longer owed before all else obedience to their parents – especially if those parents had refused to become converts – nor even to the public authorities. Instead, they owed it to the missionaries and their Master of Heaven. There were similar reactions in Japan. The Japanese, Fabian Fucan, notes in a work written in 1620:

The first commandment says: 'Love your God above all else.' You must therefore place him above both sovereign and parents and disobey the orders of your sovereign and your parents if they are not in agreement with the will of God. Is this not proof that they desire to destroy the religions and state of Japan?

And Fucan asks:

What does 'refusing God's will' mean? What it means is abandoning Christianity to adhere to Buddhism and the religions of Japan. Thus, Japanese Christians must rebel against their sovereign and be ready to sacrifice their lives and submit to any punishment if he commands them to return to Buddhism and Shintô. That means that the orders of the Bateren [transcript of the Portuguese *Padre*] come before all those of the sovereign and of one's parents.[64]

In their ignorance of the relationship between ritual and dogma in Christianity, the majority of educated Chinese regarded the Christian ceremonies and sacraments as no more than magical practices. As Louis Wei, a Chinese Catholic priest, writes, in the nineteenth century: 'Chinese intellectuals consider the liturgical ornaments, holy images, medallions and holy water ... as charms in a perverse and fanatical witchcraft.'[65]

Accusations of witchcraft do indeed recur throughout the history of Christianity in China, right from its beginnings in the seventeenth century. But here we should emphasise the role of capital importance that the Christian rituals played in the minds of the common people: for them too, very often, these were a matter of magic but – as we have seen – magic that was effective and beneficent. Failure to recognise the connection between these two aspects of a single but ambiguous phenomenon would make it impossible to understand both the hostility of the literate classes and also the conversions of the common people.

The charge brought against Fathers Vagnone and Semedo in 1616 by Shen Que, notes that death penalties exist for those who upset the public order with deviant doctrines and stir up the people on the pretext of performing good works. It explains that Buddhism and Taoism have become completely acclimatised to China and both work towards the same ends as Confucianism. In contrast, anything that smacks of magic and witchcraft must be suppressed with the greatest severity to avoid causing disturbance or excitement among the common people.[66]

Lack of comprehension with regard to the Christian rituals and the very secrecy with which the missionaries and Christians were obliged to surround themselves explain how it was that they were accused of resorting to deviant and magical practices.

Twenty years after the Nanking affair, Huang Zhen was writing:

Can it be said that worshipping Heaven consists in sprinkling oneself with holy water, rubbing oneself with holy oil, carrying a cross around – and thereby burdening both one's body and one's soul – and attracting people at night, secretly seducing them and mingling men and women together?[67]

In an address to Buddhist monks, in which he exaggerates the danger to make it seem more acute, the same Huang Zhen writes:

How few are wise and how many are foolish; less than two generations after the arrival in China of the monster, Ricci, the peoples of the coasts who were so disturbed by the teaching of these Barbarians that they ended up by following them and, sprinkled with holy water and rubbed with holy oil, were ready to die for them, these people now certainly number several hundreds of thousands of families.[68]

From Fuzhou in Fujian province, at about the same period, Chen Houguang writes as follows:

We Confucians follow a level and unified path. Confucius used to say: 'Whosoever knows me, is that not Heaven?'[69] And also: 'To study realities of the most humble kind in order to raise oneself to the comprehension of the highest matters,[70] what is that if not "serving Heaven"?'

This author goes on to cite a number of passages from the Classics relating to the cult of Heaven and respect for Heaven, passages to which the missionaries had also appealed, but giving them a quite different meaning. And he concludes:

To abandon all this in order to rally to this Yesu who died nailed to a cross, of whom Ricci speaks and whom he identifies as the Sovereign on High, to prostrate oneself before him and pray with zeal, imploring his supernatural aid, that would be madness. And to go so far as to enter darkened halls, wash oneself with holy water and wear amulets[71] about one's person, all that resembles the vicious practices of witchcraft. Was there ever anything of this kind in our Classics and our Four Books? All these Riccis and other Barbarians falsely claim to serve the Sovereign on High in order to extend their influence.[72] It is imperative that our holy emperor prosecute and expel them for, trusting in the words 'to serve Heaven and the Sovereign on High', simple folk are all taking to following them without examining the matter in depth. How deplorable this all is![73]

A certain Xie Gonghua of Zhicheng in Fujian province writes:

They speak of anointing themselves with charmed water and making marks with charmed oil. They say that to drink wine is to drink the blood of the Master of Heaven; to eat flour is to eat the flesh of the Master of Heaven. They have a stone which they place on a table and then they call it a bone of the Master of Heaven. If people are capable of accepting the holy water and holy oil, then even if they have behaved badly in their lifetimes, the Master of Heaven shows mercy if they but desire for a moment to come to him, and entirely forgives them all their earlier crimes. Now, the Master of Heaven, Yesu, was condemned by justice to die nailed to a cross for having stirred up the people with his strange speeches. He was not able to get himself acquitted. How then could he acquit others?[74]

Xu Dashou also accuses the missionaries of resorting to magic:

The sûtra of the Master of Heaven say: 'Our Father, which art in heaven.' They ask him for bread today. Tomorrow they will ask him to free them from their debts. At dead of night they go to make invocations to him, indulge in magic manipulations and weary the spirits.[75]

The mystery surrounding the Christians and the lack of understanding about Christian rituals and certain of their practices gave rise to some absurd beliefs, which persisted right down to the twentieth century. The missionaries were suspected of drugging their followers in order to obtain absolute obedience from them. 'They render their lies even more forceful by using magic procedures', writes a man of letters in the region of Quanzhou, who had received his doctorate in 1619, and he goes on:

In every country, they wait for fifty years after having buried the bones of their dead, then they take these bones, reduce them to dust and, using magic means, they turn them into oil and water, which they then distribute . . . This is the oil they use to rub on people's foreheads. After that the people become stupid and follow them blindly. Our Chinese foolishly believe that it is holy oil and holy water.[76]

The same author, who claims to know about what happens in other countries, reports that in Luzon, the missionaries inflict punishments on the local women, accusing them of 'secret crimes' and forcing them to expiate these day and night before Yesu. They choose the prettiest women and make them do domestic work, shut up in their residences. As for the men, they drape them from head to foot in a great garment of white canvas and have them whipped until the blood runs with a whip made of six or seven thongs with iron nails attached to the ends.[77] We may no doubt see in this the echo of an auto-da-fé witnessed by the Chinese of Manila. Such flagellations have indeed persisted down to the present day in the Philippines.

In his memoirs, Matteo Ricci relates how his own possession of a crucifix almost caused serious trouble for himself and his companion, Diego de Pantoja, on the road to Peking in 1600. The eunuch, Ma Tang, noticed his crucifix carved in wood, painted with blood and seemingly alive, . . . and began shouting that this was an artifice [a charm] that they had made in order to kill the king and that people who resorted to such procedures could not be honest folk.[78]

We may doubt the good faith of Ma Tang, who wanted to seize the objects carried by the Fathers and thereby compromise them. But the idea that came into his mind was quite a natural one: he thought that he had come upon a *defixio* procedure involving a statuette into which pins had been stuck to bring about the death of an enemy. Ricci himself comments: 'And he truly did believe that this crucifix was some kind of evil spell.'

The sacrament of extreme unction, combined with the missionaries' practice of collecting new-born babies so as to baptise them before they died, gave rise to the belief that they used the pupils of the eyes of the dead for magical purposes, or even to make magnifying glasses. There are a number of testimonies to these beliefs.[79] The missionaries were also quite simply suspected or accused of eating the children they took in to bring up as Christians. Xu Dashou writes:

According to *Urgent Comments on Chenopodes and Peas*,[80] these Barbarians are extremely cruel. They often get hold of children of less than nine years and cook and eat them. Such children fetch an average price of one hundred gold coins. Young good-for-nothings exploit the fact and trade in them to such an extent that the Cantonese are very apprehensive for the lives of their offspring . . . It is obviously in accordance with their ideas to have the children die rapidly once they have attracted them into their clutches.[81]

One Chinese trader from Batavia assured a neophyte that the missionaries had come to capture the souls of the Chinese by means of spells because they did not have enough of them in Europe.[82]

Right from his very first years in China, Matteo Ricci was suspected of engaging in alchemy, and it was because he believed the missionary to possess exceptional talents in this domain that Qu Taisu (Qu Rukui) decided to take him as his master and thus became one of the first converts among the men of letters.[83] This belief in alchemical manipulations performed by the missionaries was reinforced by the mystery surrounding their sources of income: not knowing where their funds came from, people concluded that they produced money by magic means. It seems to have been a belief that sometimes operated to the advantage of the missionaries. Thus, one Chinese Christian tried to draw a friend of his over to them by telling him that they knew the secret of refining cinnabar (*lian dan*), using eyes torn from the dead.[84]

One accusation quite frequently levelled against the missionaries was that they exploited men's cupidity to attract and convert them. One author writes in 1636 that the Barbarians appear modest and respectful.

People admire their Chinese-style politeness, he says, but they use gold to bribe people to come to them, so as to facilitate their dishonest designs. They adopt a Chinese appearance but in their hearts they are Barbarians. Once they have corrupted people with their gifts, they upset their minds by means of their pernicious books.[85]

According to Zhang Guangtian, it is only thanks to their bribes that they avoid all surveillance: 'Those in charge of neighbourhood groups and local leaders [responsible for policing] find it to their advantage to receive bribes and eventually nobody bothers to go and check up on them.'[86] Such a practice is to some extent confirmed by Father Le Comte, who notes that, to quieten mandarins who display too much curiosity or zeal, 'we would try to placate [them] with gifts'.[87]

But the most frequent charge levelled against the missionaries is that they pay people to be converted. Yu Chunxi, a man of letters and a Buddhist sympathiser, who was among the first to criticise Ricci's *The True Meaning of the Master of Heaven*, writes that if the missionaries win a common man over to their doctrine, they reward him. If he is a man of letters, the reward is ten times greater; and if he is a civil servant, it is one hundred times greater.[88] A similar accusation appears in *The Aid to Refutation*. The Barbarians tell their followers:

If you recruit one hundred followers, we will give you a clock which chimes automatically and a clavichord and as much gold and cloth. If you recruit a student, that is worth ten ordinary recruits. If you recruit a man of letters, that is worth one hundred ordinary recruits.[89]

In Nanking, in 1616, Vagnone was said to have given each convert three ounces of silver.[90] Such rumours were rife among the common people. Similar accusations still persisted in the mid-eighteenth century: Father Jean-Gaspard Chanseaume, newly arrived in Macao in 1746, reports on a recent Chinese text which lists the Chinese grievances against the missionaries and claims that 'they persuaded common folk to enter this religion by giving two crowns to each one who embraced it and by holding out hope for a paradise and fear of a hell'.[91] A little later, Zhang Zhentao (1713–80), from Fujian province, claimed that the missionaries were paying more than ten ounces of silver a year to each convert from the common people and several dozen ounces if the convert was a man of letters.[92]

A Portuguese source notes that in Japan in 1574, Father Coelho was willing to pay around three taels of silver to a Christian to get him to try to convert his brother, a Buddhist monk, and to behave as though he were acting upon his own initiative for, as a Japanese, this Christian understood the character of Buddhist monks and knew how to approach them in such a way as not to offend them.[93]

The Chinese often wondered where the missionaries' funds came from while the latter, for their part, in order to avoid scandal, were at pains to make sure that their origin remained unknown. Xu Dashou writes:

I have often wondered where their money came from. Some say that they practise alchemy but they themselves are careful to avoid mentioning the matter. It appears that their kingdoms have the most urgent need to convert people and large sums of money help them to do so.[94]

However, at the time of the inquiries undertaken in Nanking in 1616 and 1617, Vagnone was obliged to explain the route by which the money reached him from Macao. One of the contemporary records of the trial states: 'Their money is sent to Macao from the kingdoms of the West. From there, traders take it to Luo Ruwang [João da Rocha] and Luo Ruwang brings it here [to Nanking].'[95]

The missionaries were also accused of mystifications designed to enhance their doctrine's prestige. One author records the discovery of an ancient inscription in sigillary characters, said to have been found in a landslide in Sichuan province and to give an account of the life of Jesus. He claims to have questioned the people of Sichuan province but, he says, nobody anywhere had heard anything about landslides or inscriptions in sigillary characters. He concludes triumphantly: 'So the Barbarians of the West are the only ones to have heard of these things! All this is a subterfuge, just like the River Picture (*hetu*),[96] which they also use to make their doctrine holy.'[97]

Xu Dashou also writes:

They falsely maintain that the expression 'a great Saint from Western parts', which is to be found in the *School Sayings* [of Confucius],[98] alludes not to Buddhism, but to Yesu, and that the Buddhist monks twisted that expression to their own advantage in order to spread their doctrine. But how could the perfect Saint of the Zhou period [Confucius] possibly have praised in advance a Barbarian executed in a humiliating fashion during the Han dynasty?[99]

Yang Guangxian, for his part, expresses his indignation at what he considers to be a falsification of history destined to delude the world:

What is most to be condemned about them is the way in which they say that every event involving Yesu had been predicted in the official histories. History's task is to transmit things that are true and believable. How would it be possible to write a history relating to events which were yet to occur and which had been announced by some heavenly spirit? Until now, wicked people, who wanted to upset people, had at their disposal only methods of limited efficacy – magic tricks such as getting flames to break out on the altar of the god of the Soil, fox-like cries, magic writings concealed in the stomach of a fish,[100] or a stone man with only one eye [?]. But when these people declare that these things are written in the [official] histories, fools who are incapable of distinguishing truth from falsehood all clamour in a chorus: 'It must be true that a Master of Heaven exists. Otherwise how could the histories possibly have spoken of it in advance?'[101]

Miracle-workers had always been regarded as troublemakers in China. The missionaries attributed many miracles to Jesus: for Yang Guangxian this was clear proof that he had been plotting sedition. Besides, had he not finally been found guilty of rebelling against the laws of his country? He had been accused of attempting to usurp the royal power, since he had, in mockery, been dressed in an old red garment with a crown of thorns placed on his head and a sceptre in his hands to make him look like one who held supreme power.[102] Furthermore, as we have seen, the missionaries themselves had performed many miracles in China.

The hostility felt in literate circles was reinforced by the very fervour displayed by certain converts: such people appeared quite alienated and would without compunction defy the authority of the state. In the heterodox Chinese sects, those who went in fear of the laws and were not wholly committed, body and soul, to their faith, were considered bad disciples.[103]

The determination displayed by Christian converts and the sympathy won by the missionaries in the higher echelons of society made Christianity seem to some people much more dangerous even than the heterodox sects, which usually lacked such support. Thus, Huang Zhen writes:[104]

The sects of the White Lotus and Non-Action[105] are no more than skin-deep sicknesses, like mange or ringworm. There is nothing particularly alarming about them. But the fact that in the entire empire not a single individual could be found to refute the vicious doctrine of the Master of Heaven when it first entered China, is something to be deeply deplored and bitterly regretted.

The activities of the heterodox sects were assessed as actions detrimental to morality. In the *Pingshu*, a vast plan for governmental reform produced around 1700, a certain Wang Yuan (1648–1704) distinguishes eight categories of individuals who are harmful to public morality. They are listed in descending order of importance: (1) prostitutes, (2) actors, (3) Buddhist monks and nuns, (4) Taoist priests, (5) heterodox Chinese sects, (6) the Westerners (that is to say, the Christian missionaries), (7) Muslims, (8) thieves and bandits. Wang Yuan suggests that the missionaries be obliged to return to their own countries and break off all relations with the Chinese. Li Gong, a disciple of Yan Yuan and the editor of the *Pingshu*, appended to this article the comments of a number of readers and, on the topic of the missionaries, adds a note that reads as follows: 'Yet one could also keep those who have talents as mathematicians or technicians, but their doctrine would be banned.'[106] This distinction between what was useful (the sciences and technology) and what was harmful (religion) has already been noted above.

A danger of subversion

> They will not desist until they have seized all powers, both moral and political, in China, and have concentrated them all within the Society of Jesus.[107]

Were the term not anachronistic, one might say that the Chinese of the seventeenth and eighteenth centuries displayed a highly developed 'nationalistic' sensitivity. They were deeply conscious of belonging to an ancient and great civilisation, rich in scholarly traditions. Some Chinese were clearly conscious of the dangers that threatened this heritage as a result of the diffusion of Christian ideas. But this Chinese sensitivity would appear to have been further sharpened by the Manchu accession to power.

In his letter to Yan Maoyou, Huang Zhen makes a distinction between the Barbarians from the West, who are followers of the Master of Heaven, Yesu, and those whom he calls 'the Barbarians of China', who are the followers of those followers, his point being that considerable harm has already been done since some Chinese have renounced their own civilisation and become Barbarians. Huang Zhen writes:

You may be sure that the Barbarians will not immediately seek to destroy Confucianism. Their plan is to operate initially by means of seduction and to proceed in a furtive manner. Through seduction they can win a joyful welcome in the sight and knowledge of all. By proceeding in a furtive manner, they can win a secret welcome without arousing any anxiety. In the first case they immediately proceed to denigrate our Confucianism. In the second they undermine it. And one fine day, when their teeth and claws have grown and they are confident in their audacity and power, they will install themselves in the temple of the sovereign without a realm [Confucius], usurping his place and, roaring aloud, they will destroy our Confucianism.[108]

In the same text, Huang Zhen emphasises that the danger stems from the fact that the Barbarians 'have managed to interpret our writing and our Classics fraudulently and have chosen important people to spread their doctrine in China'.[109]

The same theme frequently recurs in anti-Christian polemical works: these perfidious Barbarians have come to undermine the intellectual traditions of China,[110] which are its most precious heritage. They threaten them with corruption and destruction. It is peoples' patriotic duty to come to their defence against this great danger, for China identifies with its civilisation. Those who are alarmed at these threats are inspired by 'loyalty to the sovereign and love of their country'.[111]

The politeness of the men of letters sometimes masks a certain scorn for the Barbarians. It is not usually expressed but it explains the way they sometimes behave. The author of a text produced in 1636 writes:

There are some who despise these little Barbarians, reckoning that they cannot do much mischief. So they accept their rich gifts, thinking that there is no harm done. They praise their writings so that all of high society talks about them and praises them to the skies without realising that this is precisely the way that these cunning Barbarians mean to snare the whole of China in their nets ... Others have the lowest opinion of their theories, which they deem quite unacceptable. Yet they continue to have relations with them and treat them politely instead of firmly rejecting [their speeches] and openly breaking off relations with them, thereby giving them a chance beyond their wildest dreams to establish relationships and get to know people ... Then there are others, particularly those well-versed in the Classics and historical works, who rely upon the intelligent clarity of those texts and believe that our great moral and philosophical tradition is quite invulnerable and could never be destroyed by such low and despicable notions. And when they see people involved in refuting these vicious ideas, they think they are bothering themselves for nothing, just like the man from the principality of Qi who was terrified that the sky would fall upon his head, and they regard it all as quite incongruous. They do not see that this perverse doctrine is daily making progress and that the good doctrine is daily disappearing.[112]

The last remark applies well enough to important men of letters such as Wang Fuzhi (1619–92) who, although certainly well aware of the contents of the works published by the missionaries, in their own writings make virtually no allusion to the doctrine of the Master of Heaven.

The contempt felt by the Chinese for other nations was noticed by the missionaries. In 1703, Father de Chavagnac wrote:

They cannot believe that anything that is not Chinese merits any attention at all. Just when you think you have convinced them and that they are ready to embrace the Christian religion, they reply: 'Your religion is not in our books; it is a foreigners' religion; can anything good exist outside China and can there be anything true that our wise men did not know?'[113]

In 1769, another missionary makes a similar comment together with a few other observations:

The good opinion that the Chinese hold of themselves, their conviction that nothing can equal the acuity of their intelligence, the fantasies with which they are infatuated, their extraordinary attachment to anything that flatters their own inclinations and, finally, the astonishing skill with which the Buddhist monks delude these poor people, are obstacles so great that we cannot dare to hope to overcome them without a miracle of Providence.[114]

Huang Zhen writes:

Aleni says that more than 7,000 books [of their doctrine] have entered China.[115] There are more than one hundred to be found today in Zhangzhou [in the south of Fujian province].[116] If they continue to upset everything and spread everywhere, these books will end up by destroying the tradition of our Saints. These people will never be satisfied until they have caught everybody in their nets and have spread their poison everywhere. When a small fire smoulders for a long time, you can expect a great conflagration. But can you even say that it is a small fire? They proclaim that already tens of thousands have rallied to them in the province of Fujian.[117] If this evil spreads throughout the whole of China, immense harm will be done. How could one stand by and do nothing and allow this great calamity to happen?[118]

His alarm is understandable for, from a Chinese point of view, philosophy, propriety, morality and politics are all interconnected. Huang Zhen goes on to say:

Aleni says that twenty members of their association[119] have come to China to preach their doctrine, that all of them are people of great virtue and that all of them together form one single body. Today, halls of the association of the Master of Heaven exist in both the northern and the southern metropolitan territories,[120] in the province of Zhejiang, in Wuchang in Huguang province, in the provinces of Shandong, Shanxi, Shenxi, Guangdong and Henan, in Fuzhou and Quanzhou in Fujian province and other places too. Only the provinces of Guizhou, Yunnan and Sichuan are free of them.[121] Alas! Our glorious China is disturbed by the pernicious ideas of the Barbarians. Their poison is spreading everywhere and threatens to contaminate millions of generations. Nowadays, respectable men of letters and people of good standing go along with their views. They print books of the doctrine of the Master of Heaven for them and write prefaces for that doctrine. I have seen many of them with my own eyes. All this is detestable and scandalous.[122]

Some of the accusations may seem childish but minor changes often indicate upheavals to come. The author of one short text waxes indignant at the sight of the Barbarians reversing the order of hierarchies, for they hold the first degree to be the lowest and the ninth the most noble, whereas in China the hierarchical order has always been the other way around.[123] He also fears that, as they become accustomed to seeing the Barbarians making sacrifices in their Barbarian costumes and to hearing them, the Chinese themselves will be transformed and all the moral and political traditions of China, its rituals and music, 'the heart of men' and its customs, everything will one day become completely 'barbarised'.[124]

Huang Zhen writes:

This is what the Barbarians say: 'We must teach the whole of China to revere our Yesu and follow no one but us. We shall never cease our efforts until we have achieved this aim.' Ah! If the whole of China took to following the Barbarians, I know that the stratagem that once enabled Confucius to escape death would no longer be acceptable and the affair would be vastly more serious than the attempted assassination of Huan Tai.[125] The only thing left for me to do would be to cast myself into the eastern sea to die, for how could I live in a Barbarian world?[126]

So the Barbarians' intention is to corrupt China. To that end, they are not content merely with words: they destroy the statues and tablets of the Chinese cults, attempting in this way to sever all the links that connect the Chinese with their past, as the author of one anti-Christian pamphlet clearly perceived. He writes:

The most upsetting thing of all is that they destroy [the statues of] our Saints, cut off the heads of our deities, break the tablets of our ancestors[127] and put a stop to [the continuance of] cults, endeavouring by all this to topple our Sages and Masters and sever our connections with our fathers and ancestors so as to sweep away all our moral principles and school traditions.[128]

Being convinced that the entire history of mankind is contained in the Bible, the missionaries tried to reinterpret the history of China in accordance with the Judaeo-Christian traditions. As we have seen, for most of them there could be no doubt that China had been populated by the descendants of Noah and that the floods of the time of Emperor Yao could only be the biblical Flood. This gave rise to great difficulties of chronological adjustment between Chinese and biblical dates, causing much ink to flow during the seventeenth and eighteenth centuries. To take but one example among many, Father Le Comte writes: 'The children of Noah spread through Asia and eventually pushed as far as the westernmost part of China, which is nowadays known as the provinces of Shanxi and Shenxi.'[129] This widely held belief went hand in hand with the equally common one in an ancient diffusion of biblical ideas in China, which explained how it was that expressions referring to Heaven and the Sovereign on High were present in the most venerable texts of the Chinese tradition. But by claiming that the Chinese were the descendants of peoples who had travelled from Judaea and that their most ancient traditions could be traced back to the Old Testament, the missionaries deprived them of their identity. If made to accept such theories, they would be obliged to repudiate both their traditions and their ancestors. No doubt motivated by the best of intentions, the missionaries thus proceeded in the same fashion as the colonial powers who taught the schoolchildren of Africa and Asia only the history of Europe. Moreover, the converts from Macao and the surrounding region, who were such a help to the missionaries in their role of assistant brothers, had also, on the occasion of their baptism, been given not only a Christian name, but also a Portuguese surname such as Fernandes, Pereira, Mendes or Leitão.

In the years following the installation of the Manchu dynasty in China, one of Yang Guangxian's most violent attacks was directed against Father Adam Schall and a convert by the name of Li Zubai,[130] whom he had encouraged to support the thesis of the foreign origins of the Chinese. In 1663, Li Zubai had composed *A General View on Transmission of the Doctrine of Heaven (Tianxue chuangai)*, in which he explained that the Chinese were the descendants of the inhabitants of Judaea. This was a betrayal of China's moral traditions and of the founders of its civilisation.

A preface for this text had been written by a censor by the name of Xu Zhijiang and it was to him that Yang Guangxian addressed a vehemently indignant letter on 21 April 1664. He wrote:

I could hardly believe that it was really you who had written this preface. You are an educated man, you were brought up in the schools, you are a famous doctor, a censor. It must have been some machination on the part of the people of this perverse doctrine, who sought to use your prestige as an administrator and celebrity to encourage Chinese people to believe, thanks to this preface, that they are the descendants of the heresy . . . They must have thought: 'This will help not only to upset people's minds but can also be used as evidence to support our perverse doctrine.' This text is surely not your work. Perhaps it is by one of your entourage who, lacking your own respect for the right doctrine, has borrowed your style to write this out of gratitude for a clock or some other curious article. This text is surely not your work. Or perhaps it is a matter of an old custom that demands a reply of this kind to poems or texts in prose that are addressed to you . . . Those who solicit prefaces can be so pressing that you really need to keep a sword at the head of your bed. They give you a text and you pay no attention to it. Especially someone like you, a man so busy with important duties. How could you possibly have had the time to read this work? For if you had seen that it claims that all our sovereigns and their councillors and all the rest of us too, from Fuxi down to the present day, are descendants of the heresy and that the Six Classics and the Four Books are nothing but the residue of this heresy, your hair would have stood on end and your eyes would have opened wide with horror. Far from agreeing to write a preface for it, you would have hurled the book to the floor and trampled on it. My own *Refutations of the Vicious Doctrines (Pixie lun)* and my collection of papers entitled *Let us reject all that comes from the West (Juxi ji)*[131] were engraved[132] four or five years ago and more than 5,000 copies have already appeared. Both the Court and the provinces have done me the honour of receiving them kindly. Can it be that you are the only one not to have seen or heard of them? . . . The more I think about it, the more convinced I become that this preface is not your work . . .[133]

Between 1657 and 1664, Yang Guangxian was launching attacks against both the religion and the sciences of Europe. In each case his criticisms were inspired by similar preoccupations and had a similar purpose: the foreign sciences and religion brought China's pre-eminence into question and sought to submit China to the authority of Europe, whether it was a matter of the calendar, the position given to China on the globe of the earth, the origins of the Chinese people or its most ancient religion. The dominating feature of Yang Guangxian's character is his Chinese 'cultural chauvinism'. Such sensitivity in the face of foreign pretensions was all the keener in view of the fact that since the middle of the century China had come under the power of the Manchu dynasty (1644–1911).

The aim of the mission was to establish itself as a Church. The missionaries and the most committed of their followers seem to constitute a foreign body within China, a kind of vast secret society obliged by the very conditions of its existence to operate clandestinely, with a system of constant liaison and communication between its various parts. Furthermore, the missionaries maintained their relations abroad. Added to which it became known that they both took their orders and received their funds from abroad. On such matters as these, political authorities always reveal themselves to be extremely touchy and the Chinese empire was even more so than most, given that it had over many years suffered from piracy and plots even within China itself.

One idea, quite frequently found expressed, is that the foreigners are working to spread their doctrine with the sole aim of corrupting the Chinese people, preparing them to obey the missionaries blindly and thus constituting a 'fifth column' ready to take action when the moment came and back up attacks launched from outside. The precedent of the experience of neighbouring countries seems to have supported such an analysis. In 1616, Shen Que wrote:

The Folangji [Franks: a name the Arabs gave the Portuguese and Spaniards, which then passed into Chinese] claimed falsely that they came to teach the doctrine of the Master of Heaven and in this way deceived the sovereign of Luzon and took his territory from him.[134]

An author writing in 1638 explains that on the pretext of trading, these Barbarians rented a piece of land in Luzon, then persuaded the local people to follow their doctrine and finally took possession of Luzon. They always proceed in this way: conversion is simply a preliminary step leading up to occupation. The astronomy, calendar, cannons, sciences and technology, by means of which the missionaries have insinuated themselves even as far as the Court, are merely pretexts for spreading their doctrine throughout every province and prefecture; their object in diffusing their doctrine in this way is to reach a position in which they will be able to take over China. Even today, their party is already in occupation of Jilong and Danshui.[135]

A paper signed by several leading figures from the region of Fuzhou and addressed to the academician, Jiang Dejing, in 1638,[136] runs as follows:

They have already annexed our tributory kingdom of Luzon as well as Kelapa [Jakarta], Sumatra and Kutoulang [?]. They occupy our Macao, Taiwan [now the region of Tainan in Formosa], Jilong and Danshui so as to be in a position to capture our ports in the provinces of Fujian and Guangdong. If, suddenly, external attacks are encouraged by internal conspiracies, how shall we manage to repulse them?[137]

In his letter, written in 1664, to Xu Zhijiang, the censor, Yang Guangxian expresses his opinion that China is faced with a vast subversive plot, the goal of the missionaries being to demoralise China and organise troops ready to move into action when the time comes. According to Yang Guangxian, the plan hinges upon four points: (1) they circulate their pernicious books everywhere in China in order to upset people's minds; (2) they set up their associations in every strategic spot in order to organise concerted action at the appointed time in conjunction with the invaders from abroad; (3) they have safeguarded their conspiracies by establishing friendly relations with high-ranking civil servants; (4) they stir up good-for-nothings and then use them as their instruments[138] and endeavour to win over to their side all the inhabitants of the empire. In Macao, which is a veritable capital for these people, they number more than 10,000 and maintain constant, secret contact with the outside world.[139]

Similar points are made in a request presented by a civil servant of Canton in 1717: the threat of these foreigners has spread to affect every country in eastern Asia. Christianity has been introduced into Japan in order 'to change the hearts of the Japanese' and thereupon seize their kingdom. The attempt was very nearly successful. And that is how Manila has already been overcome. The missionaries dispense large sums of money, attract crowds and make maps.[140]

The missionaries are frequently suspected of espionage,[141] particularly if they carry maps with them or engage in mapping activities.

Xu Dashou cites a work produced by a Chinese from the Macao region entitled *Urgent Comments on Chenopodes and Peas*. The work reports that:

during the Jiajing period (1522–66), the Barbarians from the West [clearly the Portuguese] limited their activities to bringing wood and stones into Macao, little by little, in order to build themselves houses. Eventually however, they made themselves an enclave for their ships and now they are building high walls to provide them with a lair and they send out spies disguised as men of letters into every province,[142] setting up a closely knit association... Even when several thousand *li* away, they remain in constant communication. Many accept gifts from them. Every year they are in contact with Luzon and Japan, receiving aid from both. They possess maps which show all the strategic points of our rivers and mountains, with the distances marked, and they regularly note down the strength of our troops and the size of reserve stocks in every region... They constantly exercise their soldiers, accumulate gunpowder and sometimes cast huge iron cannons. What can be the purpose of all this?[143]

A number of texts limit themselves to pointing out what a threat these foreigners represent to China. In his preface to the *Poxie ji*, dated January 1639, Zhou Zhikui writes:

These cunning little Barbarians are extremely skilful and are capable of constructing glass telescopes that can encompass a thousand *li*, through which they are able to see far into the distance from a vantage point. Having looked to see what is happening in the surrounding countryside, they attack with cannon. They are therefore feared, by reason of their talents, even by other Barbarians. Many of the latter have already been conquered by them... As for their doctrine, which is as common and as devoid of interest as can be, why do so many people come to support it? It is because they are led on by their cupidity. The Barbarians start by luring stupid and self-interested people with their money.[144]

Another author writes:

Every time they arrive in a kingdom, they destroy it, making use of their earlier conquests to make new ones. In this way, they have already annexed over thirteen kingdoms. It is not easy to know where the most distant of them are. But among those which are closer, are Luzon, Misuoguo [?], Java, Jilong and Danshui, all countries where they killed the king and took over the population. A few men are all they need to crush a kingdom.[145]

The much smaller Japan appears to have been even more sensitive to external threats than China was. It was, as we know, threats of this kind which unleashed the violent measures of persecution in Japan at a time when the Chinese for many years continued to do nothing more than send the missionaries back to Macao or expel them to Canton. The Japanese apostate, Fabian Fucan, writes:

They have sent troops and usurped power in countries such as Luzon and New Spain, countries of Barbarians whose nature is close to that of animals. But our country is superior to all others by reason of its proud courage. Hence their ambition to spread their doctrine throughout our land and thus take over our country even if it should take them a thousand years to do so, and that is the ambition which has penetrated deep into the very marrow of their bones. But what a gloomy future awaits them! Because of their faith, they hold their lives to be of no account. They call this 'martyrdom'. When a wise sovereign governs the empire, good is rewarded and evil punished. There is then no greater penalty than death. But the followers of the Deus,[146] showing not the least concern that their lives are forfeit, refuse to change their religion. What a dreadful and horrible thing! And where does all this flagrant malignity come from? Its origin clearly lies in the first *mandamento* [commandment]: 'Thou shalt love and revere thy God above all else.' The way this abominable doctrine is spreading is entirely the work of the devil.[147]

A text produced at the end of the Ming period claims that what makes the missionaries so dangerous is that

at the highest point of the state, the emperor is their dupe, at the level of the ruling classes they have won themselves allies among the civil servants and at the bottom they sow dissension in the minds of the common people. It is risky to attack them.[148]

The missionaries have many enemies who deplore the connivance they enjoy even among the administration, and one exclaims: 'How is it possible that people who wear the headgear and robes of the literate elite, people who have received a mandate from the sovereign and also receive funds from him can have lost all shame in this way?'[149] At the end of the seventeenth century, Father Le Comte writes:

When some [provincial mandarin] felt it his duty to impede the progress of our faith, we would try to mollify him by offering him presents[150] and presenting letters of recommendation which the Fathers in Peking would procure for us; or even, if necessary, we would bring the authority of the emperor to bear against him.[151]

The missionaries travel freely throughout the whole of China without anybody becoming alarmed and without being asked to give any account of themselves:

When it is a matter of roaming bandits, the strictest precautions are taken, inquiries are made, laws on the collective responsibilities of groups of families are reinforced. All movements are kept under surveillance, even those of one's ordinary neighbours... But when it comes to these Barbarians who have wandered in from across the seas, they can move from one province to another and one prefecture to another without anybody ever bothering to find out where they come from or where they are going. They are allowed to mingle with the common people. Those in charge of neighbourhood groups and local leaders find it to their advantage to accept large bribes and eventually nobody bothers to go and check up on them... When public spiritedness has come to such a pass, it means that men have lost all moral sense.[152]

Twenty years later, the same complaints are voiced by Yang Guangxian, who accuses the missionaries of spying and being two-faced, behaving in one way with those who are educated and quite another with the common people. Having elicited the appreciation of the former in their capacity as scholars, they exploit the trust that they have won in high places to stir up the common people with a fear of hell and promises of paradise. Spreading their influence secretly in this way, they bring a serious threat to bear upon state security:

Schall's[153] companions have opened churches in Nanking, Hangzhou, Fujian province and Guangdong province . . . Their followers are increasing in number and by now form a vast brotherhood, which maintains constant contacts overseas. Everybody admires the perfection of their instruments and fails to notice their lack of observance for the laws. Behaving in this way is like being somebody who raises tigers and leopards in his bed out of his love for furs, quite forgetting that they can eat men up.[154] If there are frontier posts at the country's entrance points, that is in order to prevent espionage and the giving away of state secrets. But nowadays the rules are no longer applied: in the case of the people from the West, nobody knows whether they are travelling by sea or by land, nor what they do or get up to in their residences; and while people of high society are going into ecstasy over the ingenuity of their instruments, their talk of paradise and hell is upsetting the common people . . . In our Sino-Manchurian empire, even the subjects of the Mongolian principalities linked with the imperial family have to carry documents of authorisation if they wish to cross frontiers. In contrast, these Westerners come and go quite unimpeded, and no questions asked.[155]

The missionaries all too often tended to consider themselves above the laws of the land and to claim a kind of unofficial extra-territoriality for themselves and their followers. This is noted in a report by the minister of justice (*xingbu*) cited in the *Lettres édifiantes et curieuses* of 1738. The report runs:

Lieou eul, who has been arrested and confined to the cangue, blundered into the Christian religion without thinking. He is not a European Christian. Do the Europeans have the right to govern all those who have embraced their religion? If it is true, as has been reported to your majesty, that Lieou eul, according to the maxims of their religion, cannot be examined by the law, the mandarins will no longer be allowed to interrogate those of our Chinese whom the Christians have led astray.[156]

Instead of displaying humility, as might have been expected of them, given that they claim to recognise the sovereignty of the emperor of China, the missionaries on the contrary show arrogance. They call their own kingdom 'the great West' (*Da xiyang*). And Shen Que explains, in the charge that he brings in 1616, that in the whole wide world beneath the heavens, whether inside or outside China, our emperor is the only true universal sovereign and that is why his kingdom bears the name of the great Ming (*Da ming*). Given that they claim to have sworn allegiance to China, how can they compare their 'great West' to our empire of the 'great Ming'?[157]

If the missionaries receive their funds from outside and take their orders from abroad, then, contrary to their claims, they cannot be loyal subjects. There had in fact been ample cause to suspect their loyalty even before the interventions of the papal envoys – which were considered as scandalous meddling in imperial affairs – made it quite plain that they were dependent upon a foreign power. In the nineteenth century, factual evidence of the links between religious propaganda and attempts to impose dominance on the part of the Western nations, that is to say between Christianity and imperialism, was further to exacerbate hostility towards the missionaries and their religion.[158]

However, during the second half of the seventeenth century, the missionaries won support at Court and from the emperors, Shunzhi and Kangxi. Those who managed to win recognition for their talents as astronomers and mathematicians in Peking, sometimes acquiring official posts there, were considered to be in the service of the emperor and under his personal protection. There is no better illustration of this than the behaviour of Kangxi, who reigned from 1661 to 1722. The Jesuit Fathers, who belonged to his entourage for a long time, entertained hopes of converting him but, as Paul Pelliot remarks:

Their relationship was based upon a misunderstanding; Kangxi displayed good-will towards the missionaries because he wanted to be sure of retaining the advantages of their scientific knowledge; the missionaries meanwhile presented themselves as scholars in order to acquire an authority which would enable them to extend their apostolate. What was essential for the one was no more than accessory for the others; but it took some years, on both sides, for this to be realised and this gave rise to conflicts which were exacerbated by national jealousies and rivalries between the different religious orders.[159]

Emperor Kangxi, who was endowed with an acute political sense, was a man of many parts. Being anxious to attach to himself the sympathy of each and every ethnic and religious group – Manchus, Chinese, Mongols, Muslims, Lamaists, Buddhists and Taoists – he would adopt the attitude most suitable to each case. There can be no doubt that Kangxi took the same course with the missionaries, who were certainly very useful to him by reason of their knowledge in all fields, not only the sciences. Nor can there be any doubt that Kangxi regarded the missionaries as the representatives of the distant kingdoms from which they came. Religion hardly came into all this at all.

In 1707, when the position of the missionaries in China was threatened by the quarrel over rituals, Emperor Kangxi was determined to protect the Jesuit Fathers, who in a sense belonged to his household, and he told them:

If your king of the doctrine [the Pope], on the basis of the report by Duolo [Monsignor de Tournon], accuses you of having committed a fault towards the

Master of Heaven through following Ricci's precepts, and orders you to return, I shall tell him that, having been so long in China, you have become completely acclimatised and in no way different from the Chinese, and consequently I shall not permit you to return.[160]

The lack of coincidence between the respective points of view of the missionaries and the Chinese is clearly conveyed by Father Le Comte's report on the request persented in 1692 by the Peking Fathers, with the object of obtaining what in Europe was to be termed the 'Edict of Religious Tolerance'. Le Comte writes:

After these fervent prayers [asking for God's aid], they secretly presented to the emperor the request which they were later to submit to him in public [through the intermediary of the Board of Rites].[161] He read it and, not finding in it any of the things most likely to make a good impression upon the minds of the Chinese (for they had only touched upon matters to do with the holiness and truth of our Religion), he himself drew up another version in the Tartar language and this he sent back to the Fathers, leaving them free to make deletions and additions as they might judge appropriate.[162]

It is worth remembering that the famous 'Edict of Tolerance' of 1692 contained virtually nothing about the Christian religion except a statement to the effect that it was not seditious. To the emperor's mind, what counted were the services that the missionaries might perform for him.

Foreigners were accepted in China as associate subjects, answerable to the laws of China. The Peking Fathers, who enjoyed Kangxi's protection and made themselves useful to his empire, measured up to that definition. But the same could not be said of the missionaries who had established themselves in the provinces, for they were concerned to stir up the people and form associations. The emperor, Kangxi, himself made that distinction, as can be seen from the following remarks with which Father Le Gobien credits him:

What I am doing at this point is something that I do out of love for them [the Fathers of Peking], taking no account of the others . . . All the same, they must warn the Europeans who are in the provinces to behave with great circumspection so as not to give the people any chance of creating a disturbance nor the magistrates any chance of lodging complaints about the Christians on the subject of their religion.[163]

The missionaries interpreted Chinese reactions in terms of their own religious preoccupations. They tended to regard any difficulties they might encounter as machinations devised by the enemies of religion and any sympathy shown them as signs indicating the beginnings of a conversion. For them, everything resulted from the manoeuvres of the devil, from trials sent by God or from divine grace, which could bring about things which would have been impossible without it. Furthermore, having hitherto been accustomed to the practices of a personal type of power that dispensed favour and disgrace in an arbitrary fashion, they now found themselves in the presence of a centralised state in which every decision depended upon long legal inquiries and was the subject of debates in which contradictory views were put forward and considered. The situation was much too novel for them to avoid making mistakes in their interpretations of whatever befell them, whether to their advantage or to their disadvantage.

The pomp and ceremony of the funeral rituals accorded to Father Verbiest on 11 March 1688, following deliberations on the part of the Board of Rites and upon its orders, were of a kind judged suitable for a guest who had enjoyed familiar relations with the emperor. But the Peking Fathers interpreted this political decision as homage done to the priest himself and also to their religion. 'To people in Europe it will seem unbelievable, taking place in the capital of a pagan and superstitious kingdom',[164] wrote Father Le Comte. This kind of reaction explains how it was that the missionaries always attempted to capitalise upon whatever they had obtained in a personal capacity, to extend some benefit to the Christian community as a whole. Shen Que, the vice-minister of the Board of Rites in Nanking, who was behind the first lawsuit against the missionaries of that town in 1616–17, observes that the missionaries had assumed official authorisation to stem from what was a purely diplomatic and personal gesture of respect for the memory of Ricci: the administrative organisation set in motion by his friends had designated for his tomb a plot of land which was later turned into the first Christian cemetery in Peking. Shen Que explains that it had merely been an act of politeness considered to be the due of an eminent foreigner and conforming to 'the kindness one must show to those who have come from distant lands' (*rou yuan*).[165] The favour to Ricci fell into the same category as that granted in former times by Emperor Yonglo to a king of Borneo who had visited China on an ambassadorial mission and had unexpectedly died in Nanking in 1408.[166] But the missionaries had tried to exploit the favour to Ricci as a pretext for winning acceptance for themselves in China. And Shen Que comments: 'Can you imagine the people of Borneo coming to establish themselves all over China just because a piece of land was granted them for a tomb for their king?'[167] Xu Dashou, who had no doubt read Shen Que's memorandum, makes a similar remark:

Ricci died in the 38th year of Wanli [1610]. Pantoja and the rest of them asked to be given a plot of land for his tomb. Their pleas were so insistent that they were granted this plot of land, on a personal basis. It is our holy dynasty's rule to treat foreigners from far away with kindness . . . [But, lo and behold] they then presented the fact that Ricci had been accepted, as evidence testifying to respect for Ricci, and they told people that Ricci had been honoured by the emperor.[168]

It was not only the Court that recognised the ancient adage according to which one should be good to those from distant lands. Ordinary individuals would also invoke it. Despite all his prejudices and grievances against the missionaries, even Zhang Guangtian, the friend of the monk, Total Enlightenment, says he is sorry for 'these people who have left their own country and come from so far away, who respect the Sovereign of Heaven and want men to aspire to good and eliminate evil'. And he goes on:

it is just that it is unfortunate that they are attached to a completely erroneous idea of the fundamental nature of things and, in their ignorance of the concepts of Buddhism, have reached such false conclusions on the causes [of the universe].[169]

In his preface to the *Poxie ji*, the large collection of works refuting Christianity, Jiang Dejing, who had remained on friendly terms with the missionaries despite his rejection of their idea of a Master of Heaven born during the period of the emperor, Ai, of the Han dynasty, records that he has made interventions on their behalf, mindful that one should have pity for foreigners who have come from distant lands. He writes:

Recently [in 1637], the governor of the province [of Fujian] issued an order to the civil servants, demanding that these foreigners be expelled, their statues destroyed, their residences demolished and all their followers arrested. The matter being a pressing one, they came to me to ask me to intervene. I happened to know the censor, Zeng, and I told him that their doctrine should be condemned but that men who had come from so far away deserved our compassion. The censor agreed with me and to some extent moderated the earlier measures.[170]

The way the administrators more favourable towards the missionaries reasoned was as follows: the Christians, like the Chinese, respect Heaven. The emperor is the son of Heaven and makes his sacrifices in the southern suburb to this cosmic power which is the most eminent of all. By declaring that they respect and revere Heaven, the missionaries by the same token appear to integrate themselves into the political and religious order of China. Such was the line of reasoning apparently taken by Emperor Kangxi who, as a sign of the protection he accorded the missionaries in Peking, offered them a piece of calligraphy in his own hand carrying the two characters *jing tian*, meaning 'respect Heaven'.[171] These two words were both a tactful reference to what Kangxi took to be the essential point of Christianity and at the same time an invitation to them to conform with the order of China, which was simultaneously cosmic, social, political and religious. There was nothing particularly novel about the formula for it was also to be found in the synagogue of Kaifeng, inscribed over the entrance door in a combination of four characters, *jing tian zhu guo*, meaning 'Respect Heaven and pray for the good fortune of the empire'. In this synagogue, as in all Buddhist monasteries, there was also, in a prominent position near the altar, a votive tablet requesting ten thousand years for the emperor or *wansui pai*.[172]

However, any interpretation tending to integrate the foreigners from Europe and their doctrine into the Chinese world was possible only provided that the missionaries refrained from attempting to gain followers among the people and from laying too strong an emphasis upon the transcendent nature of their religion, which placed God above even the emperor. In fact, Kangxi himself gave them advice to that very effect, saying: 'Why do you not speak of God as we do? Then people would be less resistant to your religion.'[173]

The distinction between the spiritual and the temporal is fundamental in Christian thought: each individual is both body and soul: a free conscience and a person subject to the laws of his country. It is possible to be both a good Christian and at the same time a loyal subject. The missionaries of China often protested their good faith and their submission and devotion to the emperor, declaring that affairs of state did not fall within their domain[174] and that they had never had any of the subversive intentions of which they were accused when it was claimed that they were stirring up the common people. They had come solely in order to convert China to the true religion, not to upset the laws of the country. As Father de Mailla wrote, in reply to a civil servant's demand for the expulsion of the missionaries and his description of Christianity as a doctrine of European origin: 'The Holy Religion of God is the general Law for the entire universe. It has touched peoples' hearts but it has not changed the laws of empires.'[175] The fact is that there exists a real and fundamental difference between the eternal realities which are the objects of religion and the transitory realities of this world, just as there is no common measure between man's eternal soul and his perishable body. These distinctions seemed so natural to the missionaries that they could not conceive them to be absent from the minds of the Chinese, or if they did happen to notice that absence, they did not follow up its implications. They were incapable of admitting that their own mental framework might not be universal and that highly developed civilisations could have been established upon quite different bases.

Chapter 4

Chinese morality and Christian morality

Apparent analogies

One of the most certain causes of the missionaries' success in China at the beginning of the seventeenth century was, in conjunction with their mathematical teaching, the body of works on morality which they produced. As has been noted above,[1] the solemn atmosphere and moralising style of the academies (*shuyuan*), which at the end of the Ming period included many men of letters, were in harmony with the salient characteristics of the missionaries' preaching. The men of letters appreciated the maxims of Europe and those of European classical Antiquity, discovering in them many resemblances with their own traditions. 'Conquer yourself' (*keji*) was a precept which appeared in Confucius' *Sayings*.[2] This work also contained a phrase identical to one in the New Testament: 'Do not unto others what you would not have them do unto you.'[3] The missionaries were just as struck by these analogies as the Chinese men of letters were. In his report to the Jesuit General, Acquaviva, in 1595, Ricci, who had begun to read the Classics, writes that in his view Confucius is another Seneca and that the Four Books are 'good moral documents' (*buoni documenti morali*).[4]

Ricci's first work in Chinese, in 1595, was a brief collection of maxims on friendship inspired for the most part by the authors of European Antiquity. In a letter dated 14 May 1599, Ricci makes the following remark about his little work, the *Jiaoyou lun* or *On Friendly Relations*, composed at the request of a Ming prince of Nanchang: 'This treatise on friendship has brought more credit to me and to our Europe than anything we have done hitherto.'[5] In another ethical work, *Ten Chapters of an Uncommon Man (Jiren shipian)*, first published in 1608, Ricci also draws his inspiration from Greek and Latin authors. Following his illustrious example, Father Martino Martini brought out in Hangzhou in 1661 another treatise on friendship, the *Qiuyou pian*, composed of extracts from Cicero, Seneca and Scribani. It was for its moral precepts, not its Christian theses, that Ricci's great treatise, *The True Meaning of the Master of Heaven*, had won acclaim from a number of men of letters. In one of his letters Ricci reports that pagans had twice had it reprinted at

141

their own cost and that this book 'seemed to them a useful guide for good living'.[6] And when the academician, Huang Hui (1562–?), annotated Ricci's works,

he approved all that they said about contempt for the world and the vanity of worldly pleasures but, notwithstanding, severely criticised the Father and the Chinese men of letters who follow such a doctrine [that of this work] in the passages which argue against the doctrine of idols [Buddhism].[7]

One of the books best received after Ricci's short ethical works was the *Qike*, or *The Seven Victories*, produced by Father Diego de Pantoja in collaboration with Xu Guangqi. The number of prefaces for this book, published in 1614, testify to its remarkable success.[8] It contains practical advice for the struggle against the seven deadly sins. It was after reading this work that Wang Zheng (1571–1644), initially drawn to the Peking Fathers by their works on mechanics, decided to become a follower of the doctrine of the Master of Heaven.

No doubt part of the charm of these works stemmed from their novelty but in part it derived from their strong reliance upon the Chinese traditions. They reminded the Chinese of their own books on morality or good behaviour (*shanshu*) and so, in a particularly rigorous reactionary period, they were made welcome.[9]

Chinese morality is Stoic in tone. It teaches that one should quietly accept fate and be content with one's lot. There are many classic texts that could be quoted on this topic – the *Mencius*, for instance: 'The Sage is indifferent as to the length or brevity of his life. He strives to perfect himself and waits [for whatever fate has in store for him].'[10] Now, the works composed by the missionaries were inspired by the Stoic authors of Antiquity, which were fashionable at the time in Europe. Ricci's *The Twenty-five Utterances (Ershiwu yan)* (1604) was a carefully polished translation of Epictetus' *Enchiridion* or *Manual*.[11] In it, the things that depend upon ourselves and those that do not were set in opposition just as they are in the *Mencius*,[12] written in about 300 BC.

A contemporary of Ricci's, Gao Panlong (1562–1626), one of the two scholars responsible for restoring the famous Donglin academy, develops the opposition in a little essay entitled *A Discussion of the Personality and the Mind (Shenxin shuo)*. In it, he explains that the only things that depend upon ourselves are our personalities and our minds, in contrast to what he calls 'external things' (*waiwu*). Gao Panlong had no need of the influence of the missionaries, even if he had read their works: he could quite well have appealed to Mencius, but it is to Cheng Hao, a philosopher of the eleventh century, that he refers, citing a passage in which Cheng Hao deplores seeing men who attach themselves to the pursuit of external things instead of concentrating upon perfecting themselves.

Gao Panlong declares that such behaviour causes a wastage of mental energy (*jingshen*). In the agitation that it involves, the personality and mind are humiliated and vilified and life passes by without one having the time to notice it. In contrast, what one ought to do is apply one's mental energies to study, for that is a source of satisfaction and peace of mind. Whoever accedes to the wisdom that stems from a life of study will consider all external things as his worst enemies.[13]

So it is not hard to understand the success of Ricci's *Twenty-five Utterances*, in which, as he says, 'all that is talked about is virtue and the way to lead one's life correctly, by appealing to natural philosophy'.[14] And Ricci makes one remark that it is worth stressing: his book is 'read and welcomed with gratitude by all the existing sects',[15] which means that it won favour even in Buddhist circles and among Buddhist monks.

Although Ricci considered his principal enemies to be Buddhism and its monks, in reality it was precisely the Buddhist element of the ethics of the time that was most in tune with his own teaching. Buddhism preached contempt for the world and the senses, which were the cause of attachments and rebirth. Buddhist, like Christian morality, is prohibitive and ascetically inclined. The theory that the part of Buddha's nature inherent in each being is obscured and soiled by the passions and thoughts had been transposed by the neo-Confucian thinkers of the eleventh and twelfth centuries into the terminology of the Confucian tradition: they had opposed the 'principle of heavenly order' (*tianli*), of which every person receives a share, to the 'human desires' (*renyu*), which are born from egoistic thoughts. The effort to achieve individual perfection, therefore, which was Confucius' main object, consisted, according to them, in rediscovering within one's self one's own share of this heavenly principle and developing it, whilst overcoming the passions and thoughts which obstruct the development of the five cardinal virtues: humanity, righteousness, propriety, wisdom and sincerity. Hence, despite starting from very different concepts, the evident analogies with the moral attitudes of the Christian world.

But there was more to it than just general analogies: the Christian examination of conscience found its counterpart in the literate circles of the seventeenth and eighteenth centuries.[16] Here it went by different names: 'daily examination' (*rixing*), 'solitary surveillance of oneself' (*shendu*)[17] or, more often, 'self-examination' (*zixing*).[18] Yang Tingyun (1557–1627) who was, as we have seen, one of the three most famous converts of the early seventeenth century, had fixed his own rules for his daily examination of conscience, in the course of which, employing neo-Confucian methods which owe nothing to Christianity, he strove to 'calm his mind and purify his thoughts'.[19]

The philosopher, Liu Zongzhou (1585–1645), had also devised a

Method for Accusing one's Faults (Songguo fa), which later served as a model to Li Gong (1659–1733), a disciple of the philosopher, Yan Yuan (1635–1704).[20] Liu Zongzhou describes his method as follows:

I place a bowl of water and a lighted incense stick on a small, spotless table. In front of this table I arrange a rush mat upon which I sit, at sunrise, facing the table, in the lotus position, holding myself erect and full of reverence. I control my breathing and adopt a serious attitude, as if there was some majestic and imposing presence there to which I could confess my bad actions without hiding a single one.[21]

The religious atmosphere of this whole setting and the allusion to a 'majestic and imposing presence' explain how it was that Ricci discerned a definite piety among the Chinese men of letters.[22]

At the end of the Ming period, great popularity was enjoyed by certain works called *Rules [for noting down] Merits and Faults (Gongguo ge)* which provided, as it were, scales for checking one's good and bad actions. They were sometimes criticised as being excessively utilitarian and for the mechanical nature of the whole procedure, but they derived their inspiration from the same principles as the *Registers for Self-examination* and other handbooks with similar names.[23]

One man of letters, Huang Wan (1480–1554), had in his youth had a master who had taught him to keep a register in two parts, one with the heading, 'The principle of heavenly order' (*tianli*), the other headed 'Human desires' (*renyu*).[24] Good thoughts and good actions deriving from the *tianli* were to be recorded with a red mark, the others with a black one.[25] The total of good and bad marks, added up every ten days, made it possible to control one's behaviour better.[26]

But it was not simply in the daily examination of conscience that Christianity found an equivalent in various forms in China. Practices of self-mortification were not unknown: the same Huang Wan, upon the recommendations of his master, was supposed to shut himself up in his library and fast for the entire day 'so as to develop his sincerity'. To correct his faults, he was to strike his shoulders and hands with a rope and keep inside his sleeves little plaques inscribed with the moral precepts he needed to reread the most frequently.[27]

Such procedures were not at all unusual and the men of letters who were the contemporaries of Ricci and his successors often resorted to practices of austerity, forcing themselves to remain motionless for long periods of time, meanwhile controlling their breathing. This was what was called 'sitting in calmness' (*jingzuo*), a method of yoga borrowed from the Buddhist monks, the purpose of which was to calm the senses and mind. Some men of letters would withdraw into isolation for periods of retreat, during which they performed this exercise while leading a very frugal life. Ascetic tendencies appeared early on in 'neo-Confucianism': Huang Zongxi records how Hu Yuan (953–1059), the master of Cheng Yi, betook himself to Mount Taishan with two companions, there to lead an ascetic life, eating crude and tasteless food and not sleeping at night. During this same period, Xu Zhongxing imposed a similar regime upon himself 'with no fan in summer, no fire in winter, no pillow at night'. He built himself a hut and there he would sit all day long, his body held erect and completely motionless.[28]

The reference to Heaven, the appeal for efforts to overcome one's proclivities and passions, the preoccupation with self-examination and the ascetic tendencies all seemed to establish links between the men of letters and the missionaries or 'men of letters from the West', as their friends called them. It also explains how it was that the missionaries' moral preaching found an echo in China. As the author of an anti-Christian pamphlet entitled *The Accusation* remarks:

With their *Seven Victories* [Diego de Pantoja's work on methods for guarding against the seven deadly sins] and their ten prohibitions [the Ten Commandments], they win over to them those men of letters who are preoccupied with morally perfecting themselves.[29]

No doubt the similarities in moral attitudes did encourage people to come over to the doctrine of the Master of Heaven.

But things that resemble one another are not necessarily identical and, in fact, the preoccupations of the Chinese were fundamentally different from those of the missionaries. Ricci was hoping that the distinction between what depends upon ourselves and what does not would lead the Chinese to think about the salvation of their souls, but for Gao Panlong that very distinction had no purpose other than to set one on the road to wisdom and teach one to live in harmony with the immanent order of the universe. The Chinese men of letters did not undertake their examinations of conscience in order to beg heaven to pardon their faults, but in order to understand their own defects better and correct them. They submitted themselves to austerities not in order to humiliate themselves before God, but so as to win greater control over themselves in order to come to achieve a greater harmony with 'the principle of heavenly order', which they believed to be actively present in nature, in society and even in themselves when they could silence their egoistical reflections and thoughts. The fundamental idea in Chinese morality was that of the individual perfecting himself, whereas a Christian thinks only of the salvation of his soul. Fearful of compromising his eternal life and falling into sin, he offers his sufferings up to God: for him the present has meaning only insofar as it relates to the Beyond.

Body and soul

The hesitations of the missionaries show how difficult it was to find Chinese words which correspond to the cardinal concepts of Christianity. An example of this was the idea of a rational soul contrasting with the body and the senses. The missionaries resorted to the word *hun*, which denoted the more volatile of the two souls attributed to men by the Chinese. But this soul, which was inseparable from vital energy, was sooner or later dissipated after death, just as was the *po*, the grosser of the two souls.[30] This had nothing in common with the Christian distinction between an eternal soul and a perishable body. The concept of *hun* did not play a role of importance in the philosophical ideas of the Chinese and was so lacking in substantiality that sometimes the missionaries had recourse to a transcription from the Latin, in the form of *yanima*. After Ricci's death, some missionaries opted for yet another term, that of *xing* or 'human nature'. Giulio Aleni, who lived in China from 1613 onwards, was one who did so. He was followed by Lodovico Buglio (in China from 1639 to 1682), the author of a *Xing ling shuo*, 'In which it is explained that the soul is intelligent'. But the term *xing* was one of the most important in neo-Confucian philosophy and there was a danger of it leading in directions not at all Christian. All in all, the dangers of its use were greater than those of the insubstantial soul evoked by the word *hun*.

It was nevertheless indispensable to get the Chinese to understand that the rational soul (*linghun, lingxing* or *yanima*) was of a substance radically different from that of the body and inanimate things, and that this soul was the exclusive privilege of mankind. Such ideas were in contradiction with their entire philosophy. For the Chinese, the universe was composed of one single substance, so everything in it was a matter of combinations and degrees, the realities of the world being – to use our terminology – all more or less spiritual or material. Thus the spirit of man was held to be more subtle and sharp than that of animals but not different in substance. Ricci had poured scorn upon such a mad idea. He writes: 'If I were to tell foreign kingdoms that in China there are educated men who say that animals, plants, metals and stones are all intelligent and of the same kind as man, they would be dumbfounded.' To which a Chinese man of letters whom Ricci introduces into the discussion, replies, as would any other Chinese:

It is true that some people in China say that animals have the same nature (*xing*) as man, but that is because the nature of the animals is imperfect, whereas that of man is perfect.[31] If we say that animals possess intelligence, it is an elementary intelligence, whereas man has received a vast and extensive intelligence. That is what makes the difference between their species.[32]

Ricci obviously rejects these ideas and replies that one can only conceive of degrees within a single species. Now, man and the animals have different natures, for man is endowed with one attribute which is his alone (*ben fen*): the faculty of reason.[33]

We know that the inquiry undertaken after Ricci's death with the approval of the Provincial, Valentim Carvalho, had as its object to 'discover whether there was anything at all in the Chinese sciences that related to these three things: God, the Angels and the rational soul'.[34] Some missionaries gave an affirmative answer to this question because they believed they had found such ideas expressed in the Classics and thought that the Chinese of their own period had been corrupted by Buddhist idolatry and by the materialist and atheist philosophy of the Sung. Others, on the basis of the unanimous opinion of contemporary men of letters and the interpretations of the most authoritative commentators, denied that the Chinese had ever known any equivalent of these ideas. However, whatever the case might be, they would have to be brought out of their state of error. Ricci had deemed it necessary to devote two whole chapters of his great treatise to proving the existence and immortality of the soul, drawing upon evidence of the most divers kind. The chapters in question are III ('That the soul of man, unlike that of animals, does not disappear') and IV ('Which presents a refutation of heterodox views concerning the spirits and the soul of man and an explanation showing that Heaven, Earth and the Ten Thousand Beings cannot be said to be of one substance'). In these pages, he reminded the reader of the Aristotelian distinction between the three souls: the vegetative soul of the plants, the sensitive soul of the animals and the rational soul of man, explaining that the first two disappear at death while the third, in contrast, is immortal. He had insisted upon the duality of the human personality, declaring that man has 'two hearts' (*er xin*),[35] one animal heart and one human heart and consequently two natures, a bodily nature (*xing xing*) and a spiritual nature (*shen xing*), and that this explains the contradiction in our feelings and the struggle between our reason and our passions.[36]

Not only was the substantial opposition between the soul and the body something quite unknown to the Chinese, all souls being, in their view, destined to be dissipated sooner or later,[37] but so was the distinction, originally inseparable from it, between the sensible and the rational. The Chinese had never believed in the existence of a sovereign and independent faculty of reason in man. The concept of a soul endowed with reason and capable of acting freely for good or for evil, which is so fundamental to Christianity, was alien to them. They, on the contrary, associated the mind and the feelings, the heart and reason, within the single concept of *xin*. They amalgamated moral sense and intelligence. And if they recognised a difference between man and the animals, it was not of an intellectual order but of a moral one: it was a difference that it was important to preserve and, if one did not take care to do so, it could be abolished. The author of one refutation writes:

The missionaries say that only the soul of man is intelligent. But there are some men so stupid that they think of nothing but drinking, eating and indulging in lust while there are dogs and monkeys so devoted to their master that they will sacrifice themselves for his sake. So they clearly possess a sense of righteousness (*yi*). Mencius was quite right when he said that the difference between men and animals depended upon very little and that vulgar men lost that very little, while worthy men were able to preserve it.[38] How could one falsely institute a separation between men and animals, thus holding the souls of the former to be eternal while those of the latter are not?[39]

The distinctions drawn by the missionaries seemed artificial and arbitrary. Xu Dashou writes:

[According to Ricci, Aleni and Longobardo], animals have no previous or subsequent life,[40] whereas men, who have no previous life, have a subsequent eternal life. Why is that? It is because the soul of man is created by the Master of Heaven and, once created, there can be no end to retribution for it in the form either of sufferings or of joys. Only the nature of the Master of Heaven was born before the cosmic beginning ([*tai*]*ji*)[41] and will endure beyond it. Why is that? It is because that nature is capable of creating all things whereas no thing is capable of creating it. They also say: 'That which is superior encompasses that which is inferior. That is why the soul of the animals contains that of the plants and that of man contains that of the animals. Finally, the soul of the Master of Heaven contains those of man, animals and plants, all at once.' Such are the divisions of every kind and the countless incomprehensible things to be found in their discussions. Again, for example, they say: 'The souls of animals are suddenly annihilated [when they die]. Only the soul of man goes on to undergo torments [or to enjoy happiness].' Now, before the Barbarians arrived in China, not a single soul belonging to any of us Chinese went up to paradise while the number who fell into hell is incalculable. This is quite the reverse of what happens to animals which, once killed, disappear forever. This comes down to saying that the Master of Heaven has far greater love for the animals than for us men.

And then Xu Dashou proceeds to pose the following – to his mind, embarrassing – questions:

Where has the Master of Heaven stored away the souls he gives to human beings? Is creation of souls something real or something magic? Is the soul distinct from the body and not one with it? Does the Master of Heaven transmit the soul with his very own hand? And how could there be things which, like the soul of man created by the Master of Heaven, have a beginning but no end?[42]

Xu Dashou also claims to have questioned the missionaries on the item in the creed which says: 'I believe in the life everlasting', and that they told him:

'When man goes down to hell, his soul is as dead' ... Having said that the soul is immortal, why do they then say that it is dead? And if it is truly not dead, why seek for life eternal? Alas, all these vicious and mistaken ideas stem from their desire at all costs to set up a Master of Heaven where there is none.[43]

The Chinese accuse the missionaries of destroying the unity of human nature (*lie xing* – which is the title of the third chapter of *The Aid to Refutation*) by postulating the existence of these heterogeneous substances of the soul and the body within man. But it is not true that one can achieve the highest wisdom if one ignores the body and man's place in society, nature and the cosmos.

The monk, Tongrong, writes:

With his long discussions on the three souls, Ricci deceives everybody and leads people into error. The harm that he is doing is incalculable. Let us endeavour to refute his theses by appealing to our Confucian Saints. Mencius says: 'The body and feelings are [one expression of] heavenly nature (*tianxing*). Only the Sage knows how to make use of his body correctly.'[44] He who knows how to make use of his body correctly accedes to the true principle ... He becomes united with the nature of Heaven, becoming one with it ... The senses and the mind are not two, the spirit and the body have no separation between them ... Ricci turns his false notion of a wandering soul into something with which to bind men. But what more profound mistake could there be than to count three souls in a single man, explaining that the vegetative and sensitive souls disappear at the end of human life! For if there is disappearance on one side and no disappearance on the other, there can be no unity and no harmony with heavenly nature. And then, all that is left are conflicts [between the rational soul and the body], between what one loves and what one detests, what one accepts and what one rejects, what lives and what dies.[45]

Such a doctrine is therefore a source of anxiety and torment. It encourages a contempt for life and for the wisdom that is constituted by balance and a right sense of the order of the world.[46]

Knowing nothing of the radical distinction between reason and the passions, the Chinese were unable to conceive that the mind might be entirely independent of the senses. When the philosopher, Gao Panlong (1562–1626), was seeking to understand what the master, Cheng Hao (1032–85), had meant by 'the mind must remain a part of the body as a whole', he eventually hit upon an explanation altogether to his satisfaction: 'the body as a whole' is simply a way of referring to the body; and Gao Panlong declares: 'I was very happy with this discovery, for [in that case] the mind was not simply an attribute of a "squared inch".[47] It was the entire body which made up the mind.'[48]

Human nature and cultivation of the self

If the Chinese word *hun* in no sense evoked the rational and eternal soul, as a spiritual substance distinct from the body, the word *xing*, or 'nature', did so even less.

One day in 1599, in Nanking, Matteo Ricci had been present at a discussion between a number of men of letters on the subject of human nature. He writes:

In the middle of the symposium, they began to argue about a subject which is often disputed in the schools of China, namely whether human nature is, in itself, good, bad or indifferent. They said: 'If it is indeed good, what is the source of the evil that it does? If it is bad, what is the source of the good that it does? And if it is neither good nor bad, what is the source of the evil and the good that it does of its own accord?' And because they have no logic and are incapable of distinguishing between moral goodness and natural goodness, acquired goodness and goodness given by nature, and because they are even less aware of nature corrupted by original sin and of God's aid and grace, this question has remained unresolved and undecided right down to the present day.[49]

Ricci accuses the Chinese of having no logic and pities them for knowing nothing of the teachings of Christianity. In the end, he seems to conclude that the question of the bases of morality has never been solved by them. But the questions they were posing and the very manner in which they were posing them must have been unfamiliar to Ricci. We do not know exactly what the discussion at which he was present was about. Perhaps it was reconsidering the themes of Part I of the *Mencius*. Perhaps it was concerned with the neo-Confucian distinction between nature of a heavenly order and nature as an individual temperament.[50] In any event, the debate must have been purely academic, since the idea that man possesses predispositions for good was universally accepted in China. It was also accepted that these predispositions were fragile and needed to be developed. This was the position of Mencius, around 300 BC:

The [natural] sentiments of compassion are the seeds[51] of the virtue of humanity; the [natural] sentiments of shame and aversion [for what is evil] are the seeds of righteousness; the [natural] tendency to be humble out of decency is the seed of propriety; the [natural] tendency to approve of what is correct and reprove what is not is the seed of wisdom.[52]

The Chinese thought as Diderot did, or rather, Diderot had come to think like the Chinese: 'No, my dear friend,' he wrote to Sophie Volland, 'nature did not create us wicked; it is bad education, bad examples and bad legislation which corrupt us.'[53]

For Mencius, the first roots or radicles of the virtues of Chinese morality (*ren*, *yi*, *li* and *zhi*) were to be found in human nature, and it was in that sense that he called human nature good.

The meaning that the Chinese gave the word 'nature' (*xing*) may be illuminated by a passage from the works of Gao Panlong (1562–1626). He writes:

Nature is the principle of life. Thus, in plants and in trees, in which there is nothing but nature, it is what causes there suddenly to be branches and roots, suddenly flowers and seeds. With the seed comes the fulfillment of the nature of the plant or the tree and new birth. But it may happen that the plant or the tree is dried up or damaged. And then it withers away. It is the same with the nature of man. If it is developed in such a way that it prospers and blooms, its energy (*qi*) expands greatly to the point of filling the universe. Then its nature is fulfilled. Such are the flowers and fruits of man.[54]

The text is clearly inspired by the following passage from the *Mencius*:

In the olden days, the trees of the mountain of oxen were splendid indeed. But because it was on the borders of a great kingdom, they were felled with axe and club. How could they have retained their splendour? Yet, nourished by the effluvia of the days and the nights, moistened by rain and dew, the buds and shoots nevertheless grew. But when the oxen and sheep came along, they ate them. That is why the mountain is so bare. Seeing it so bare, one cannot believe that it ever bore great trees. But how could that be in the nature of this mountain?[55]

The same applies to the feelings which man receives from nature.

The development of man as a moral being is thus conceived of as a natural development and compared to that of a plant or a tree. There is no opposition between nature and culture. The latter must be inspired by the former and be nothing but an extension of it. Just as the Chinese were at pains to accommodate nature, they also sought to direct the instincts and passions by means of the rituals.[56] The agricultural and botanical comparisons may not be as arbitrary as might be supposed. The linguist and historian of technology, André G. Haudricourt, has put forward the extremely attractive and likely idea that, among societies both of herdsmen and of farmers such as the Chinese, who did not practise herd-raising on a large scale, the society's particular, dominant activities influenced not only the metaphors it used and its traditional representations, but also its modes of behaviour and concepts of human action.[57] Animals are trained and driven by spoken commands and the use of the stick. In man's relations with animals, direct human intervention and constraint are indispensable. When dealing with plants, on the other hand, it is necessary to wait for them to grow. All one can do is see to it that the conditions for growth are as favourable as possible:

prepare the soil, dig, hoe, prune, and water, taking care not to cross nature but to conform with its ways. Such modes of indirect action clearly contrast with the direct modes of action of the stock-raiser and herdsman. This no doubt accounts for the differences between, on the one hand, the Chinese concepts of education, morality, religion and political power and, on the other, those of the West, with its Judaeo-Christian traditions. The God of the Jews and Christians is a god of shepherds – one has only to think of the biblical metaphors – who speaks, gives orders and imposes his will. The Heaven of the Chinese does not speak. It is content to produce the seasons and act in a continuous fashion by ensuring that they follow one another.[58] Haudricourt sets up an opposition between 'the Chinese garden' and 'the Mediterranean sheepfold' and concludes, somewhat humorously:

Is it absurd to wonder whether gods who command, moral systems which issue orders and philosophies which are transcendent perhaps have something to do with sheep ... while moral systems which give explanations and philosophies of immanence might have something to do with the yam, the taro and rice?

One should, no doubt, beware of too hasty conclusions, for great civilisations are eminently complex, but there can be no doubt that Haudricourt's intuition is correct: the Chinese evidence confirms it. 'Following nature, that is what is called the Dao',[59] runs the first sentence in one of the Four Books, *The Invariable Middle (Zhongyong)*, which appears to reproduce the Stoic expression, 'to follow nature', that is to say, to derive one's inspiration from it or even guide it (*shuai*), not repress but cultivate and channel it.

The argument of the *Mencius* is famous: any man will leap to save a child about to fall into a well, without thought of the glory or advantage that he might thereby gain. That indicates a natural propensity for the good which has but to be encouraged. Similarly, filial piety, the virtue considered to be the model for all the others, has as its origin the child's spontaneous affection for its parents. Rituals and social duties are conceived to express a natural order. The origin of morality, which derives from seeds of goodness inherent to human nature, is not solely to be found in man: it conforms objectively to the order of nature, as the philosopher, Zhang Zai (1020–77), explains: the order of the succession (*xu*) of births laid down by Heaven is the principle which governs the relations between the elder and the younger and between the successive generations; it is a principle that has a wide application in Chinese society. Similarly, the lots apportioned to each individual by Heaven (the inequalities in talents and capacities and the ranks of dignity that stem from these) are at the origin of the hierarchical order (*zhi*), respect for which constitutes propriety. 'The different degrees in the manifestation of respect towards those who are older and more noble all therefore express the principle of heavenly order', concludes Wang Fuzhi (1619–92), in his commentary.[60]

Chinese morality is thus seen as translating in terms of man and society norms which are universal. But the fact that nature, in its principle, is good does not mean that it is invariably so: its perfection falls not into the category of absolute truth but into that of statistical truth. In all its exuberant activity of production, there are bound to be a few failures. Wang Fuzhi writes:

Nature's activity of creation–transformation (*zaohua*) is entirely without intention (*wuxin*) [that is to say, it is entirely spontaneous] and it causes beings to be born in the greatest abundance. It is therefore inevitable that at the moment of their formation [literally, at the moment of union through coagulation, *ninghe*], not all beings are perfect in their physical constitution.[61]

Commenting upon Confucius' proposition: 'Men are close to one another by nature but differ from one another through their habits',[62] Gu Yanwu (1613–82) explains that physical and moral anomalies are both of the same kind. It sometimes happens that monsters of inhumanity are born but only in extremely rare cases. Such were the tyrant, Zhouxin, the last sovereign of the Yin, who invented terrible tortures, or the bandit, Zhi, who would massacre innocent people every day. This was because, from their births, they had been different from other men. The same is true as regards physique: all men are similar as regards their organs and bone structure, but some are born deformed either in heart or in body. As it says in Confucius' sayings: 'Man is upright by birth. Those who are not live only as the result of chance.'[63] And Gu Yanwu concludes: 'So we can definitely say that human nature is good.'[64]

These truly Chinese ideas were enriched and modified by the influence of Buddhism. Buddhist and Chinese themes were superimposed upon one another and amalgamated by the neo-Confucian thinkers of the eleventh and twelfth centuries. The Buddhist idea according to which all things possess a nature of Buddha which is simply concealed and obscured by the passions and a false belief in the reality of the self and the world, was complemented by the neo-Confucian idea according to which human nature, being a reflection of the principle of heavenly order (*tianli*), is fundamentally good but usually disturbed by reflective and egoistical thoughts. It was therefore necessary to return to that original state of absolute calm which is our true nature, a state in which thoughts and feelings of every kind have not yet been produced, for it is from our fundamental nature that our spontaneous inspirations towards the good are born. To reach this state, the Chinese thinkers of the eleventh and twelfth centuries recommended certain techniques inspired by practices used in the monasteries. The most current consisted in sitting cross-legged and controlling one's breathing. As we have seen, this was called *jingzuo* or 'sitting in calm'.[65] In this way, they came to distinguish two kinds of nature: one, which was perfectly good, was a reflection of the principle of universal order; the other, which corresponded to individual temperament and physical nature, was responsible for desires and passions. They wanted to 'eliminate human desires (*renyu*) in order to return to the principle of heavenly order (*tianli*)'. This gave rise to a repressive morality which seems Christian in tone. But at the same time, the neo-Confucian theses were heretical and blasphemous from a Christian point of view for they implied a confusion between God and his creatures: the absolute was not transcendent and situated in the Beyond but, on the contrary, resided in man himself.

In *The True Meaning of the Master of Heaven*, Ricci introduces a Chinese man of letters who maintains that human nature is good because it is an expression of universal order, and goes on to say:

So it can be said that the Master of Heaven, the Sovereign on High (*tianzhu shangdi*)[66] is within every being and is one with it. This encourages men not to behave badly so as not to tarnish their basic goodness; not to contravene their duties so as not to violate the principle of order, which is fundamentally within them; not to harm others so as not to insult the Sovereign on High, who is within them.

These heretical statements provoke the indignation of the 'Western man of letters' who exclaims: 'This mistake is even worse than all the others I have heard so far',[67] and concludes by saying: 'To say that creatures and their creator are identical is an arrogant declaration of the devil Lucifer.'[68]

In another passage in this same work, the 'Chinese man of letters' uses a comparison in the Buddhist style to explain that a mind which is obscured by passions loses the Master of Heaven, who is within him, just as a scarab covered in filth loses its brilliance.[69]

The Chinese concepts were so unlike the Christian theses that many Chinese initially formed a crudely mistaken idea of the real meaning of the missionaries' teaching. Thus a certain Wang Jiazhi, wishing to praise a short ethical work composed by Ricci, mistakenly believes himself to be at one with his author when he, too, expounds the theme of the identity of the principle of order within all creatures. He writes: 'My spirit is the same as Ricci's; Ricci's is the same as that of all men and that of all men is the same as that of Heaven and Earth':[70] in other words, the Sovereign on High is within each one of us.

A certain Li Can, aiming to refute the missionaries' theses, writes as follows:

The teaching of our Confucian Saints and Sages finds its source in the spirit of man. That is why it is said that 'man is the spirit of the universe'. I have never heard it said that a Heaven exists outside the spirit of man . . . If it is said that one must lift one's head to find Heaven, then creatures endowed with life and feeling will lose their roots.

And Li Can proceeds to explain that one of the following must be true:

Either the Master of Heaven has no spirit, in which case he is as stupid as a block of wood or stone. Or else he does possess a spirit and that spirit is his own Heaven, in which case their thesis is reduced to nothing.[71]

The argument is typically Buddhist: the absolute is internalised and identified with the fundamental basis of the spirit.

But however deep the Buddhist influences may have been, the general inspiration remained Chinese. It is always to the Classics that reference is made. According to the concepts of the Chinese, true goodness is spontaneous because – according to the *Mencius* – its origins lie in the natural impulses common to all men or – according to the Buddhist traditions – because the absolute can be identified with the basic nature of all creatures. In contrast, Christianity does not accept that nature and virtue coincide: in Christianity, all virtue, on the contrary, implies some victory gained over oneself. True goodness is dictated by reason. Ricci was therefore quite right to reject Chinese concepts of morality, which are based upon the notion of an immanent order and which rate spontaneity as the supreme value. He writes:

If people did good despite themselves, how could one call it good?[72] What merit is there in loving one's parents if in doing so one is merely following one's natural inclinations? It is therefore necessary to make an absolute distinction between the two kinds of goodness: the goodness which comes from nature and is spontaneous goodness (*liangshan*) and the goodness which comes from virtue and is the goodness that is acquired through effort. Spontaneous goodness is a virtue which was allotted to us in the very beginning by the Master of Heaven and we can claim no merit for it. What I call merit (*gong*) results from a personal effort to act virtuously.[73]

Ricci was thus brought to contradict the theses of Mencius. He writes:

Tiny children love their parents. Any man, whether good or bad, will leap to save a child who is about to fall into a well. What is involved here is simply a spontaneous goodness (*liangshan*). What virtue does a man without goodness or an animal have in acting in this way? Virtue consists only in doing one's duty when one sees it.[74]

Around 1635, one Huang Zizhen from Fuzhou writes:

Here is what the Barbarians teach: Zisi [a disciple of Confucius] said: 'Following nature is what is called the Dao [good morality].' But what we [the missionaries] say is: 'Overcoming nature is what is called the Dao. The fact is that before nature was corrupted, to follow it was to conform with morality. But today the nature of men is not at all what it was originally. It is therefore impossible to reach the perfection of the Dao without overcoming it.' In the Classics and the commentaries that contain the tradition of our Saints and Sages, there is not a single word which does not express the heart and nature. How can these animals criticise that tradition, getting it all wrong? I would prefer not to lower myself to making the slightest comparison [between what they say and the teaching of our Saints and Sages], but fearing lest ignorant folk be made stupid by these people, I find myself obliged to clarify these matters in writing and words. As an example of the Dao which consists in following nature, Zisi refers to wood or stone which has not yet been sculpted or engraved, and he compares this to the nature which is given with life. Whoever acts in conformity with this nature can never contravene the norms of Heaven. That hardly seems controversial. But when we allow ourselves to be carried along by passion and calculation, then this is no longer our true nature. That is why he says: 'Whatever is allotted by Heaven is nature and following nature is the Dao.'[75] If one says that overcoming nature is the Dao, what can it be that one is calling nature? Confucius said: 'Men are close to one another by nature. They differ from one another by their habits.'[76] Thus nature is what is first and innate and habits are subsequent impregnations. If these people spoke of overcoming [bad] habits within man, that would be acceptable. But they speak of overcoming nature. But nature is not something that comes to us from outside. What would be the good of overcoming it? If our nature is overcome and eliminated, what will remain of ourselves? They also say: 'One cannot reach the perfect Dao without overcoming nature.' Does that mean that the Dao is within us and nature external to us?[77]

Another text develops a similar argument:

Master Dong [Dong Zhongshu, about 175–105 BC] has said that the great source of the Dao comes from Heaven. Zisi, the disciple of Confucius, has said that what is allotted by Heaven is nature. How could one say that our holy doctrine has never spoken of Heaven? But this Heaven has nothing in common with what the Barbarians call Heaven. Their books say: 'Everything good is the work of the Master of Heaven and everything bad comes from ourselves.' If that were so, human nature would always be bad. Where could the Master of Heaven possibly have found all these seeds of evil, to distribute them among men [so that] all the good that men do turns into falsehood and error? . . . And besides, even from Antiquity, it has never been a matter of anything but respecting Heaven, not flattering it. Now, these Barbarians do not respect it but they do flatter it. The great zeal that they display day and night resembles exercises in austerity, but people of their kind think of nothing but obtaining good fortune by irregular methods. They are not content to remain in their place as is fitting (*su wei*).[78] What they call honouring Heaven is really defiling it . . . These Barbarians reject the precepts [of our Classics] such as: 'Conform with the norms [of Heaven and Earth without transgressing them][79] and participate in the work of Heaven and Earth.'[80, 81]

The distinction between the soul and the body and between duties to the world and duties to Heaven introduces a duality in man and, as it were, a duplicity which tends to ruin the simplicity of heart or the sincerity (*cheng*) which, according to Chinese ideas, should inspire every action: true goodness could not result from any deliberation; it can only come from the inspirations of the heart.

The Jesuits, who were so anxious to reach agreement with the classical traditions of China, did not perceive the opposition between the Christian and the Chinese moralities so clearly as the Franciscan, Father Antonio de Caballero, who, in his treatise produced in Canton in 1668, writes:

What we call the light of reason in man, they call the Commandment and Law of Heaven.[82] What we call the natural satisfaction of obeying justice and the fear of contravening it, all of this they call inspiration sent by the Xamti [the Sovereign on High]. To offend Heaven is to act contrary to reason, to ask for Heaven's pardon is to correct oneself and return with sincerity both in word and deed to submitting, as one should, to this same law of reason.[83]

We can have no quarrel with his conclusions. But Caballero could not appreciate the relationship that existed between the morality of the Chinese and their religious ideas and attitudes, nor the cosmic mysticism from which that morality was inseparable. Whereas in Christianity a clear distinction is made between secular and religious realities, in China these appear simply as two sides of a single reality.

Fully to develop every potentiality of human nature (*jin xing*)[84] from the seeds of goodness inherent in each of them is thus the ultimate aim of Confucian morality. The fundamental idea is that man is perfectible and that the cultivation of the self must be the aim of every life. A text from Wang Yuan (1648–1710) expresses this humanist ideal well enough:

The Sage has said that man is the spirit of the universe[85]. . . Something essential would be lacking in the life of plants if they had no seeds. It would mean the end of the vegetable kingdom. Similarly, something essential would be lacking in the life of the universe if Heaven had not given birth to man. It is in this sense that it can be said that man is the spirit of the universe. Could one say that of his physical person? No, it is rather of his spirit, that is to say of his virtue of humanity (*ren*) that it can be said. Ruin and prosperity depend upon destiny. Whoever is incapable of changing destiny and uses his intelligence only for the essential good of his own person and family does not deserve to be called a man. How could he be called the spirit of the universe?[86]

The Chinese concept of saintliness is associated with that of a sovereignty in which, as we shall see, there is a fusion between the cosmic and the ethical, the religious and the political. Saints are considered to be those exceptional individuals who have known how to perfect their nature and thus identify with the order of the world and apply themselves to accomplish it. Such were those ancient sovereigns whose virtue could operate from a distance upon other beings and without the latter being aware of it and who gave China its essential institutions and technology, organised space and made the world habitable. The term 'Saint' (*shengren*) was also applied to Confucius himself, who was considered to be a sovereign without a kingdom, and – by analogy with the founders of Chinese civilisation, who were regarded as the patrons of Confucianism – the title of *sheng* was attributed to the emperors and the ruling dynasty.

But Ruggieri and Ricci and, following them, the rest of the missionaries, had borrowed the word *sheng* from the Chinese to translate their word for 'saint'. Thus, *shengjiao*, 'the holy [saintly] doctrine', was used to refer to Christianity and *shengren* to denote saints of the Church. The missionaries were obliged to define the meaning that they gave this word.

In *The True Meaning of the Master of Heaven*, Ricci ascribes the following remarks to the Chinese man of letters whom he introduces into his work:

Assuredly, the virtue of the Sovereign on High is very great. But we men, too, have a perfect virtue. The Sovereign on High assuredly possesses limitless capacities. But our spirit, too, the spirit of man, is also capable of responding to the ten thousand opportunities that may present themselves. Consider, for example, our first Saints, who arranged the world and founded civilisation, established the right doctrine and the social rules, nurtured the people thanks to ploughs and weaving looms and made life possible for them with boats, carts and wares that could be traded.[87]

Having censured such scandalous ideas, Ricci, in another part of his work, explains the correct meaning that should be given to the word 'saint' (*shengren*). He writes:

The word 'saint' is more rigorously applied in Western Law than in China... Those whom we call saints are those who, revering the Master of Heaven, humiliate themselves and master themselves, those whose words and actions surpass those of other men and cannot be achieved by human strength alone.[88]

And Ricci belittles the Chinese concept, not understanding its cosmic and religious significance: 'To instruct men in the affairs of the past and the present, it is not necessary to be a saint. Whoever is determined to do so and seeks a fine reputation can achieve this if he tries hard.'[89] And he explains that saintliness comes only through God and in relation to him:

If one teaches people and transmits to them the doctrine relating to the Sovereign on High, if one tells them of events that are to come, how could it be by using simply human powers? Curing by means of drugs is possible for those who have studied medicine. Governing the state by means of a just system of rewards and punishments can be managed by men of letters. These are not actions that can be used as proofs of saintliness. If, in contrast, by some exceptional virtue and with an efficacy equal to that of the Creator, one cures incurable diseases without any drugs or if one raises the dead, those are things that are beyond the power of men and are due to the Master of Heaven. Those whom we call saints in our kingdoms are all people of that kind.[90]

The point definitely is that only miracles operated with the help of God can prove saintliness.

However, Yang Guangxian, comparing Jesus to the Chinese Saints, takes up precisely the opposite position to that of Ricci. He writes:

When he came to be born on earth to save mankind, the Master of Heaven ought to have promoted rituals and music, distributed the virtue of humanity and righteousness (*ren, yi*), in order to usher in an era of good fortune for men everywhere on earth. Instead of that, he only performed minor beneficent acts (*xiao hui*), such as healing the sick, raising the dead, walking on the water and producing food by magic means, and he only concerned himself with matters of paradise and hell.[91]

Yang Guangxian lists the exploits of the great Saints of Chinese Antiquity and compares them favourably with the miracles performed by Jesus:

Ji distributed the one hundred cereals. Qi made known the five rules which govern human relations. Yu the Great drained away the flooding waters, the Duke of Zhou arranged the rituals and music. Confucius took for his models Yao and Shun, Mencius refuted Yangzi [the apostle of absolute egoism] and Mozi [the apostle of absolute egalitarianism]. Those are real exploits which saved the world. In the case of Yesu, there is not a single one that is comparable. Healing the sick and raising the dead are things that can be done by great magicians, not actions worthy of one who is supposed to have created Heaven, Earth and the Ten Thousand Beings. If one considers those to be exploits, how is it that he did not arrange for people never to be sick again and never to die? That *would* have increased his merit. But as he is called the master of men's sickness and death and at the same time the master of curing and resuscitating them [it is clear] that he is quite incapable of controlling anything at all. How can anybody have the audacity to speak of merit?[92]

The differences between the Chinese and the Christian moralities are radical ones, not only because Christianity holds human nature to be corrupt but also because China is unfamiliar with the idea of the sovereign good. Chinese and Christians consequently adopt totally opposed ways of proceeding. Christian morality relates to a transcendent God and thus its starting-point is what to the Chinese appears to be what is the most distant and inaccessible, namely divine perfection. It is God himself who laid down the Ten Commandments and there is no good except through him and in relation to him. One's first duty is to love, not one's parents, but God. According to Chinese concepts, in contrast, it is through respect for the rituals that man can develop within himself his natural predispositions for the good: even the most humble realities of life are a reflection of the principle of universal order. As Confucius' *Sayings* put it, one must learn to start from the bottom, that is to say from what is simplest and most immediate, in order eventually to reach what is highest (*xia xue er shang da*).[93] Perfecting oneself is thus fundamental to everything and the way to contribute to the universal order. Ricci, on the other hand, maintains that 'if study has no object other than the self, there is nothing very elevated about it', and adds: 'The correct goal of all efforts to perfect oneself is the Master of Heaven.'[94]

Christian charity and the Chinese virtue of humanity (*ren*), which are confused by the missionaries, cannot possibly be the same. Loving others, which is preached by Christianity, stems from loving God and has no meaning or value except in relation to him; one must love others out of love for God. In contrast, Chinese morality teaches people to remain responsive to the sentiments of humanity and compassion, which are natural to man provided he has not been corrupted. It is by developing his natural sense of reciprocity and humanity that man can move closer to the model of spontaneous action which is Heaven and that he can accede to the true wisdom which is an apprehension of the world order.

A passage from a short work entitled *Humble Remarks on the Distinction between the Doctrines* clearly shows the opposition between Chinese and Christian ideas on the subject of filial piety:

The following evening, my guest, who was drunk with Western doctrine, came back to see me and said: 'You revere the Sovereign on High but you do not dare to usurp a right which is not yours nor to profane him with your prayers, and in this you are obeying the laws.[95] But Ricci says that the Master of Heaven created Heaven, Earth and the Ten Thousand Beings. He is therefore our supreme and universal father. Furthermore, he rules and supports them constantly. He is thus our common sovereign, with no superior. All those who love and respect him build temples and statues to him. How could we not but be supremely lacking in loyalty and filial piety if we did not show reverence and address our prayers to the one who is our supreme father and the sovereign of all of us?'[96] I replied: 'True morality is to hand and yet you go looking for it in distant ideas. Our father is the one who engendered us, our mother the one who raised us. Filial piety consists solely in loving our parents. All good fortune and prestige depends solely upon the sovereign. Loyalty consists in respecting him. To love one's parents is to have heart (*ren*), or humanity; to respect one's sovereign is to have a sense of righteousness (*yi*). These are sentiments in which heavenly nature (*tianxing*) manifests itself of its own accord. Why go seeking morality in obscure and distant ideas? By revering the Master of Heaven as the supreme father of all mankind and as the sovereign of the universe, by having to love and worship him morning and evening, Ricci [is led to] consider parents to be negligible and unworthy of affection and to turn the sovereign into an ordinary individual. He is therefore encouraging everybody to behave in a fashion contrary to filial piety and loyalty. That is inevitable.[97] Besides, reading Ricci's works, I have discovered many errors. To prove it, here are just a few: "Animals are also capable of loving their parents", he says, "and uncouth men are capable of loving their country. Only a worthy man who is altogether good is capable of extending his love to what is distant." That comes down to holding that there is no difference between a loyal subject and an uncouth fellow, between a pious son and an animal. That is the first mistake. "Charity (*renzhe*) consists in loving the Master of Heaven." That means that Ricci contradicts Confucius, who said that "to be a man is to possess humanity (*ren*)[98] and to love one's parents is the most important thing in the whole world". So that is the second mistake. Then he says: "Those who are the closest to us, such as our parents, are still strangers to us compared with the Master of Heaven."[99] That boils down to considering filial piety as adventitious and seeking the virtue of humanity outside [human nature]. Ricci has understood nothing about true human nature, for which there is only one basis.[100] That is the third mistake. He also says: "We have three fathers in the universe: the first is the Master of Heaven, the second our sovereign, the third our father [the master of the family]. When a father of inferior rank does not obey a father of superior rank he misappropriates the homage of his sons. Whoever is a son owes obedience to the superior orders. If, in so doing, he infringes inferior orders, that should not prevent him from being considered a pious son."[101] All these propositions are quite intolerable. Even when one of our parents behaves in a tyrannical fashion, we must try to reason with him or her. Even if a sovereign behaves in an unjust way, we must try to get him to return to human sentiments. How could one justify criticising one's parents or resisting one's sovereign on the grounds of filial piety towards the Master of Heaven?[102] That is the fourth mistake.'[103]

In that it opposes religious duties upon which eternal salvation depends to worldly duties, Christian morality is inevitably a source of conflicts. But from a Chinese point of view, no radical contradiction is imaginable: every conflict of duties should be soluble for all duties stem from the same universal order.

Whereas Christian morality is egalitarian and abstract – all men are

equal before God – Chinese morality is totally preoccupied with relations that are both hierarchical and complementary, the model of
which appears to be provided by the universe itself: *yin* and *yang*,
Heaven and Earth, husband and wife, sovereign and subject are all similar.

Xu Dashou observes that some of his compatriots are attracted to the
doctrine of the Master of Heaven by the resemblance between Christian
and Chinese precepts. It is quite true that the object of rituals is 'to correct defects and make people entirely good'[104] and that 'their doctrine
aims in all things to lead men to goodness'. However:

Nothing could be more serious than ignoring the differences between the relations between prince and subject, father and son, husband and wife respectively. If there is the slightest thing lacking in what is most important of all, even
while for the rest everything is perfect, the fault is unpardonable... Thus, in
their book entitled *The Seven Victories*, overcoming one's pride is placed in a
position of the first importance. But the simple axiom from 'Little rules of seem-
liness',[105] 'One should not allow one's pride to grow', is quite enough to exhaust
that subject. What is the point of becoming attached to the inelegant and obscure
ideas of these people? What is the point of speechifying on and on forever?

And Xu Dashou explains that behaving as a pious son is quite enough to
expel all one's pride, for 'filial piety is the basis of all behaviour'.[106]

Thus, the Barbarians concern themselves with nothing but details and
neglect what is essential. Huang Wendao writes:

What they call the seven [things] to be overcome are pride, avarice, envy, anger,
greed, jealousy and sloth. Although all this involves the cultivation of the self,
they are only clumsy methods for controlling oneself. What Confucius told Yanzi
had to do with a far more elevated concept: he considered the virtue of humanity
(*ren*) as the basis, and propriety (*li*) as the substance. When one knows how to
preserve humanity within oneself, whatever is contrary to humanity disappears
of its own accord. When propriety is re-established, whatever is contrary to the
rituals eliminates itself of its own accord.[107]

The Christian morality is individual and introspective, taking reason as
its guide and free will as axiomatic: one must conquer pride, which leads
to forgetfulness of God. The Chinese oppose this with a morality of behaviour in which modes of conducting oneself and feelings are complementary and lend one another mutual support. They oppose the
Christian distinction between an eternal soul and a perishable body with
an overall concept of man as a social being, situated within a complex of
relationships which is considered to be an extension and expression of an
immanent and universal order. The missionaries reason about abstract
virtues; thus Ricci writes: 'It is one's understanding that decides what is

right (*yi*).'[108] But the Chinese take into consideration only social practices in their concrete reality and the relationship between 'the exterior' (behaviour) and 'the interior' (feelings).[109] The *yi* is not, as Ricci thought, what reason judges to be right, but instead the overall modes of behaviour which, respectively, are proper in the relations between sovereign and subject, father and son, husband and wife, elder and younger, friend and friend.

The Chinese traditions recognise man to possess naturally good dispositions, which it is important to preserve (*cun, quan*) and develop (*yang, hanyang*). This Chinese optimism is countered by Christian pessimism, which recognises no goodness in man and no virtue without effort. Ricci said: 'Loving one's parents is too easy. There is therefore no merit in doing so.' He was thereby attacking the first of all Chinese virtues, filial piety, the model of all ritual modes of behaviour.

The analogy between Chinese and Christian precepts can be no more than a deceptive appearance, for in Chinese morality there is no such thing as aspiration towards a God external to this world. On the contrary, it hinges upon the idea that one must find within oneself, and there develop, the innate sense of good which is there as a reflection of 'the principle of heavenly order'. The process of each man's endeavour to perfect his social being is the basis for everything and there is something religious about the effort that perfecting oneself involves. As the Chinese texts put it, it is that very process which is 'serving Heaven' (*shi tian*). Good behaviour consists in accomplishing one's duties as a man correctly and, in the place that is one's own (*su wei*),[110] and also in respecting the ritual attitudes which govern the whole complex of social relations. That is the way to 'conform to Heaven and Earth's norms of behaviour without transgressing them'[111] and to 'contribute through one's own actions to the work of Heaven and Earth'.[112] The rituals and the morality, of which they are simply an expression, are the means by which man can achieve harmony with the order of the world, realising it within himself, and also through which he can contribute to it. Thus, even the humblest actions fall within a cosmic order which gives them a more general and elevated meaning than they would seem to have. Ricci considered Confucianism to be a purely civil and political type of teaching which, in its essentials, was compatible with Christianity. But that idea, which was often echoed after his time, implied a peculiarly Christian separation between the domain of eternal truths and that of worldly realities, between religious and secular duties. For Ricci, Confucianism was a purely worldly doctrine.

Montesquieu was probably the first to have an accurate intuition of the spirit of the Chinese mores. When he read the accounts of missionaries, he sensed that the connections between the various domains of social reality were very much closer than those in Europe. He writes: 'The legislators of China confounded their religion, laws, manners and customs ... all these were virtue.'[113] Then, trying to convey how the private virtue of filial piety could be important politically as well as religiously and morally, he explains:

The principal object of government which the Chinese legislators had in view was the peace and tranquillity of the empire; and subordination appeared to them as the most proper means to maintain it.[114] Filled with this idea, they believed it their duty to inspire a respect for parents and therefore exerted all their power to effect it. They established an infinite number of rites and ceremonies to do them honour when living and after their death. It was impossible for them to pay such honours to deceased parents without being led to reverence the living. The ceremonies at the death of a father were more nearly related to religion; those for a living parent had a greater relation to the laws, manners and customs; however, these were only parts of the same code, but this code was very extensive.[115]

Montesquieu's idea of a deliberate intervention on the part of the legislator, which is typical of the eighteenth century, is clearly mistaken. It ignores the extremely ancient origins, both religious and political, of the ancestor cult.[116] However, his great merit is to have sensed how, in the ritual system of the Chinese, religion, politics, morality, attitudes and compulsory modes of behaviour and feelings were all intricately interdependent.

Retribution

A constantly recurring theme in the tradition of the men of letters is that one should act without expecting any reward. Self-interest would remove all value from a good action. Wang Fuzhi writes:

A worthy man is not motivated to act virtuously by any thought of reward. When the sovereign encourages people to good behaviour by offering rewards, men of great heart receive them only with shame whereas men who are worthless feign virtue out of a desire for rewards and in this way falsity spreads everywhere and rewards quite wrongly multiply. Similarly, among the common people one comes across a belief in the possibility of acquiring merit in the eyes of invisible powers and some claim that this belief encourages people to act virtuously ... [It is by these means that the Buddhists] stir up the stupid common people and intimidate worthy men, and so it is that within men's hearts the Dao is lost.[117]

The Invariable Middle, one of the Four Books, says:

The worthy man quietly awaits what fate has in store for him, leading a peaceful life. The worthless man seeks to attract good fortune through perilous actions... The worthy man behaves in conformity with the condition allotted to him and desires nothing more than that.[118]

This is what Longobardo is referring to when he declares that the Chinese say that one must act without concerning oneself about the ends, with neither punishment nor recompense.[119]

By promising a better rebirth to those who observed its prohibitions and gave gifts to the monks, Buddhism had sometimes laid itself open to the accusation of appealing to self-interest. Thus Gu Yanwu (1613–82) criticises those Chinese men of letters who late in life turn to Buddhism or Taoism (whose techniques were reputed to prolong life):

Although the conduct of these people is different from that of people who have their heads full of thoughts of acquiring land or constructing buildings, they are just like them in that they are guided by the passion of self-interest.[120]

Understandably enough, the doctrine of the Master of Heaven was also accused of seeking to attract people with promises of infinite felicities and frightening them with threats of eternal flames, since, according to the Christians, all their future life was supposed to be decided in this single present one. There was an important difference between this concept and that of the Buddhists, according to whom every life is but a link in an indefinite chain of rebirths which can only come to an end when the state of Buddha is achieved. In contrast to the terrible alternative proposed by the doctrine of the Master of Heaven, the automatic fructification of all actions in Buddhism has a reassuring quality, as the Buddhist monks were well aware. The Buddhist monk, Total Enlightenment, writes: 'They aim to dazzle and frighten the stupid common people with promises of happiness without end [and threats of eternal suffering].'[121] The missionaries were astonished to find among the literate elite, more often than not, a singular lack of interest in matters to do with the other life. Caballero writes: 'They expect neither paradise nor hell, neither punishment nor recompense in the other life because, since they believe that everything is annihilated, they neither fear nor hope for anything.'[122] Longobardo, for his part, cites the following opinions of a number of men of letters:

Doctor Li Sung Lo, the president of the financial court, believes that after death there is neither reward nor punishment (in the sense of the Christian belief) and that men return to the void from which they emerged. He rejects the idea of an immortal God who punishes and rewards and also the existence of a paradise and a hell. And Doctor Ching Lun Lu, the mandarin of the court of rituals, says that one should not bother about the other life, but only about this one.[123]

This refusal to recognise the existence of paradise and hell did not imply that there was no form of retribution at all. But it was effected in *this* life or through the family lineages, through the good or bad reputations the dead left behind them. The fact was that most men of letters retained a quiet confidence in fate. Lu Shiyi (1611–72) writes:

Although it occasionally happens that men full of loyalty and filial piety fall into misfortune while, in contrast, traitors and good-for-nothings are fortunate enough to escape the punishments they deserve, sooner or later, either in the course of this life, once things are sorted out, or in later generations, the worthy are the objects of praise and rogues receive their punishment. How could one possibly put one's trust in vain pronouncements about things that one can neither see nor hear?[124]

As one man of letters during the Sung period explained:

If there is no paradise, there is no more to be said; and if there is one, it is right that worthy people should ascend to it. If there is no hell, there is no more to be said; and if there is one, it is right that the good-for-nothings should enter it.[125]

His remarks were intended as criticism of the pious actions which make it possible, in Buddhism, thanks to the transference of merits, to obtain a more favourable rebirth for one's deceased relatives. His conclusion was that 'to address prayers to Buddha in favour of one's deceased relatives is to regard them as good-for-nothings'.

His remarks are echoed by Ricci in *The True Meaning of the Master of Heaven*, in which he puts the following words into the mouth of a Chinese man of letters:

A Sage of olden times has said: 'What need is there to believe in the existence of paradise and hell? If paradises exist worthy people certainly ascend there. And if hells exist, the wicked surely go there. All we have to do is act as worthy people.' These are assuredly fine words.

But the retort of the Western man of letters is: 'If one does not believe in paradise and hell, one is certainly not a worthy man.'[126]

The Chinese and Buddhist idea of the automatic nature of retribution indeed rendered all divine intervention unnecessary. It implies that there is no distinction between the sphere of worldly realities and that of religious truths. In Buddhism and according to the Chinese ideas, there were, despite claims to the contrary, no sins in the Christian sense, that is to say faults committed against God as opposed to faults committed against men. One single term applied to every kind of crime or fault: it was *zui*. As a Protestant missionary wrote at the end of the nineteenth century: 'Who has been fortunate enough to discover a name for sin which does not dash us on to the Scylla of civil crime or engulph [*sic*] us in the Charybdis of retribution for the faults of a former life?'[127] The remark is perceptive and testifies to a good understanding of the situation in China. The elimination of 'sins' (*chu zui*), which is discussed at length in certain texts of the school of the Pure Earth, has nothing in common with the remission of sins in Christianity. In Buddhism, 'sins' are of many kinds, some religious, some secular. For Buddhists, the important thing is to reduce the stock of bad *karma* by means of acquiring merit (*punya*) through performing pious actions.

Whereas, for the Chinese, accomplishing the rituals in a spirit of perfect sincerity is the way to 'serve Heaven and contribute to the world order', from a Christian point of view, good behaviour has neither value nor meaning unless sanctioned by faith. Nicole wrote: 'In states where [charity] has no entry, people can nevertheless live in as much peace, safety and comfort as if they were in a republic of saints.'[128] The fact is that self-love 'imitates the principal actions of charity' and produces 'human worthiness', humility, kindness and moderation. In making these remarks, Nicole probably had China very much in mind, the country praised so highly by certain Jesuits for its public tranquillity and for the gentleness of its mores. Whoever is unaware of God cannot act well whatever he does, for there is no good without him.

Father Le Comte relates the following anecdote: a Chinese had returned a lost purse to its owner and the local mandarin decided to print and post up an account of this good action. But a convert, duly instructed by the missionaries, told the man who was thus honoured: 'It only befits Christians to perform such actions and in the state that you are in, however many your virtues, they will not prevent you from being damned.'[129]

The close link between salvation and faith and the eternal nature of that sanction, which were Christianity's contributions to solving the question of retribution, seemed shocking to many Chinese. While consigning to the eternal flames all those who knew nothing of the Revelation, the Christians promised total absolution for their faults to all those who, being instructed in the Christian religion, performed a sincere action of repentance.

The author of a pamphlet dated 1634 writes:

It is enough for the most villainous of bandits to enter their residence just once for him to ascend to the Heaven of eternal happiness, whereas Yao and Shun, the Duke of Zhou and Confucius [the great Saints of Chinese Antiquity] can never enter there but must remain imprisoned in the purificatory hell.[130]

Similarly, in about 1635, a certain Lin Qilu writes:

Only the followers of their religion can be virtuous. Even if they outrage Heaven and Earth, insult the spirits and the gods and rebel against their sovereign and their parents, the Master of Heaven protects them and opens paradise for them. Those who do not accept their doctrine are acting wrongly. Even if they honour

Heaven and Earth, respect the spirits and the gods, love their sovereign and their parents, they provoke the wrath of the Master of Heaven and are cast down into hell.[131]

And Xu Dashou writes:

How could our Saints and Sages of Antiquity possibly have abandoned cultivating their virtue in order to concentrate upon cultivating favours from Heaven? But there is even worse to come: what these Barbarians consider to be good and evil are the exact opposite to what our Saints and Sages mean. The books of the Barbarians say: 'If you have done good throughout your life but have not made yourself agreeable to the Master of Heaven, all your goodness will have been in vain. If you have done evil all your life but for one single instant did make yourself agreeable to the Master of Heaven, all the evil you have done will immediately be absolved.' How could it be possible to have given birth to Heaven and Earth and be Master of Heaven and yet make such ignoble calculations founded upon self-interest?[132] ... These Barbarians believe in a Heaven external to nature and that is why they criticise the idea of submitting to and conforming with the natural order.[133] If our Heaven depended upon this Master of Heaven whom the Barbarians have falsely set up, it would not tolerate his rebellious conduct and whims and would be filled with an extreme hatred for him.[134]

Furthermore, by introducing rifts within families, between the pagan and the converted, the doctrine of the Master of Heaven strikes at filial piety. Xu Dashou writes:

As for fathers and mothers now deceased who never in their lifetimes heard of their vicious doctrine, the Christians certainly condemn them unjustly to the purificatory hell even if they were full of virtue and wisdom. And if they happen to have been quite ordinary people, they are immediately consigned to eternal torments. According to them, if these people have pious sons willing to flatter the Master of Heaven, they will be able to enter paradise. But the wrath of Heaven is terrible and extremely difficult to appease; [if one is not Christian], however pious a son may be, that can be of no help to one's deceased parents.[135]

The definitive nature of retribution in Christianity seemed every bit as unjust as did the connection established between faith and salvation. The total discrepancy between faults and their punishment, merit and its reward, violated a principle which was fundamental to the Chinese ideas of justice and religion: namely, that there should be an exact correspondence between the crime and the punishment, between the fault and the retribution exacted for it. Furthermore, the everlasting torments inflicted upon the damned testified to an unprecedented cruelty on the part of the Master of Heaven and this belied the virtue of infinite compassion with which he was credited. Conversely, complete and definitive absolution for faults and crimes also appeared arbitrary and unjust. Xu Dashou writes: 'So these people have never known what the Buddhist canonical writings announce: once good and evil are exhausted, one goes either up or down on the ladder of good and bad destinies.'[136]

In Buddhism, paradise and hell are part of the system of the six possibilities for rebirth, corresponding to rebirth as a god (*deva*) or an infernal being (*naraka*). Like all the other rebirths, they are pure illusions for they stem from what is relative and composite and these things have no being in themselves. These are differences that Yang Guangxian points out in his *Refutations of the Vicious Doctrines*:[137]

Hells and paradises were thought up by the Buddhists as a means to encourage stupid people to be good. It is not as if there are really any hells or paradises: the blessings that result from good actions and the misfortunes that come in the wake of bad ones – these are the only true paradises and hells of the present world . . . But these people teach, absurdly, that paradises and hells truly do exist above and below us and they say that those who honour their doctrine of the Master of Heaven go up to paradise while the rest go down to hell. Their Master of Heaven is just a rogue then, inciting people to flatter him. How could he possibly be capable of directing the world? It might still be conceivable if all those who honoured him were worthy people and those who did not were all good-for-nothings. But if the opposite were true, would this not be an intolerable reversal of goodness and evil? Buddhist repentance is in line with what Yanzi, the disciple of Confucius, taught when he spoke of 'not committing the same fault twice' (*bu er guo*). Buddhism has never spoken of a definitive wiping-out of crimes. But when this doctrine maintains that if a person sorrowfully implores Yesu and his mother, they will forgive his crimes and he will go up to paradise, it suggests that all criminals and cheats can become heavenly beings. In all conscience, their paradise must be a proper den of thieves! These people, having picked up what was left over from what Buddha had spat out,[138] say that Buddha has been cast down into hell and will never be able to leave it. Everything indicates that their hearts are full of hatred and their words are even more poisonous than those of jealous women. If it was a good doctrine for the world, they ought to set out great and good principles like those that Confucius expounds, which teach us integrity and sincerity and consider that the fundamental things are perfecting oneself and harmonious relations within the family and, similarly, when it comes to putting these virtues into practice, good government and public peace. [In that way], even without expecting people to respect them, they would be respected spontaneously. But whatever is this behaviour that consists in rejecting Buddhism as false and then setting up a diabolical and vicious doctrine of one's own?[139]

The Japanese apostate, Fabian Fucan, adopts an equally virulent tone when he explains his abomination of the remission of sins:

Even if a man has committed acts of banditry and piracy, if he has killed his father and mother, committed the five abominable crimes [listed in the Code], even if he has been guilty of treason and rebellion against the state or other capital crimes, provided that the Fathers, having heard [his confession], forgive him, his crimes are absolved. That is what they claim. This is a truly diabolical doctrine ... The Fathers ought to be branded with a red-hot iron as supporters of banditry and instigators of rebellion and assassination.[140]

They detest life

Christianity appears to its enemies as a doctrine devised to torment men by persuading them that they are faced with an appalling choice – that of eternal damnation or everlasting bliss – and to increase their dissatisfaction by comparing the joys of paradise to all the miseries of this world and, finally, with its introduction of the duality of soul and body within man, to tear them asunder within themselves.[141]

In Ricci's great work in Chinese, there is a long passage on the pains of existence and man's permanent dissatisfaction. He cites this distress of the soul and man's inexhaustible thirst for happiness as proofs that man is an exile on this earth. He writes: 'Who is ever contented with what he has and does not seek outside for more? If men were given all the riches and all the peoples of the world, they would still not be satisfied. The fools!'[142] But the Buddhist monk, Tongrong, answers Ricci with the retort that a doctrine which preaches permanent dissatisfaction, claiming that our true homeland is Heaven, has no right to censure men for being incapable of contenting themselves with their lot. He exclaims:

How blind Ricci is! He falsely claims that beyond our minds there exists a Master of Heaven whom one must love and serve and that everything depends upon him, which comes down to not contenting oneself with one's lot and ceaselessly seeking outside for something more. And then, after that, he accuses people of not knowing how to content themselves with what they have! ... He knows absolutely nothing at all about what it is that each man assuredly does possess, namely a basic spirit, a basic nature, the great Dao, this thing that is given us together with our body and to which all the Saints and Sages [of Confucianism] have, in all periods, devoted all their efforts, this thing that they have made known to the world and which is the source of social tranquillity and good political order ... Ricci is quite mistaken on the subject of the basic spirit and wrong about the basic nature of man. He is therefore in rebellion against the constant principles of morality.[143]

Not content to struggle against their passions, the Christians place all their hopes in the existence to come and detest the whole of this life. Huang Zhen writes:

Their obsession is to seek the Master of Heaven and they feel no regret at exhausting their entire lives in flattering him. Thus, they pass their lives in upholding illusions. Their life is an unreal life (*xusheng*). Their entire ambition is summed up in this lure of paradise. Therefore they make no fuss about leaving this life in order to seek it and, as they die, they are still deluding themselves.

Their death is an unreal death (*xusi*).[144] But, for the rest of us, life and death are great things. These sinister Barbarians thus claim exactly the reverse of what Confucius and Mencius say about the good control of desires . . . For our Saints and Sages, to be blessed with life is a true joy. They therefore have nothing in common with what these cunning Barbarians say about the intelligent soul, which, according to them, is shackled at birth and liberated at death as if it were emerging from a dark prison. They teach people to regard life as a torment and death as a joy. The fact is that these Barbarians know nothing about the true basis of all things [which is within ourselves] and cling to the idea of a Master of Heaven outside themselves. Obsessed by the hope of paradise, they seek by any means to ascend to it. They crucify themselves without reason and although they have committed no crimes, they beat their breasts, begging to be saved. Where, in them, can be found that taste for bountiful life and that peace of heart which the Sage can achieve?[145]

And Xu Dashou writes: 'They said of a man who had been ill for many years: "This illness is really a blessing from the Master of Heaven, who will reward him in the other world." But who had ever seen this other world?'[146]

In *The True Meaning of the Master of Heaven*, Ricci had been unwise enough to relate an anecdote the effect of which was to make many Chinese think of Christianity as a doctrine 'in which one presents condolences at births and congratulations when deaths occur' (*diao sheng qing si*).[147] He had written:

I have heard that not so very long ago there was a kingdom where there was a ritual – I do not know whether it still exists – which consisted in presenting one's condolences to the parents of a new-born child since it had been born into a world of pain and suffering, and to congratulate the relatives of somebody who died, since he had left this world of pain and suffering. That is excessive but it indeed shows an understanding of what this world is. It is not the world of men. It is the original place of animals . . . Man is only in this world as a temporary guest.[148]

The author of *The Aid to Refutation* lavishes his irony on this idea, saying:

They teach one to hope, albeit vainly, for the soul one day to live eternally and that, for the present, the most important thing is to seek death. They relate that, in their country, when a birth takes place, relatives and friends come together to weep at the door and present their condolences. When a man's father or mother dies, they make music and offer him their congratulations. They also say that this world is a world for animals and regard death as a favour from Heaven. Not only do they not shun it, but indeed they rejoice at it. There was somebody who lost both his eyes. They said that this was a great favour from the Master of Heaven, who had in this way rid him of two enemies, and other things of a similar kind. Confucianism says that one must not dare to destroy or wound one's body[149] and that assuredly one cannot bring oneself to perfection without taking it into account. And even when Buddhism says that one must accede to the Law by forgetting one's body, how could one aspire to the fruit [deliverance from the cycle of rebirths and deaths] by detesting the means [of that deliverance, which is the body]? These people also say that those who die in suffering for the Master of Heaven are reborn in a higher Heaven, and they even go so far as to excite stupid common folk day and night, daring them to court death. I really do not know what their intentions can be.[150]

And on the subject of the baptism of children who die as infants, he writes:

They also say that there are not a great number of hells,[151] just four, one on top of the other: the purificatory hell, the one for children, the one where one purges one's crimes and the one for eternal sufferings. The purificatory hell was designed for our emperor Saints and enlightened sovereigns, our masters and our heroes. The one for children is to provide favoured treatment for the wicked who die prematurely. The hell where crimes are purged and the one for eternal suffering are the ones to which are consigned all those who do not adhere to their doctrine in this world.[152] I asked them what was the significance of this hell for children. They told me that the Master of Heaven had thought that children, having no knowledge, could be accepted. That is why, in this hell, he purifies them lightly of their original sin. When their punishment is purged, they leave the world.[153] Their body remains forever the size of a child and they rejoice within themselves eternally. If, having lived only for a little while, children are lucky enough to have been sprinkled with holy water by these people, their good fortune is even greater. In this way, they excite stupid folk to rejoice when their children die at a tender age and to lament if they have not been sprinkled. I hate that way they have of exciting people.

I asked them: 'What age do you fix for those whom you call children?' They replied: 'We take intelligence into account. One who, while yet a child, acts as though he is older is considered to be intelligent; one who, although already grown, acts as a child is considered foolish.' That means that when a child is born to a family, they should make wishes for it to die young and be an idiot, and it would be better to die prematurely and be an idiot than to live to a hundred and be intelligent. Is there any common sense in all this?'[154]

Buddhism appears to have been the target of similar criticisms among the literate elite. Thus Yan Yuan writes:

Buddhism despises the body and says that we are embarrassed and burdened by it. The diversity of sounds, colours, tastes, smells, images and ideas[155] perceived by our ears, eyes, mouth, nose and mind[156] is something that we should rid ourselves of as soon as possible. The Buddhists thus consider our senses to be our enemies. And if we were to follow their thought through to its conclusion, the best thing to do would be to die without delay: then we should no longer suffer from the burden and obstacle that is our body.[157]

But the Buddhist schema is different from the Greek one, which opposes the intelligible to the sensible, and also from the Christian schema, which makes a distinction between the rational soul on the one hand and the body and senses on the other. In Buddhism, the mind or *mana-indriya* is rejected as being the source of ideas, images and thoughts. Reflective thought, reason itself, which can only touch upon what is relative, is incompatible with an absolute which is attained in states of profound calm and is consequently beyond discussion. The mind is one of the 'six bandits' (*liu zei*) which represent an obstacle to deliverance, that is to say the faculties of the eye, the ear, the nose, the body and the mind or thought (*xin* or *yi*).[158]

Analogies between Buddhist morality and Christian morality cannot be pursued very far. The same applies to the rigorist tendencies in neo-Confucianism, which were one of the results of Buddhist influence on thinkers of the Sung period.[159]

The opposition between the 'principle of heavenly order' (*li*, a term which the missionaries translated as 'reason') and 'human desires' (the passions), which had been stressed by Zhu Xi in the twelfth century, seemed to tally with the teaching of the missionaries. But, as we have seen, this opposition in no sense implied a distinction analogous to that which separates the soul from the body. Moreover, in the seventeenth century, there was among certain thinkers a reaction against what has none too accurately been called the 'idealism' of neo-Confucianism, that is to say the tendency to hypothesise a 'principle of order in nature'.[160] They saw this as one of the unfortunate effects of Buddhist influences upon the true Confucian tradition. Wang Fuzhi writes:

It was only Buddhism which set up a principle of order [an absolute] distinct from the passions. That was surely prompted by a disgust for and rejection of the things of the world and their norms and [this leads to] abolishing all human rules... Wufeng [Hu Hong, 1105–55] was right when he said that 'the principle of heavenly order and human desires are two expressions of the same reality'.[161] The Buddhists consider the body and senses as an inexhaustible source of bad *karma* but they do not realise that what is most humble in us is the reflection of heavenly nature (*tianxing*) and its norms. Developing what is most noble in ourselves [as Mencius urged] does not mean that we should reject what is most humble. If the most humble part [the senses] were to harm the most noble [the mind], the sole fact of possessing a body would prevent anybody from becoming a Saint or a Sage[162] ... The desire for riches and sexuality are the means whereby Heaven secretly controls the Ten Thousand Beings.

Wang Fuzhi defines evil as a lack of harmony and writes: 'I am very much inclined to think that those who despise desires also despise the principle of universal order.'[163]

In the same spirit but in a more superficial fashion, Wang Yuan (1648–

1710) makes a distinction between repressing and channelling the desires. He writes: 'There is no law against the natural feelings of man that
does not introduce trouble into the world.' All the efforts of the Saints,
the founders of civilisation, were directed towards regulating human desires by means of the rituals. All that is done in accordance with the
rituals is legitimate. All that is done in opposition to them is to be condemned:

The Saints gave us the rituals as norms: they never dreamed of suppressing desires. Why go beyond the law established by our Saints, with useless austerities?
Out of ten thousand men only a few heroes are capable of renouncing everything. All the rest are people with ordinary capacities. But, on the pretext that
sensuality and alcohol upset virtue, Buddhism prohibits them. On the pretext
that meat as food leads one to kill living creatures, Buddhism prohibits it.
Heroes will observe these prohibitions without even thinking about it. But ordinary followers will never be able to forget their senses and desires. They will
resort to imposing constraints upon themselves and will behave all at odds with
themselves in order to make themselves masters of their impulses. In the end,
the result will be a hundred times worse, for their senses will be exacerbated by
this struggle. Han Yu (768–824) and Ouyang Xiu (1007–72) in the past
denounced the errors of Buddhism: they never imagined that the situation would
become as bad as it is nowadays when the Taoists have followed in the steps of
the Buddhists as have, in their turn, the Muslims and the Westerners [that is, the
missionaries]. That is why heterodox sects are multiplying among the people.[164]

In the eighteenth century, a similar line of criticism was to be adopted by
the great philologist, Dai Zhen (1723–77), against the excesses of rigorism: our elementary needs are a manifestation of the cosmic order, so
they should not be despised. Just as moral faculties cannot exist in
abstraction, no more can intelligence be disincarnate. The *li*, or principle
of order in nature, cannot prevail in society or in men when the most elementary and legitimate needs are not satisfied. And Dai Zhen echoes a
sentiment to be found in Yan Yuan: 'To try to suppress the desires is
more dangerous than to try to stop the course of a river.' Virtue does not
consist in blocking and repressing the passions, but in regulating and
channelling them by means of the rituals.[165] So it is folly to try to conquer
nature.

Ricci had misunderstood Confucius' statement: 'Man can develop the
Dao; the Dao cannot develop man.'[166] Huang Zhen produces an interpretation which does conform to the moral traditions of China: the
Dao is the directing principle for man. It is our 'innate knowledge', our
'innate capacity'.[167] When man does not follow the Dao, he is not following his own nature, he becomes a tyrant to himself and destroys himself.
The Dao is the basis of everything. So how can one call it 'dependent'
(*yilaizhe*) as Ricci does (explaining that it belongs to the sphere of acci-

dent)? With his argument on the expression 'white horse',[168] the Barbarian, Ricci, ends up by maintaining that the Dao is dependent and can be abandoned. He even goes so far as to say that, even if there were no Dao, there would still be men. But the *Book of Odes* (*Shijing*) says: 'To be a man and not have rituals? It would be better to make haste to die!' That means that men are less important than rituals.[169] What the converted men of letters are doing is scorning virtuous nature in order to honour Yesu, despising sincerity of the heart in order to revere the Master of Heaven, disparaging the virtue of humanity and the natural sense of righteousness in order to set greater store by paradise.[170]

The damnation of the Saints and gods of China

> Tell me now, my sons, of all the men born on this earth before the Spaniards came to preach the Holy Gospel, how many had been saved? How many? How many went to heaven? – Not one– How many Incas went to hell? – All of them – How many queens? – All of them. For in the *huacas* they worshipped the devil.
>
> Father Avendaño, preaching to the Indians
> Cited by Jean Delumeau, *La Peur en Occident*, p. 257

The missionaries installed in Macao, a Portuguese enclave and stronghold, felt no compunction in proclaiming all the Saints of Confucianism – Yao, Shun, Yu, King Wen and Confucius himself – to be devils.[171] But in China itself, it was necessary to be more prudent for there such declarations would have alienated many of the missionaries' sympathisers and compromised results which had been so slowly and painfully achieved. There could be no question of condemning to the eternal flames the founders of Chinese civilisation and the most perfect models of the Confucian virtues. Ricci, who was much impressed by Chinese morality, was for his part inclined to favour salvation for the Chinese Saints: Confucius was a Sage who would have been worthy to be saved and King Wen was already in Heaven, according to the *Book of Odes* (*Shijing*), which Ricci himself used to prove the existence of a paradise. The founder of the mission at least hoped that 'thanks to the great goodness of the Lord, many of their ancients had been saved according to natural law and with the special aid which God is accustomed to provide for those who do all they can to receive it'.[172] He writes in his letter to the Visitor, Francesco Pasio, dated 15 February 1609:

An extremely distinguished person who is a follower of the sect of idols has even called me an adulator of the literate elite in a letter he has written to me because, he says, I have placed some ancient scholars in paradise.[173]

Not that Ricci was displeased by this for, as he said, 'we should have much too much to do if we were obliged to fight against all three sects [Buddhism, Taoism and Confucianism]'.

However, possibly as they grew more sure of themselves, the missionaries subsequently showed less tolerance and an intermediary solution in between paradise and hell was favoured: the Saints of the Confucian tradition thus now found themselves in the limbo of the patriarchs.

The first catechism in Chinese, published in 1584, mentioned only three infernal regions 'which are in the middle of the earth, like the pips in the middle of a pear': the hell of the damned, 'the one into which there fall all of those who, from Antiquity down to the present day, have violated the Laws of the Master of Heaven'; limbo, 'in which there reside those children who died suddenly before knowing what good and evil are'; and purgatory, in which there reside those of the sect of the Master of Heaven whose slight crimes have not yet been purged'. No provision was made for the Chinese Saints. But a reworked version of the same catechism produced half a century later, possibly in 1648, adds a fourth infernal region, with them in mind: it is none other than the limbo of the patriarchs. This catechism reads as follows:

The Master of Heaven has created five different places for the souls of men.[174] In the centre of the earth there are four large holes. The deepest is the prison into which the Master of Heaven casts the wicked of the past and the present and also the devils. The second, which is not so deep, is where the good men of the past and of today reside and purge their crimes. Once their crimes have been purged, the Master of Heaven takes them and has them ascend to paradise. The third place is for children who have not yet come to the doctrine. As they have not yet done anything good, they cannot ascend to paradise and enjoy its bliss. But as they have never yet done evil, it would not be fitting for them to go down to the deepest hell and suffer its torments. However, they inherited the crime of Yadang, the first ancestor. In the place where they are, they feel neither pleasure nor pain. The fourth place is the residence of the Saints of Antiquity. According to their merits, they ought to ascend to Heaven, but the door of Heaven remains closed to them on account of the crime of Yadang. These Saints of Antiquity were obliged to wait for Yesu to come, after his Passion, to liberate them and have them ascend to Heaven[175]...

The fifth place is paradise.

Nevertheless, the missionaries sometimes hesitate to reveal the fate of the figures most revered in the Confucian tradition. In his letter to the censor, Yan Maoyou, written around 1639, Huang Zhen relates how, having gained entry to Father Aleni by passing himself off as a sympathiser, he managed by dint of cunning and determination to elicit his opinion on the fate of King Wen, a kind of paragon of virtue in the literate tradition. He writes as follows:

Their doctrine also has ten prohibitions, one of which says that if one takes a con-cubine when one has no son, one is violating a great prohibition[176] and that [consequently] one will surely go to hell. That comes down to saying that, of all our saintly sovereigns and enlightened kings throughout the entire history of China who had favourites and concubines, not one has escaped the hell of the Master of Heaven. So I put this question to him: 'King Wen had many empresses and concubines. What do you make of that?' Aleni sighed deeply for a long while and made no reply. The following day I put the same question to him again. Once again, deep sighs and no answer. The day after that, I questioned him again and said: 'The matter must be discussed in depth and clarified. A great record of all the past should be set up and then, enlightened by its explanations, people could be encouraged to rally to you and would no longer harbour any doubts.' At this, Aleni sighed again for a long time and then said solemnly to me: 'I did not want to tell you at first, but now I will.' Then he sighed again for quite a while and gravely announced: 'I will tell *you*, my old brother, but I would not tell it to others: I very much fear that even King Wen himself has been cast down into hell.' Then, reconsidering and changing the subject, he said: 'I am speaking of the principle of the matter; I am not speaking of the man himself, for it could be that, having subsequently sincerely repented, King Wen was not damned after all.'[177]

But whether King Wen was saved or damned, the very thought of inflict-ing punishment upon him was, in itself, scandalous.

The monk, Purun, writes:

It is enough for evil-doers of every kind to come but once to their residences for them to ascend to the Heaven of eternal joys. But our Saints, Yao, Shun, the Duke of Zhou, Confucius, who never had access to their doctrine, are for a long time prisoners in the purificatory hell (*lianqing diyu*).[178]

And Xu Dashou writes:

As for our Confucius, who explained the wisdom of our ancient kings and handed their model down to us, there is no person of flesh and blood who does not revere him. But these people say that he is in hell along with Fuxi, Yao, Shun and all our Saints. According to *Urgent Comments on Chenopodes and Peas*, the Barbarians of Macao have no compunction in calling Confucius a devil. How can creatures who appear to be human say such things? When I myself heard them speaking in such a fashion, I could not prevent myself from becoming violently indignant. But these Alenis and Longobardos said to me: '[Where they are] is a kind of purifying hell. There is nothing particularly painful about it.' All those who have followed their doctrine but have not pursued it to the end also go into this hell. It is a kind of secondary paradise . . . They also told me: 'Those who follow our doctrine go up to Heaven, the rest do not.' I said: 'So, from one moment to the next, people can go up to Heaven, whereas Confucius fell into hell. Since the very beginning of humanity, there has never been a man more admirable than Confucius. You should have your tongues torn out! If you condemn Confucius to hell, how much you must despise him! Whereas, as for you, you are destined [for paradise]. What arrogance on your part!'[179]

But if the Saints of the Confucian tradition were the beneficiaries of extenuating circumstances and condemned to no more than a stay in the purificatory hell, no such indulgence was admissible for the Buddhist and Chinese deities. They were all condemned to the eternal flames:

Buddha, Bodhisattva, Spirits and Immortals – they insult them all, calling them devils and say that they have all been cast into hell. Their books say that by making sacrifices to Heaven, Earth, the Sun and the Moon, to the Bodhisattva, the Spirits and the Immortals, and other beings of that kind, one is, by doing so, each time infringing one of the great prohibitions of the Master of Heaven and that, in this way, one becomes guilty towards him.[180]

In place of the Sovereign on High [of China], these people set up one by the name of Yesu, brought into the world by a barbarian woman, and they have bestowed upon the devil the name of Buddha Sâkyamuni.[181]

In conformity with this consignment of the Chinese deities to the eternal flames, in the immediate instance their statues were condemned to be burnt.

For the Christians, every cult is diabolical except for that of God, the Virgin and the saints. The Christian faith insists that every evidence of paganism should be destroyed. Anybody wishing to receive baptism had therefore first to get rid of everything in his home which might remind him of superstition: Taoist and Buddhist books, works of divination, statuettes and images of deities. This was customary right from the early days of the mission, as we can see from a letter written by Ricci from Zhaoqing on 24 November 1585:[182]

Another repentant man who, in penitence, had for a long time eaten no meat or fish or eggs or milk,[183] having seen and read the Catechism,[184] brought his idol and his books to us to be burnt and, falling on his knees and repeatedly striking his head upon the ground, he begged us to make him a Christian.

A certain Li Yingshi, who was baptised in 1602, was a well-known specialist in matters of geomancy[185] and all questions concerning horoscopes and almanacs. Ricci writes:

He had an excellent library and it took him three whole days to inspect it and destroy by fire the works which were forbidden by our Law and of which he possessed a large number, especially those that related to this art of divination – mostly manuscripts – which he had collected with great zeal and at much cost.[186]

This Li Yingshi had been convinced by the Fathers that if he did happen to make correct divinations, it was thanks to the devil and a pact he had, unknowingly, made with him.[187] Another passage in Ricci's memoirs records the difficulties experienced by one Chinese who aspired to baptism, 'when the moment came to throw out the idols in his home'. Ricci writes:

At this time [about 1601–2] one great consolation was the conversion, among the small number of new followers, of a mandarin of soldiers and the death of another of the town's [Nanchang] inhabitants. This mandarin was an old man by the name of Zou, 78 years old, who lived quite close to our house but had never conversed with any of us. He had learned something of Christianity through the intermediary of a Christian who had worked in his house and, touched by God, he suddenly abstained from worshipping idols and sent two of his servants to our house, for them to become Christian. After their baptism, he came to us in person, declaring that he, too, wished to become Christian.

But when the time came for him to throw out the idols from his home, the devil incited his son to prevent him from doing so, using both arguments and force, for it was this son who controlled the household, his father having voluntarily abandoned to him his responsibilities as mandarin which, for many years, had been hereditary in that house.[188] His son argued that he should not throw out of his house idols which they had kept there for so long with so much prosperity[189] and that if he desired to be Christian, he could do just as he pleased but that he, his pagan son, intended to keep his deities: without these images, his house would, after all, seem a poor place to his friends and neither his wife nor his children nor any other member of his family could live without them. And when he saw that his words were having little effect, he declared that he would not allow them to be removed for, just as he [his father] wanted to have his God in his home, so did he and his family wish to have theirs.

The old man thus found himself in a great dilemma, considering that while he could not force his son to become a Christian, neither could he prevent him from keeping his own idols in his room. But if he allowed him to keep them in his own room, he could not forbid him to keep them in the main room [either], since his son had already been promoted to be head of the household and it was he who was in control of everything. Yet, despite all this, the father was anxious to throw the idols out of his house without delay, both on account of the scandal that would be provoked among the Christians if they saw them in a house that belonged to him, even if his son was master there, and also on account of the risks he was running of denying his faith by reason of the presence of these idols and allowing himself to slip back into some form of idolatry. So this poor old man was in the greatest distress, coming and going every day to our church to ask for baptism and arguing that his servants had received it so quickly and so easily and that, at his age, he could not afford to delay and promising that he would never worship these idols and that even if he did take them away, his son could quite easily buy some more or have new ones made.

But in the end, encouraged by the Fathers, he resolved to throw them out of his house and, having asked a servant from our house to assist his two servants who were already Christians, he ordered them to gather them all up and take them to the Fathers. And they did so in the presence of the son, who had not the heart to resist his father by force, seeing that he was so determined. But he took his revenge upon the three servants who accomplished this fine action, heaping insults upon them all the time they were there [but being unable to prevent the three] on account of their numbers from managing, despite the insults, to carry the idols to our house. Thus, the old man received, with great consolation, the holy baptism to which he had so earnestly aspired.[190]

The Chinese texts are full of echoes of such destructions of religious statues and images. Thus, Huang Zhen's letter to the censor, Yan Maoyou, runs:

They order their supporters to bring them the statues of the Bodhisattva Guany-in, the sovereign lords, Guan [Yu][191] and Zitong,[192] the lord, Kuixing,[193] and the sovereign lord, the patriarch Lü [Dongbin].[194] And they cut the heads off all of them and put them down the latrines or throw them into the fire. The very thought of all this makes the hair on one's head and on one's whole body stand up on end and fills the heart with pain and wounds the soul. These are things that I myself have seen with my own eyes. So in this way, they incite people to revolt against the Saints [of China]. There is no greater cruelty. These are great crimes and sacrileges.[195]

In effect, every Christian was bound to consider it his duty to destroy the statues of pagan temples. This represented a striking difference from Buddhism, which always got along well with local cults and limited itself to putting an end to blood sacrifices: 'Buddhism protects the gods, the spirits and men', writes the author of a *Collection for the Refutation of Heresy*. 'In contrast, their Master of Heaven wants everything for himself – all the glory and all the profit.'[196]

'Wherever they have passed, the skulls of the Buddhas are crushed to dust and the texts of the sûtra are reduced to ashes.'[197] Some converts displayed great zeal in destroying representations of the gods, possibly acting thus in conformity with certain iconoclastic traditions.[198] Xu Dashou writes:

As for the five household gods to whom sacrifices were laid down by the Classics, as for the square altar of the god of the Soil, as for the spirit of the Harvests, those mentioned in the rituals, the heroes who averted great calamities, who brought help to the people in catastrophes, who died out of devotion to the common good or who served the state well, as for all these gods and the souls of all those people, including that of our Saint, Confucius, those who belong to the Barbarians' sect call the whole lot of them devils, spit before them without giving them a glance and think that such behaviour constitutes a magic formula to win the favour of the Master of Heaven. And they always get people to throw these gods into the latrines. They order those who keep gods in niches or in the main room of their house to bring them to the halls of the Master of Heaven, which the leaders of their towns have built without any authorisation, in order to burn them there. How painful it is to see these gods which are our greatest Saints and

Sages and our heroes of loyalty and duty mutilated and subjected to the flames of destruction. Is it not a crime [in the eyes of the law] to destroy without authorisation and just as they please the [statues and tablets of] the great Sages whom all the successive dynasties have honoured and, for example [those of] Guan Yu, who was granted the title of sovereign just a few years ago by our holy emperor? Furthermore, the private foundation of sanctuaries and temples is explicitly forbidden by the Code. I do not know what imperial order people are obeying when they order the common people to build halls of the Master of Heaven or to set up a cross in their homes. Is this customary? Is it acceptable?[199]

Zhang Guangtian, who had been a disciple of the great Buddhist master, Zhuhong, also refers to the destruction of Chinese statues and temples, at the same time pointing out that the ancestor cult continued to be allowed by the Barbarians:

They say that, in their country, people revere only the Master of Heaven, that they make no sacrifices to other gods and build no temples other than those of the Master of Heaven. All over China, they are setting up halls of the Master of Heaven where they do honour to his statue. Those who have accepted their doctrine are allowed to continue with their family cults in their homes, but if they have other sanctuaries and revere other gods they are infringing a prohibition of the Master of Heaven. They are therefore absolutely obliged to destroy the temples of our Confucius and the altars of the deities of the Mountains and Rivers and those of the protector gods of the Soil and equally the temples built since Antiquity, by imperial decree, to the memory of heroes of loyalty and filial piety. And they must throw all their statues into the cesspits. On top of all this [the Barbarians] order that a hall of the Master of Heaven be set up in each locality, prefecture and sub-prefecture so that this criminal condemned to die on the cross may be worshipped there. Whatever are these perverse Barbarians who dare to upset the veneration of the masters and models of our empire from time immemorial and in their place substitute their own barbarian custom of one single religion?[200]

There was something both incomprehensible and at the same time scandalous about the Christians' determination to destroy the Chinese cults.

Outrages against the Chinese mores

It is well known what a scandal was caused in Europe around 1700 by the quarrel over Chinese rituals and also that it centred upon two questions that were judged to be of capital importance: should the Sovereign on High of the Chinese Classics be identified with the God of the Bible? Should converts be allowed to continue with their ancestor cults and the cult of Confucius? Antonio de Caballero Santa Maria, the Franciscan who travelled to Fujian province from Manila by way of Formosa in 1633, had been amazed to discover that Chinese Christians were continuing to worship their ancestors, Confucius and even the local town god. With his very own eyes, he had seen pagans and converts together taking part in these superstitious practices and the scandal was all the greater given that the Jesuits themselves had, in the first instance, forbidden this. A treatise published in Manila stated that:

at the beginning of the missions to China, the missionaries would not tolerate any of the ceremonies that have been mentioned; but later on, to remove some of the difficulties which were impeding the progress of the missions, they began to tolerate them as a political measure.[201]

It was quite true that their ancestors were so dear to the hearts of the Chinese and the ancestor cult was so essential to the social and political system of China that to condemn it would have meant compromising everything. It was for similar reasons that the attacks made by missionaries in India against the distinctions of the caste system had provoked such a strong reaction. Vincent Cronin remarks, on the subject of the arrest of Father de Nobili and his companions in Madurai, that they were imprisoned not for preaching a heterodox doctrine – for, for a Hindu, any path that leads to the Truth is a good one – but because of the war being waged by the Portuguese, with whom they were known to be connected, and above all because some of the missionaries were not observing the separation of castes, preaching during the day to Brahmins and during the night to untouchables.[202]

In 1645, the Chinese rituals were condemned by Innocent X but were subsequently authorised by Alexander VII, following a mission to Rome by Father Martino Martini, a clever man sent by the Jesuits to defend their point of view to the Pope. Caballero gives an account of his meeting with Father Martini in Hangzhou in 1659, after his return from Europe. He reports that Martini argued that, so long as the political and civil origin of all the Chinese cults was borne in mind, a totally pagan action could be justified on the grounds of the fine intention behind it. Caballero's retort was:

If that is permitted, the missionaries will find themselves spared the most arduous part of their work and their worst problem, which is how to persuade converts to abandon the public cult of their idols. All their difficulties would thus be solved with regard not only to the cult of Confucius and their ancestors, but also to everything relating to the idols in China. The original institution and intention can save everything.[203]

It reads like an excerpt from Pascal's *Les Provinciales*.

When the adversaries of the Jesuits triumphed, at the beginning of the eighteenth century, the Chinese rituals were on three occasions condemned as superstitions by Pope Clement XI in 1704, 1707 and 1717;

then authorised for Chinese Christians, provided they observed eight very restrictive conditions, by the Pope's legate, Mezzabarba, in 1721; and finally absolutely and definitively condemned by the Papal Bull, *Ex quo singulari*, by Benedict XIV in 1742.[204]

To judge by the claims of their accusers, the Jesuits were guilty of extreme laxity. But such tolerance would seem to be belied by the Chinese sources, which refer far more frequently to the prohibition against the ancestor cult than to any authorisation to practise it. No doubt the truth lies somewhere in between: if the Jesuits allowed converts to continue with their ancestor cults, it was because it was dangerous to clash head-on with what constituted the very basis of the social, political, and religious order of China, the essential consideration being eventually to succeed in changing Chinese mores and Chinese minds. In fact, the better educated and most convinced converts do appear to have ceased to make sacrifices to their ancestors. Furthermore, within the Jesuit mission itself, not all the missionaries appear to have shared an identical attitude with regard to ancestor worship.

Zhang Guangtian, whom we have already cited, remarks that 'those [of the Chinese] who adhere to their doctrine are authorised to continue their family cults' provided they forgo all others.[205] Xu Dashou notes the same tolerance and even expresses indignation at seeing in some converts' homes the Master of Heaven, supposedly the supreme deity, cohabiting with the humble figures of the family ancestors, for this represented an intolerable infringement of the ritual hierarchies.[206]

Conversely, however, a proclamation of the inspector of the judiciary of Fujian province, dated 20 December 1637,[207] notes that some of the converts made by Manuel Dias the Younger, who arrived in China in 1610 and died in Hangzhou in 1659, were not making sacrifices anymore. Manuel Dias categorically condemned all Chinese cults in his *Simple Explanations concerning the Ten Commandments of the Holy Doctrine of the Master of Heaven (Tiangzhu shengjiao shijie zhiquan)*,[208] in which he wrote:

None of your gods of the Soil nor any of your wise and holy men, as you call them, to whom you ascribe foreknowledge of future happenings[209] as is possessed by the angels and prophets of the true God, nor any of your ancestors are, nor can be, the friends of God. And yet you honour them with a supreme cult of sacrifice, you prostrate yourselves before their images just as you would before the true God . . . How mistaken! What blindness! What a mass of superstitions and impiety![210]

In 1616, Shen Que, the vice-president of the Board of Rites in Nanking, wrote:

I have learned that they [the missionaries] were leading astray the minds of humble folk and telling them, without compunction, that they should not make sacrifices to their ancestors, that it was enough to revere the Master of Heaven and that, by doing so, it was possible to ascend to paradise and avoid hell. Buddhism and Taoism also speak of hells and paradises, but they use them to encourage people to be pious sons and obedient younger siblings and to show what punishments lie in wait for impious sons and disobedient younger siblings. So that helps to strengthen our Confucian morality. But these Barbarians do precisely the opposite; they encourage people not to sacrifice to their ancestors, and that is teaching them filial impiety.[211]

So sometimes the attitude of the Jesuits had not been, and still was not, all that different from that of other orders which strictly forbade converts to continue to make sacrifices to their ancestors – a fact that is confirmed by a proclamation dated 16 December 1637, issued by a certain Shi Bangyao, maritime inspector for Fujian province. The missionaries whose names it cites are said to have come from Luzon to Fu'an, in the north-east of Fujian province. We know from other sources that they were Spanish Dominicans, who had arrived in the region in 1632.[212] In his proclamation, Shi Bangyao declares that, contrary to the claims of the missionaries, the doctrine of the Master of Heaven does run counter to the teaching of Confucius since it urges people to give up making sacrifices to their ancestors. And he mentions the case of two graduates who, when brought before the magistrate, declared in an outrageous fashion that sacrifices to ancestors were a piece of nonsense (*xu wen*) and only the Master of Heaven was true. Shi Bangyao is full of indignation at the obstinacy of these converts who obdurately refuse to revert to their better feelings.[213]

Forty or so years after the criticisms of Shen Que, the tone has become more violent, as can be seen from Yang Guangxian's diatribe:

Given that the Barbarians vilify Heaven [by saying that it is brute matter organised by the Master of Heaven], there is nothing surprising about the fact that they order their followers to destroy the sacred tablets of Heaven and Earth and of relatives and masters. They have respect neither for Heaven nor for Earth nor for the son of Heaven. They have no respect for parents since Yesu had no father and even less for masters, and so they destroy the wooden tablets of our Saints. Of all the doctrines that exist, this is the only one which goes so far as to destroy everything: Heaven, Earth, and social rules too. When they say that every great country from the East to the West observes and practises their doctrine,[214] they are certainly boasting. The fact is that I have never heard of a Saint ever inciting people to ignore their fathers and their sovereign. And if all those great countries have really accepted that law, they must be countries for animals.[215] All the more so, if they practise and observe it.[216]

Yang Guangxian establishes a close connection between the fact that Jesus 'was not born from his father' and the filial impiety of the Barbarians. And he goes on to specify that the 'followers of their doctrine are not allowed to worship the tablets of their grandfather and father'.[217]

The permission granted to converts to continue with their ancestor worship must, in any case, have been qualified by restrictions which, from the Chinese point of view, constituted manifest proof of filial impiety. But conversely, even when accompanied by restrictions, this permission could encourage converts to interpret the fourth commandment in a heterodox manner.[218] This did not escape the notice of Antonio de Caballero, who cites a short work written by a Chinese neophyte, to defend the Christians against the accusation so often brought against them of not honouring their parents. The author reproaches his compatriots for their custom of burning papers for the dead[219] and advises them instead to make them offerings of food which can then be distributed on their behalf amongst the poor. He goes on to say: 'Pray to God to increase their happiness; that is the good and reasonable way to honour your ancestors correctly.' Caballero reports this to be the official position of the Jesuit hierarchy, 'for nothing can be printed without the approval of the Society'.

These recommendations were based upon the fourth commandment, but their purpose was to attempt to adapt Christianity to a society in which filial piety was considered fundamental. Caballero observes:

The Chinese Christians are thus in danger of believing that offerings made in accordance with the fourth commandment have the power to deliver the dead from the sufferings of Purgatory and Hell.[220]

Had he been better acquainted with the history of China, Caballero might have remembered that Buddhism, which came from central Asia and India, had in the past acclimatised itself to China precisely by responding to the needs of filial piety. Thanks to the Buddhist theory of the transference of merit, pious actions (reciting and copying out the sûtra, giving alms to monks, donating contributions for the construction of monasteries or the casting of statues) had become a means of aiding one's deceased relatives and continuing to serve them after their deaths as in their lifetimes, in accordance with the prescriptions of the *Sayings* of Confucius.

A Chinese manuscript of 1640, quoted above, tells of a descent to a Christian-style hell in which one of the damned requests that his nephew be asked 'to recite in his favour 3,800 sûtra of the Master of Heaven so as to deliver him from hell'.[221] It is an example of a transposition of Buddhist traditions and ideas which demonstrates just how superficial Christianisation remained.

Echoes of the quarrel over rituals reached the Court and the missionaries there even appealed to Emperor Kangxi (1661–1722) for his opinion on the matter. So when a Chinese translation of the Papal Bull, *Ex illa die*, condemning ancestor worship and also the cult of Confucius, was communicated to him, Kangxi, in his own hand, wrote on it as follows:

Having read this proclamation, I ask myself how these uncultivated Westerners dare to speak of the great [philosophical and moral] precepts of China . . . Most of what they say and their arguments are ridiculous. Seeing this proclamation, I at last realise that their doctrine is of the same kind as the little heresies of the Buddhist and Taoist monks. These are the greatest absurdities that have ever been seen. As from now I forbid the Westerners to spread their doctrine in China; that will spare us a lot of trouble.[222]

Whether or not the missionaries were authorising ancestor worship, the Chinese were well aware of the difference between Chinese and European mores. Zhang Guangtian writes:

Among them, when a father or a mother dies, they offer up no sacrifices and erect no temple. They are content to recognise the Master of Heaven as the father of all and show little regard for those who gave them birth, considering them simply as their brothers. If they did not behave in this way, they would be infringing one of the great prohibitions of the Master of Heaven. Are we to discontinue the sacrifices we offer to our ancient kings and abandon the offerings we make to the nine ancestors of the imperial temples, and thus encourage the people to follow them?[223]

The very behaviour of the missionaries proved that they were lacking in filial piety:

Only the Barbarians never reflect that every tree has its roots, every river its source. That is why, right at the beginning, they truly did forbid people to make sacrifices to their ancestors. Later on, having been criticised for doing so, they changed their tune. And now, among the populace, people are allowed to honour their father and grandfather in the same sanctuary as the Master of Heaven. It is as if they had made their earlier prohibition taboo. Now they say that one must make sacrifices to one's ancestors. But what do they really mean by that? When their own parents die, these people never consult the omens to find a propitious place for their burial, for when they see the experts in geomancy make their pronouncements, they criticise them and mock. So, do they abandon their own dead in wild places? And how is it that these people who have, after all, lived now for many years in China, have never been seen to possess the slightest tablet of their barbarian ancestors?[224]

Furthermore, the missionaries never mention filial piety in their works:

Reading the books that they have written, among all the hundreds of thousands of characters that go to make up, for example, *The Seven Victories*,[225] *The True Meaning of the Master of Heaven*,[226] *The Ten Sayings*,[227] *The Twelve Beliefs* [the

Credo], the *General Remarks on Western Studies*,[228] whether it be a matter of canonical texts, or treatises on discipline, or even the essay, *On Friendly Relations*,[229] or the *Elements of Geometry* [!],[230] not once does the word *xiao* [filial piety] appear. On the contrary, plagiarising all that is most superficial in our three doctrines [Confucianism, Buddhism and Taoism] and in our philosophers of Antiquity in order to add some lustre to their baseness, they speak of 'overcoming one's pride and arrogance'. This is a thesis the like of which has never been heard before: that one should love not one's parents but other people, respect not one's parents but other people.[231]

In the opinion of the Japanese apostate, Fabian Fucan, the missionaries invented the fourth commandment purely to please the Japanese: 'So you speak of filial piety, you followers of the Deus! In our empire, filial behaviour is regarded as the way of all goodness: hence your purely formal adherence to this virtue.'[232]

For Li Can, Ricci, who abandoned all his own family, has no right to speak of filial piety:

Ricci set off on a sea voyage of 10,000 *li* to come to China. Did he ever take with him father or mother, wife or children? I am not accusing him of filial impiety on that account. I am accusing him of committing a great impiety by speaking of filial piety when he himself has abandoned all his family.[233]

Ricci had already provoked a scandal by declaring that it was sometimes necessary to disobey one's superiors and one's parents – as clearly went without saying in the cases of converts. But his successors had shown equally little compunction about expressing views that were just as contrary to Chinese morality. Manuel Dias the Younger, in his *Simple Explanations concerning the Ten Commandments of the Holy Doctrine of the Master of Heaven* (1642), declared that it was a crime to obey the orders of one's parents if they ran contrary to one's duty and that there was even some merit in disobeying them. Father Francesco Brancati, in a work on the Ten Commandments which appeared in 1650, was even more explicit, saying: 'One should not obey the orders of one's father and mother if they run counter to reason; if these orders are contrary to those of the Master of Heaven, one should obey the Master of Heaven and not one's parents.'[234] That came down to saying that converts should put their faith before their filial piety and obey the missionaries rather than their parents and their superiors.

Not only were the missionaries lacking in filial piety from a Chinese point of view: they were also devoid of compassion and modesty.

In order to distinguish themselves from the Buddhists, who forbade the killing of any living creature, the missionaries had had to translate the fifth commandment as 'Thou shalt not kill any man' (*wu sha ren*). But as Zhang Guangtian pointed out, was it not a well-established law in China that every murderer should be put to death? What need had they of lessons from these people who had just arrived from so far away?[235] Xu Dashou expresses a similar reaction:

They say that it is no crime to kill living creatures and teach only that one should not kill other men. Could it be that it might ever be permitted to kill other men? Of what use is such a prohibition? And if they forbid the killing of men, why do they write at such length about the military art and pyrotechnics?[236]

One theme which frequently recurs in the writings of Buddhist monks and men of letters influenced by Buddhist traditions is that the doctrine of the Master of Heaven teaches that no pity should be shown to animals. Ricci himself, in *The True Meaning of the Master of Heaven*, had explained at length that, given that animals have no rational and eternal soul, it is permissible to kill them. But for Xu Dashou, as for many others, the only purpose of such theories was 'to encourage people to kill animals so as to allow free rein to gluttony'. He writes:

That is why these Barbarians deny so obdurately that there is transmigration. So they do not know what the Buddhist canons proclaim, namely, that so long as mental activity never ceases, migration never comes to an end. How can they insist so crudely that there is no transmigration?[237]

And the monk, Tongrong, writes: 'Having rejected the ideas of our Saints and our Sages and having counted three souls in man, when it comes to encouraging the slaughter of animals, is that not to reach an even further depth of error?'[238]

The distinction that Christians make between meat and fish seems absurd:

They make a distinction between the aquatic species and the animals that are butchered [saying that the former] are suitable for fast days. That is as laughable as the Muslim's practice of denying themselves pork and eating only animals that they themselves have killed.[239]

As well as having no compassion for living creatures, the missionaries are devoid of respect for the rules of seemly conduct. They have no shame about approaching women and allow the sexes to intermingle in their assemblies. There is nothing more variable than modesty and rules of seemly behaviour. These things are determined by the particular society and the particular time. Father Le Comte, such a perspicacious observer, had noted that the Chinese, who were so concerned about decorum in public, showed no embarrassment in intimate circumstances and showed themselves 'practically naked among their friends, wearing no more than a pair of underpants of taffeta or transparent material'. On the other hand, they were horrified by the paintings of Western nudes.[240] There was a similar disagreement between China and Europe on the matter of the distances to be observed between the opposite sexes. Chinese mores required a strict separation in this domain. As early as the age of seven, girls and boys were brought up separately.

One of the reasons why the Nanking missionaries, Vagnone and Semedo, were found guilty in 1616 was that they approached women 'to rub them with oil and sprinkle them with water', which constituted a serious infraction of the correct mores.[241]

As the Chinese saw it, there was a contradiction between the tenth commandment and the behaviour of missionaries:

As well as their general rule against lust, they have established a prohibition which runs: 'Thou shalt not look at thy neighbour's wife.' But they order the wives and daughters of their followers to mingle with the crowd to receive secret instruction. They sprinkle them with holy water, rub them with holy oil, hand them the holy box, make them drink holy salt, light holy lamps [in their presence], share holy flour with them, wave the holy fan, cover themselves with red robes and wear strange clothes, and all these things they do half-hidden in the darkness.[242]

Montesquieu had clearly recognised the obstacle that the Chinese mores presented to the diffusion of Christianity. He wrote on the difficulty of altering the mores of the Chinese:

There follows hence a very unhappy consequence which is that it is almost impossible for Christianity ever to be established in China. The vows of virginity, the assembling of women in churches, their necessary communication with the ministers of religion, their participation in the sacraments, auricular confession, extreme unction, the marriage of only one wife – all these overturn the manners and customs of the country and with the same blow strike at their religion and laws.

The Christian religion, by the establishment of charity, by public worship, by a participation in the same sacraments, seems to demand that all should be united; while the rites of China seem to ordain that all should be separated.[243]

Chinese critics claimed that the missionaries permitted themselves to take liberties with the women who became their followers, but displayed great severity towards their male converts, insisting that every candidate for baptism should get rid of his concubines. Now, the possession of concubines was justified by the obligation to produce male descendants to perpetuate the lineage and the ancestral cult. It was common to find concubines in wealthy families, much less so among the common people, who would more often resort to adoption in order to assure their descendancy in the event of their not producing any sons. Father Le Comte writes:

One of the obstacles to the conversion of the Chinese is the multitude of wives, at least in the homes of people of quality, and this polygamy causes a dearth of any other forms of distraction apart from banquets or the theatre: no games, no excursions, no hunting, no public assemblies. A few take refuge in study, but the majority pass the whole time in their seraglios. The missionaries allow their converts to marry one of their concubines in cases where the legitimate wife refuses to become a Christian, but that is a marriage that is forbidden by the laws of the country.[244]

The legal code did indeed punish repudiation of a legitimate wife without cause and subsequent remarriage, during her lifetime, with a concubine. This text by Father Le Comte, which provides us with direct evidence of the kind of life led by people of high society, also confirms what we already know of the scant attention paid by the missionaries to the Chinese laws.

The rule was that any man seeking baptism should first get rid of his concubines and there are a number of well-known examples where this indeed happened. But one Chinese text suggests that, where influential figures were concerned, the missionaries saw fit to be more accommodating. Xu Dashou writes:

They forbid their followers to look at the wives of others but the Barbarians do not forbid themselves to approach them. They insist that their followers show their concubines the door, but the most distinguished of their disciples sometimes continue to keep several.[245]

Having reminded the reader of the strict prohibitions laid down by the rituals on the relations between men and women and the traditional subordination of the wife to the husband, Xu Dashou goes on to criticise the missionaries for their incorrect views on marriage:

The Barbarians say that the husband should also consider his wife as his master and that when she dies he should not regard her as dead: if a man remarries, they do not consider him respectable, even if he has no son. They claim that all the countries they have visited observe their doctrine[246] and that once people adhere to it, they do not allow them more than one wife, even if they are emperors or kings. If that is the case, Shun and King Wen [Saints of Chinese Antiquity] behaved unworthily in the past and must be in the hell which they call a purificatory hell (*lianqing diyu*)[247] ... My friend Zhou Guoxiang was old, poor and had no son. Fortunately, he had been able to buy a concubine and by her had a son who was just one year old. These Barbarians told him that, in their country, it was believed to be virtuous not to have any concubines and thought to be of no importance not to have a line of descendance. My friend obeyed them and ejected the mother of this child. I do not know whether the child is still alive.[248]

Zhang Guangtian, for his part, writes:

In their countries, among sovereigns and common people alike, the only unions are between a single husband and a single wife. They have neither favourites nor concubines. They consider of no importance the idea according to which it is very serious not to have any descendants. Consequently, according to them, the Saints of our kingdom – Yao, Shun, Yu, Tang, Wen and Wu – cannot have escaped the purificatory hell. Not only are the common people forbidden [by them] to have concubines, for this would violate their prohibition against bigamy, but, according to them, even our emperors ought to send away all their women and keep only one wife, just like the common people, whereas the *Rites of Zhou (Zhouli)* speak of three women's quarters and nine classes of imperial favourites. So what are we to make of these calamitous Barbarians who seek to upset our venerable canonical traditions with their barbarous custom of monogamy?[249]

And Xu Dashou writes:

They would like all kings and sovereigns to adhere to their vicious doctrine, expel all their concubines from their women's quarters and live like common people with but a single wife. But in their residences they themselves invite ignorant women at nightfall to enter a room draped with red hangings, where they close the doors and practise unction with holy oil, give them holy water and place their hands on five places of their bodies: these are impure and secret rituals. How could one possibly contravene the rule on the separation of the sexes any more seriously than that?[250]

Not only do the Barbarians violate the rule on the separation of the sexes and seek to impose strict monogamy; they also preach in favour of an unnatural chastity. A text from the mid-eighteenth century criticises the missionaries for urging women to forgo all coquetry and for encouraging girls to remain celibate: 'Christian girls and women make a point of not wearing garments of silk and not decorating their heads with flowers and precious stones and some girls renounce marriage for ever.'[251] Celibacy was also disapproved of in Japan. Fabian Fucan writes: 'Jesus was born from a couple who had sworn chastity. What kind of a virtuous ideal is that? . . . The universal norm is that every man and every woman should marry. To go against that natural law is evil.'[252]

It is quite clear that to its enemies the doctrine of the Master of Heaven appeared as a reversal of all things both moral and commonsensical. In a short work dated 1637, the Buddhist monk, Chengyong, wrote:

They regard their father as a brother and their sovereign as a friend. They present condolences for births and congratulations for deaths. Their works are composed of an accumulation of improbabilities and nonsense . . . They prohibit sacrifices and obliterate social rules.[253]

Morality, which is a social matter, also depends upon particular concepts of man and the world. In the Christian view, the only truth and perfection lie outside this world; man must fight against his own nature, against his body and all its temptations, for the only thing that matters is the salvation of his soul. Chinese morality, in contrast, is founded upon the idea of an immanent order that is present not only in the cosmos and society, but also in man himself. Thus, for each person, to act correctly means to develop the aptitudes for good that that individual possesses and to integrate himself into the order of the world. There is no true goodness nor true wisdom if man's place in society and the universe is disregarded. Pure spontaneity, not yet vitiated by the reactions of the egoistical self, is valued above all else.

Chapter 5

Chinese Heaven, Christian God

The Heaven of the Chinese

Ricci's first concern had been to seek out anything in the Chinese traditions which might have been in agreement with Christian teaching. This inevitably meant applying to China mental frameworks which were alien to it and committing oneself to errors of interpretation. In trying to assimilate the Chinese Heaven and the Sovereign on High to the God of the Bible, the Jesuits were attempting to bring together concepts which were irreconcilable.

The classical formulae, 'respect' and 'fear Heaven', really meant something quite different from the sense given them by Ricci and by many other missionaries after him, who were led on by the mirage of a 'natural religion' or the idea of an ancient transmission of the message of the Bible to the Chinese. These formulae did not refer to a single, all-powerful God, the creator of heaven and earth, but instead evoked the ideas of submission to destiny, a religious respect for rituals, and serious and sincere conduct. As for the Sovereign on High, the *shangdi*, a projection of the sovereign below in representations of the heavenly order, his, functions appear to have been intimately linked with the exercise of royal power. The Chinese character which served to designate him (*di*) on the bones and tortoise shells of the end of the second millennium, in all probability originally represented some kind of sacrifice. The word *di*, which had been applied to the emperors ever since the founder of the united empire at the end of the third century BC, had in the old days been applied to deceased sovereigns. The Sovereign on High was inseparable from a ritualistic and polytheist context the spirit of which was radically different from Judaism. Just as Heaven was associated with Earth, the Sovereign on High was associated with the sovereign Earth (*houtu*).[1]

The Christian faith relates to a personal and transcendent God of pure spirit and it sets up an opposition between the earth below, where man plays out his eternal destiny, and a Beyond, which is totally incommensurate with it. In contrast, the Heaven of the Chinese is a concept in which secular and religious aspects merge. Whereas for the Christians the word 'heaven' is simply a metaphor to refer to God and his angels, and paradise and its elect, for the Chinese the same term has a multitude of meanings. It expresses an order that is both divine and natural, both social and cosmic. As the author of a preface to a work by a missionary puts it, it is a 'global' notion (*hun*). It is a crossroads where the religious and the political, observational sciences and mathematics, and concepts of man and the world all meet.

In association with Earth, with which it forms a couple, Heaven produces all creatures and ensures their development. With its seasonal surges of activity, it regulates the plant cycle. It provides norms for the weather and, by its signs, it makes it possible to establish a calendar which organises work in the fields. It is easy to understand how it was that this cosmic power became so important in a civilisation in which agriculture became so predominant an activity at a very early date.

We should at this point recall the possible influences that pastoral or agricultural traditions may exert upon concepts of human activity.[2] The God of the Christians is an interventionist God: he has created the world on his own initiative, he gives each man a soul and manifests himself in the course of individual existences. In contrast, the Heaven of the Chinese acts only in an indirect fashion: its action is silent, imperceptible and continuous. 'Heaven and Earth, in their majestic perfection, are dumb', declares the *Zhuangzi*, echoing the sayings of Confucius ('Heaven does not speak'). The course of the seasons, in its clear regularity, is not the result of a conscious will. Beings do not have to speak for their organisation to be fulfilled. The Saint draws upon the source of Heaven's perfection and penetrates the principles for the development of all beings. Taking Heaven as his model, he acts without making any intervention and without speaking.[3] Concepts of sovereignty in the Christian and Chinese traditions respectively are quite different. The power exercised by the sons of Heaven is one not of constraint but of setting the world in order and transforming mores. The most perfect sovereigns of Antiquity, who are promoted to the status of Saints, managed to imitate Heaven with respect to its invisible and efficacious action: 'King Wu allowed his robe to hang free, clasped his hands and order reigned beneath Heaven', says one of the Classics.[4] Similarly, the Sovereign on High (*shangdi*) is confused with the dynamism of nature and its power of order and generation. Its action never ceases for a single moment. On the subject of the Incarnation, Yang Guangxian writes.

If the Sovereign on High had come to be born on earth and had lived here for 33 years, the universe would have been deprived of its master during those years. Heaven would therefore have had to stop turning and Earth stop producing, men would have had to stop being born and dying and animals would have had to stop reproducing themselves. It would have been the end of all the species.[5]

In China, there are close links between Heaven and the supreme power, which is the organiser of time and space. The polar and circumpolar stars, which play a role of capital importance in the equatorial astronomy of the Chinese, evoke the royal couple, the Court and the administration of China.[6] The observation of signs in the heavens and the establishment of the calendar are royal privileges. The first sovereigns, the founders of civilisation, managed to interpret the signs of Heaven and Earth and were thus able to establish the rituals and institutions in conformity with the norms of the universe. According to ancient traditions, natural dis-asters and abnormal celestial phenomena indicated a lack of virtue in the sovereign. The son of Heaven, solely responsible for the order of the world, would then have to mend his ways and, through acts of contrition, re-establish the equilibrium that had been compromised. Similarly, he alone had the right to make sacrifices to Heaven. Heaven was informed when a new dynasty acceded to power and sovereigns reigned by virtue of a 'mandate from Heaven' (*tianming*).

According to the Chinese ideas, there was no justification for dissoci-ating the visible sky from Heaven considered as the principle of universal order, that which is body or substance (*ti*) from that which is activity (*yong*).

As we have seen, for most of the Chinese at the end of the Ming period, Jesuit teaching formed a unified whole: calculations relating to the calendar, astronomy, 'respect for Heaven' and morality – for them, all these things went together. Thus, the teaching brought by the mission-aries was frequently referred to using the general term, 'heavenly studies' (*tianxue*). That is the term used by an anonymous author at the end of the Ming period, in a short work in which he casts himself as a defender of the 'theories of the Master of Heaven'. For him, 'the heavenly studies' consist firstly in the study of Heaven itself: the mission-aries are astronomers. Now, Heaven regulates time and the numbers that express time reflect the Master of Heaven's activity of creation–transformation (*zaohua*). Each season in effect corresponds to a definite function: springtime is for sprouting, summer for growing, autumn for harvesting, winter for withdrawing and renewing energies. The action of Heaven is characterised by the sequence of these connected functions. The author then undertakes an exposition of the *Book of Changes*, the *Yijing*, the 'ancestor of heavenly studies'. The theories of the Master of Heaven are none other than the teachings of the *Yijing*, which he calls a 'Heavenly Book', by a different name. And the work concludes with an astonishing interpretation of the symbolism of the images of the Holy Mother (the Virgin) and the Master of Heaven by reference to the hexa-grams of the *Yijing*. The Holy Mother is symbolised by the hexagram of the Earth (*kun*). *Kun* is the mother, that is why she carries a child in her arms; and the Master of Heaven is the son to whom she gave birth. The symbol of the Master of Heaven is the hexagram *zhen* (lightning). According to the formula in the *Yijing*, *zhen* is the 'eldest son' of the symbol *qian*, which is the hexagram for the sky or Heaven. He takes the place of Heaven in order to exercise his power. That is why he holds in his hand three heavenly pieces of wood struck by a thunderbolt(?). The Trinity corresponds to the hexagrams *zhen*, *kan* and *gen*, all three produced by the mother, *kun*.[7]

Just as some Jesuits, called 'figurists', believed that in the Chinese Classics they had discovered a whole complex of Christian symbols and transparent allusions to Christianity, similarly, the author of this little work interprets what he thinks he knows of the doctrine of the Master of Heaven by means of symbols taken from the *Book of Changes*. It is all very Chinese and not very Christian. In this text Heaven appears not as a way of referring to a personal, creator God, but as the anonymous power whose continuous action ensures the alternations and equilibrium of nature.

Yang Guangxian was often ridiculed for his pretentiousness in the field of astronomy and accused of bad faith. However, he was most perceptive when it came down to what it was that distinguished the Chinese from Christian, or more generally, Western modes of thought:

Ricci declares: 'The blue sky – or heaven – is something organised by the Sovereign on High [God]. It is sometimes in the east, sometimes in the west and has neither head nor stomach nor hands nor feet. This heaven does not deserve to be honoured. Even less so does the earth which everybody tramples underfoot and into which all rubbish goes. So heaven and earth do not deserve to be honoured.'[8] To say such things is surely the talk of a beast capable of speaking the language of men. Heaven is the great origin of all beings, all things and all principles of order. Where there is a principle of order (*li*), there is also energy (*yin* and *yang*); if there is energy, numbers are produced; if there are numbers, there is body. Heaven is a principle of order which has assumed a body. When bodies have reached their full development, the principle of order is revealed in them . . . Apart from the principle of order, there is nothing that can be called a principle of order, and apart from Heaven there is nothing that can be called Heaven . . . To refer to it with a word that covers it all, we use the term 'Dao'. But if we envisage it in its different aspects, as a visible body we call it Heaven; as an organisational power we call it Sovereign [on High] (*di*); as a marvellous efficacy we call it spirit (*shen*); as innate nature we call it universal dynamism (*qian*).[9] In this way of speaking, which is both global and at the same time analytical, we never emphasise the particular aspects without saying something about the totality. *The totality is the substance; the particular aspects are simply its manifestations.*[10] In contrast, the mode of discussion of the followers of the Master of Heaven consists in concentrating exclusively upon the aspect of activity and in giving concrete form to what Master Cheng [Cheng Hao, 1032–85] calls devils and spirits (*guishen*). But how is it possible to select only the aspect of organisational power? Master Zhu [Zhu Xi] used to say: 'The universal dynamism (*qianyuan*) [the original virtue of Heaven] is inherent to Heaven just as the spirit is inherent to man.' How could one say that man is man [independent from his spirit] and that the spirit is the spirit [independent from the man]? By reasoning in this fashion [it is clear that] Heaven cannot be Heaven [independently from the Sovereign on High, who is its organisational power] and that the Sovereign on High cannot be the Sovereign on High [independently from Heaven]... When man raises his head and sees Heaven, he calls it the Sovereign on High: that does not mean that above Heaven there is also another Sovereign.'[11]

The Chinese thesis is that there is no meaning outside the world and that body and spirit cannot be separated. The Dao appears only through its manifestations and in the alternation and complementarity of the *yin* and the *yang*. A Saint is one who is able to work back from the diversity of what is visible to the unity of the principle. Wang Fuzhi (1619–92) writes:

In the order of nature [starting from the top], it can be said that Heaven possesses the Dao, that human nature is formed from the Dao and that, through the manifestation of human nature, we can know the Dao. Working in the opposite order, it can be said that the spirit makes it possible to develop human nature until it is fulfilled, and thus one can become united with the Dao and in this way serve Heaven (*shi tian*).[12]

In a letter to a friend, in which he discusses the search for the principle of heavenly order (*tianli*) and man's fulfillment of his nature, a certain Li Suiqiu (1602–47) writes as follows:

Ignorant people believe that the recent doctrine of the Master of Heaven is close to our Confucianism, but that is a serious mistake. If one examines what it is that Confucianism calls Heaven from the point of view of heavenly phenomena as well as from that of social relations and the organisational principle for all beings,[13] one realises that there is a definite difference [from the teaching of the Barbarians]. How could there possibly be in Heaven a man presiding there like the one they call Master of Heaven?... If one has a correct understanding of what the Heaven of Confucianism is, one must reject totally the Western concept of the Master of Heaven. If not, one will end up by no longer understanding the meaning of respect for Heaven (*jing tian*).[14]

The author of a refutation of Christianity denounces the missionaries' assimilation of their Master of Heaven to the Sovereign on High of the Classics. He maintains that this assimilation reveals a total misunderstanding of the Chinese ideas. He explains that Confucianism understands Heaven to have three different senses and to manifest itself simultaneously as:
- the immense, luminous, blue sky;
- Heaven as the source of retribution for good and evil. 'They only know

this one. Furthermore, for us, this Heaven simply has an organisational power like that of a sovereign who rules the world. It is a gross error on their part to speak of creation';

Heaven as the permanent source of the universe, a source which combines the principle of order (*li*) and universal energy (*qi*), and also substance and activity (*ti* and *yong*); and which is spontaneous action and reaction.[15]

For Zou Weilian, who died in 1635, the identification of the Barbarians' Master of Heaven with the Chinese Sovereign on High is simply a clever manoeuvre intended to fool the Chinese. He writes:

There is a Barbarian from a kingdom of the distant West situated beyond the seas, named Li Madou [Matteo Ricci], with the surname of Xitai, who arrived in China at the beginning of the Wanli period [1573–1620] with a few companions. He wrote a number of books, one of which is entitled *The True Meaning of the Master of Heaven*. In it, he exalts this doctrine, and he published his book in order to spread it far and wide. His comments and ideas are extravagant and contradictory, apparently profound and subtle, but in reality superficial and uncouth. In a wicked and wordy style, he glorifies himself . . . He fraudulently likens his Master of Heaven to the Sovereign on High of our Classics for, knowing that the Sovereign on High often appeared in these works and that sacrifices to Heaven and the god of the Soil (*jiao* and *she*) had been instituted on account of him, he could see that he was accorded the highest dignity. But the great scholar [Zhu Xi] has explained that the Sovereign on High is the organisational power of Heaven. The Sovereign on High and Heaven are, in fact, interchangeable terms. To honour Heaven is to honour the Sovereign on High. Why does he say that Heaven does not deserve to be honoured and why does he substitute the name of the Master of Heaven for that of the Sovereign on High, which he then bans?[16] He starts off by saying that the Master of Heaven is the principle of universal order (*li*). He goes on to declare that he is a spirit (*shen*) and ends up by maintaining that he is Yesu, a criminal of a Western kingdom in the Han period.[17]

In 1623, Wang Qiyuan explains that 'the two aspects of Heaven [the physical (*xingerxia*) and the metaphysical (*xingershang*)] are like the two aspects of a person who has both an exterior and an interior, a body and a spirit, an individual temperament (*ming*) and also a heavenly nature (*xing*)'. Then he adds: 'And these people claim that our concept of Heaven leaves something to be desired! How absurd!'[18]

The inseparability of the visible sky and Heaven considered as the active principle of the order of the world, and the correlation between the concepts of body or substance (*ti*) and activity (*yong*) are as fundamental to the ideas of the Chinese as the distinction between the Creator and his creation is to those of the Christians.

Huang Zhen is another who denounces the confusion, deliberately encouraged by the missionaries, between the Christian concept of a creator

God, who is distinct from his creation, and the Chinese concept of Heaven as immanent order. He writes:

The danger of confusing vermilion with violet[19] is as great as that which threatens the five characters that represent the 'Sovereign on High', 'the order of Heaven' and 'Heaven' (*shangdi, tianming, tian*). These Barbarians, who are so full of cunning, think that they have discovered an admirable stratagem. The barkers [those who resemble dogs which bark when they hear others bark] and greedy people on the look out for anything profitable come forward to respond to them and, in every province, the Barbarians thus find encouragement and support. The barkers have no eyes: they simply respond to others barking. Greedy people have lost their natural goodness: they have eyes for nothing but money . . . Every day, the statues of our models of loyalty and filial piety and our heroes of devotion and duty fall beneath their axes.[20] The heavenly Dao and good nature gradually become obscured. In all this there is truly cause for tears and lamentation. The Barbarians should not bring their teaching to upset the ideas of our Saints and Sages on the worship of Heaven and knowledge of Heaven. Confucius said: 'At the age of fifty, I knew what was the destiny fixed by Heaven.'[21] Nobody knew better than Confucius what Heaven is. The great object of his teaching was good conduct and the inspirations of our hearts. That is how the ceaseless quest for perfect sincerity should be summed up. He never taught that Heaven should be defiled by an unclean cult. For what makes Heaven Heaven remains hidden in its inexhaustible perfection.[22] It is the universal Dao. It is the spirit and heart of man. It is human nature. Its mode of action is marvellous and has a guiding power . . . That is why our Confucianism says that it is only by preserving our innate spirit and developing our nature that we can worship Heaven. He says that it is only by regretting our faults and reforming ourselves that we can pray to Heaven.[23] Any other discourse on Heaven, any other ways of worshipping it, are contrary to the fundamental idea of Confucius, who was called the sovereign without a kingdom. I have read that Zilu said to Confucius: 'In prayers for the dead, one says "We pray to you, spirits from above and below"', and the Master replied: 'I have been praying for a long time'[24] . . . Confucius and Zilu always associate Heaven and Earth together[25] . . . That is why these Western monsters disrupt the ideas of our Confucianism on the subject of Heaven and the Sovereign on High. That is why they are absolutely set against speaking of prayers to the spirits of the Earth and why they dare not say that Heaven is our innate spirit, our state of perfect sincerity. It is clearly because such concepts reduce to nothing all that they say about the Master of Heaven, Yesu. To believe, as some of our compatriots do, that the Master of Heaven, Yesu, is the same as the Sovereign on High of our Classics is to accept that the cry of the bat is in tune with the song of the phoenix.[26]

As this text indicates, Heaven is reflected in man himself. It is his innate spirit and the moral sense that is inherent in every individual.

One short anti-Christian work runs as follows:

The Master of Heaven of our Confucianism is at once Heaven and Sovereign [on

High]; every man and every creature in the world possesses a Master of Heaven within himself. The Master of Heaven of the Barbarians is just a devil.[27]

The same opinion is expressed, rather less crudely, by one of Longobardo's interlocutors:

Doctor Che Mo Kien, a mandarin of the court of rituals, who has read Ricci's books, one day asked us what we understood by *Tien cheu* [*tianzhu* – Master of Heaven]. We replied that we understood him to be a living, intelligent substance, without beginning or end, who had created all things and governed them from Heaven *as the king* in his palace governs the entire kingdom; but he mocked at us and said *that we were using extremely clumsy comparisons, for the Tien cheu or King on High is not really like a living man, seated in Heaven, but is simply the virtue which dominates and governs Heaven, which is in all things and in ourselves, and so we may say that our hearts are the same thing as Tien cheu and Xamti* [the Sovereign on High].[28]

Around 1635, a certain Lin Qilu writes:

In China, we have always said that it was necessary 'to fear the orders of Heaven'; and we say that Heaven is the principle of universal order. When we speak of the Sovereign [on High], it is to refer to his regulatory power. It is Heaven that causes men to be born. And every creature possesses within himself the norms of Heaven. It is because each one is capable of conforming with the principle of heavenly order and complying with the norms of the Sovereign on High that man can exert his domination over the Ten Thousand Beings, rule the universe, put right the defects of the world and see that the current teaching is correct. That is what our Confucianism calls the Master of Heaven. How could one possibly abandon without a backward glance these superior and fine ideas in favour of a doctrine of devils and demons? Are we going to destroy the temple of our ancestors, cast away their holy tablets, repudiate our rituals and laws and, instead, sprinkle ourselves with holy water, rub ourselves with holy oil, revere an instrument of torture in the form of the character ten and turn a man with blue eyes and a big nose into the Master of Heaven?[29]

Just because some men of letters of the seventeenth century, such as Gao Panlong and Huang Zongxi, deplored the fact that their contemporaries had lost their respect for Heaven and reproached them for now seeing in Heaven no more than the visible sky or an abstract principle of order, this did not mean that they had suddenly become converted to the ideas of the missionaries or that, under their influence, they adhered to the idea of a substantial difference between a creator spirit and his creation. Quite the contrary, indeed: they refused to make any separation between the visible and the divine, between substance and activity. For Gao Panlong, Heaven was within man himself and it was when this fundamental truth was forgotten that the religious sense of universal order was weakened. He writes:

What our contemporaries call Heaven is no more than the blue expanse above us. They do not know that above the nine heavens and below the nine earths, everything, from the hairs on our skin and the marrow in our bones to all that is to be found within and beyond the limits of the universe, everything is Heaven. Thus, as soon as I have a good thought, Heaven necessarily knows of it. As soon as I have a bad thought, it also knows of that ... Knowing the good, it rewards it with what is good, knowing the bad, it provides retribution with what is bad. The retribution is automatic and follows action as a shadow follows the body.[30]

The truth is that man is one with the universe. Cheng Hao (1032–85) had said: 'The man of worth considers Heaven, Earth and the Ten Thousand Beings as a single and unique substance' (*tiandi wanwu yiti*) and it was an axiom that was often cited. His disciple, Xie Liangzuo (1050–1103), wrote: 'The spirit of man is but one with the universe ... What am I saying – it is but one? It is, on its own, the entire universe.' And Huang Daozhou (1585–1646) writes:

My body and my spirit are not fundamentally two distinct things ... Everything under Heaven is but one single thing and comprises no duality. The sun, the moon, the four seasons, the spirits and gods, Heaven and Earth are but one thing and comprise no duality.[31]

According to a 'Chinese doctor' quoted by Longobardo, 'the spirit is in no way distinct from substance but is the same substance considered in the form of action and government'. The 'King on High' is simply 'the operative virtue of Heaven'.[32] 'Substance and spirit are not two things, but the same considered from the point of view of two modalities.'[33]

Universal dynamism

The Chinese tendency was to deny any opposition between the self and the world, the mind and the body, the divine and the cosmic. Faced with such concepts, some missionaries concluded that the Chinese, whose ancient texts appeared to suggest that they had at one time revered a Supreme Being, had been corrupted by Buddhist idolatry and by the atheistic and materialistic philosophy of the 'new interpreters', the neo-Confucian thinkers of the eleventh and twelfth centuries. However, the reason why the Chinese contemporaries of the missionaries refused to make any radical distinction between nature and its power of organisation and generation was that they never *had* made any such distinction, for Chinese thought never had separated the sensible from the rational, never had imagined any 'spiritual substance distinct from the material', never had conceived of the existence of a world of eternal truths separated from this world of appearances and transitory realities. For the Christians, the inheritors of Greek thought and medieval scholasticism, such distinctions were, in contrast, so fundamental, so self-evident and natural, that their historical character was no longer perceptible. Placing their confidence in 'the light of natural reason', the missionaries endeavoured to warn the Chinese against what they regarded as errors of judgement. They did not realise that they were faced with a conception of the world and modes of thought that were fundamentally different from their own and that these modes of thought related to the morality, the religious attitudes and the social and political order of the Chinese. Chinese philosophy rested upon different bases from European philosophy. Ricci was therefore obliged to devote almost the whole of his great treatise, using every possible argument, to demonstrating the existence of purely spiritual substances. Transposing the Chinese concepts into his own language, he writes: 'If one fuses Heaven and the animating spirit in a single, living substance, it is the most ridiculous nonsense.'[34]

Similarly, in a work published around 1626, the *Countless Proofs that the Master of Heaven Governs the World* (*Zhuzhi qunzheng*), Father Adam Schall von Bell explains that:

the God of the Christians, in opposition to even the most elevated Chinese concepts, is in his substance radically different from Heaven, Earth and the Ten Thousand Beings ... he does not proceed from the Taiji [the cosmic origin], nor does he derive from the *yin* and the *yang*, but, on the contrary, the Taiji and the *yin* and the *yang*, too, were created by him; he created everything and there is nothing that does not obey his rule.[35]

Another example is provided by Father Giulio Aleni, who, before his expulsion in 1639, had been preaching in the south of Fujian province. He also attempted to persuade the Chinese of the errors of their ways. Huang Zhen summarises his preaching as follows:

This doctrine glorifies in an exclusive manner a being who is supposed to have created Heaven and Earth, men and all the other beings. They call him the Master of Heaven. They say that his substance is omnipresent, omniscient and omnipotent. They say that this Master allotted to man an intelligent soul, which they call 'human nature' (*xing*).[36] According to them, it is wrong to say that Heaven and Earth are the Master of Heaven, for Heaven and Earth, the Master of Heaven and man constitute three distinct realities the substances of which cannot be united. They consider that our Chinese thesis according to which the Ten Thousand Beings are one single substance is false; that Wang Yangming's thesis according to which the whole universe, Heaven, Earth and the Ten Thousand Beings, is the product of an innate knowledge (*liangzhi*)[37] is mistaken. This is what has come to upset our traditions, which have been most excellently established for ten thousand generations.[38]

The missionaries not only denounced these confusions but also drew the conclusion that the Chinese were materialistic. For Father Le Comte, the 'new interpreters', that is to say the neo-Confucian thinkers of the eleventh and twelfth centuries,

spoke of the Deity as if it was no more than nature itself, that is to say the force or natural power which produces, arranges and preserves every part of the universe ... It is no longer the sovereign Emperor of Heaven, just, omnipotent, the first of all spirits and the arbiter of all creatures: in their works one finds nothing but a refined atheism and an alienation from all religious worship.[39]

And he also inveighs against the

sect of scholars [the men of letters], of whom it can be said that they pay no more than lip service to God because they are continually repeating that one must worship and obey Heaven, but in their hearts they are a long way from doing so for they give those words an impious meaning which destroys the Deity and stifles any religious feeling.[40]

Other missionaries go even further and deny that the Chinese have ever had any knowledge of God. Longobardo writes: 'Their secret philosophy is pure materialism',[41] and he entitles Section 10 of his treatise: 'That the Chinese have never known any spiritual substance distinct from matter ... but one sole material substance in different degrees'. Father Sabatino de Ursis, summoned to Peking in 1607, is of the same opinion. He writes: 'According to the principles of their philosophy, the Chinese have never known any spiritual substance distinct from matter ... And consequently they have never known either God or the Angels or the Rational Soul.'[42] In his *Chinese Monarchy*, the Jesuit Father, Antonio de Gouvea, who was in China from 1636 to 1677, writes:

The Chinese know nothing about creation, do not believe in the immortality of the soul, do not distinguish the soul of men from those of animals except insofar as they imagine the latter to be more gross and the former more refined; they recognise no Angels or Spirits pure and simple, only material and corporeal ones ... They recognise no paradise or hell, no punishments or rewards in the other life, because they believe that everything is annihilated; they neither fear nor hope for anything.[43]

The Franciscan, Antonio de Caballero, says that the sacrifices to the Sovereign on High, that is to say the imperial sacrifices to Heaven, 'are in effect addressed to the material principle of the universe and constitute a categorical and veritable idolatry'.[44]

However, in one sense, from the Chinese point of view it was the missionaries who were the real materialists since they deprived the universe of its invisible forces, turning it into brute matter directed from outside and lacking the spontaneous intelligence that all creatures display. Huang Wendao from Fuzhou demands:

Is it reasonable to use the pretext of the Master of Heaven to declare that Heaven and Earth are totally lacking in intelligence, that the sun, moon and planets are brute matter, that the gods of the Mountains and Rivers, the gods of the Soil and the Harvests are devils and that it is not necessary to make sacrifices to ancestors?[45]

Having set out the missionaries' teaching on creation and the birth of Jesus, Yang Guangxian exclaims:

Even to such lengths do they go with their extravagant and baseless claims! Heaven is the product of the combination of the two primordial energies, the *yin* and *yang*. It is not true that it was created. Confucius said: 'Why should Heaven speak? The four seasons follow upon their course and all beings are born.'[46] If Heaven had been created by a Master of Heaven it would be no more than brute and insensible matter. How could it give birth to the Ten Thousand Beings? However divine (*shen*) their Master of Heaven may be, he is in reality a form of energy (*qi*) produced by the two primordial energies. Does it make any sense at all to say that he was able to create the two primordial energies which give birth to all beings?[47]

In short, the spirits and gods are simply a more refined and subtle form of the universal energy which, through the intermediary of its two opposed and complementary modalities, the *yin* and the *yang*, is at the origin of all things in the world.

To speak of fetishism, idolatry or materialism, as the missionaries did, was to make no effort to analyse the Chinese idea in such a way as to penetrate their meaning more deeply or attempt to seize upon their originality.

Believing that the universe possesses within itself its own organisational principles and its own creative energy, the Chinese maintained something that was quite scandalous from the point of view of scholastic reason, namely that 'matter' itself is intelligent – not, clearly enough, with a conscious and reflective intelligence as we usually conceive it, but with a spontaneous intelligence which makes it possible for the *yin* and the *yang* to come together and guides the infinite combinations of these two opposite sources of energy.[48] It is this form of elemental intelligence that Ricci rejects in his great treatise. The man of letters whom he introduces into this work says: 'When the *li* [the principle of order inherent in the universal energy] goes into action to produce the *yin* and the *yang*, there is a kind of spontaneous intelligence at work' (*ziran zhi lingjue*). But for Ricci, what is of an inferior order cannot give birth to something of a superior order. God, who is pure spirit, was able to create the world; the *li*, which, he says, is only an attribute, not a substance, cannot do so.[49]

The Barbarians wish to separate the creator from creation, the subject from the object of its action, the active spirit from brute matter. But that is not the model according to which the universe in reality functions. Huang Zhen writes:

The mode of action [the Dao] of Heaven and Earth can be summed up in a word. It is not double. How could it be controlled by the Master of Heaven, Yesu? How could the universe have been created by him in seven days? In effect, it is through the perfection of this mode of action of Heaven and Earth that the Ten Thousand Beings are born... How could it be something produced by the Master of Heaven, Yesu?[50]

In other words, there is too much spontaneity in natural mechanisms for them to involve the intervention of a reflective, deliberating will analogous to that of an artisan.

For Huang Zhen, the Dao penetrates and informs everything in the world. It inspires the Saints and the true Sages, simple folk and also the animals as they pursue their lives. He writes:

Everything between Heaven and Earth, the coursing water, the flowers in bloom ... participates in the flow of this principle of universal order (the *li*)... If even the disciples of Confucius have not managed to understand that, how could these barbarian monsters be capable of doing so?... Is it knowing Heaven to say, as the Barbarian Ricci does, that the Master of Heaven came down to be born on earth and that he was Yesu, that Yesu then returned to Heaven and once more became the Master of Heaven? Is it knowing Heaven to know how many hells and paradises there are piled up one on top of another?[51]

To show the Chinese how absurd their ideas were and to guide them to the true religion, the missionaries used in their arguments the static concepts of Aristotelian philosophy: those of form, matter, soul, substance, accident. And it was also with such concepts in mind that they tried to understand the philosophical traditions of China. But since the Chinese imagined the universe as a continuous process of development, the notion of an opposition between being and appearance was alien to them and they recognised only dynamic notions.

Longobardo, attempting to explain what they understood by the idea of *li*, the principle of internal and immanent order, writes:

By this they mean Being, Substance and the Entity of things, believing there to be one substance that is infinite, eternal, uncreated, incorruptible, with no beginning and no end. It is not only the physical principle of heaven, earth and the other corporeal things, but also the moral principle of virtues, customs and other spiritual things.[52]

And he warns against likening this concept to the idea of God:

I can well imagine that some people might think that this Li or Taikie [Taiji] is our God because they attribute to it qualities and perfections which can only belong to God. Take care not to allow yourselves to be dazzled by such specious descriptions which conceal hidden poison. For if you penetrate to the root of the problem, you will see that this Li is nothing other than primary matter.[53]

In contrast, Leibniz, who learned of the Chinese ideas through Longobardo's treatise, denied that the *li* could be primary matter. He wrote: 'I do not see how it could be possible for the Chinese to derive from primary matter – as our philosophers describe it in their schools – which is a purely passive thing without control or form, the origin of all organisation and forms'; and he also writes that 'one should reflect above all upon their *li* or rule, which is the first actor and reason for other things and which I believe to correspond to our deity'.[54]

But there is no possible solution: the Chinese concept cannot be an equivalent of primary matter since it is not 'a purely passive thing, without control or form'. Nor is it an equivalent of our deity since it is not endowed with understanding and acts without reflection 'solely through its own propensity and through a natural order'.[55]

The word *li*, which originally referred to the idea of the organisation of space,[56] appears very early on to have acquired the sense of natural order not imposed from outside but inherent within nature – the kind that is discernible in the rings of a tree trunk, the veins of a stone or those of a leaf. It is the idea of a principle of development inherent in the universe and in all beings. It is worth noting that Wang Yangming, the most influential philosopher of the sixteenth century, fell ill as a result of attempting, at the suggestion of Zhu Xi, to penetrate the principle of development in bamboos, in front of which he had remained seated in contemplation for a number of days on end.[57] It has been suggested, on an analogy with modern science, that *li* should be translated 'programme',[58] but the notion is clearly intuitive rather than scientific. It is a concept inseparable from that of *qi*, which is not necessarily either spirit or matter but may equally well be either. The *qi* is universal energy, uncreated and omnipresent, which fills space, in which it is invisible (*wu*), or becomes visible by condensing itself and taking the form of visible bodies (*you*). The *qi* is by nature active and in a state of constant evolution by reason of its division into the *yin* and the *yang* and the combinations which give rise to the association of the *yin* and the *yang*; its action consists of condensing itself to form substances and bodies the various elements of which must necessarily sooner or later return to the undifferentiated mass of universal energy. Invisible forces and spirits, and human intelligence, are all nothing but more or less subtle and refined forms of the universal energy, while visible bodies are the grosser forms produced by its accumulation.[59]

In contrast to Ricci, who had ascribed to the terms *wu* and *you* the meaning of being and nothingness, Longobardo, who as a result of his inquiry into Chinese ideas had become better informed on the matter, had understood that in reality these two terms denoted the two aspects that it was possible for the 'universal substance' to take. He explains that *you* is 'that which has consistency, *wu* that which can neither be seen nor touched and which is very simple, very pure, very subtle, as we Christians conceive the spiritual substance to be', but it is not spiritual substance

for (1) it cannot exist on its own, given that it is but one of the aspects of the primeval air [the *qi*]; (2) it supports all material accidents and thus composes the being of all things: it is both their being and their substance; (3) because all things which appear to be spiritual are called *ki* [*qi*] ... by all the philosophers both ancient and modern and above all by Confucius, who, when asked by his disciples to explain what the spirits were, replied that they were nothing but air.[60]

Longobardo also writes:

The Chinese have known nothing of an infinite power producing something from nothing. They have only known of a universal, immense and infinite substance from which emanated the Taikie [Taiji] or the primeval air which contains within it the universal substance and which, sometimes through movement, sometimes through rest, assumes various qualities and accidents and thus becomes the immediate matter of things.[61]

Father Le Comte, for his part, writes:

They recognise in Nature nothing but Nature itself, defining it as the principle of movement and rest.[62] They say that it is *par excellence* Reason [the *li*] which produces order in the various parts of the universe and which is the cause for all change.[63]

There is no reason that is external to the world, no eternal being apart from becoming. Wei Yuan (1794–1857) writes:

Heaven turns towards the left [when one looks towards the south] while the sun, the moon and the five planets turn towards the right. It is from the close combination of the chain and the web that order and elegance (*wen*) are born. That is why, in man, the right eye is more piercing, the right hand stronger. A man's hair, a spider's web, the spirals of a snail's shell, the spreading stems of marrows and melons – all these things achieve a perfect elegance (*zhang*) by turning to the right. And it is precisely in this opposition to the [direction in which] Heaven turns that lies their supreme obedience to the order of Heaven.[64]

The universe owes its order entirely to the alternations and combinations of the *yin* and *yang*. So there are no immutable realities nor any Master of Heaven as conceived by the missionaries, nor is there any immortal soul. Xu Dashou puts it as follows:

The Barbarians say: 'I believe in eternal life.' It is easy to see from this that they have understood absolutely nothing at all about the meaning of the word 'life'. Confucianism speaks of a ceaseless proliferation of life (*shengsheng*).[65] It does so by referring to nature's uninterrupted flow to which there is no end. Buddhism speaks of an absence of life [an absence of production]. It does so by referring to that departure and that absolute rupture [which constitutes deliverance] which is like a disappearance that leaves no traces. Taoism knows very well that the universe cannot maintain itself indefinitely but [being convinced that one can] deepen one's roots and strengthen one's trunk, it preaches 'prolonging life', making use of the two words *chang sheng* . . . to lead people to an understanding of the mysteries. Now, these people, with their vicious ideas, have changed the expression 'long life' (*changsheng*) into 'eternal life' (*changsheng*).[66] But life is a springing-forth (*qi*). How could a springing-forth be eternal?[67]

Ultimately, what the Chinese criticisms of Christian ideas bring into question are the mental categories and types of opposition which have played a fundamental role in Western thought ever since the Greeks: being and becoming, the intelligible and the sensible, the spiritual and the corporeal. Does all this not mean that Chinese thought is quite simply of a different type, with its own particular articulations and its own radical originality?

Creation

The missionaries took it upon themselves to refute two Chinese errors: the ideas that (1) the universe was the product of an omnipresent, uncreated primordial energy and (2) that all the beings in the world were, as the universe itself was, the products of natural and spontaneous mechanisms. In his work in Chinese entitled *On the True Origin of the Ten Thousand Beings* (*Wanwu zhenyuan*), Father Aleni puts it as follows: 'Heaven and Earth cannot have created men and other beings on their own. The primordial energy cannot have separated Heaven and Earth on its own.'[68]

Such absurd ideas ought not to have withstood for an instant the logical demonstrations of the missionaries who, for their part, were convinced that they possessed an overriding argument that proved the existence of a creator God: namely, that nothing can create itself, every work implies a worker. 'Houses do not build themselves,' Ricci wrote, 'they are constructed by builders. So Heaven and Earth cannot have made themselves spontaneously.'[69] All the works written in Chinese by the missionaries return to this argument and develop it. The order and perfection of the world and all its beings are the proof of the existence of a creator God. But oddly enough, the argument, instead of convincing, seemed ridiculous. Father Longobardo writes:

When we would tell them that the Xangti [the Sovereign on High] was the creator of the world in the way that we conceive him to be, they would laugh and scoff at us, being quite convinced that, in accordance with the principles of their sect, the Xangti is Heaven itself, or is the virtue and power of Heaven, and that consequently he cannot have existed before Heaven, but only when Heaven came into existence or after it did so. And if we tried to carry the dispute further and prove in our own way that the Architect comes before the house that he builds, they would interrupt us, stopping us short by saying: 'Well then, since your God is our Xangti, you have no need to explain to us what he is since we know, better than you do, what the Xangti is!'[70]

Building is a task for a drudge, not worthy of a power as eminent as that which presides over the ceaseless activity of creating and transforming (*zaohua*) the universe:

Ricci says: 'Houses do not build themselves. A builder is necessary.' But a builder only works to orders. So who ordered the Master of Heaven to construct Heaven and Earth? The builder is not the master of the house he builds. Now, according to you, the Master of Heaven is both the builder and the master.[71]

And Xu Dashou writes: 'How is it possible to go so far as to denigrate Heaven to the point of likening it to a workman and, quite without basis, attribute to him the creation of man and woman?' It is childish to transpose to the domain of the cosmos and universal order a line of argument suggested by the activities of a human builder:

Their books also say that Heaven, Earth and the heavenly spirits were all created from nothing by the Master of Heaven in six days and six nights. So their Master of Heaven is certainly inferior to the original virtue of Heaven (*qianyuan*), which acts faster than the eye can detect, since he was exhausted after six days and six nights.[72]

To prove the existence of a creator God, Ricci, in *The True Meaning of the Master of Heaven*, had appealed to Aristotle's four causes, explaining that God is the supreme, efficient and final cause.[73] In a dialogue produced by an author hostile to the Christian theses, a convert is introduced who, attempting to impress his adversary, counters his arguments with Aristotle's four causes, but without producing any proofs:

The Chinese Christian said: 'Everything has an efficient, a formal, a material and a final cause. If there was no Master of Heaven to direct the universe, what could Heaven, Earth and the Ten Thousand Beings have been formed from in the beginning?'

The author replies:

'The *yin* and the *yang* fuse [in cosmic space] and the Ten Thousand Beings are born through a process of transformation.[74] You ask who is in charge of all this?

Even the spirits and the Saints were unable to find a name for it. That is why they were obliged to call it Taiji [the cosmic origin]. When Ricci says that the Master of Heaven created the world in seven days, that implies feeling and knowledge, action and an object of the action. The mechanism of creation–transformation (*zaohua*) cannot be like that.' Thereupon the convert burst out laughing loudly. He said: 'The Taiji is nothing but an empty principle. Ricci settled the matter when he said that it was of the order of accident rather than substance.[75] How could [an empty principle] have created Heaven, Earth and the Ten Thousand Beings?' The other replied: 'All Ricci's citations of the term "Sovereign on High" stem from an amalgamation or vague resemblance. The truth is, he does not know what Heaven and the Sovereign on High really are. How could he know what the Taiji is? The Taiji is the source of all principles of order. But one cannot speak merely of principles of order: it is also the origin of the universal energy. But one cannot speak merely of universal energy: if one goes right back in time, it has no beginning yet can cause the beginning of beings. If one goes forward in time, it has no end but can cause the end of beings. Ricci is blinkered and judges everything by his own yardstick, saying: "It is impossible for a principle which is in the void not to fall", and "In the beginning, how could it give birth to beings without being set in motion?"[76] He also says "Take the principle of a cart. Why does it not give birth to a cart?"[77] and a lot of other crude nonsense which any sensible man would deem ridiculous. If one returned to Ricci the same kind of arguments on the subject of his Master of Heaven, what explanation would he give?'[78]

The difference between the philosophical ideas inherited from Ancient Greece and those of the Chinese emerges clearly here. According to Aristotle, it is normal for all things to be at rest, whereas for the Chinese, in contrast, universal dynamism is the primary assumption. The Taiji, or original mass of energy in fusion, contains within itself the principles of organisation which are at the origin of the universe and its beings. Ricci could not understand how the Chinese ideas could be dynamic ones. For him, the cosmic origin (Taiji) is an abstract concept; the principle of organisation (*li*) is the equivalent of the Platonic *eidos*.

A certain Huang Wendao attacks the notion that the world could have been created by a personal god because, to him, that idea appears to be in contradiction to the ideas of spontaneous organisation and natural dynamism that are so fundamental in China. He writes:

I have read the books of these foreigners. Their essential idea is that [of the existence] of a Master of Heaven. Their principal rule consists in overcoming the seven [deadly sins]. They consider that prayer consists in repentance and asking for good fortune and that the ultimate destinies are paradise or hell. [Laozi's] *Daode jing* says: 'There is one thing which formed itself out of chaos and which in the beginning gave birth to Heaven and Earth. I do not know what its name is, so being unable to do otherwise, I call it the Dao.' But our Confucianism judges that concept to be still too mysterious and not really to correspond to what the

Dao is. *A fortiori* nor does [the idea of these people correspond to it] for they add, over and above Heaven, a master who is represented by statues, who is endowed with a will and takes action and now hides in the highest and purest regions of Heaven, now descends into the world of men, now is condemned as a criminal and reviled, and now comes back to life and ascends into Heaven.[79]

What the Chinese reject is the idea of a conscious will at the origin of the world and organising it. The opposition with Christian ideas even emerges from the remarks of the missionaries themselves. Ricci writes: 'If they finally came to realise that the Taiji is the first, substantial, intelligent and infinite principle, we should agree to call it God and none other.'[80] And Longobardo, on the subject of the heavenly principle of order, observes:

It is through its operation that all things are ordered, with the weight and dimensions in accordance with their particular state, but it is without intelligence or reflection and operates solely by virtue of its own propensity and natural order.[81]

The Chinese texts do, in effect, state that Heaven acts without intention (*wuxin*) and in total impartiality: it is devoid of egoism. That is the source of its dignity and greatness. Its action is entirely spontaneous and impersonal. From the point of view of the Chinese concepts, this was a superior form of intelligence, but the missionaries denied that, since, for them, will, reflection and intelligence were closely associated.

Attempting to refute the concept of the Taiji, Ricci had written in *The True Meaning of the Master of Heaven*: 'I have heard it said that the people of worth of Antiquity respected the Master of Heaven, not the Taiji. If this Taiji was the ancestor of the Ten Thousand Beings, why did the ancient Saints never mention it?'[82] Xu Dashou's retort was:

What audacity on the part of these Barbarians, to dare to criticise our Saints in this way and to publish such works contradicting the teaching of our ancient masters! Besides, in the *Book of Changes* (the *Yijing*) it is written: 'The Taiji gave birth to the two principles [the *yin* and the *yang*], which produced the four symbols,[83] which gave birth to the eight trigrams,[84] which gave birth to the Ten Thousand Beings.' These Barbarians who speak in this way were born blind.[85]

As the ideas of the Chinese are so alien to him and as he cannot conceive of the world as the product of an evolutionary process, Riccio refuses to go into them, declaring: 'I have seen the diagram [of Zhou Dunyi] on the "Cosmic origin without an origin" (*Wuji er taiji*): it is just a collection of strange symbols chosen at random.'[86] The author of one refutation writes:

The Barbarians say: 'Your Taiji is nothing but a couple of characters, *li* [the principle of organisation] and *qi* [the uncreated universal energy]. It is not intelligent. So it cannot direct the ten thousand transformations.' My reply would be that the *yi* [the change which produces the infinite combinations of the *yin* and the *yang*][87] is a natural power (*benxing*) of perfect intelligence. Without reflection, without intention, in absolute calm, without agitation, it reacts and its effects are communicated. But this intelligence *does not* really *direct* the ten thousand transformations; if there was some being directing them, those transformations would all be good and fortunate whereas they sometimes turn out to be bad and bitter.[88]

The Christian idea of a personal God, now angry, now merciful, who created the world and governs and intervenes in the details of individual existences and who has a history since he became incarnate in a particular place at a particular time, is countered by the Chinese idea of an impersonal Heaven which is at one with the order of nature and its limitless power of production. For the Chinese, there is something divine in the very functioning of the universe, but it is a divine quality that is immanent in the world. There is no being or truth which transcends it.

Xu Dashou contrasts Christian creation, which he calls 'a personal, external creation starting from the uncreated' with the Chinese concept of a continuous creation–transformation which is 'an impartial and spontaneous non-created creation'.[89]

The disagreement between the Chinese men of letters and the missionaries did not stem solely from the fact that the latter preached of a creator God while the former imagined the universe to be regulated by an immanent principle of order manifesting itself at even the most elementary level. It was also occasioned by their radically different cosmological concepts. The missionaries taught of the existence of a static world, created once and for all and limited in both space and time, concepts which they tied in with their theory of the existence of a creator God. The Chinese, on the other hand, believed the world to be the product of a ceaseless evolution, limitless in extension and duration. Xu Dashou writes:

These people say that the universe has only a certain number of layers [these are Aristotle's crystalline spheres] and that it has a size limited in all directions . . . It is as if they were insisting upon setting up walls in the great void in order to close the universe in. How could the great void possibly accommodate such limitations? They even go so far as to claim that from Antiquity down to the present day this world is only seven thousand years old and that before that there was no world . . . To speak in such a way is to recognise a present but not a past . . . They also say that the number of souls is limited and that, apart from them, there is no thread of life.[90]

Not only was this Master of Heaven, whom they claimed to be wiser and more powerful than all the great Saints of China and all the Buddhas, obliged to labour for six days and six nights to create the world – which showed how limited his powers were – but, furthermore, he was not capable of filling space since, according to the missionaries' astronomical concepts, he left half of it outside the nine Aristotelian crystalline spheres.[91]

Besides, these Barbarians' picture of the world was quite ridiculous:

They also say that the twelve heavens, which resemble balls, are forever at rest upon the Master of Heaven's lap. But where, I wonder, does the body of the Master of Heaven himself rest? They also say that the earth inhabited by men floats upon the surface of the waters, occupying the smaller area; that the Master of Heaven, in his compassion, spared this little ball of mud from being totally engulfed by the waters so as to provide man with a place to live . . . These are the absurd things that they say.[92]

It was quite natural for the Chinese, who were accustomed to the concepts of a vast duration in the evolution of the universe or universes, to be shocked by the recentness of the date of creation taught by the missionaries. At the beginning of the eighth century, the Buddist monk, Yixing, had calculated on the basis of numerological considerations that the beginnings of the present universe had taken place around 97 million years earlier.[93] Equally, it is quite natural that they should have regarded the missionaries' teaching on the end of the world at the time of the Last Judgement as fantastical nonsense. In his letter to the censor, Yan Maoyou, Huang Zhen gives a version of this teaching which is probably a relatively faithful reflection of Father Aleni's pronouncements on the subject:

When Heaven and Earth are on the point of being destroyed, the Master of Heaven will appear in person in space, surrounded by countless heavenly spirits. At that moment, all the dead, ever since the remotest Antiquity, will recover their souls and be reborn. One by one they will be judged. The good will return to paradise with their own bodies of flesh and the bad will go to hell in the same fashion. Then, for all eternity, there will be no further change. At that point, although Heaven will exist, it will no longer revolve. The sun and the moon will no longer shine. Although there will still be an Earth, it will no longer be able to produce and all the plants will disappear . . . Such is the insane nonsense that they put about.[94]

The story of earthly paradise and Adam's fall contradicts the Chinese idea of a gradual development of the arts and of the human order. Chen Houguang writes:

It was only after a gradual arrangement of the wild world that men eventually found their place. We have never heard tell of a great happiness in the beginning with sorrows afterwards. By first deceiving and upsetting men's minds, they seek to blind our worthy people and get them to follow them.[95]

Buddhist criticisms

Jesus secretly studied Buddhism; but he could not penetrate its won-
drous hidden depths.
          Taiji jashûron (1648). Cited in *Deus Destroyed*, p. 231

The missionaries believed Buddhism to be no more than a vulgar idolatry and they refused to make any effort to understand a doctrine which
they regarded as inspired by the devil. In reply to a letter from Yu
Chunxi, who urged him not to attack Buddhism before reading the
Buddhist texts, Ricci had said: 'Since entering China, I have learned of
only Yao, Shun, the Duke of Zhou and Confucius [that is to say the Confucian tradition] and I do not intend to change.'[96] The missionaries frequently declared that they wished to have no dealings or contacts with
the Buddist monks. Nicolas Trigault writes: 'Our Fathers should, so far
as possible, avoid the company of this wretched race.'[97] For them, the
Buddhist religion could be summed up as a cult of statues and an absurd
belief in metempsychosis. But there was no more fetishism involving
images and statues among the Buddhist faithful than there was among the
Christians of Europe and the term 'metempsychosis', which indicates a
belief that the same soul successively animates a series of different
human or animal bodies, was not at all appropriate since Buddhism
denies the reality of the individual and any idea of a permanent soul. The
Buddhists held the theory of *nirâtman*, or the unreality of the self,
according to which beings were never any more than temporary aggre-
gates. The term 'transmigration' is much more suitable as a translation of
the word *samsâra*, which evokes the flux of births and rebirths. But
Ricci's knowledge and that of his companions stopped at Pythagoras,
and it was their belief that the ideas of Pythagoras had travelled to India
from Greece and from there to China and Japan.

In truth, the philosophical bases of Buddhism entirely escaped them
and there lurked, unseen by them, behind what they took to be superstitions pure and simple, postulates quite different from those upon
which Christian ideas are based.

In the second chapter of *The True Meaning of the Master of Heaven*,
Ricci had poured scorn upon the Buddhist ideas according to which being
emerged from nothingness and had accused Buddhism of aiming solely
for nothingness.[98] He explained that nothingness is the absolute anti-
thesis of being. So neither nature nor bodies nor beings nor substances
could develop out of the void (*kong*) as the Buddhists held, or out of
nothingness (*wu*) as the Taoists claimed.[99]

But what Buddhism teaches is simply the unreality of the world of phenomena and the existence of an absolute which is above and beyond all limitations and co-substantial to beings, each of which possesses in the profoundest depths of its spirit, the nature of a Buddha. Buddha is the 'awakened one', the one who was the first to see that a false belief in the reality of the self and the world was the cause of the attachment which kept beings in a state of illusion and confined them to the sufferings of their successive existences. The world perceived through the senses stems neither from being nor from nothingness: it is a pure fantasy (*mâyâ*) and devoid of being in itself. It is empty (*sûnya:kong*). As for the Dao of the Taoists, the inexhaustible receptable of all differences and particular realities, it is similar to the Buddhist absolute because it consists in an absence of all characteristics (*wu*).[100]

It is only in a state of the deepest calm, when all distinctions disappear, that a being can attain the absolute as conceived by Buddhism.

The Christian and the Buddhist images speak for themselves, revealing the fundamental opposition of the two religions. The Christian saints sometimes raised their eyes heavenwards, while the Buddhas are seated with half-closed eyes, their gaze turned in on themselves, their faces lit by a half smile: the respective images convey two different worlds of thought and feeling. For the Christians, the only truth, the only being, the only happiness lie outside this world, in the kingdom of God. For the Buddhists, the absolute is to be found nowhere but in ourselves. Christian ecstasy, which is a dramatic struggle between the soul which seeks to become united with God and the body which holds it prisoner, stands in opposition to the Buddhist states of deep calm in which all distinctions between the self and the absolute are abolished. In that it declared that each one of us is a Buddha unrecognised by himself and that the absolute constitutes our fundamental nature, Buddhism was regarded as a dreadful heresy by the Christians: it seemed to be making a god out of each individual. But that view takes no account of the fact that the realisation of the absolute within the individual is, precisely, incompatible with the persistence of the illusion that a self or individual soul exists at all.

A number of twentieth-century authors have underlined the differences between the Buddhist and the Christian ideas. Masao Abe writes: 'For Buddhists, the idea of a personal God is the hardest thing to understand in Christianity.'[101] Similarly, according to Buddhadâsa, a Thai Buddhist:

In the religious language of Buddhism, God[102] is neither a person nor a spirit nor a body nor a body-with-a-spirit. It is simply impersonal nature devoid of any self. It has neither attributes nor form nor dimensions... It is endowed with no characteristics that would make it possible to define it.

Now, 'this God of the Christians, who has created the world, has the characteristics, feelings and thoughts of a person'.[103] A true 'God', a mysterious power beyond all human description, would have demeaned himself by creating the visible world.[104]

Furthermore, while for the Christians the world is a unique and real creation, for the Buddhists it is not created and not real, situated in a space and a time which become dilute as they are infinitely multiplied: there is a plurality of worlds and of times.[105]

The limitless multiplicity of worlds in Buddhism was, for the monks and followers of that religion, an argument against the idea of a creation limited to this world alone: the monk, Tongrong, describes the universe in terms which would be acceptable to a modern astronomer, for stars are indeed born and do live and die. He explains that:

Space, worlds and beings have neither a beginning nor an end if one considers them, not in themselves and individually, but as a whole. From this point of view they are inexhaustible. They proliferate unceasingly and, in the course of incalculable cosmic periods, pass through successive phases of formation (*cheng*), stability (*zhu*), disintegration (*huai*) and return to the void (*kong*). The worlds are inexhaustible although one particular one may be in the process of formation, another of disintegration, another in a stable state, while yet another has already returned to nothingness ... If this particular world disintegrates, it does not mean that all the others are doing the same ... It is like the situation that obtains with a town and its houses. Even if some of them burn down in one quarter, later on they will be rebuilt just as they used to be ... Seen from a distance, the town will appear no different and it will not be possible to distinguish the houses that were destroyed from those that were not. From a point of view in which all differences are as one, space, beings and worlds are inexhaustible ... and consequently have no beginning and no end.

Tongrong also criticises Ricci for pursuing his deductions and calculations on the universe and its creatures right through to the limit, in a ridiculous fashion, taking into consideration nothing but discursive thought or immediate evidence. He explains that this is what accounts for the obscure and incomprehensible ideas from which Ricci himself cannot extricate himself, and for his mistaken belief in a Master of Heaven without beginning or end, capable of producing the universe and all its beings.[106]

There is no *creation*, since creation has always been there and everything is in the mind. For anybody who has managed to understand this, the sensible and the absolute worlds are but one.

The first Buddhist monk to respond to Matteo Ricci's attacks was the great master, Zhuhong. He criticises the missionaries' ideas using arguments taken from the Buddhist cosmology:

An old man told me: 'There are men from a foreign country who have invented the doctrine of the Master of Heaven. Why do you not attack it?' I replied: 'In my opinion, it is a good thing to teach people to respect Heaven. Why should I attack it?' 'But', the old man insisted, 'the fact is that these people seek to use it to change our ways and customs and at the same time to destroy our Buddhist Law; and many worthy men of letters and excellent people among our friends are rallying to their doctrine.' Then he showed me one of their books and I was anxious to refute a few of their theses.

Although these people exalt the cult of the Master of Heaven, they have, in fact, understood nothing at all about the nature of Heaven.[107] If one consults the Buddhist sûtra, what they call the Master of Heaven (*tianzhu*) is the King of Heaven, *Daoli* [the heaven of the 33 gods or *Trâyastrimsa*, the second of the six heavens of the world of desire or *kâmadhâtu*, the dwelling-place of Sakra Davendra, known as *tianzhu*, which is a translation of *devapati*, that is to say 'Master of gods'].[108] There, there is a little kiliocosmos and consequently one thousand Masters of Heaven and, above it, a medium-sized kiliocosmos, that is a million Masters of Heaven and, still higher above this, a large kiliocosmos, that is a thousand million Masters of Heaven. And the one who presides over the whole collection of these kiliocosmoses is the great Brahmâ, the king of the gods. The one whom these people call Master of Heaven, revered to the highest degree and inferior to none is, in comparison to the god Brahmâ, like one of the 1,800 princes of ancient China in comparison to the son of Heaven of the Zhou. The Master of Heaven that they know is but one of thousands of millions of Masters of Heaven. And furthermore, they know nothing of all the other heavens of the world of desire and, above that, those of the world of appearances (*rûpadhâtu*), and even higher up, those of the world of the absence of appearances (*arûpyadhâtu*).

Thus, they also say that the Master of Heaven has no body, no colour and no voice. So what they call the Master of Heaven is none other than the principle of universal order. How could he possibly direct ministers and peoples, give orders and apportion rewards and punishments? Although these people may be intelligent, they have not read the Buddhist sûtra. So it is not surprising that their reasoning is all wrong![109]

It should be added that, according to Buddhist ideas, every god – even a supreme God – is necessarily inferior to the Buddha, for the gods remain subject to transmigration and stem from what is conditioned. Rebirth as a god is one of the six possible ways of being reborn: as gods, men, asura (a kind of spirit), infernal beings, starving devils, or animals. Only the Buddhas have managed to escape from a conditioned state and from the cycle of rebirths and deaths.

When pressed by Huang Zhen to refute the doctrines of the missionaries, the Buddhist monk, Total Enlightenment,[110] observed that these people, having set up a Master of Heaven in whose name they fought against Buddhism, in fact knew absolutely nothing about Buddhism. He consequently saw no reason to refute them. However, seeing that these people were declaring that all they were attacking was Buddhism and that they criticised the Buddhist vow which was to endeavour to save all beings, he eventually decided to reply.

Total Enlightenment regards the missionaries' beliefs as a typical example of an attachment to false ideas. The truth is that:

they cling to the idea that the Master of Heaven is the Master of Heaven, that the Buddha is the Buddha, that beings are beings . . . They resort to distinctions between the self and others, this and that, yes and no. That is their fundamental error . . . If they were not so attached to the idea of a Master of Heaven, they would not be attached to the idea of a Buddha either nor to the idea of beings, and then they would begin to understand the profound thought of our Buddhism and the meaning of the expression 'to save all beings'. Seeking to refute Buddhism as they do, while at the same time being attached to false ideas, they in effect attack themselves, destroy themselves, refute themselves. It is as the sûtra says: 'Heretics are intelligent but they have no wisdom.'[111]

In reply to Ricci's charge that Buddhism had no foundation other than nothingness, Total Enlightenment cites Emperor Hongwu's preface to the Sûtra of the Heart (*Hrdayasûtra*), in which the founder of the Ming dynasty explains that the Buddha is not unreal (*kong:sûnya*); it is the phenomena of the world that are unreal: once the unreality of phenomena is eliminated, what remains is basic nature, that is to say our nature of a Buddha. Total Enlightenment goes on to say:

All retributions, all transmigrations stem from the fact that one has been incapable of penetrating one's own nature and that, in consequence, one produces false ideas. If their Master of Heaven did not realise that himself, he too is no more than an individual who floats or sinks, blown about on all three worlds.[112] How could he give man a soul? These people are attached to empty words and illusions. They derive satisfaction by thinking of the joys of paradise instead of concentrating upon the sole, real and fundamental thing, namely our basic nature.[113]

For Buddhism, all the realities of the sensible world are devoid of being in themselves because they are impermanent and composite and are therefore subject to decomposition, causing pain. The only reality that is not composite is the absolute, which the Buddhas attained by passing beyond the relative at the end of incalculable cosmic periods of time. *Nirvâna* is an extinction in which beings are fused with the absolute. At that point they escape from the painful, ceaseless cycle of rebirths and deaths caused by their attachment to what is relative. They are delivered for ever. The Christians are a long way from ever achieving this, victims as they are of their belief in the reality of the self and the reality of the sensible world. Precisely by affirming the existence of a Master of Heaven and attributing to him a will and other positive qualities, they reveal themselves to be profoundly steeped in error.

To the monk, Tongrong, the doctrine of the Master of Heaven seems the very epitome of a vulgar heresy based on an attachment to what is relative. Since the Master of Heaven of the Barbarians is endowed with a personality and clearly defined virtues (omnipotence, omniscience and infinite mercy), he cannot be identified with the absolute. It is contradictory to say that he has no beginning and no end and at the same time to attribute particular qualities to him. The Christians' Master of Heaven is just like all the rest: a figment of the imagination, for everything is in the mind: plants, animals, Heaven, Earth. All these are the object of distinctions made through discursive thought. But if this discursive thought and these distinctions are suppressed, that is the Dao (the absolute). The whole world of appearances then merges with the absolute, which is without beginning and without end. For whoever manages to penetrate the illusory nature of this world, which is the product of our own mental activity, the 'sensible' and the absolute are but one and the same thing.[114]

The monk, Purun, of Hangzhou, is another who regards the doctrine of the Master of Heaven as no more than a vulgar heresy. He explains that:

these people who, to make a good impression, resort to technological expertise and invent miracles in order to get others to believe in their vicious ideas, these people have not understood that everything is in the mind and is of a single substance [that of our basic spirit]. That is why they cling to the idea of realities external to the mind and declare that the Ten Thousand Beings of the world were produced by a Master of Heaven.[115]

Xu Dashou is of the opinion that the Barbarians have stolen the expression 'without beginning or end' from the Buddhist texts. But the Buddhist expression refers to the absolute which is the true substance of all the phenomenal world while, in contrast, when used by the Barbarians, it implies an attachment to what is relative.

There are thus three possibilities. Either (1) this 'without beginning or end' is a principle of universal order, in which case there seems to be no reason why it should suddenly give birth to the Master of Heaven, and if it did so there must have been a time when he did not exist; or (2) this 'without beginning or end' is wisdom, in which case it is the basic substance of our spirit, something possessed by all men and impossible for these people to appropriate as their particular property; or (3) this 'without beginning or end' stems from discursive knowledge, in which case it implies a subject and an object, a time of happening and a duration – so how could it know no beginning or end?

Then, on the subject of the dogma of the Trinity:

> In addition [to the thesis of the Master of Heaven possessing three souls],[116] these people hold to the thesis of the non-identity and non-difference of the Master of Heaven's single nature in three persons. If I had not read the Buddhist books, I would have considered that admirable and subtle. But who could fail to see that they have quite simply stolen from Buddhism the idea of the three bodies of the Buddha – the spiritual body, the body of retribution and the body of transformation – and that they have totally misinterpreted it?

> If the Master of Heaven possesses three souls, one vegetative, one sensitive and one rational, such a mixture is in contradiction to the perfection that is ascribed to him.[117]

Similar criticisms are advanced by the Japanese apostate, Fabian Fucan, who points out that the Buddha's spiritual body is beyond all differentiation.[118] It is therefore superior to the God of the foreigners who, for his part, is endowed with positive qualities. The word *mu* (*wu* in Chinese: an absence of all characteristics) is a word which the followers of the Deus[119] will never be able to understand. If there is wisdom and virtue, there is love and hatred. If the Deus feels love and hatred, he does not deserve to be placed on the same level as the Buddhist 'thusness'. To say that the Deus possesses this or that quality is, by the same token, to make him full of defects. The ultimate reality is invisible, inaudible, intangible, inexpressible. It is from this lack of differentiation that all differences are born. And in support of this, Fucan cites Laozi's *Daode jing*, one of the most famous Taoist texts: 'The Dao gives birth to the one, the one to the two, the two to the three and the three to the Ten Thousand Beings.'[120]

As has often been emphasised, Buddhist influences are detectable in the philosophical tendencies of the Sung period bequeathed to seventeenth-century China. And yet, neo-Confucianism had originally represented a reaction against Buddhism and Taoism, which were considered to be anti-social doctrines. In contrast to them, the thinkers of the eleventh century had stressed the positive and practical nature of the tradition of the literate elite. However, they had not been able to shake off habitual modes of thought in which the Chinese tradition had long been steeped, with the result that, without realising it, they borrowed much from Buddhism, producing a synthesis between fundamental Buddhist ideas and those of the classical Chinese tradition. The Buddhist concept of the absolute, total indeterminacy which is beyond discursive reason became fused with the Chinese idea of the Dao and *li*.[121] One of the fundamental theses of neo-Confucianism is that, in its state of absolute calm, our spirit resembles Heaven: then, its inspirations are perfectly adapted to all circumstances for the precise reason that they are devoid of all egoism and are entirely spontaneous.

The critique that stemmed from the tradition of the Chinese literate elite echoed one of the themes of Buddhist thought in its refutation of the Christian concept of a personal, creator God: if he is absolute, he is pure indeterminacy, an absence of all characteristics. If he is endowed with particular qualities and with a will, he cannot be absolute. But it would be misleading to attempt to draw clear distinctions between Buddhism, Taoism and Confucianism as the missionaries did, in the belief that they were dealing with quite separate philosophies and religions. It was in association with the traditions of the literate elite and the Taoists that Buddhism had been understood and interpreted in China; and, given the absence of any inclination towards systematisation, the partitions separating one doctrine from another were very much more permeable in China than they were in the West.

The Incarnation

One thing that the Chinese had found difficult to accept, even before coming to the Incarnation, was the – in their view – contradictory nature of a Master of Heaven that stemmed both from the Hebrew concept of a personal, wrathful yet merciful God and the Greek concept of an eternal being that is absolute perfection.

The author of one refutation of the Christian theses writes:

Does this great governor of the universe who created everything have a corporeal substance? If he does, who created him and where was he before Heaven and Earth existed? If he has no corporeal substance he is what our Confucianism calls Taiji [the cosmic origin]. But the Taiji can have neither love nor hatred. And how could it demand that people obey it? How could it dispense rewards and punishments? ... But there is worse to come: they claim that the Master of Heaven descended to be born on earth as a man ... So where was he before he descended? If he was in paradise, paradise must have existed before the Master of Heaven did. In that case, how can the Master of Heaven be said to have created paradise? If one says that he created paradise, to live there, as men make houses to live in them, where did he reside before he made paradise? If he had no dwelling-place, he must have been one and the same as the Taiji and had no need of any paradise. But in that case, it is absurd that a being identical to the Taiji should come down to earth as a man.[122]

It does not make sense for a perfect and absolute being to be endowed with feelings and passions. Xu Dashou writes:

If the Buddha or the principle of universal order (the *li*) clung to the slightest privilege to increase their prestige, it would be impossible to call them venerable ... Now, by virtue of the very fact that he is particularised by his powers and the places where he resides, the Master of Heaven is nothing but a heretic. By virtue of the fact that he freely abandons himself to his delight or wrath, he is a vicious devil. Furthermore, he praises the murder [of animals] and slanders Heaven,[123] denigrates sovereigns and places fathers on the same level as sons;[124] he appreciates gifts prompted by self-interest, encourages shamelessness,[125] and slanders the Classics and the Saints;[126] in all these respects he is like an irreligious person who has committed the worst of crimes. Wherever is his dignity?[127]

Xu Dashou also writes: 'To say that a being attached to the self [endowed with passions] has been capable of creating Heaven is to accept that passions can precede nature',[128] his point being that the principle of heavenly order (*tianli*) comes before the passions, which are a product of the imperfections of nature.

The missionaries had identified the flooding waters of the period of Yao, in the legendary tradition of China, with the biblical Flood – which was to pose difficult chronological problems – and they explained that this catastrophe had been provoked by God, who had been angered by men. The same author writes: 'They say that the overflowing of waters which occurred during the period of Yao was occasioned by the wrath of the Master of Heaven... A being of perfect virtue does not lose his temper.'[129]

The fact that the Master of Heaven of these Barbarians only recognises the good that is done in his own name and that the only people to be saved are those who believe in him, proves that he is 'an egoistical being, endowed with passions, self-centred and self-interested, a hundred, a thousand or ten thousand times more so than ordinary men'.[130]

This egoism stands in contradiction to the universal compassion of the Buddhas and Bodhisattvas as much as it does to the absolute impartiality of the Heaven of the Chinese tradition. The Japanese, Fucan, writes:

Whatever shines with a dazzling light retains nothing of its brilliance for itself. A great goodness keeps back nothing for itself when it comes to love. But listen, in contrast, to the words of the Deus: 'This is mine, all mine', or 'This is exactly what I expected.' This Deus is a being with a self and is full of human whims. To believe that a human whim can be compared with the order of Heaven testifies to an abysmal ignorance.[131]

To claim that the Master of Heaven has communicated his injunctions and warnings to men is to descend to the level of popular superstitions and resort to a vulgar stratagem:

Confucius said: 'How could Heaven speak?',[132] and Mencius said: 'Heaven does not speak. It is content to manifest itself through its movement and action.'[133] Now, they say that in Antiquity the Master of Heaven transmitted from on high the ten prohibitions [the Ten Commandments]. What difference is there between that and the heavenly writings which were forged under the Han and Sung dynasties? [To resort to such tricks] is to upset and delude the world.[134]

Roger Bastide regarded the Incarnation as something irreducible, with a universal meaning, independent of all civilisations. He wrote:

Catholicism is founded upon the dogma of the Incarnation; consequently, it is not so much a matter of destroying existing structures [in countries where missionary work is undertaken], but rather of transmitting new values to them – values which will no doubt transform them but will do so from within; at the limit, it is a matter of creating an African Christianity or an Asian Christianity just as a Western Christianity already exists through its incarnation in a Graeco-Roman culture.[135]

But perhaps the matter is not so simple after all, and, in the light of the Chinese situation, we may well wonder whether the dogma of the Incarnation can really be separated from Judaeo-Greek concepts and whether it does not necessarily imply an opposition between a transcendent eternity and a worldly transitoriness, between the two of which, precisely, it operates as a mediator. Given that that opposition was unknown to the Chinese and in contradiction to their traditions as a whole, it followed inevitably that either the Christian ideas would have to undergo a serious distortion or else modes of thought would have to be totally remoulded. It is, at all events, worth noting that the seventeenth-century Chinese Christians never make any allusion to Jesus in their writings, limiting themselves to paying homage to the Sovereign on High, or *shangdi*.

We have noted the approval that the missionaries won through their constant allusions to Heaven and the Sovereign on High. These men from so far away appeared to be expressing themselves like the Chinese, and the importance that they attached to moral rigour was also in tune with the needs of the period. But so long as that was how the situation remained conversions were out of the question: the situation remained one of total misunderstanding. Accustomed as they were to the idea of a principle of order inherent in the universe, the Chinese found nothing shocking in the Christian thesis of a divine Providence. On the contrary, many rejoiced to see foreigners who thought as they did and who declared that it was necessary to respect Heaven. The difficulties began when it came to revealing the mysteries that are the very essence of Christianity. While the Chinese men of letters were delighted by the analogies that they thought they had discovered between the teaching of the 'men of letters from the West' and their own traditions, they nevertheless expressed total disapproval when it came to 'this Yesu who died nailed down' and all that, to them, smacked of magic practices: the sprinkling of holy water, applications of oil, liturgical formulae.

At the end of the seventeenth century, Father Le Comte was writing:

Men of quality and those who pride themselves on their learning usually stopped me when I came to the mysteries. Their minds balked above all at the Trinity and the Incarnation. To them, as much as to the Jews, the idea of a vulnerable God, a dying God, was scandalous and somehow mad.[136] The existence of an eternal, sovereign God, infinitely just and infinitely powerful did not appear to upset them so much, and the manifest proofs that I provided would often prevent them from committing themselves on the subject by entering into dispute with me.[137]

Father Parennin was still making similar remarks half a century later:

When it comes to preaching to the great or the men of letters of this country,[138] one is not as a rule successful if one starts with the mysteries of our holy religion; to them, some of these seem obscure, others incredible. Their conviction that foreigners do not know anything about religion that can be compared to their great doctrine is such that even if they do listen to us for a moment, they immediately turn the conversation to some other subject.[139]

This is confirmed by Father Parennin's account of the words of the Manchu prince, Sunu, the cousin of the emperor, Yongzheng, who had acquired a number of Christian books. He writes:

I was enchanted by the order, clarity and weight of the arguments that proved the existence of a sovereign being, the creator of all things,[140] one such that nothing greater or more perfect could be imagined. The simple revelation of his magnificent attributes pleased me all the more as I found this doctrine to be in conformity with that of our own ancient books. But when I reached the place where it is taught that the son of God became a man, I was astonished that people so enlightened in other respects should have mixed in with so many truths a doctrine which seemed to me so improbable and which shocked my reason. The more I thought about it, the more I found my mind balking at this point.[141]

People could not remember ever having heard such an absurd proposition in China:

When the Ming sent ambassadors to the West[142] across India, all the way to Arabia, the people of those kingdoms honoured one sole Heaven.[143] When disasters or great good fortune occurred, they raised their eyes to Heaven to address their prayers to it, exactly as we in China respect Heaven. They had never heard tell of a Master of Heaven who died nailed to a construction in the shape of the character ten.[144]

The Chinese did not, in general, understand that the Christian mysteries are beyond human reason and that it is vain to attempt to refute them. When Father Aleni declared that: 'Only the Master of Heaven was there before the earliest Antiquity and never grows old', Xu Dashou asked him: 'Who gave birth to the Master of Heaven, then?' 'His mother', he replied. 'He has a mother, yet he is eternal?' Aleni said: 'That is the Master of Heaven who came down to be born on earth, for there is also a

Master of Heaven who was born of himself who is really eternal.' Xu Dashou writes:

So I went on to ask him whether the Master of Heaven was a principle of order or a man. He made no reply. I also asked him whether, before being born, the Master of Heaven was present or absent.[145] Again he made no reply. I then said: 'On what grounds do you declare him to be eternal?' All he would say was: 'The Master of Heaven is inconceivable; if one were to conceive him, one would be committing a very grave fault.'[146]

For the men of letters, the historical and localised existence of Jesus was incompatible with the universal nature of the Sovereign on High or Master of Heaven. Yang Guangxian writes:

If one accepts that Yesu is truly the Master of Heaven, then the Master of Heaven is a man among men and can no longer be called the Master of Heaven. If there really was a Master of Heaven in Heaven, not one of the kingdoms between Heaven and Earth ought to escape his government. He ought not to preside solely over the kingdom of Judaea.[147]

Huang Wendao is also of the opinion that it is unfair for the Master of Heaven to have descended into one particular kingdom, leaving all the others to their misfortune. It is not logical that he should have descended at one particular moment and not before or after that moment. And besides, he asks, who continued to save men once he had returned to Heaven?[148]

One author mockingly records the following conversation with acquaintances of his:

'Did the Master of Heaven really descend to be born on earth?' asked one. 'That is what has for many years been handed down amongst malevolent Barbarians. But it is hardly credible. The Master of Heaven presides over Heaven, Earth and the Ten Thousand Beings and that is how it is that the activity of transformation in the universe never ceases for a single moment. If he had descended to be born on earth and had lived there for 33 years, the one hundred gods would no longer have had a master and the activity of the transformation of the universe would soon have ground to a halt. Heaven, Earth and the Ten Thousand Beings would have been entirely destroyed.[149] So it would all be quite incomprehensible.' But the first speaker thought of a solution: 'Perhaps there was a Master of Heaven who remained in Heaven and [continued to] preside over the work of creation–transformation in the universe, while another Master of Heaven descended to be born on earth.' 'In that case,' I said, 'there would be two Masters of Heaven. That would be just as incomprehensible.'

The same text pursues the subject of the life and death of Jesus:

'If the Master of Heaven descended to live on earth, that is because he could not do otherwise: he had to save mankind. He chose twelve disciples in religion to spread his doctrine. Now, amongst them, there was one who was in charge of the doctrine and had been taught the correct tradition, but who had then practised alien rituals. He was full of pride and no longer respected the Master of Heaven. He therefore lodged a complaint with the administration, accusing him of wishing to usurp the throne of the sovereign of the kingdom, and the Master of Heaven was obliged to undergo a beating and blows from canes and to wear a crown of thorns and a bamboo cage on his head [!], and finally he died nailed to a construction in the shape of the character ten. Then he went down to hell, rose again and ascended into Heaven'[150] . . . I then said: 'The whole business is incomprehensible. If the Master of Heaven wished to save men, why could he not have a Saint born to spread the heavenly Dao in order to save them? Why did he need to undergo tortures himself and die nailed down?' Somebody else then said: 'The Master of Heaven had announced all these events in advance and he acted deliberately.' 'Impossible![151] The Master of Heaven is assuredly totally sincere. How could Heaven not be totally sincere and act with the intention [of deceiving people]? Besides, the Master of Heaven is supremely wise. How could he possibly have made such a mistake as to appeal to the wrong man?'[152]

Redemption also raised difficulties. Another man of letters writes:

They say that the Master of Heaven paid in person for the crimes of the ten thousand generations. That is totally incomprehensible. Since the Master of Heaven is majesty without equal and infinite compassion, why did he not simply issue an amnesty to men for their crimes, and what need had he to redeem their crimes with his own person? . . . And if he was capable of redeeming the crimes of men with his own person, why was he not capable of arranging that men should commit no more crimes? . . . Although he is said to have redeemed all crimes, the fact that there are still people who are cast into hell proves that the redemption was incomplete.[153]

Another inconsequentiality on the part of the Barbarians was that they produced representations of the Master of Heaven. Chen Houguang writes:

The Sovereign on High can have no visible form. So he cannot be represented in images. Yet Matteo Ricci took the Yesu of those distant lands and made him the Sovereign of Heaven. [He represents him] with wild hair, wearing a cangue [!] and he has drawn him an imaginary face. Can there be any worse insult [towards this universal power]? The books of these Barbarians say: 'The Taoists have made statues of the Sovereign on High,[154] with a human form. But could a man be the august Sovereign of Heaven?' They criticise among the Taoists what they praise highly in their own doctrine. Is that not contradictory?[155]

Jiang Dejing asks one missionary: 'How could Heaven possibly be represented? And even if it could, I very much fear that it would not be as your figure, with a large nose, deep-set eyes and a thick beard'. And he goes on to say:

The Western man of letters could find no answer to that. Some people will say that when the Buddha came from the West, he was given an image and that when Ricci came from the greater West he too produced images of Yesu; and that Ricci wished in this way to oppose the greater West to the West.[156]

In short, some people thought that it was only to match the Buddhists with their statues of Buddha that the Barbarians had made pictures of their Master of Heaven. That was the only excuse that could be found for them.

The Jesuits had soon learned from experience how imprudent it was to reveal the mysteries of Christianity to the Chinese without first giving them a lengthy preparation. The Chinese considered it scandalous that Jesus had been condemned to death in accordance with the laws of his country, and the degrading execution to which he had been submitted seemed to them incompatible with the supreme dignity of a master of the universe. Most men of letters, in particular in the early seventeenth century, therefore had but a limited knowledge of the doctrine of the Master of Heaven, derived from the little works on morality produced by the missionaries and Ricci's great treatise, in which no more than a handful of lines on the life of Jesus were to be found, right at the end.[157] However, the Jesuits' enemies in Europe were quite wrong to accuse them of preaching not of a suffering Christ but only of a glorious one. The little works composed for catechumens and neophytes, and their pious pictures too, left no room for doubt on the matter. But in the eyes of men of letters who were hostile to the missionaries, it was precisely this that proved their deceit and cunning. Having acquired some works reserved for the edification of Christians together with a number of pious pictures, Yang Guangxian accused the Barbarians of duplicity. In his book, Ricci had taken good care not to reveal the fact that Jesus had been put to death ignominiously for having violated the laws of his country. He had limited himself to writing that 'once his work of salvation was completed, he reascended to Heaven'.[158] Yang Guangxian, using an *ad absurdum* argument, writes:

One might just speak of honouring the Sovereign on High without honouring Heaven and Earth. But one cannot speak of honouring Yesu as Sovereign on High. One might just speak of honouring an ordinary man as a Saint or as the Sovereign on High. But one cannot speak of honouring as a Saint or the Sovereign on High a criminal who has transgressed the laws ... The one whom they call Master of Heaven is the one who directs the universe. And, according to them, it is by virtue of the fact that he could direct the universe but was not able to direct his own life until he died a natural death that he can be recognised as the Master of Heaven! In their books of doctrine, they mention Yesu's correct laws. Why do they say nothing of the way that he died nailed down?[159]

Elsewhere Yang Guangxian writes:

If Yesu's only merit is that he died nailed down following a just sentence, all the great criminals who have suffered slow deaths, decapitation or strangulation could claim an equal merit. It is all a lot of vicious writing and vicious talk, which contradicts the principle of universal order and the Dao. How can we tolerate these things in China even for a single day?[160]

Adopting an argument attributed to the Jews in the Gospel, Yang Guangxian writes:

Not only was Yesu not able to save mankind as a whole, but he himself was sentenced to the most ignominious of deaths. Could this be the Master who created Heaven? His bid for power having failed,[161] he did not submit quietly to justice but prayed to Heaven on his knees ... If he prayed to Heaven on his knees, does that mean that among the spirits of Heaven there is a spirit to be more revered than the Master of Heaven? Who could accept that he should kneel to him, who could accept that he should pray to him? To pray on one's knees when one is the Master of Heaven is clear proof that one is not the Master of Heaven.[162]

The virginity of Mary as well as the Incarnation became the butt of Yang Guangxian's blasphemous sarcasms. He writes:

If the Master of Heaven is Yesu, who put him in the stomach of Maliya? Even in the fantastical stories recounted in the *Tales of Qi*,[163] there has never been such nonsense. 'All beings are born from the union of the seeds of males and females.'[164] That is the constant rule for mankind. Among the four types of birth,[165] only birth through humidity is a birth without father or mother. For all the rest, collaboration between a father and a mother is necessary. To have a mother but not a father is, in my opinion, something which – even in their country – ought not to be viewed with approval. So, *a fortiori*, how could it elicit approval in all the other kingdoms on earth [as they claim it does]? Animals are the only creatures in the world which know only their mother, not their father. It is unimaginable how, in their doctrine, the father can be quite unknown. But if he is not unknown, then why do they honour with such reverence the ghost of a man who had no father? To revere as a Saint a son without a father comes down to making a woman without a husband the founder of a religion. Since Maliya gave birth to Yesu, it cannot be said that she engendered him and yet remained a virgin. How could a virgin joyfully accept becoming a mother? And has anyone ever verified whether she really was a virgin or not? In *The Ritual* it is written: 'What is said in the women's quarters should not be disclosed', and also: 'One does not speak of the affairs of women in public.'[166] That is to show that one feels shame about such things. A virgin mother is something one would not dare to mention even in the case of animals, but for these people it is a title of saintliness and glory that they have the audacity to trumpet abroad throughout the universe. Master Yesu and his disciples are even lower than animals. But perhaps they were trying to cover up the shameful thing of not having a father when they spoke of virginity. Nevertheless, all they achieved was to draw attention to the fact.[167]

As Vincent Cronin observes,[168] in India, the missionaries came up against a radical difficulty when they attempted to explain the historical nature of the Incarnation. Given that, for the Indians, the truth lies beyond this world of appearances and that everything perceived through the senses is an illusion (*mâyâ*), for them there could be no such thing as history in our sense of the word: creation and the Incarnation were incomprehensible in the sense of historical events which happened once only in a real and unique world. The Incarnation could only be imagined as an avatar, that is to say an unreal manifestation, a mere game or deception on the part of a deity. From the Indian point of view, the personality and historicity of Jesus were indications of limitation and imperfection.

In China, too, we come across this comparison of the life of Jesus to an avatar. An anti-Christian work on the Incarnation explains that there are two possible solutions: either the Master of Heaven did descend to be born in person and, in that case, Heaven remained for the duration without direction; alternatively, the Master of Heaven remained in Heaven in person and appeared on earth only in the form of an avatar. This would amount to a plagiarisation of the Buddhist theory of the two bodies of Buddha: the spiritual body (*dharmakâya*) and the body of transformation (*nirmânakâya*). But this 'single avatar is inferior to the unequalled marvel constituted by the thousands of hundreds of tens of millions of bodies of transformation [of the Buddhas]'.[169]

For the Buddhist monk, Ruchun, however, the life of Jesus cannot be an avatar. On the contrary, it is proof of the universality of transmigration. In his great treatise, Ricci had claimed that the Buddhists had stolen that theory from Bidawola (Pythagoras) and were using it to frighten people; that before Buddhism came to China, nobody had heard of such a thing and that it was therefore something that did not merit credence. To this, Ruchun retorted that transmigration is clearly the product of *karma* and ignorance and that there was therefore no need to invoke Pythagoras. Besides, it was quite untrue that nobody had heard of transmigration before the arrival of Buddhism since there are many historical examples of transformations of men into animals in former times. Only the actual word 'transmigration' (*lunhui*) was new. But the clearest proof of its universal reality was what the Barbarians themselves said about Yesu, who, having descended from Heaven, was born among men; from the world of men fell into hell; from hell was reborn as a man; and who, from being the man that he was, ascended once more to

Heaven. Ruchun goes on to observe that transmigration is also a cease-less succession of thoughts. So why should it be as Ricci claims, namely that transmigration only takes place as from 'when there are horns and fur', that is to say animal rebirth.[170]

It is necessary to understand that in a Buddhist interpretation such as Ruchun's, Jesus has passed through three of the six possible ways of rebirth: those of god (*tian*: *deva*), man, and infernal being (the three others being those of a spirit (*asura*), a hungry ghost, and an animal). For the monk, Ruchun, then, Jesus is simply a being submitted to transmi-gration. He has not yet emerged from the cycle of rebirths and deaths; he is therefore inferior to the Buddhas, who have attained definitive and external extinction.

In contrast to the Indians, the Chinese believed in the reality of the world and possessed an essential sense of history, so that, in their case, it was not the historicity of Jesus that raised problems but his double nature. They could not conceive how the Incarnation could be a me-diation between a transcendent eternity and a transitory earthly life, for such an opposition was quite alien to them. The solution of the men of letters who were most favourable to the missionaries was to consider that Jesus, like Confucius, had been a man whose saintliness and virtue had made it possible for him to become identified with the heavenly principle of order (*tianli*). This Confucian interpretation is remarkably well expressed by a Chinese man of letters in 1625. Longobardo writes:

Doctor Cien Lin-vu, who was a friend of ours and who had often heard our Fathers speak of the true God who had come into this world to save us, was never able to imagine him in any way but as he imagined Confucius for [for the Chin-ese] there is but one universal nature: the most perfect men ... best represent the universal nature of the first principle and their excellence consists in being at one with it. From which it must be understood that what Jesus is in Europe, Con-fucius is in China and Foé [the Buddha] is in India.

And when Longobardo explained that Europeans followed the Law given by God himself, this Cien Lin-vu remarked that the Law was the same as that of Confucius, 'for the legislators in both cases were none other than Heaven and the first principle'. Longobardo was anxious to reply but Doctor Michael, the famous convert, Yang Tingyun, re-strained him 'for fear that his friend might be hurt, especially since it would be extremely difficult to refute a sentiment considered to be so correct in China'.[171]

A close friend of the missionaries, the grand secretary, Ye Xianggao (1562–1627), always a precious ally to them, expresses himself in a simi-lar fashion. Longobardo tells us that in *An Explanation of the Ten Com-*

mandments composed by Yang Tingyun, he wrote that the Sovereign on High or Master of Heaven

became incarnate in China several times in the persons of Iao [Yao], Xun [Shun], Confucius, several kings and even a number of ordinary individuals: so it was quite possible that he could similarly become incarnate in the West in the person of Jesus, just as the Jesuits claim . . . Jesus in the West is just what Confucius or any other distinguished man of letters is in China.[172]

The Chinese men of letters were certainly extremely accommodating and it is not hard to understand how it was that in the early seventeenth century a kind of syncretism of Confucian and Christian ideas was very nearly successful – a syncretism which, however, the more perspicacious of the missionaries and their Chinese enemies were at pains to combat, by pointing out its absurdity.

This is perhaps the point at which to add a note on the avatars of Jesus in the Taoist mode. Spiritualistic practices which appear to have been extremely ancient and very much alive made it possible to enter into contact with immortals and illustrious figures from the past. Furthermore, rather than such illusory apparitions as the Buddhas' bodies of transformation, the Chinese traditions included avatars conceived of as tangible phenomena which could be situated in time and space. These flesh-and-blood avatars were said to be particular deities or historical figures. At the time of the great Taiping rebellion, in the mid-nineteenth century, the Westerners believed at first, on the strength of a number of reports, that the Taiping were Christians and that this was a miracle produced by their reading the Bible. Soon, however, they were obliged to accept what was manifestly true: the Christianity of the Taiping, who had adopted a number of Christian ideas and practices, was more than somewhat heterodox. Their king, Hong Xiuquan, claimed to be the younger brother of Jesus and, as such, declared himself to be even better informed than the latter about the latest revelations of the Sovereign on High. It was therefore up to him to convert the Western missionaries who had come to his court. Hong Xiuquan was, himself, in constant touch with God the Father and his eldest son, thanks to the messages which he received directly from them and the mediumistic seances in the course of which either he himself or his associates got them to descend. Thus Hong Xiuquan had seven times, between April 1848 and January 1851, made contact with the Sovereign on High (the translation of God used by the Protestant missionaries) and with Christ three times. For Hong, Christ was the son and heir of the Sovereign on High, but he had other brothers. Since he was not God himself, his rank of dignity came immediately below that of his father. And Hong Xiuquan one day remarked: 'My elder brother [Christ] has clearly declared that there is only one supreme God, so why did his disciples subsequently make the mistake of saying that Christ was God?'[173]

The critique of original sin and the divine perfections

> He had too many failures, this potter who had not learned his craft!
> But that he took vengeance on his pots and creations because they
> had turned out badly – that was a sin against good taste.
>
> Nietzsche, *Thus spake Zarathustra*[174]

Those who criticised the doctrine of the Master of Heaven claimed that it was impossible not to hold a creator and omnipotent God responsible for the defects in his creation. One author writes:

As Confucius says: 'Man can perfect the order of the universe . . . being good depends upon ourselves'.[175] But these people, on the contrary, ascribe all the power of creation to the Master of Heaven. If he was able to produce spirits and men, why did he not create only good spirits and good men? . . . If he created everything, why did he not limit himself to what was good? Why did he create these bodies of flesh, these detestable mores, these malignant devils? Why did he not eliminate them? A good workman does a good job and, if he does not, he scraps what he has made.[176]

The author of one short work explains that, according to the missionaries, man was created entirely good by the Master of Heaven. It is man himself who is the source of evil. But how did it come about that man could do evil if the Master of Heaven is all-powerful? Their answer is that it is as with parents who desire their children to be worthy people. If those children behave badly, it is not their fault. Possibly, but then parents are not all-powerful. All they have done is give birth to their children so they cannot be held responsible for their children's natural characters and dispositions. But the same cannot be true of the Master of Heaven: why did he not arrange it so that the natural characters and dispositions of men always restrained them from doing wrong?[177]

The same type of argument is put forward by the author of *Humble Remarks on the Distinction between the Doctrines*:

The Master of Heaven has created a world perfect down to the last detail. So when he created the ancestors of mankind, he should have made them supremely wise and quite exceptional. Why were the individuals called Yadang and Ewa such bad people? It is as if a workman had made objects unfit for use: the fault cannot be ascribed to the objects themselves so it would appear that the workman was inept. How is it that the Master of Heaven was capable of skill when he created Heaven, Earth and the Ten Thousand Beings but proved himself inept when he created man? So far as we Chinese are concerned, even if we go back into the past as far as Pangu[178] and the separation of Heaven from Earth [at the beginning of our universe], in each generation we had wise kings such as Fuxi, Shennong, Huangdi, Yao and Shun to assist Heaven and Earth [in their task]. We have never heard anything about good-for-nothings such as Yadang and Ewa... They start off by introducing such misleading and confusing concepts so as to disturb the minds of our compatriots so much that they will go over to them.[179]

However, as Xu Dashou points out, it is really as early as the fall of Satan that the question of the responsibility of the Master of heaven arises:

I also asked Aleni what was the origin of the one whom he calls the devil. He told me: 'When the Master of Heaven made the world in the beginning, he immediately proceeded to create countless spirits. The first and greatest of all was called Luqifu'er. He is the ancestor of the Buddha. He said that his wisdom was as great as that of the Master of Heaven and the Master of Heaven became angry and demoted him by despatching him to hell. He is the present King Yâma.[180] However, despite the fact that Luqi[fu'er] was sent to hell to suffer torments there, one half of his soul made the devil and walks through the world. He deprives people of their right thinking and the Master of Heaven immediately hands these unfortunate individuals over to him.' I then said to him: 'Before mankind was created, for the Master of Heaven to have put the Buddha in charge of hell, must there not have been beings which were shut up there already?' Aleni replied: 'Countless fallen spirits were indeed imprisoned there. It was therefore a foregone conclusion that there should be men there.' I then said: 'What kind of a penal law is it that makes the greatest of wrongdoers a king and [at the same time] makes him undergo tortures?'[181] Besides, if the Buddha, who has become King Yâma, walks through the world and does as he likes there, that proves that his power is greater than that of the Master of Heaven. Furthermore, the Master of Heaven feels an infinite anger towards him. This shows that the object of that anger enjoys an existence which, equally, is without end. That proves that his strength is equal to that of the Master of Heaven. And, finally, was not the one whom you call the devil created by the Master of Heaven's own hands? How has all this come about? You said just now that Yadang and Ewa were not virtuous; that is understandable enough: they were men, and [as such] were already some way distant from the Master of Heaven. But as for Luqi[fu'er], he was the first of the spirits which he created by transformation and he was accused before they were. It is clear from all this that the Master of Heaven is the source of all evils and that it is justifiable to ascribe every crime to him. Is not all this enough to make one burst out laughing?[182]

If the Master of heaven is full of mercy, he should have warned Adam and Eve before they committed an irreparable crime:

The monk, Ruchun, writes that the doctrine of Heaven [Christianity] holds that the Master of Heaven is omnipotent, omniscient, the creator and ruler of Heaven, Earth and the Ten Thousand Beings. First of all he created Yadang and Ewa, who are the ancestors of humanity. Their nature and their bodies were perfect and they enjoyed total happiness. But having once contravened the holy orders of the Master of Heaven, they lost all his favour and thereafter became subject to sickness and misfortune. They would have liked to escape from this state but the way to Heaven was barred to them. The defilement from that crime of those ancestors was transmitted to the entire human race. That is why all men, from the moment of their conception, are affected by that defilement and all their later crimes stem from that root of evil.

Refutation: the Master of Heaven thus gave birth to good men devoid of vice. Why did he not make sure that Yadang and Ewa preserved their good nature and felt no desire so that they could be a pure source for their innumerable descendants? At the moment when these first humans were about to feel some desire, the Master of Heaven should have displayed some of his miraculous powers to prevent them from acting badly. Would that not have been the easiest of things for him to do? Omnipotent and omniscient as he is, he must be capable of detecting the evil intentions of all men. So he ought to have rid them [of desires] which contravened his orders and thus protected those who were to come afterwards. In that way, men would have been good from start to finish. He would have stopped the evil at its root . . . When it is a matter of pulling up weeds, one always takes care to remove their roots; to cure an illness, one tackles the primary cause. Man makes great efforts to attack evils before they can develop. So why did the Master of Heaven, who is all-powerful, instead develop the tumours and tares in this way?[183]

For Yu Chunxi, a man of letters with Buddhist inclinations, who died in 1621, and one of Ricci's earliest adversaries, the Master of Heaven, being all-powerful, should have made sure that the first humans did not need to be put on their guard:

Ricci says that the body is the external man while the soul is the internal man. Tigers and wolves threaten the external man but they bring peace to the internal man [by reminding him of the existence of God]. In the last analysis, they are useful to man. In the beginning, tigers and wolves did man no harm. It was man's revolt against the Sovereign on High which attracted them in his direction.[184]

And Yu Chunxi goes on to say:

But I sometimes wonder how the tigers and wolves knew that man had rebelled against the Sovereign on High. That would mean that these animals are superior to man. If the power of the Master of Heaven can arrange for these animals to put men on their guard, why was it not able to arrange for man to have no need to be put on his guard? Since tigers and wolves are so easy to convert,[185] paradise should have been established for the souls of tigers and wolves.[186]

By not intervening and allowing evil to happen, the Master of Heaven showed a singular lack of compassion. The Japanese, Fucan, makes the same point: God gave Adam and Eve no protection against Lucifer, unlike the Buddhas who protect men against the devils. He allowed them to act as they did and then expelled them from the *Paraiso terreal* (earthly paradise). And now he wishes to burn in hell not only Adam and Eve but all men.[187]

The monk, Ruchun, writes:

If it is said that at that time [after the Fall], the Master of Heaven would have liked to destroy Yadang and Ewa but was afraid that then there would be no human race, why did he not start all over again and create a man who was truly good, since he possesses the inexhaustible power to create men? And if it is said that he had not the heart to cut the evil short [by eliminating the guilty] because the evil was not yet very serious, how is it that he could leave things as they were, knowing full well that little streams turn into big rivers and that great fires begin with tiny sparks?[188]

Nor can it be held that the Master of Heaven wished to test the man he had created by leaving him free to act in order to see whether he would resist the temptation of doing evil. Omniscient as he was, he must have known in advance that Adam and Eve would transgress his prohibitions. Knowing for certain that they would fall into sin, he simply set a trap for them. The thesis of free will is incompatible with the creator's omniscience:

If it is said that he knew in advance from the moment man was created that he would surely commit a fault but that he allowed him to act as man himself decided, either for good or for evil, so as to decide whether he should be rewarded or punished, that is what is called 'trapping people with a net'.[189] How does that show him to be the master [of all beings]? So what do these words 'omniscient' and 'omnipotent' mean?[190]

It was precisely upon the contradictions that resulted from the Master of Heaven's omniscience and omnipotence that many criticisms focused. Fabian Fucan explains: God, who is omniscient, was not able to foresee that the angels he had created would fall into sin. If he did not know that they would, it is absurd to say that he is omniscient. If he did know yet created them none the less, he is a malignant and cruel being, not full of mercy as they claim. If he is omnipotent, why did he not create the world free of all sin? Why did he create harmful devils? He bungled his creation.[191]

A Chinese author takes a similar line: if he did not know that Lucifer, having received such power from him, was going to rebel, the Master of Heaven was lacking in wisdom. If he did know, he was lacking in goodness since it was he who created Lucifer. Anyone lacking in wisdom and goodness cannot be called the Master of Heaven.[192] Xu Dashou writes:

The intelligence of the common run of men is limited and they do not know too well how to cope with devils. How can it be that, with his omnipotence, the Master of Heaven was not capable of preventing a devil from making his own descendants fall into crime? . . . When men of average wisdom and virtue have unworthy sons . . . it is said that such was Heaven's will and they themselves could do nothing about it. But if a being as divine and holy as the Master of Heaven goes to a great deal of trouble to produce two individuals who are to be his very first heirs and then incites them to commit a theft which will make them the very first criminals, is that behaviour worthy of a being so divine and holy? . . . When one's dignity is as eminent as that of the Master of Heaven, one does not lose one's temper. And if one thinks of all the countless faults committed by the whole descendancy [of Adam and Eve], is it not illogical to lose one's temper only with the eldest son and daughter just for stealing a fruit? Yadang and Ewa's descendants who are lacking in virtue can blame them for having started the evil. But if one looks further, who was really at the source? I do not see what the Master of Heaven could reply to that.[193]

The Master of Heaven has no pity. Buddhism, on the other hand, shows a true compassion, for it seeks to save even the worst criminals, whereas the Barbarians say that once one has fallen into hell, one remains shut up there for all eternity.[194]

If the Master of Heaven is omnipotent, it is impossible to see how devils can have the audacity to defy him:

They say that when the emperor, Ming, of the Han dynasty [AD 58–75], dreamed of a man of gold,[195] it was in fact the Master of Heaven [who appeared to him] but that the devil twisted the apparition to the advantage of Buddhism. But if the power of the Master of Heaven is limitless, what being or devil could have dared to steal from him? And even supposing he had had such audacity, he should have been punished in less than the twinkling of an eye. And, after all, after revealing himself in a dream, why should he have slept more than one thousand years and only awoken in our time?[196] Why did the Master of Heaven not show himself in flesh and blood to Emperor Ming right away and why did he wait so long after his execution before proclaiming all this?[197]

As Fabian Fucan had noted in Japan, in original sin there is a massive disproportion between the sin committed and the punishment meted out. In 1620, he wrote:

A holy law forbade Adam and Eve to eat the *macan* [this Portuguese term had been used in Japan to denote a kind of persimmon]. It is really the height of absurdity! It is like setting out to fool an old woman or gull a child. A persimmon could not possibly be a direct or an indirect cause in an affair as important as attaining the highest Heaven or else falling into hell. In all the five prohibitions and ten laws of Buddha and in all the Buddhist codes of discipline, I have never found any precept that warned against persimmons.[198]

And Xu Dashou writes:

The ancestors of mankind had only committed a tiny little crime, yet you condemn their entire descendancy to a heavy penalty to last for all time. That is contrary to the principle according to which the guilt of a criminal does not extend to his kin. For an ancestor to involve his entire descendancy in his crime is much less just and equitable than what is taught by the Buddhist theory of transmigrations, according to which each individual suffers the effects of his own actions.

Xu Dashou then relates the following anecdote:

Shang Yang, a minister of the Qin prince and the reformer of the Qin laws, had promised a large reward to whoever would carry a big tree from one place to another, an action without any useful purpose but which received the reward that had been promised.

Xu Dashou reminds the reader that 'it was so that people should believe in the laws of the kingdom. But what could be more absurd than this terrible punishment for the theft of one fruit?'[199]

Ricci, for his part, had certainly sought to combat the widespread belief in the occult influence that good or bad actions could have upon the family lineage by emphasising the injustice of it.[200] However, the dogma of original sin, by its very generality, seemed even more irrational to the Chinese. Xu Dashou writes:

Ricci declares that each one of us is responsible for his actions. He says: 'If I myself have done good or committed an evil action, the Master of Heaven will certainly not visit retribution upon my sons and grandsons instead of upon myself.' But why does the Master of Heaven, on the pretext that the first ancestors [of mankind] have become guilty of a crime towards him, inflict the evils that derive from that crime upon the endless sequence of their descendants? Quite apart from the extreme cruelty of this punishment, does it not involve a total contradiction with what he said before?[201]

The punishments that result from original sin are, moreover, not distributed equally amongst all mankind. According to the missionaries' teaching, man has been sentenced to live by the sweat of his brow and woman to give birth in pain: 'But there are many wealthy men who eat without having to plough and women without husbands or children who never suffer the pains of childbirth.'[202]

In Buddhism, the fructification of actions, *karma*, accounts for social inequalities and the diversity of individual destinies. But Christianity seems incapable of producing any such explanation. Xu Dashou asked Father Aleni:

'If there are no earlier lives, why are there rich and poor, lowly and great, long lives and existences that end prematurely and so many other profound differences between men?' Aleni replied: 'It is as your Confucian men of letters say: the cause lies in the chanciness of the transformations of the primordial energy.'

Xu Dashou's reply was:

Confucianism says that some things are impossible even for a Saint and that Heaven and Earth do sometimes produce imperfections.[203] The fact is that in Confucianism everything depends upon natural processes.[204] But in your doctrine you say that the Master of Heaven is omnipotent and that Heaven and Earth were created by him. How could natural processes possibly constitute an obstacle for him? Would that not imply that the Master of Heaven is not omnipotent?[205]

Furthermore, it is hard to know what to think of this world created by the Master of Heaven. Should it be praised because he has filled it with perfections or should one lament at finding in it nothing but miseries and pains? In the discourse of the missionaries, these two contradictory representations exist, the one alongside the other, as is noted by Chen Houguang, who introduces a convert as spokesman:

My guest said: 'I agree with you that loyalty towards the sovereign and filial piety are fine virtues. But who has endowed us with a nature capable of acting virtuously? The Chinese speak only of cultivating their virtue and do not know how to raise their heads to see the Sovereign of Heaven and pray to this merciful father to help them. That is why perfect virtues are so rare amongst them.' I replied: 'Let us leave to one side the question of a nature that is capable of acting virtuously, for we have no time to discuss it thoroughly. Let us talk, rather, of the mistakes and confusions that Ricci made with regard to his Master of Heaven, for I do not feel like adding my comments without proofs. He says on the one hand that he created Heaven, Earth and the Ten Thousand Beings and that he created them solely for the benefit of man; that the sun, moon and stars are attached to the heavens in order to give us light; that the five colours were made for our pleasure, the five sounds for our delight, the savours and perfumes in order to satisfy our tastes and all material things, whether hot or light, for our comfort; and that consequently, we should give thanks to the Master of Heaven and always use these benefits with respect. However, he also says that, having felt compassion for men at seeing them thus plunged into the abjection of this world that has no care for Heaven, their first homeland, nor for the important matters that await them after this life, the Master of Heaven filled this world with bitter sufferings so that men might desire to wrench themselves away from it. Thus, having created some things for the good of mankind, he created others for its misfortune. So, what the Master of Heaven does for the life of mankind and what he does for mankind's destruction are in contradiction.'[206]

Language and thought

The wonderful family resemblance of all Indian, Greek and German philosophising is easily enough explained. In fact, where there is affinity of language, owing to the common philosophy of grammar –

I mean owing to the unconscious domination and guidance of similar grammatical functions – it cannot but be that everything is prepared at the outset for a similar development and succession of philosophical systems: just as the way seems barred against certain other possibilities of world interpretation. It is highly probable that philosophers within the domain of the Ural-Altaic languages (where the conception of the subject is least developed) look otherwise into the world and will be found on paths of thought different from those of the Indo-Europeans and Musulmans.

Nietzsche, *Beyond Good and Evil*[207]

Our examination of Chinese reactions to the writings and preaching of the missionaries has often revealed differences in mental categories and frameworks in all sorts of areas: for example, the relation between politics and religion, the role of reflective consciousness or spontaneity in morality, concepts of spiritual substance or of a principle of organisation inherent in the cosmos, beings, and society. The originality of Chinese thought is evident at every turn. It is particularly noticeable in the Chinese refusal both to envisage a sphere of constant truths quite separate from the phenomenal world and to draw a distinction between the rational and the sensible.

We would ask what, if any, could be the part played by linguistic peculiarities in the obvious divergencies between Christian and Chinese ideas. Perhaps we could pose the following simple question: taking a language such as Chinese as a starting-point, would it have been possible for Greek philosophy or medieval scholasticism to develop? To which the answer would probably be 'no'. But what proofs can we adduce to justify that immediate impression?

The Protestant missionaries of the nineteenth and early twentieth centuries complained about the difficulties involved in expressing Christian ideas in Chinese. One of them exclaims: 'Chinese is such an imperfect, unwieldy instrument for conveying spiritual truths!'[208] And, as we have already noted, another comments: 'The language itself is one of the most unsuitable means for making new truths known.'[209] The fact is that in Chinese, it is, for example, so difficult to express how the abstract and the general differ fundamentally, and not just occasionally, from the concrete and the particular. This was an embarrassment for all those who had, in the course of history, attempted to translate into Chinese concepts formed in inflected languages such as Greek, Latin or Sanskrit. Thus, linguistic structures inevitably pose the question of modes of thought. Surprised at not finding the mental frameworks to which they themselves were accustomed, among the Chinese, the missionaries accused the latter of lacking logic. And it is quite true that logic comes from *logos*.

Benveniste writes:

We can only grasp thought that has already been fitted into the framework of a language ... What it is possible to say delimits and organises what it is possible to think. Language provides the fundamental configuration of the properties that the mind recognises things to possess.[210]

Benveniste shows that Aristotle's ten categories encompass nominal and verbal categories that are peculiar to the Greek language: 'what Aristotle presents as a table of general and permanent conditions is simply a conceptual projection of a given linguistic state'. And he goes on to make the following observation, which is crucial to any explanation of the general differences between the Chinese and the Western concepts of the world:

Beyond the Aristotelian terms, over and above that categorisation, there is the concept of 'being', which is all-enveloping. Greek not only possesses the verb 'to be' (by no means a necessity for all languages), but furthermore puts this verb to quite singular uses ... It is the language that has made it possible to make 'being' an objective concept and, as such, possible for philosophical thought to manipulate, analyse and class in the same way as any other concept.[211]

Benveniste's analysis illuminates two characteristics of Greek – and, more generally, Western – thought, both of which are closely related to the structure of Greek and Latin: one is the existence of categories the obvious and necessary nature of which stems from the use to which the language is unconsciously put. The other is the fundamental importance of the concept of being in Western philosophical and religious thought. Throughout its history, the West has sought being beyond appearances. From which it might be supposed that, to use Benveniste's words: 'All varieties of philosophical and spiritual experience unconsciously depend upon a classification imposed by the language simply by virtue of its being a language and the fact that its function is to symbolise.'[212] Similar remarks could be made about the relation between Indian thought and its particular language of expression, Sanskrit, it, too, an Indo-European language, the general structure of which resembles that of Greek or Latin. In the Indian world, grammarians, logicians and philosophers are close to one another. Although it followed different paths from those of Greek thought, Indian thought, too, was founded upon a set of categories of linguistic origin and it assigned capital importance to the concept of being. Sanskrit, too, possessed a verb to denote existence (the root being -*as*) and derivatives from that verb: *sant*- (real, true, just, good), *satya* (true, real), *sattva* (being, reality, spirit). *Âstikya* is belief in the existence of the deity; *nâstikya* is negation of being, nihilism, unbelief.

The only civilisation to leave considerable evidence of elaborated philosophical thought which did not use a language of the Indo-European type was the Chinese civilisation. Now, a model of a language more different from that of Greek, Latin or Sanskrit cannot be imagined. Of all the languages in the world, Chinese has the peculiar, distinctive feature of possessing no grammatical categories systematically differentiated by morphology: there appears to be nothing to distinguish a verb from an adjective, an adverb from a complement, a subject from an attribute. The fact is that, in Chinese, these categories only exist by implicit and arbitrary reference to other languages which do possess them. Furthermore, there was no word to denote existence in Chinese, nothing to convey the concept of being or essence, which in Greek is so conveniently expressed by the noun *ousia* or the neuter *to on*. Consequently, the notion of being, in the sense of an eternal and constant reality, above and beyond that which is phenomenal, was perhaps more difficult to conceive, for a Chinese. It is a point that was noted by the Chinese philosopher, Liang Shuming, who, in a work which appeared in 1921,[213] drew an opposition on this precise point between China and, not just the West, but India too:

The metaphysical questions which have been discussed in China are entirely different from those explored in the West and in India. The questions posed by Western Antiquity and Indian Antiquity have never been debated in China. Those questions were certainly not identical in the West and in India but they were similar in that they involved a quest for the reality of the world. It is inasmuch as they resemble one another that the West and India definitely differ from China. Among Chinese philosophers, have you ever seen some favouring monistic, others dualistic and yet others pluralistic ideas? Or some favouring idealistic while others favour materialistic ones? The Chinese have never discussed ideas such as these, which stem from a static and immutable reality. The metaphysical inquiry traditional in China ever since the earliest Antiquity and which has provided the basis for all knowledge great or small, learned or popular, has been concerned with nothing but change and not at all with static and immutable realities.

The only observation to add, perhaps, is that, for Chinese thought, the only permanent reality is the Dao, the spontaneous order which presides over all change. If one bears in mind the essential linguistic facts, it is Liang Shuming who is right, as opposed to the majority of contemporary Chinese historians, influenced as they are by Western philosophy and, in particular, by simplified and dogmatic forms of Marxism. In point of fact, these modern interpreters have the greatest difficulty in classifying Chinese thinkers as idealists or materialists and their very hesitations prove that Western categories are inapplicable to the Chinese situation.[214]

Given that Chinese is an uninflected language,[215] all that helps to guide one through a phrase, with the aid of a very limited number of particles, are the links between terms of similar meaning, the oppositions between terms of opposite meaning, the rhythms and parallelisms, the position of 'words' or semantic unities and the types of relationship between them; and yet the infinite possible combinations of two semantic units are the source of an inexhaustible fund of meanings. At every level, meaning stems from the way terms are combined. No doubt this is what accounts for the predominant role played by complementary pairs of opposites and correspondences in Chinese thought and above all for its fundamental relativism.[216] Nothing has meaning except through opposition to its contrary. Everything depends upon position (*wei*) and timing (*shi*).[217] This is the type of thought to be found in the *Yijing*, the ancient Classic which fuelled philosophical thought in China for so long. The 64 hexagrams of the *Yijing* were, so to speak, a superior and refined form of the language itself. They sharpened the Chinese sense of what is relative or opportune.

Our own philosophical traditions, which owe so much to 'the suggestions stemming from certain grammatical functions',[218] are founded upon categories considered to be universal and are concerned with abstractions and ideas that are stable. Chinese thought, in contrast, recognises only functional classifications and oppositions. It is concerned not with 'yes' or 'no', being or non-being, but with contraries which succeed, combine with and complement one another; not with eternal realities but with potentialities and tendencies, phases of flowering or decline. In the place of the idea of law as an immutable rule, it favours that of a model or schema for development.

The lack of those mental categories which we take to be constitutive of all rational thought does not imply an essential inferiority, but rather different modalities of thought, the strength and flexibility of which may, on further consideration, be seen as advantages. In the manipulation of the Chinese language, the mental mechanisms and aptitudes that are at work are different from those which have been favoured in the West. Comparisons and combinations are preferred to logical articulations.

Accustomed as they were to manipulating the abstractions of scholastic philosophy in their schools, the missionaries considered the Chinese to be poor at reasoning. Ricci reflects upon the fact that 'they have no logic and do not know how to distinguish moral goodness from natural goodness or acquired goodness from that which is given by nature'.[219] And Father Foucquet, for his part, considers them to have 'little aptitude for the subtleties of dialectic' despite the fact that 'for the most part, they have good minds'.[220]

The Chinese, meanwhile, accused the missionaries of indulging in 'all kinds of breaks and separations' and 'countless incomprehensible lines of reasoning'.[221]

In *The True Meaning of the Master of Heaven*, Ricci does in effect attempt to teach the Chinese to reason in accordance with the rules of scholastic philosophy. He sets in opposition irreconcilable and mutually exclusive realities and qualities: the animate and the inanimate, the sensible and the insensible, the incorporeal and the corporeal, the organic and the inorganic, what is endowed with reason and what is not, the soul and the body, substance and accident. These are distinctions that are summarised in Porphyry's tree, where they provide categories for classifying everything in the world.[222] Ricci makes use of the entire logical apparatus inherited from classical Antiquity and medieval scholasticism: Aristotle's four causes,[223] the three types of soul (vegetative, sensitive and rational),[224] the three forms of inclusion of the inferior by the superior (for bodies, the larger includes the smaller; for natures, the rational soul includes the sensitive soul; for virtues, the Master of Heaven possesses in himself the natures of the Ten Thousand Beings),[225] the seven forms of identity,[226] what has a beginning and an end (perishable bodies), what has a beginning but no end (human souls created by the Master of Heaven) and what has neither a beginning nor an end (the Master of Heaven).

In the history of Western thought, the opposition of substance to accident had been so fundamental that a great effort was needed to free oneself of that idea. That opposition encompassed that of the noun to the adjective which is so fundamental to Indo-European languages. Here, too, the language no doubt helped to produce the concept of the existence of permanent and ideal realities, independent of the unstable diversity of what can be perceived through the senses. But for the Chinese, whose language lacked inflections, the abstract concept of substance could not have the same logical necessity as it did for the European missionaries of the seventeenth and eighteenth centuries, who were accustomed to use languages which regularly made a distinction between the adjective and the noun and who were heirs to a long scholastic tradition. To express the notions of substance and accident which were vital in proving the Christian truths and without which the missionaries considered it to be impossible to think correctly, Matteo Ricci had been obliged to resort to circumlocutions, translating substance as 'that which is established of itself' (*zilizhe*) and accident as 'that which depends upon something else' (*yilaizhe*). From the Chinese point of view the distinction was gratuitous and artificial since in their language nothing of the kind was suggested.

Desiring to justify these categories, Ricci produces an example which shows clearly that the origin of the mental schema is linguistic. He says:

Let us consider the term 'white horse', in which we have the words 'white' and 'horse'. The horse is the substance [that which is established of itself] and white is the accident [that which depends upon something else]. Even if there was no white, there could still be a horse; whereas if there was no horse there could be no white. So white is accidental. If one compares these two categories [one will say that] all that is substance is primary and [that] all that is accident is secondary and lowly.[227]

The choice of the term 'white horse' was no doubt suggested to Ricci – or, more probably – to his Chinese collaborators by the memory of the sophist, Gongsun Long (*c.* 320–250 BC), who declared in one of his most famous paradoxes that 'white horse is not horse' (*baima feima ye*).[228] But what is remarkable is that Gongsun Long gives the two words 'white' and 'horse' equal status, just as they are of equal status in the Chinese language. He declares: 'The one relates to colour, the other to form.' Form and colour are not opposed to one another as substance and accident. And Gongsun Long writes: 'The horse which is not linked with the white is the horse. The white which is not linked with the horse is the white' (*ma wei yu bai wei ma; bai wei yu ma wei bai*). What seems to us to be illogical, or clumsy and stumbling logic in the Chinese sophists is illuminated when one refers not to our mental categories but to the characteristics of the language which they are manipulating.

The distinction between substance and accident was indispensable to Ricci's proof – irrefutable in his view – of the absolute autonomy of the spirit and the existence of a rational soul. The proof consisted, precisely, in the spirit's capacity for abstraction. Only the spirit (*shen*) is capable of conceiving what is spiritual (*shen*):

If I wish to understand something, I must strip it of all that is corporeal and 'spiritualise' it [i.e. form a mental conception of it] (*shen zhi*). Then I can receive it in my mind. Take a yellow ox. If I wish to understand its nature and substance, I look at its colour and say: that is not the ox but the colour of the ox. I hear its lowing and I say: that is not the ox but the cry of the ox. I eat its meat and I say: that is not the ox but the taste of the ox. So I cannot know what the ox is until I strip it of all that was corporeal about it – its colour, its lowing, its taste, etc. – and form a mental conception of it.[229]

It was a development of the concept of substance and a Platonic idea of the ox which must have left many a Chinese completely baffled.

A comparison between the Chinese and Western situations confirms Benveniste's analysis: the structure of Indo-European languages seems to have helped the Greek world – and thereafter the Christian one – to conceive the idea of realities that are transcendental and immutable as opposed to realities which are perceived by the senses and which are transitory.

J.-P. Vernant writes:

In the intellectual world of the Greek philosopher, in contrast to that of the thinkers of China or India, there is a radical dichotomy between being and becoming,[230] between the intelligible and the sensible. It is not simply that a series of oppositions between antithetical terms is set up. These contrasting concepts, which are grouped into couples, together form a complete system of antinomies defining two mutually exclusive spheres of reality. On the one hand there is the sphere of being, of the one, the unchanging, of the limited, of true and definite knowledge; on the other, the sphere of becoming, of the multiple, the unstable and the unlimited, of oblique and changeable opinion.[231]

And Plato writes:

On the one hand, we have that which is divine, immortal, indestructible, of a single form, accessible to thought, ever constant and abiding true to itself; and the soul is very like it; on the other hand, we have that which is human, mortal, destructible, of many forms, inaccessible to thought, never constant nor abiding true to itself: and the body is very like that.[232]

The Greeks had imagined a heaven of pure, eternal ideas, a heaven of which the world of men was but a crude and distorted reflection. Thereafter, over the centuries, Christian thought deepened the opposition between the kingdom of God and the earthly world, between the rational and eternal soul and the body destined to return to dust, and between the creative spirit and brute matter.

But concepts of being and substance set in opposition to those of becoming and sensory perception are by no means universal. What is considered evident in one civilisation is not considered so in another. Words in the Chinese language do not refer to static abstractions but to dynamic ideas which are defined through opposition and complementarity. Chinese thinkers are concerned not with eternal realities revealed by the use of reason and discourse, but rather with the phenomena of growth and decline. The Chinese concept of human nature (*xing*) evokes an order of development in conformity with nature, and that is why the *Mencius* speaks of 'exhausting one's nature', the sense of the expression being that man must develop the tendencies towards the good which exist in him only as potentials. Similarly, the concept of *li*, 'the principle of order', which is so fundamental, does not in any sense refer to an immutable law external to beings and the universe; on the contrary, it evokes the idea of an internal principle of organisation and development. It is not hard to understand how it was that Ricci made the mistake of regarding the *li* as a kind of hypostasis or as the equivalent of the Platonic *eidos*. Attempting to pour scorn upon the Chinese ideas, he writes: 'Let us imagine a cartwright who has in mind the *li* of a cart. Why does he not produce a cart forthwith?' To which the Chinese man of letters whom Ricci introduces into his work replies, in conformity with the traditional Chinese ideas:

> I have heard it said that the *li* [the principle of order inherent in the universal energy] gave birth to the *yin* and the *yang* and the five phases[233] and that subsequently these elements produced Heaven and Earth. So there is progressivity in these phenomena of production.[234]

Ricci is not averse to reproducing the Chinese line of argument since he regards it as absurd and believes that simple reasoning inspired by 'natural enlightenment' is enough to demolish it entirely: there must be a cause for the existence of the world and that cause can only be a creator God. But for the Chinese, in contrast, it was the very idea that the world might have been created by a God which seemed ridiculous.[235] Sensitive as they were to the spontaneous nature of natural phenomena, they could not imagine action on the part of an external agent where, it seemed to them, simple, natural mechanisms were at work. They refused to dissociate from the universe the forces which animate it: for them, order was inherent in nature. Here again, we may ponder on the suggestive power of particular linguistic characteristics. Perhaps civilisations with languages that clearly indicated, through their morphology, which was the subject and which the object of the verb and which, furthermore, possessed both active and passive voices, were more inclined to develop an opposition between the agent and the object of its action, to form a more precise idea of the personalities and attributes of divine powers and to make a distinction between the acting spirit and brute matter. In this connection, we may at the very least note once again a remarkable parallelism between the Chinese language and Chinese thought. In Chinese, the subject is no more than whatever an assertion is being made about. There is no necessary link, made manifest through morphology, to connect subject, verb and complement. Every Chinese text has in general an impersonal tone. As conceived by the Chinese, the action of nature is impersonal and impartial. Heaven acts without intention (*wuxin*).

It is therefore possible that linguistic peculiarities may have played a covert role in human reasoning and that they may have favoured certain orientations of thought. At all events, the intellectual traditions, modes of thought and vision of the world of the Chinese differed markedly from those of Europe. Together with the social organisation and political traditions of China, these differences constituted a considerable obstacle to Christianisation, as is shown in a particularly instructive fashion by Chinese reactions to the action of Christian missionaries in the seventeenth century.

The missionaries were deeply inbued with all that the oppositions between the kingdom of God and the earthly world and between the eternal soul and the perishable body imply for the human moral and
philosophical order and they were convinced of the existence of transcendent truths. At the farthest extremity of the Eurasian continent they
had come into contact with a scholarly and developed civilisation which
differed fundamentally, not on particular points, but as a whole, from all
that had become familiar to them by virtue of their own long traditions.
Instead of the stratified world of Christianity, they were faced with a
global universe where all things – dominant ideas, morality, religion,
politics – were mutually related and echoed one another. They found
themselves in the presence of a different kind of humanity. (However, it
goes without saying that the situation is now very different, for China
and the West have both evolved since the seventeenth century.)

Around 1700, at the time of the quarrel over rituals, Europe was
passionately debating the question of whether the Chinese ceremonies
were superstitious and therefore incompatible with the Christian faith or
whether they were purely civil and political and therefore compatible.
This was to make the mistake of limiting to one detail, which had meaning only within the mental categories of the West, a question of much
wider significance: namely, whether it was possible to reconcile Christianity with a mental and socio-political system which was fundamentally
different from the one within which Christianity had developed and from
which it was, like it or not, inseparable. If the doctrine of the Master of
Heaven was regarded by many Chinese as a threat to the most venerable
traditions of China, to society, morality and the state, this cannot simply
have been a xenophobic reaction as has so often been suggested. Instead
of rejecting from the start the arguments of the Chinese, it might have
been worth taking the trouble to learn from them.

Notes

Introduction

1. Sometimes known as the 'literati'. The Chinese literate elite comprised those of mandarin rank who had received an education in the Chinese Classics and had passed the state examinations for entering the civil service.
2. *Histoire de l'expédition chrétienne*, Introduction, p. 49.
3. In histories of Christianity in China, it is customary to recall the earlier installation of a Nestorian community in the capital of the Tang dynasty in the seventh to ninth centuries, and also the foundation of a Catholic arch-bishopric in the Peking of the Mongols at the beginning of the fourteenth century. But these episodes are no more than historical curiosities. Only Nestorianism appears to have been of any importance but it remained the religion of merchants of Syrian origin.
4. In this connection we should refer the reader to the work of Georges Dumézil and the studies of the linguists, particularly Emile Benveniste, *Le Vocabulaire des institutions indo-européennes* (2 vols., Paris, Ed. de Minuit, 1969).
5. See p. 223.
6. Le Comte, II, letter to Father de la Chaize, p. 356: at the time of his departure from China in 1691, Father Le Comte estimated there to be about forty Jesuits, to whom should be added '4 ecclesiastics from foreign missions ... almost as many Dominican Fathers, 12 to 15 Franciscans, 3 or 4 Augustinians, all of them Spaniards from Manila'. This would seem to be the period of the greatest number of missionaries.

Sources

1. For the end of the sixteenth century and the beginning of the seventeenth, we can refer to the easily accessible and very interesting correspondence comprising the letters of Fathers Michele Ruggieri and Matteo Ricci, published by Tacchi Venturi. For the end of the seventeenth century and the eighteenth century there is some interesting, but widely scattered, information in the 31 volumes entitled *Lettres édifiantes et curieuses*. Father Louis Le Comte (1665–1728), who was in China from 1687 to 1691, reveals himself in his letters as a remarkable observer. He was also one of the best French writers of his time. On the other hand, the correspondence of the

Fathers in Peking, who were too preoccupied with their scientific work and their services to the emperors, tell us very little about Chinese reactions.

2. China had a start of more than five centuries over Europe in this field.

3. The books composed in China by the missionaries reached Japan, Korea and Vietnam, where written Chinese played the role of a scholarly language.

4. *Fonti Ricciane*, ed. Pasquale d'Elia (3 vols., 1942–9), I, p. 198. Henceforward referred to as *FR*.

5. *FR*, III, p. 283.

6. *Histoire de l'expédition chrétienne*, p. 641.

7. The book printed by wood-block technique seems to have played a less important role in the diffusion of Christianity in Japan, where trade in Chinese books had always been flourishing. Following the proscription of Christianity, the Tokugawa promulgated a number of severe prohibitions against the importation of Chinese books written by missionaries. Works of a scientific character were proscribed just as the religious works were. Cf. Itô Tassaburô, 'The book-banning policy of the Tokugawa Shogunate', *Acta Asiatica*, XXII (1972), pp. 36–61. On the Christian literature published in Japan by the Jesuits (who set up a European printing press there in 1590), see the references given by Mme Minako Debergh in 'Deux études sur l'histoire du christianisme au Japon', *Journal asiatique*, CCLXVIII, 3–4 (1980), p. 402, note 17.

8. Cf. Henri Bernard, 'Adaptations chinoises d'ouvrages européens', *Monumenta Serica*, X (1945), p. 314.

9. Longobardo, p. 93.

10. Xu Changzhi is mentioned in the monograph on Haiyan, now Haining, on the northern coast of Zhejiang province, of which he was a native (*Haiyan xianzhi*, chapter 17, 18a). After following classical studies, he became, in 1631, a disciple of the Buddhist master, Total Enlightenment (Yuanwu, 1566–1642), the abbot of the Jinsu monastery in Haiyan, who later installed himself in Ningbo, and subsequently of the master, Tongrong (1593–1661). It was these two monks who were the authors of the short works which appear in the last volume of the *PXJ*. Xu Changzhi's brother, Xu Congshi, is better known. Born in 1574, he successfully passed his doctorate examination in 1607. He was appointed prefect of Jinan in Shandong province in 1621 and won fame through his repression of an uprising by the White Lotus sect led by Xu Hongru in 1622. He became governor of Shandong province, was besieged in Laizhou during the rebellion of Kong Youde and was killed by a cannon ball in 1638.

11. This Xu Fuyuan should not be confused, as he is in the *DMB* (pp. 272, 1662), with another individual with the same personal name but a different family name of Xu and whose dates were 1599 to 1665.

12. See the note on him by Fang Hao at the beginning of the first volume of the *TDXB*.

13. *Chan* is the Chinese word from which the Japanese *zen* is derived.

14. Cf. Ch'en Sou-i (1936).

15. An allusion to the folkloric stories about the magic mirror that makes it possible to see the monsters which hide beneath the appearances of ordinary men.

16. A biography of Yang Guangxian can be found in Arthur W. Hummel, *Eminent Chinese of the Ch'ing Period* (Washington, 1943), pp. 889–92. It dwells upon the pretensions and ridiculous aspects of this individual, who was by no means a fool.

17. George Elison, *Deus Destroyed: The Image of Christianity in Early Modern Japan* (Cambridge, Mass., Harvard University Press, 1973), p. 542.

18. This translation seems to me more accurate than that of *Anti-Jesuit* adopted by G. Elison.

1 From sympathy to hostility

1. Letter of 25 January 1584, *TV*, II, p. 420.

2. Letter of 30 May 1584, *TV*, II, p. 422.

3. On the approval that the Chinese so frequently extend to what the missionaries say, cf. pp. 19, 82–3.

4. Letter from Ruggieri written from Macao (12 November 1581), *TV*, II, p. 403.

5. Letter from Ricci to the Visitor, Francesco Pasio, Peking, 1609, *TV*, II, p. 381. Cf. *Histoire de l'expédition chrétienne*, p. 40.

6. Ricci would have liked to abandon his Buddhist monk's robes sooner but was obliged to wait for authorisation from the hierarchy. Nevertheless, as early as the autumn of 1592, he decided no longer to call himself a monk (*heshang*). A year later, his companion, Lazzaro Cattaneo, asked Valignano, the Visitor for Japan and China, for permission for the missionaries to grow beards and long hair and, on official visits, to wear the black silk robes of the literate elite. Permission was not granted until 1594 and it was not until May 1595 that Ricci availed himself of it for the first time. Cf. *FR*, III, chronology, pp. 25–6.

7. *TV*, II, p. 215. My italics. Cf. also *ibid.*: 'we have spread our reputation as theologians and literate preachers since, among them, that is what we are'.

8. *TV*, II, p. 211.

9. *FR*, I, p. 379, note 4.

10. E. Zürcher, 'The first anti-Christian movement in China', *Acta Orientalia Neerlandica* (1971), p. 193. On the analogies between Chinese morality and Christian morality, cf. pp. 141–4.

11. *TV*, II, p. 209.

12. The Chinese appear to have been very struck by the missionaries' physical appearance. At the time of his first visit to Fujian province between 1625 and 1639, Giulio Aleni was described by Huang Wendao (*Pixie jie*, *PXJ*, V, 19a) as 'a man with blue eyes and the beard of a dragon'.

13. *TV*, II, pp. 207–8.

14. These figures are somewhat exaggerated.

15. The patron Saints of Confucianism.

16. Li Zhi's information is incorrect: Ricci arrived in Zhaoqing, the administrative capital for the provinces of Guangdong and Guangxi, on 10 September 1583 and left for Shaozhou in the north of Guangdong province in August 1589. It was in May 1595 that he left Guangdong province definitively.

17. Here, in contrast, Li Zhi's accuracy is remarkable. Ricci himself tells in his memoirs of the astonishment of the participants in a meeting of this kind where, after remaining silent for a long time, he decided to make an intervention which demonstrated that nothing in the discussion had escaped him. See *FR*, II, p. 78.

18. *Xu fenshu (Continuation of the Book to be Burned)*, chapter 1, letter to a friend (Zhonghua shuju edn, Peking, 1975), p. 35.

19. *TV*, II, p. 225. The Chinese of the seventeenth century were easily moved to tears. Cf. p. 102.

20. *FR*, II, p. 291.

21. The *Jiaoyou lun (On Friendly Relations)* (1595), the *Ershiwu yan (The Twenty-five Utterances)* (1604), and the *Jiren shipian (Ten Chapters of an Uncommon Man)* (1608).

22. The scientific, technical and artistic activities of the Jesuit Fathers at the Court in Peking became more diverse under the Manchus in response to the emperors' requests. They raise the whole question of Western contributions and influences in China during the seventeenth and eighteenth centuries – a question that extends beyond the framework of the present study and certain aspects of which are only now beginning to be the object of serious research.

   Right from the start, the Jesuit missionaries had the idea of attracting the interest of the Chinese by means of their Western scientific ideas; but the curiosity they provoked was far greater than any of them had dared to hope.

   It is true that the Jesuit missionaries did introduce a few important novelties, such as the demonstration of the sphericity of the earth – a fact which had been both claimed and accepted in China in earlier periods – the introduction of new fields of mathematics, and techniques of astronomical calculation more reliable and accurate than those that had been in use in China since the fourteenth century. But these things were not all entirely new, for China was not without its own scientific tradition. Some mathematicians among the literate elite discovered analogies between the knowledge from the West and what had been taught in China ever since the Han and Sung dynasties. Quite contrary to the thesis put about in the first half of the twentieth century, when Western knowledge of the history of Chinese science was still limited, the teaching of the missionaries contained nothing of a kind to upset existing ideas. Nor did any of the Jesuits' teaching to the Chinese bear the mark of modern science or indeed convey its spirit. Their teaching always remained in conformity with that purveyed in their colleges in Coimbra and Rome. Neither Copernicus nor Galileo were really legitimated in China. The Jesuits first taught the Chinese the astronomical theories which were current in Europe at the end of the sixteenth century, and once they had become installed in the astronomical service of the capital they limited themselves to introducing into China such new knowledge as was useful to their own calculations, which was strictly of a practical and immediate nature.

23. *Dijing jingwu lue* (Shanghai edn, 1957), pp. 60–61. The work was completed in 1635 or 1636. See the biography of its author, Li Tong, who died in 1637, in *DMB*, pp. 969–70.
24. On the effect on the Chinese of the religious paintings imported from Italy, cf. p. 87.
25. It should be remembered at this point that Chinese printing was at its peak at the end of the Ming period. The Western books no doubt surprised the Chinese more by virtue of their strangeness and, in particular, their writing, than by their technical qualities.
26. For a critique of these clocks, see p. 63.
27. *Lifa lun, PXJ*, VI, 20a–25a, which traces the history of astronomy and calendars in China down from the period of Emperor Wudi of the Han dynasty (141–87 BC).
28. *PXJ*, I, 7a.
29. It is quite true that a division of roles between the missionaries took place quite early on, those in Peking, at the Court, devoting themselves to science and technology, while those in the provinces attempted to convert the common people. Cf. pp. 45, 46.
30. Bartoli, p. 150.
31. H. Bernard, *Monumenta Serica*, X (1945).
32. For these figures, cf. Hummel, Fang Hao and *DMB*.
33. Cf. p. 19.
34. *TZSY*, pp. 628–9.
35. On the Donglin academy and the political movement of the Donglin, see the study, which has become a classic, by Heinrich Busch, 'The Tung-lin shuyuan and its political and philosophical significance', *Monumenta Serica*, XIV (1949–55), pp. 1–163.
36. That was the missionaries' thesis. Thus, at the beginning of the second part of his *Treatise*, Longobardo writes that 'the interpreters' – that is to say the neo-Confucians of the Sung period – were 'influenced by the sect of idols, which was of Indian origin'.
37. *FR*, II, p. 74.
38. Cf. *FR*, II, note to pp. 156–8.
39. Here is one, among many others: in a *Refutation of the Heresy (Yiduan bian)*, Gao Panlong, one of the restorers of the Donglin academy, expresses his indignation at the Hangzhou men of letters' inclination towards Buddhism. He writes as follows: 'At the time of the second moon of the summer [in 1605], I went to Wulin [Hangzhou] and stayed by the Lake of the West. I learned that the men of letters of that place adhered to heterodox doctrines and I felt very sad about it within myself. I asked them whom they followed. They told me it was Lianchi [the great Buddhist

monk, Zhuhong, 1535–1615] and they showed me several books that he had written. Most of them denigrated Confucianism and praised Buddhism. This monk had first been brought up in the schools of Confucianism, but one fine day he revolted and went over to the heresy ... I cannot understand such ingratitude towards the doctrine of our Saints and the teaching of our schools. This monk has written a book in which he attacks Zhu Xi [the most eminent representative of neo-Confucianism, 1130–1200] with all his might' (*Gaozi yishu*, III, 52a *et seq.*).

40. Ricci had written a *Mnemotechnical Method* (*Jifa*), in Chinese, probably published between 1628 and 1631. The ability to learn texts by heart was much appreciated in China.
41. Cf. p. 141.
42. *FR*, I, pp. 108–9.
43. A way of referring to Buddhism.
44. My italics.
45. Letter written in 1609 to the Visitor, Francesco Pasio, *TV*, II, p. 386.
46. Cf. *FR*, I, p. 108, note 1.
47. *TZSY*, p. 416. The Jesuit missionaries were later to learn that the Jews of China also used the terms *tian* and *shangdi* to translate the name of Yahveh as, for instance, on the steles in the synagogue of Kaifeng in Henan province, which are dated 1489, 1612 and 1663. Cf. *FR*, I, p. 108, note 1b. See Joseph Dehergne and Donald Leslie, *Juifs de Chine* (Paris, Les Belles Lettres, 1980), pp. 63–9. Note also that the term *shangdi* was used by Protestant missionaries as a translation for God, in the nineteenth century.
48. Letter of 4 November 1595, *TV*, II, p. 207.
49. Those who have been called the 'figurists', namely Fathers Bouvet (in China from 1687 to 1693 and from 1707 to 1730), J. de Prémare (in China from 1698 to 1726), Foucquet (in China from 1699 to 1720) and Gollet (in China from 1700 to 1741), saw the Chinese Classics as cabalistic books in which all the Christian mysteries were hidden.
50. *FR*, II, p. 296.
51. This date is obviously invented. The term 'Taiji' appears for the first time in the appendix of the *Yijing*, the *Xici*, which is dated to the third century BC, but the concept of Taiji acquired a particular importance among neo-Confucian thinkers from Zhou Dunyi (1017–73) on, and occupies a place of central importance in their work.
52. On the question of the *li* or the principle of universal order, see pp. 204–6.
53. Elsewhere, Ricci declares that the Chinese have no logic. It brings us to the fundamental question of the relation between language and thought. See pp. 239–46.
54. My italics.
55. The letter is preserved in the Casanatense Library in Rome, ms. no. 2136. Cited by Father D'Elia, *FR*, II, note to pp. 297–8.
56. *TZSY*, p. 468. Cf. *Lunyu*, VI, 22.
57. *TZSY*, p. 619.
58. *TZSY*, p. 616.

59. The work is the *Tianru yin*, a title that might be translated as *On the Perfect Coincidence [like that of a Seal and its Imprint] between the Doctrine of Heaven and Confucianism*. This work is introduced by a preface dated 1664 and was reprinted in the second volume of the *TDXB*, pp. 989–1042.
60. *TZSY*, p. 551.
61. Longobardo, p. 18.
62. The vocabulary and, indeed, the thesis itself, suggest that Father Noël received considerable help from a Chinese convert.
63. Letter from J. Bouvet of 30 August 1697, cited by Henri Bernard, *Sagesse chinoise et philosophie chrétienne* (Tientsin, 1935), p. 145.
64. Le Comte, II, letter to Cardinal de Bouillon, p. 141. Cf. also, *ibid.*, pp. 146–7: 'People do not realise that China preserved knowledge of the true God for more than two thousand years and practised the purest maxims of morality while Europe and almost all the rest of the world were sunk in error and corruption.' Le Comte goes on to specify that he means the two thousand years 'before the birth of our Lord'.
65. J. Dehergne, *Répertoire*, pp. 209–10.
66. *LEC*, XIX, p. 483; the letter is not dated.
67. Ch'en Shou-i (1935).
68. Although the Jesuits sometimes entertained illusions about the Shangdi of the Classics, which they were prone to liken to the God of the Bible, they certainly entertained none on the score of the ideas of the Chinese of their own period. As early as 1581, the man who was to be Ricci's first companion in Guangdong province, declared in a letter dated 12 November and written in Macao (reproduced in *TV*, II, p. 402): 'This nation has no knowledge of the true God or of the first and supreme cause, attributing all things to Heaven, which they call Tien. And this is the greatest word they have and they say that Heaven is like their father, from whom they have received everything. They pay homage to the Earth, which they call their mother, who produces for them whatever is necessary for their survival. They say that this world came to be by chance, by itself, and so too did all the things which are in it and are governed by destiny, and that punishment and recompense come from Heaven, punishment being a bad life and recompense a good one.'
69. At this period, there was only one famous convert, who had been baptised John. This was Zhong Mingli, a native of Xinhui, near Macao, who entered the Company of Jesus in 1610 as a subordinate brother. It is not known whether this João Fernandes (his Portuguese name) was in Peking between 1610 and 1620. In 1621 he was expelled from the Company for a reason that is not known. Cf. Fang Hao, I, p. 91.
70. Longobardo, Foreword. This is the source for the information given here. The text reads: 'the meaning of our books to theirs', which is in contradiction to the rest of the phrase and, besides, does not make sense. So it must be a mistake.
71. João Rodrigues, known as 'the interpreter' (Tçuzu, that is Tsûji in Japanese), had arrived in Japan as early as 1561 and was obliged to move to

Macao in 1610. He was one of the most determined opponents of the assimilation of ancient Chinese traditions to Christian ones.

72. Qu Rukui came from an important family in Jiangsu province. He had first met Ricci, then still wearing the robes of a Buddhist monk, in Caoqi, near the present-day Shaoguan in Guangdong province, in 1589, and had been his first pupil in mathematics. It was he who advised Ricci to adopt the costume of the men of letters.

73. Longobardo, p. 19.

74. The term *shangdi* had the further disadvantage of expressing a concept very different from that of the Christian God: it was one of the current names of a Taoist deity, the Sovereign of Jade. It was a title that had been officially conferred upon the latter by Emperor Huandi of the Han dynasty, who reigned from 147 to 168.

75. Sainte-Marie, p. 55.

76. In the later, nineteenth-century edition of the missionaries' works in Chinese, the terms Heaven and Sovereign on High were systematically replaced by *tianzhu* (Master of Heaven), *shangzhu* (Master on High), and *zhuzai* (Sovereign Governor), even in quotations from the Classics (which was obviously absurd). Cf. Ch'en Shou-i (1935).

77. Longobardo, p. 21.

78. This is the *Xixue shijie zhujie (An Explanation, with Commentary, of the Ten Commandments of Western Studies)*, a work mentioned by Fang Hao (I, p. 138) among the works by Yang Tingyun. This particular work does not appear to have survived.

79. On these ideas, cf. pp. 204–6.

80. Longobardo, pp. 96, 98. Contrary to the claim made by Longobardo in his treatise, Yang Tingyun does not always speak favourably of Buddhism, but here it is solely a question of the thesis common to the 'three sects', namely that of the unity of the world: 'Heaven, Earth and the Ten Thousand Beings form but one substance' (*tiandi wanwu yi ti*). The hostility that Buddhism, as an anti-social doctrine, attracted, did not prevent some men of letters from borrowing certain ideas and drawing analogies on a philosophical level.

81. My italics.

82. Longobardo, p. 98.

83. Sainte-Marie, p. 104.

84. *Ibid.*, p. 105.

85. Longobardo, pp. 99–100.

86. *Ibid.*, p. 100.

87. *Ibid.*, p. 21.

88. Li Yingshi's preface to the 1606 publication of Ricci's map of the world; the preface is reproduced in Fang Hao, I, p. 160. L. Yingshi, who is called Paul by Ricci and was baptised on 21 September 1602, had been a military commander in Korea at the time of the invasion of the Japanese armies led by Hideyoshi. Like other converts of the early seventeenth century, he was attracted to the missionaries by their mathematics. Cf. *FR*, II, pp. 261–4.

89. Preface to the *Qike (The Seven Victories)* by Diego de Pantoja, first published in Peking in 1604, cited by Ch'en Shou-i (1935).
90. Cited by Ch'en Shou-i (1936).
91. Longobardo, p. 97.
92. The *wulun*, the 'five social relationships' of Confucian morality.
93. Preface by Wang Jiazhi to the *Jiren shipian* by Ricci (1608), Xu Zongze, p. 151.
94. Preface by Chen Yi to Aleni's *Xingxue cushu* (1646), reproduced by Xu Zongze, pp. 212–13.
95. Xu Zongze, p. 212. On Chen Minzhi, cf. *FR*, II, p. 172, note 3.
96. Proclamation made by Shi Bangyao, the maritime inspector of Fujian province on 16 December 1637 (*PXJ*, II, 32b). We should note that in Fuzhou, Father Aleni was called 'the Confucius from the West' by his admirers.
97. Cf. Hummel, p. 876.
98. *Tianxue chuangai, TDXB*, II, p. 1050. On this work and its author, see Hummel, p. 890.
99. *Shangdi kao, TDXB*, I, pp. 49–92.
100. Preface by Feng Yingjing to the *Tianzhu shiyi* (1604), *TZSY*, p. 361.
101. Cf. pp. 129–30.
102. Preface by Chen Yi to the *Xingxue cushu*, Xu Zongze, p. 212.
103. In his *Tianxue chuhan (First Collection of Heavenly Studies)*.
104. These are the great Saints of Confucianism.
105. The principal neo-Confucian commentators of the Classics in the eleventh and twelfth centuries.
106. Xu Zongze, p. 147, and vol. 23 of the Zhongguo shixue congshu editions, pp. 353–6, who provides a better text.
107. Bibliothèque Nationale, Chinese archive no. 7348. The preface is dated 1634. Cf. E. Zürcher, 'The first anti-Christian movement in China', p. 194.
108. *Poxie lun*, in *Zhaodai congshu*. In his notes on the *Songyuan xue'an*, left unfinished by his father, the youngest son of Huang Zongxi, Huang Baijia, born in 1643, frequently cites the physical and astronomical theories introduced into China by the Jesuits. See, in particular, chapter 6 in his commentaries on the *Zhengmeng* by Zhang Zai.
109. The author takes it that the missionaries were not attacking Buddhist philosophy, about which they knew nothing at all. Cf. p. 214.
110. This is a reference to the critique by Yu Chunxi (who died in 1621) on the subject of the permission to kill animals given by Ricci (see *PXJ*, V, 12a–15a) and the pages on Christianity by the Buddhist monk, Zhuhong, at the end of his *Zhuchuang suibi* (1614) (*PXJ*, VII, 1a–4b). A reply to these criticisms appeared under the title, *Bianxue yidu*, several years after Ricci's death.
111. *Hao'an xinhua* (1670), chapter 1, p. 13, in the Congshu jicheng edition. On Zhang Erqi, see Hummel, pp. 34–5.
112. The author seems to be confusing India and the Sukhâvatî, the paradise of Amitâbha situated in the West.

113. *Xifang yaoji*, in *Zhaodai congshu, ji*, p. 5.
114. J. Dehergne, 'Les chrétientés de Chine de la période Ming (1581–1650)', *Monumenta Serica*, XVI, 1 (1957).
115. J. Delumeau, *La Peur en Occident aux XIVᵉ–XVIIIᵉ siècles* (Paris, Fayard, 1978), p. 260.
116. Letter dated 15 February 1609, *TV*, II, p. 381.
117. On the absence, in China, of this distinction between the spiritual and the temporal, considered so fundamental in the West, cf. p. 108.
118. As we have seen above, the number given for this same date is 2,500. These variations testify to the difficulty of keeping an exact count of those baptised: they included people who were dying (children and old or sick people) and there appear to have been many apostates.
119. The correspondence of Nicolas Trigault, published in Antwerp in 1613. Letter cited by Joseph Shih, *Histoire de l'expédition chrétienne*, Introduction, p. 20.
120. Cf. the mission records in Latin and Portuguese provided by these three priests (*FR*, II, pp. 192–244, 484–529).
121. Later periods show a radical change from Ricci's policies: large numbers of converts were aimed for, rather than converts of high quality, and almost all conversions were among men of the people. Father Le Comte provides the following figures for the end of the seventeenth century: 'more than 200 churches or private individual chapels . . . 4 priests from foreign missions, about the same number of Dominican Fathers, 12 to 15 Franciscans, 3 or 4 Augustines – all of them Spaniards from Manila'. But at the time of his departure from China in 1691, there were, above all, 40 Jesuits, making a total of approximately 65 priests. He goes on to say: 'Virtually each one would baptise 300–400 people a year, which comes to more than 50,000 idolaters over five to six years. Furthermore, the 4,000 to 5,000 children abandoned in the streets of Peking each year are all baptised' (Le Comte, II, letter to Father de la Chaize, pp. 355–6).
122. On these figures, cf. Hummel and Fang Hao.
123. It is possible that the religious attitudes of the Manchus, who were formerly nomadic shepherds, remained different from those of the Chinese, despite their relatively profound sinicisation. That is what would appear to be suggested by the remark made by Le Comte at the end of the seventeenth century that 'the Chinese are more docile and easier to convert' than the Tartars (that is, the Manchus) but that 'in times of temptation, they have much less courage. In contrast, the Tartars, who are much rougher by nature, find it hard to submit to the yoke of faith, but those in whom faith has once triumphed display a strength of a kind to withstand the greatest persecutions' (Le Comte, II, letter to Father de la Chaize, p. 360). It would also appear that Muslims were more appreciative of the Christian works composed by the missionaries than the Chinese were. Ricci writes: 'Many people from the sect of the Saracens purchase the *Tianzhu shiyi*, for it seems to conform with their doctrine' (*FR*, II, p. 179). Cf. Ricci's letter cited *ibid*. in a note: 'Someone has told me that many people from the sect

of the Moors who are in this country purchase this book, for it seems to them that it speaks of God better than the other books of China.' Paul Pelliot (*T'oung Pao*, XXI (1921–2), p. 415, note 2) cites a Muslim work which seems to be an Islamic version of the *TZSY*.

124. *Daiyi bian* (1622), passage cited by Ch'en Shou-i (1936).
125. Preface by Chen Yi to Giulio Aleni's *Xingxue cushu* (1646), Xu Zongze, p. 212.
126. Letter from Huang Zhen to the censor, Yan Maoyou, *PXJ*, III, 11a.
127. Preface by Jiang Dejing, who received his doctorate in 1622 and died in 1646, to the *Poxie ji* (1638), *PXJ*, III, 1a.
128. Preface to the *Poxie ji* (1639), *PXJ*, III, 22b.
129. *Rangyi baoguo gongjie, PXJ*, VI, 10a.
130. *Zuiyan, PXJ,* III, 26b.
131. *PXJ*, I, 22b.
132. *Xiedu shiju, PXJ*, III, 33b.
133. *ZP*, 33a.
134. Le Comte, I, pp. 54–5.
135. On this map of the world, see the bibliography provided by Father d'Elia in his *Fonti Ricciane*.
136. *PXJ*, III, 37a–b.
137. Shi Bangyao (1585–1644), who received his doctorate in 1621, later committed suicide by poison in Peking, when the town was captured by the troops of Li Zicheng in 1644.
138. *PXJ*, II, 32a.
139. Cf. p. 123.
140. *Zuiyan, PXJ,* III, 27a.
141. *Zhuzuo jiyuan qi* (1634), *PXJ*, VIII, 21b.
142. The technique of translation into Chinese of Western works was much simpler than that of translation from Indian works of the fifth to eighth centuries AD, a period during which the technique became increasingly systematic, involving large teams of Indian, bilingual and Chinese collaborators, each member of which would have one specific task. Generally speaking, where the works originally written by the missionaries were concerned, it seems that an oral translation would be followed by a version in the written language, and men of letters played an essential role both in producing that version and in the final work of 'polishing' (*run*). Lastly, the *imprimatur* of the Jesuit hierarchy would be needed.
143. *TZSY*, p. 628.
144. Arthur F. Wright ('The Chinese language and foreign ideas', p. 298) cites the case of a Chinese pastor who, wanting to provide a decisive proof of the fact that Jesus was truly the son of God, could find no better proof of that relationship than their very names: they both came from the Ye family since the one is called Ye su (Jesus), the other Ye Hehua (Jehovah). The anecdote can be explained by the importance attached, in China, to proper names and family relationships. It is worth noting that, in the nineteenth century, the Taiping regarded the relationship between God, the Father,

and Christ as a family one, imagining there to be an entire divine family. Hong Xiuquan was Jesus Christ's younger brother. Cf. p. 232.

145. C. W. Mateer, 'Lessons learned in translating the Bible into Mandarin', *Chinese Recorder* (November 1908), p. 608. Cited by A. F. Wright, 'The Chinese language and foreign ideas', p. 291. On the absence of any Chinese concept equivalent to the Christian concept of sin and on the metamorphoses of the Incarnation in China, see pp. 167, 229.

146. *FR*, II, p. 295. Cf. Ricci's letter of 4 November 1595, *TV*, II, p. 207: 'As we desire to prove the things of our Holy Faith by their books also, I have during the past years had excellent masters explain to me not only the Four Books but all the six doctrines (the Classics), and I have noted in them many passages which are favourable to the things of our Faith.'

147. M. J. R. Stevenson, cited by A. F. Wright, 'The Chinese language and foreign ideas', p. 302, note 8. The Jewish community of Kaifeng went back to the eleventh century and still existed at the time of the first Jesuit mission.

148. This is the most likely sense.

149. *Pixie jie* by Huang Wendao, *PXJ*, V, 19a–b.

150. *Ibid.*, 21b.

151. The period during which the first Jesuits arrived in China.

152. Letter from Huang Zhen to the censor, Yan Maoyou, *PXJ*, III, 8a–b.

153. *TXZZ*, p. 951.

154. *Siku quanshu zongmu tiyao*, chapter 125, note on the *Ershiwu yan*.

155. Father da Rocha, who arrived in Macao in 1591, died in Hangzhou in 1623.

156. *Shengxiang lueshuo*. Cf. Xu Zongze, p. 176.

157. *Pixie ji*, preface.

158. *PXJ*, I, 22b.

159. *Pixie lun*, p. 1129.

160. On the meaning of this expression, see p. 152.

161. *Zhuzuo ji yuanqi* (1634), *PXJ*, VIII, 21a.

162. Letter of 15 February 1609, *TV*, II, p. 387. My italics.

163. On this expression, cf. pp. 210–1.

164. See p. 55.

165. *ZP*, 15b–16a. The author mentions the converts made by Father Giulio Aleni in Fujian province between 1625 and 1639.

166. *Qingshu jingtan*, cited by Ch'en Shou-i (1936).

167. *Zhuyi lunlue*, *PXJ*, VI, 2b–3a.

168. *Ru si* (like death) is a mistake for *zhi si* (to know death). An allusion to the *Lunyu*, XI, 12: 'May I ask you about death?' Jilu asked Confucius. 'For whoever does not know what life is, how is it possible to know what death is?'.

169. An allusion to a passage in the *TZSY*, p. 407, in which Ricci criticises the concept of the Taiji.

170. On this question, see chapter VI A of the *Mencius*.

171. *Bianxue chuyan* by Chen Houguang of Sanshan, that is Fuzhou in Fujian province, *PXJ*, V, 1a–b. The accusations made by the author look libellous

at first sight, but an analysis shows that, from the point of view of Chinese traditions and ideas, they are well-founded.

172. On the meaning of this expression, see p. 193.
173. *PXJ*, III, 1a, 2a. Jiang Dejing nevertheless believes that indulgence should be shown towards those who have repented of their errors: 'But as for those who, leaving the doctrines of Yang and Mo, returned to the good doctrine, Mencius was prepared to welcome them and he considered it to be wrong to reproach the piglet which had escaped [once it had returned to the pigsty].'
174. An expression to be found in the *Shujing, Wenhou zhi ming* and in the *Shijing, Daya*, the *Daming* poem.
175. Letter from Huang Zhen to Yan Maoyou, *PXJ*, III, 10b.
176. *TZSY*, pp. 404–5.
177. *Ibid.*, pp. 562–70.
178. *Ibid.*, p. 578.
179. *Ibid.*, p. 418. Ricci claimed that sacrifices to Earth were a later addition to sacrifices to Heaven or the Sovereign on High.
180. *TZSY*, p. 417. On the Chinese refusal to dissociate the universe from its organisational principles, cf. p. 198.
181. *TZSY*, p. 532. In reply to a Chinese man of letters who claimed that the *Chunqiu* spoke only of what is correct and what is not (*shi fei*), Ricci maintained that in reality the *Chunqiu* mentions one of the three kinds of vulgar (i.e. profane) interests, namely those relating to fame, whereas he, Ricci, spoke of the interests of the existence to come.
182. *Pixie guanjian lu*, *PXJ*, VI, 8b.
183. *TZSY*, pp. 564–5.
184. *Ibid.*, pp. 567, 569.
185. *Ibid.*, p. 578.
186. *Ibid.*, p. 578.
187. *Ibid.*, p. 615, in which Ricci refutes Mencius' remarks on the duty of providing a descendance.
188. *Ibid.*, p. 619, where Ricci explains the theory of the 'three fathers'.
189. For the complete text of the formula used by Cheng Hao and repeated by Zhu Xi, see p. 196.
190. *Liji, Zhongyong*, 14.
191. *Pixie shuo* by Li Can, *PXJ*, V, 24b, 26a.
192. On the differences between the Chinese and the Christian moralities, see chapter 4.
193. *Pixie lun,* p. 1122.
194. *FR*, II, p. 297.
195. This title does not appear in Xu Zongze's bibliography.
196. *Huihuo xiedang hou gaoshi*, *PXJ*, II, 22a–b.
197. *Pixie lun*, p. 1118.
198. The *Jincheng shuxiang* is an illustrated work which Xu Zongze (p. 373) mentions among the works of Father Adam Schall von Bell, who was born in Cologne in 1592, arrived in Macao in 1619 and died in Peking in 1666.

Schall had been summoned to Peking in 1630 to collaborate on the reform of the calendar. In 1645, one year after Peking was taken by the Manchus, Schall had become director of the astronomical service (*Pixie lun*, pp. 1129–30).

199. This word, which means receptacle or utensil, should not be confused with its homophone character which is used to refer to the universal energy.

200. Letter from Father Parennin dated 28 September 1735, *LEC*, XXIV, p. 23. At this period, however, in the literate and best informed circles, a distinction was made in the missionaries' teaching between the sciences and religion.

201. The men of letters no doubt regarded the sciences as a means to combat superstition. In his memoirs (*FR*, II, p. 55), Ricci mentions the case of a young Chinese who was sent to learn mathematics from him, who assured him that it was not necessary to refute the sect of idols (Buddhism) and that all he need do was teach mathematics. 'Thus, the Chinese, knowing the truth about things of the material earth and heavens, could see for themselves the falsity of the books of idols.' And Ricci goes on to comment: 'and it has indeed happened that many, having learned our sciences and mathematics, subsequently laughed at the Law and the doctrine of the idols, saying that they put forward so many mistakes that it was not possible to believe them in otherworldly and supernatural matters'. In his *TZSY*, p. 595, Ricci cites the Indian mythological themes taken over by Buddhism as scientific absurdities and as proof of the lack of understanding of the true cause of all things, which is God.

The same tactics were later employed against Christianity. A certain Yang Xianji, a pupil of the English missionary, Joseph Edkins (1823–1903), who had arrived in Tianjin in 1861, sought to prove that the Bible was irreconcilable with the facts established by modern science. Cf. Paul A. Cohen, 'The anti-Christian tradition in China', *Journal of Asian Studies*, XX, 2 (February 1961), pp. 177–9.

202. W. J. Peterson, 'Fang I-chih's Western learning', in *The Unfolding of Neo-Confucianism*, ed. W. T. de Bary (New York, Columbia University Press, 1975), pp. 398–9.

203. As has been mentioned on p. 57, from a Chinese point of view 'Western studies' made up a whole which included all the missionaries' teaching, both their religious and moral doctrines and also the sciences.

204. The men of letters who were taking an interest in Western science and technology at the beginning of the seventeenth century.

205. *Siku quanshu zongmu tiyao*, chapter 134, note on the *Tianxue chuhan*.

206. On the categories adopted by Li Zhizao for the classification of the works written by the missionaries, cf. p. 58.

207. *Siku quanshu zongmu tiyao*, chapter 125, note on the *Huanyou quan* by Francisco Furtado (1628).

208. *Ibid.*, chapter 106, note on the *Tianwen lue* by Manuel Dias the Younger.

209. This thesis is developed in Zhang Zai's *Zhengmeng* at the end of the eleventh century. The idea of the evolution of a multiplicity of universes is

taken up in a critique of Buddhist origin on the creation of the world. See p. 194.

210. *Nangong shudu, PXJ*, I, 8a.
211. *Ibid.*, 7b.
212. *Ibid.*, 8b. One thing which appears to have greatly shocked the Chinese is that the missionaries wanted to do away with the intercalary months which periodically made it possible for the lunar calendar to catch up with the solar calendar. They considered the missionaries' claim as scandalous because the use of intercalary months dated from the earliest Antiquity and was consecrated by the entire tradition.
213. See p. 105.
214. *PXJ*, II, 23a. In the trial, the astronomical instruments found in Father Vagnone's possession were used as items of evidence against him. Cf. *ibid.*, 26a.
215. *Pixie zhaiyao lueyi, PXJ*, V, 30a.
216. The two most famous works of Western technology appeared at the beginning of the seventeenth century. Xu Guangqi (1562–1633), under instruction from Father Diego de Pantoja, translated a treatise on *Irrigation Methods of the Great West (Taixi shuifa)*. This work was printed in Peking in 1612 and reproduced in the *Tianxue chuhan*, produced by Li Zhizao in 1628, and also included in the famous agricultural treatise by Xu Guangqi, the *Nongzheng quanshu*, published after his death in 1639. Wang Zheng (1571–1644), who had been passionately interested in mechanics ever since boyhood, collaborated with Father Johann Schreck to produce a work entitled *Illustrated Explanations concerning the Strange Machines of the Distant West (Yuanxi qiqi tushuo)*.
217. Cf. p. 188. It is well known that the Jesuit Fathers of Peking acted as intermediaries in the purchase of cannons from the Portuguese in Macao at the end of the Ming period. Also well known are the efforts of Father Verbiest to set up a little foundry for producing cannon, following the installation of the Manchus in Peking.
218. *Li shuo huangtang huoshi, PXJ*, III, 39a–b.
219. *ZP*, 36a–b.

2 Religious attitudes and the phenomena of assimilation

1. This is the Mahâyâna concept of the *upâya*: the means of achieving awakening are legion; none should be rejected, but none is of any value on its own. At a deeper level, it is the whole question of the concept of truth that is posed by the Chinese attitudes. The concept of one transcendent and immutable truth is alien to Chinese thought. Cf. pp. 238 ff., on the relation of language to thought.
2. All forms of worship and all forms of saintliness may be useful. None is exclusive.
3. *FR*, I, p. 132. In his *TZSY*, p. 599, Ricci inveighs against the monstrosity of uniting all doctrines in one.

4. *FR*, II, pp. 65–6. In his *Zhuzi yulei ping*, Yan Yuan (1635–1704) cites, in support of the thesis of the equal holiness of all three doctrines in the seventeenth century, Lu Shanji (1575–1636), Sun Qifeng (1585–1675) and Du Yue (1595–1682).
5. See the article on Lin Zhao'en in *DBM*, pp. 912–15 and the recent study by Judith A. Berling, *The Syncretic Religion of Lin Chao-en* (New York, Columbia University Press, 1980). In our own day, Caodaism in Vietnam has been inspired by the same syncretist ideas. Cf. p. 232, note 173.
6. Sainte-Marie, pp. 4, 5. Caballero had lived in Jinan in the early 1660s.
7. Longobardo, p. 21.
8. Le Comte, II, letter to Cardinal d'Estrées, p. 228.
9. Xu Zongze, p. 308.
10. This is the neo-Confucian formula: *tiandi wanwu yi ti* ('Heaven, Earth and the Ten Thousand Beings are all the same and single substance').
11. Longobardo is referring to the Taoists.
12. The name given by the missionaries to the neo-Confucian philosophers who had produced new commentaries on the Classics during the eleventh and twelfth centuries.
13. He is thinking of the missionaries who held the opposite view on the question of 'whether there was anything in the Chinese sciences that related to these three things: God, the Angels and the Rational Soul'. See the Foreword of Longobardo's *Treatise*.
14. Longobardo, pp. 97–8.
15. Cf. *TZSY*, pp. 599–602.
16. J. J. M. de Groot, *Sectarianism and Religious Persecution in China* (2 vols., Amsterdam, 1903, 1904).
17. Le Comte, III, Preface to the 2nd ed.
18. *TZSY*, p. 452.
19. Longobardo, pp. 94–5. On the fundamental thesis of the unity of the world in Chinese ideas, cf. p. 146. 'Matter' and 'spirit' are not two fundamentally heterogeneous substances.
20. *Lunyu*, VII, 22.
21. *Ibid.*, VII, 21.
22. *Ibid.*, XI, 12.
23. Cf. *Dutongjian lun*, chapter 3, p. 77, lines 1–5 in the Peking edn (1975).
24. On the Chinese ethic of the perfecting of the individual as man's supreme goal, cf. p. 163.
25. Sainte-Marie, p. 131.
26. *Zhouyi waizhuan*, V; *Xici, shangzhuan*, 8, pp. 189–90 of the Peking edn (1977).
27. *Lunyu*, XI, 12.
28. *ZP*, 8a–b (summarised text). The doctrine of the Master of Heaven had been accused of creating dissatisfaction and anxiety in the followers of Christianity. Cf. p. 150.
29. *Qingshu jingtan*, chapter 15, cited by Ch'en Shou-i (1936).
30. Huang Zhen's preface to the *Poxie ji, PXJ*, III, 22b.

31. Le Comte, II, letter to Cardinal de Janson, p. 398.
32. That is to say, the Sovereign on High, whom the Chinese identified with the immanent order of the universe.
33. The last sentence alludes to the Taoist cult of the Sovereign of Jade, also known as the Sovereign on High (Le Comte, II, letter to Cardinal de Bouillon, p. 186).
34. Letter from Ricci, written in Zhaoqing, 20 October 1585, *TV*, II, p. 55. Ricci was nevertheless obliged to recognise a certain piety among the upper classes. In 1609, he wrote: 'They also have pious inclinations, as I am gradually realising, although many others may believe the contrary.' Cf. *TV*, II, p. 385.
35. Remember that the costume and tonsure of the Buddhist monks had been first adopted by the Jesuit missionaries of Japan and, in China, these were not exchanged for the costume of the literate elite – beards, and hair worn long – until 1595, twelve years after the arrival of the first Jesuits.
36. *Histoire de l'expédition chrétienne*, Introduction by Joseph Shih, p. 32.
37. *Ibid.*
38. *Ibid.*, p. 26.
39. Cf. p. 68.
40. *Histoire de l'expédition chrétienne*, Introduction, p. 33. On the natural tendency to integrate Christian teaching into the religious system of China, cf. pp. 76–7.
41. Namely the 'three jewels': Buddha, the Community of Monks and the Buddhist Law (Buddha, Samgha, Dharma).
42. But the Buddhist hell and paradise are places of temporary abode, whereas for the Christians they are eternal.
43. In a posthumous article ('Notes on Buddhist hymnology in the Far East', in *Buddhist Studies in Honour of Walpola Rahula* (London, Gordon Fraser, 1980), Paul Demiéville studies this analogy and the enigmas that it poses.
44. Cf. *TV*, I, pp. 123–4.
45. *Histoire de l'expédition chrétienne*, Introduction, p. 32.
46. J. Delumeau, *La Peur en Occident*, p. 256.
47. *TXCZ*, pp. 921–2.
48. *Tianshi mingbian (On the Distinction between [the Doctrine of] Heaven and Buddhism, TDXB*, I. In 1585, the civil governor of Guangdong province wrote to ask Ruggieri and Ricci for 'the doctrine of the West [that is, Buddhism], which had arrived in China many years ago but had then been corrupted'. On early confusions between Christianity and Buddhism, encouraged among the Chinese by the missionaries disguising themselves as Buddhist monks, cf. J. Gernet, 'La politique de conversion de Matteo Ricci et l'évolution de la vie politique et intellectuelle en Chine aux environs de 1600', in *Sviluppi scientifici, prospettive religiose, movimenti rivoluzionari in Cina* (Florence, L. S. Olschki, 1975), pp. 116–19, and 'Sur les différentes versions du premier catéchisme en chinois de 1585', in *Studia Sino-Mongolica* (Wiesbaden, Franz Steiner, 1979), pp. 409–10.
49. *Weitan airen jilun*, Bibliothèque Nationale, Chinese archive no. 6868, 18b.

50. *Histoire de l'expédition chrétienne*, p. 504.
51. *TXZZ*, p. 919.
52. *TXZZ*, p. 942.
53. John E Wills jun., 'Maritime China from Wang Chih to Shih Lang', in *From Ming to Ch'ing*, ed. J. E. Wills jun. and J. D. Spence (Yale University Press, 1979), p. 219.

    In an address to the international conference of sinology held in Taipei in August 1980, Li Chia-yuan notes that a certain Xu Yun (1569–1618), the author who is the subject of his study, favoured a syncretism incorporating Taoism, Buddhism and Christianity.
54. Bibliographical note on the *Tianzhu shiyi, Siku quanshu zongmu tiyao*, chapter 125.
55. This remark was made by Emperor Yongzheng to the Fathers of Peking on 21 July 1727 on the occasion of the arrival of a Portuguese ambassador, Antoine Gaubil (*Correspondance de Pékin* (Geneva, Droz, 1960), pp. 1189–1290). The text of the address neatly sums up the classic position adopted by the Chinese literate elite towards Christianity.
56. Cf. *Histoire de l'expédition chrétienne*, Introduction by Joseph Shih, p. 47.
57. *TXZZ*, pp. 949–52.
58. On Zhuhong, cf. *DMB*, pp. 322–4 and the work by Chün-fan Yü, *The Renewal of Buddhism: Chu-hung and the late Ming Synthesis*.
59. This is a reference to the *Tianshuo* (*Explanations on Heaven*), which appears at the end of the third volume of Zhuhong's writings, the *Zhuchuang suibi*. Father d'Elia also attributes the *Bianxue yidu* to Ricci.
60. Cf. *Bianxue shuo* (January 1636) by the Buddhist monk, Yuanwu (Total Enlightenment), and *Zhengwang shuo* by Zhang Guangtian, *PXJ*, VII, 13a–30a and 32b–33a.
61. Literally, 'the *dharma* of the world'.
62. *ZP*, 23a–24a.
63. It was only relatively late on that some members of the literate elite had themselves baptised. Thus Qu Rukui first met Ricci in 1590 and was not baptised until 1605, while Li Zhizao, who first made contact with the missionaries in 1601, did not receive baptism until 1610.
64. Letter from Father Foucquet, written in Nanchang (1701), *LEC*, V, p. 151.
65. Letter dated 12 November 1581, written in Macao, *TV*, II, p. 403.
66. It was not long before Ricci became aware of the full proliferation of Chinese deities. Cf. p. 83.
67. Letter dated 13 February 1583, *TV*, II, pp. 28, 31.
68. *Histoire de l'expédition chrétienne*, p. 493.
69. Le Comte, II, letter to Cardinal d'Estrées, p. 157.
70. *Ibid.*, pp. 159–62.
71. Pfister, I, p. 30.
72. This remark suggests he is referring to the temples which contain images of often as many as five hundred Buddhist saints (*arhat*), or the one thousand and one Kannon with a thousand arms of the Sanjûsangen dô in Kyôto, a

complex of temples dating from the Kamakura period (1185–1333).

73. *FR*, I, p. 131.
74. Cited by Chen Shou-i (1936).
75. On the destruction of the statues, see pp. 178–80.
76. *Sh'er shenkai (Twelve Reasons for Profound Grief)*, *PXJ*, VI, 14a–b. Text dated 1636.
77. *Histoire de l'expédition chrétienne*, pp. 504–5. Cf. also *ibid.*, p. 495: 'another neophyte had brought one of his friends to the point where he was receiving the catechism. But when it came to speaking to him of giving up his idols, he could not be persuaded to give them up so ignominiously'.
78. Le Comte, II, letter to Father de la Chaize, p. 277.
79. Father Pierre-Martial Cibot was born in Limoges in 1727 and arrived in Macao by way of Rio de Janeiro in 1759. He was 'an expert on mechanics and botany, and a polygraph' (J. Dehergne, *Répertoire*, p. 176).
80. Letter from Father Cibot, Peking, not dated, *LEC*, XXX, p. 104.
81. The Chinese interest in Western painting is also noted by Ruggieri in a letter dated 25 January 1584 in which he asks to be sent 'a fine picture of the Virgin with Christ, which these gentlemen of China are very keen to see, and a few images of the mysteries of our faith, painted on paper so that they can be shown more easily, for they are extremely interested in painting' (*TV*, II, p. 420).
82. *FR*, I, pp. 193–4. The Virgin, at first called Shengmu niangniang (goddess holy mother), was possibly confused with the goddess of sailors, the Mazu po, also known as Tianfei (heavenly lady), or Tianhou (heavenly empress). But there was also some confusion with Guanyin, the giver of children.
83. Apparently a reference to little sticks of incense of the Chinese type: the setting encouraged comparison with the Chinese cults in the minds of the spectators.
84. *Histoire de l'expédition chrétienne*, p. 493.
85. *FR*, II, p. 110.
86. *Ibid.*, pp. 125–6.
87. Le Comte, II, letter to Father de la Chaize, p. 277.
88. *Histoire de l'expédition chrétienne*, p. 493.
89. *Ibid.*, p. 278.
90. *Ibid.*
91. Letter from Father Dentrecolles, Peking (1726), *LEC*, XX, pp. 65–6.
92. 'Etat de la Religion dans l'empire de la Chine en l'année 1738', *LEC*, XXV, p. 242.
93. Extract from a number of letters on Tonkin province, *LEC*, XXVIII, p. 277. It would be of little interest to collect together the very numerous examples of miracles performed with holy water, since the information is very imprecise.
94. *TV*, II, p. 448.
95. One of the most ancient references to charmed water comes from the Yellow Turbans of the late second century.

96. *Histoire de l'expédition chrétienne*, p. 509.
97. Louis Wei, p. 44.
98. *Histoire de l'expédition chrétienne*, pp. 494–5.
99. Letter from Father Chavagnac, Fuzhou (1703), *LEC*, IX, pp. 345–7. A similar tale of exorcism followed by conversions is to be found in a letter from Father Foucquet, writing from Nanchang (1701), *LEC*, V, pp. 174–83.
100. Memoirs of Father Noël (1703), *LEC*, V, pp. 94–5.
101. On the destruction of statues, see. p. 129.
102. The original text, which appears in *FR*, II, p. 200, is more precise, stating that this was a king's daughter who had not wished to marry and had become the goddess of child-bearing. She was probably Miaoshan, the younger daughter of a more or less mythical king, who, having refused to marry, was punished and then committed suicide. This goddess was sometimes confused, as in the present case, with the Guanyin of a thousand eyes and a thousand hands. But she is not usually known as the goddess of child-bearing. See Glen Dudbridge, *Legend of Miao-shan*, Oxford Oriental Monographs no. 1 (London, 1978); and Henri Dore, *Recherches sur les superstitions en Chine*, VI, pp. 94–138. I am indebted for this information to M. Soymié. It seems likely that, as Father d'Elia suspected, Coima (or Choima) was the result of a faulty transcription from the manuscript and that this strange name in fact masks that of Guanyin. On Guanyin, the giver of children, see H. Maspero, *Taoism and Chinese Religion*, translated by Frank A. Kierman jun. (Amherst, University of Massachusetts Press, 1981).
103. *Histoire de l'expédition chrétienne*, p. 496. Cf. *FR*, II, p. 200. Here is another example of a similar substitution: when Father Aleni returned clandestinely to Fujian province after his expulsion from there, he transformed into churches two Buddhist temples of Wuyi shan on the border of Jianxi province in the north-west of Fujian province. The Buddhist statues in it were replaced by statues of Christ.

  This was a common procedure which made it possible for non-Christian traditions to perpetuate themselves under a Christian disguise. Vincent Cronin (*A Pearl to India*, p. 225) records a remark made by Gregory the Great, cited by Father de Nobili: 'Tell Bishop Augustine that after pondering the question of the English for a long time, I have adopted the following decision: do not destroy their temples, but only the idols inside; so that this act of grace may induce these people . . . to come and adore [the true God] in places familiar to them.'
104. Cf. p. 83.
105. Pfister, I, p. 84, following Bartoli. Father de Silva died on 9 May 1614, two years before the lawsuit was brought against the missionaries of Nanking.
106. Pfister, I, p. 259. The author claims to have been told these details by Monsignor Delaplace, who was the apostolic vicar to Zhejiang province at the time.
107. See the detailed article by Paul Demiéville, 'Momies d'Extrême-Orient',

Journal des Savants, 3rd centenary (Paris, 1965), pp. 144–70.

108. Le Comte, II, letter to Cardinal de Bouillon, pp. 224–5. Cf. Pfister, I, pp. 202–7, which uses the expression *fang tudi*.

109. Le Comte, *ibid.*, p. 227.

110. *Revue des missions catholiques*, IV (Lyons, 1872), p. 701.

111. Fang Hao, II, p. 33.

112. *Relations de la Chine* (Paris, 1935), p. 242. There are two works by Father Rossi, SJ, on Father Etienne Faber, both mentioned by Pfister (I, p. 207): one is *La Cause du P. Faber* (T'ou-sè-wè, *c.* 1904–5), the other a *Biographie du P. Faber* (T'ou-sè-wè, 1909).

113. Bibliothèque Nationale, Chinese archive no. 6881, a xylograph entitled *Preuve du jugement par le Maître du Ciel (Tianzhu shenpan mingzheng)*.

114. *Zuigen* (root of evil), an expression of Buddhist origin.

115. An abbreviation of *[sacer] dote* (priest).

116. A note explains that this is Saint Paul, Paul being Kuibin's baptismal name. 'The second founding disciple' means the second apostle.

117. Two saints thus appear in the story, one after the other. Only the second is the saint on duty.

118. Note to the text: 'This was Zhang Shi of Quanzhou. His saint's name was Mige. He was a zealous Christian who had performed many meritorious actions and had been called to heaven in 1623. There exists a work entitled *A Collection of the Miracles of Mige*.' Mi'e'er and Mige are both transcriptions of Michael.

119. Literally, 'he was not able to avoid following the vulgar crowd'.

120. Note to the text: 'This was a co-religionary of Kuibin's, a native of Quanzhou, who died in the *dingchou* year [1637].'

121. Note to the text: 'They too were from Quanzhou and had died a few years earlier.'

122. Note to the text: 'They too were from Quanzhou and were fervent Christians. Wang died at the age of 86. Nian had followed the doctrine for over twenty years. They both died peacefully in the *jimao* year [1639].'

123. Sainte-Marie, p. 140.

124. Letter from Father Foucquet, *LEC*, V, p. 232.

125. Father Noël's report on the state of the missions in China (1703), *LEC*, VI, pp. 80–1.

126. Jean Delumeau, *La Peur en Occident*, p. 291.

127. Le Comte, II, letter to Father de la Chaize, p. 272.

128. *PXJ*, VII, 18b, 26a.

129. The dogmatism of the missionaries and their refusal to enter into any discussion were noted by a number of Chinese. Cf. in particular pp. 79–82.

130. *PXJ*, II, 9b–10a. The file on the trial of Zhong Minren and his consorts.

131. On this common reaction, cf. p. 226.

132. *PXJ*, II, 9b.

133. *Ibid*.

134. The massive scale of the conversions that took place in Japan on the orders of daimyô with interests in trading with the Portuguese do not appear to

have unduly shocked the missionaries, nor to have prompted them to any misgivings.

135. Le Comte, II, letter to Father de la Chaize, p. 329.
136. Cf. p. 244.
137. Le Comte, *ibid.*, p. 332.
138. *Ibid.*
139. On the cult of pious images, cf. p. 86.
140. Le Comte, *ibid.*, pp. 337–40.
141. *Ibid.*, p. 341.
142. Letter from Father de Fontaney (1704), *LEC*, VIII, pp. 116–19.
143. Letter from Father Desrobert, Petsiuen chan, Hubei (1741), *LEC*, XI, p. 379.
144. Letter from Father Dentrecolles, Raozhou (1715), *LEC*, XIII, pp. 329–30.
145. Le Comte, II, letter to Cardinal de Bouillon, pp. 165–7.
146. Coffins, in the form of three biers enclosed one within another, were frequently kept in the home until such time as enough money had been saved to pay for the funeral rites and a festival day had been picked for the ceremony.
147. *ZP*, 31b.
148. Letter from Father Parennin, Peking (1735), *LEC*, XXIV, p. 43.
149. Le Comte, II, letter to Father de la Chaize, p. 311.
150. Letter from Father François d'Ollières, Peking (8 October 1769), *LEC*, XXX, pp. 169–70.
151. Le Comte, letter to Cardinal de Bouillon, pp. 170–71.
152. Le Comte, II, letter to Father de la Chaize, p. 278.
153. *Ibid.*, p. 297.
154. *Ibid.*, p. 278.
155. Letter from Father Dentrecolles, Raozhou, Jiangxi (1712), *LEC*, X, p. 200.
156. This detail is a reminder of the importance ascribed, in Buddhism, to copying and reciting sacred texts.
157. Letter from Father de Neuvialle, *LEC*, XXVI, p. 363. To judge by its contents, this letter must date from Father de Neuvialle's stay in Hubei, from 1740 to 1746.
158. Fang Hao, I, pp. 259ff.
159. *Zhuzuo jiyuan qi, PXJ*, VIII, 21b. The custom of clicking fingers (*tanzhi* – in Sanskrit *acchara*) to express joy and satisfaction is of Indian, Buddhist origin.
160. *ZP*, 34b.
161. In Buddhist teaching, the eight forms of knowledge are those of sight, hearing, smell, taste, touch, thought, the spirit and the inmost knowledge of the basic truths.
162. *ZP*, 31b.
163. Le Comte, II, letter to Father de la Chaize, pp. 388–93.
164. Yan Yuan, *Cunren bian*, chapter 2, *Huan mitu*, p. 22 in the Congshu jicheng edn, no. 989.
165. *Xiaoluan bu bingming shuo, TDXB*, I.

3 Religion and politics

1. Cf. E. Chavannes, *Les Mémoires historiques de Se-ma Ts'ien*, chapter 28, 'Les sacrifices *feng* et *chan*', on the royal sacrifices to Heaven and Earth.
2. *Sapientia sinica* by Father Intorcetta, printed in 1662 and cited by Sainte-Marie, p. 130.
3. On the concept of Shangdi, cf. p. 193.
4. *FR*, I, p. 117: '*Anzi vogliono che a questo Re del Cielo solo il Re deva servire e sacrificare, e se altri lo volessero fare sarebbono gastigati come usurpatori della iurisditione regia.*'
5. There is a kind of pun here on the word *zhu*, which means both 'ancestral tablet' and 'master'.
6. *PXJ*, III, 1a–b.
7. *ZP*, 20a.
8. Cf. *Liji, Wangzhi*, 31. There are analogous passages in *Liji, Quli*, B, 21.
9. *Pixie jie* by Huang Wendao, *PXJ*, V, 20b.
10. See, p. 152.
11. The analogy clearly does not relate to the existence of a single God since Buddhists and Taoists believe in nothing of the kind.
12. *TXCZ*, 22nd absurdity, p. 923.
13. *Nangong shudu*, *PXJ*, I, 6b–7a. On the notion of Heaven, conceived of both as nature and as the organisational principle of nature, cf. p. 194.
14. *ZP*, 25a. The equality of the sovereign and his subjects stems from the institution of a Master of Heaven to whom even the emperor owes obedience. On the egalitarianism of Christianity, cf. pp. 117–19.
15. *Pixie lun*, p. 1125. By declaring the sky (or Heaven) to be no more than matter, the missionaries do, in effect, deprive Heaven of the very attributes upon which its majesty rests according to the Chinese concepts.
16. *Pixie zhaiyao lueyi, PXJ*, V, 28b.
17. *ZP*, 20b. One quite often comes across this idea, namely that it was the missionaries themselves who *invented* the doctrine of the Master of Heaven. In his *Pixie shuo* (*PXJ*, V, 23a), Li Can regrets being born so many millennia after Confucius and Mencius, so many centuries after Zhou Dunyi, the brothers Cheng and Zhuxi, and more than one hundred years after Wang Yangming, in a period when vicious ideas are rife. He mentions having recently heard of the so-called doctrine of the Master of Heaven, 'a doctrine the origin of which goes back to the Western illusionist, Matteo Ricci'.
18. In the Musée Guimet, in Paris, there is a copy of this stele engraved in 781. The fullest study of the stele is by Father H. Havret, *La Stèle chrétienne de Si-ngan-fou* (3 vols., T'ou-sè-wè, 1895–1902), *Variétés sinologiques*, nos. 7, 12, 20.
19. As does the author of a short preface to Father Aleni's *Shengmeng ge*. Cf. Xu Zongze, p. 343. On Nestorianism in China, see Yoshiro Saeki, *The Nestorian Documents and Relics in China* (Tokyo, Maruzen, 1951).
20. *TZSY*, p. 378. It is worth noting, in passing, that from the Han period to the Ming, the Chinese knew a greater area of the world than the West did,

since their geographical knowledge extended from Japan to the shores of the Mediterranean.

21. As Buddhism did. It was the treasure-hoarding of which the Buddhist Church was guilty that was the primary cause for its proscription in the years 843–5.

22. Cf. *TZSY*, p. 534: 'Interest in the world to come distracts from interest in the present world. If it could be arranged for all people to aspire to the advantages of the world to come, where would be the difficulty in governing them?' This is an argument also adopted by the convert, Wang Zheng (1571–1644), in his *Treatise on the Supreme Principle of Fear of Heaven and Love of Men (Weitian airen jilun)*, 18b.

23. The work in which this passage occurs, the *Bianxue yidu*, was published several years after Ricci's death but probably to some extent borrows from some of Ricci's posthumous writings.

24. The first certain evidence of the presence of Buddhism in China goes back only to the first century AD.

25. Literally, 'the present is not worth the past' *(jin bu ru gu)*. Buddhism in China was often criticised on account of the brevity of the dynasties whose emperors were fervent Buddhists. This was seen as proof of its inefficacy. Han Yu (768–824) resorted to this classic argument in his famous attacks against Buddhism.

26. *Bianxue yidu*, in *Tianxue chuhan*, vol. 2, p. 647.

27. *Xifang wenda*. A study and translation of this text by John Mish is to be found in 'Creating an image of Europe for China: Aleni's *Hsi-fang wen-ta*', *Monumenta Serica*, XXIII (1964).

28. An expression used to denote periods of perfect morality.

29. *Bianxue shugao*, *TDXB*, I, pp. 25–6.

30. *Zengding Xu Wending gong ji* (Shanghai, 1933), I, p. 13.

31. Preface by Zheng Man (1594–1636), a figure connected with the Donglin, for the work by his friend Wang Zheng. Cf. p. 110, note 22.

32. It complements it on points where the ancient traditions are supposed to have been interrupted by the Burning of the Books by the first Qin emperor in 213 BC.

33. Xu Zongze, p. 123. On this Zhang Xingyao, baptised Ignatius in 1678. See Fang Hao, II, pp. 99–104.

34. *Bianxue shugao*, *TDXB*, I, pp. 29–30.

35. A town in the south of Shanxi province which the missionaries made one of their most active centres at the end of the Ming dynasty.

36. On his return from exile in Macao from May 1617 to March 1624, Vagnone took the Chinese name of Gao Yizhi and from December 1624 on lived in Jianzhou. In 1633 he was in Fuzhou, in the neighbouring province to Shenxi. He died in April 1640 in Jiangzhou.

37. This proclamation appears in the Chinese archives in the Bibliothèque Nationale, no. 6875 (3rd text). My italics.

38. Chinese archives of the Bibliothèque Nationale, no. 6875 (1st text). This work should not be confused with the famous *Tianxue chuangai* composed

by Li Zubai in 1663 (cf. p. 36, note 98). It is earlier and should be attributed to a native of Fujian province by the name of Huang Mingqiao.

39. On this frequent accusation of buying conversions, cf. p. 123. Keeping up-to-date records of the families of converts appears to have been standard practice for the missionaries.

40. *Nangong shudu*, *PXJ*, I, 11a–14b. Shen Que, who received his doctorate in 1592, had been appointed vice-minister of the Board of Rites in Nanking in 1615. His memoranda against Vagnone, who had started setting up Christian communities in Nanking when he settled there at the beginning of 1605, are dated June and September 1616 and January 1617. For a biography of Shen Que, see *DMB*, pp. 1177–8.

41. Proclamation issued by the legal inspector's office in Fujian province, 20 December 1637, *PXJ*, II, 36a; and Proclamation issued by the prefecture of Fuzhou, Fujian province, same date, *PXJ*, II, 38a.

42. *Xiedu shiju* (1638), *PXJ*, III, 33b–34a.

43. Although the latter did become a necessary precaution once the public authorities became alarmed at the increase of associations of the Master of Heaven among the people.

44. *Xiaoluan bu bingming shuo*, *TDXB*, I, pp. 39–47. According to Fang Hao (I, p. 132), Yang Tingyun composed his pamphlet in 1617 in response to the accusations of Shen Que, who, in his memorandum, compared Christianity to the Chinese sects of the White Lotus and the Non-Action.

45. Cf. *Can yuan yi shu*, *PXJ*, I.

46. See J. J. M. de Groot, *Sectarianism and Religious Persecution in China*.

47. 'Proclamation following the arrest of the irregular association', *PXJ*, II, 23a–b.

48. Cf. Yan Yuan, *Cunren bian*, chapter 2, *Huan mitu*, p. 22 in the Congshu jicheng edn, no. 989.

49. *LEC*, XXVII, pp. 283–4.

50. *ZP*, 19a. Each convert has to give the names, official addresses and dates of birth and death of his father, grandfather and great-grandfather.

51. The file of charges against Vagnone and others, *PXJ*, I, 22b.

52. *ZP*, 19b–20z. On the intermingling of the sexes, cf. p. 189. Beating one's breast and letting down one's hair are gestures of mourning. They are also adopted by Chinese Christians performing acts of contrition.

53. *ZP*, 31a.

54. Christianity teaches of the existence of souls, angels and Satan.

55. The usurper and founder of the short-lived Xin dynasty (9–23 AD).

56. *ZP*, 35b.

57. *ZP*, 21a.

58. *TZSY*, VII, p. 378.

59. *Bianxue chuyan*, *PXJ*, V, 4a.

60. *PXJ*, *Pixie guanjian lu* by Zou Weilian, 8b–9a. Cf. also *ZP*, 21b: the Barbarians would like 'to force egalitarianism' upon the hierarchies of sovereign and subjects, etc., using the single word 'friend'.

61. *ZP*, 16b–17a.

62. *ZP*, 18b.
63. *TZSY*, p. 719.
64. George Elison, *Deus Destroyed*, p. 283. Fucan was writing at a time when the power of the Shogun had begun to extend control over the whole of Japan and subsequently found it necessary to eliminate the enclaves of Christians.
65. Louis Wei, p. 44.
66. *PXJ*, I, 5b–6a.
67. Letter to Yan Maoyou, *PXJ*, III, 19a.
68. *Buren buyan, PXJ*, VII, 11a.
69. *Lunyu*, XIV, 35. Whoever needs to reproach himself for nothing and performs his duties as a man to the best of his abilities should derive satisfaction from that alone. It is through such behaviour that he 'serves Heaven'.
70. *Lunyu, ibid*. On these moral ideas, see p. 160.
71. Literally, 'magical invocations' (*mizhou*).
72. *Bu ming yu xia*. The expression is borrowed from *Shujing (Proclamation of Zhonghui)*.
73. *Bianxue chuyan, PXJ*, V, 8b–9b.
74. *Lifa lun, PXJ*, VI, 22b–23a.
75. *ZP*, 22b.
76. *Quyi zhiyan, PXJ*, III, 30b. The belief is attested by a letter from Father Pélisson, Canton (1700), *LEC*, I, pp. 87–8. The missionaries are accused of making ointments out of the bones of the dead with which to put spells upon the common people, who then follow them blindly. The *Xiedu shiju* (*PXJ*, III, 34a–b) also refers to magic procedures and drugs which cause followers to lose all their personal will-power. According to a letter from Father de Fontaney (1704) (*LEC*, VIII, pp. 96–7), the conversions effected by Father Baborier, on the border between the provinces of Fujian and Jiangxi, were compromised by an individual who spread the rumour that the missionaries prepared the oil for baptisms by boiling the intestines of the dead, swearing that he had seen this with his own eyes in Manila, where he had lived for three years.
77. *Quyi Zhiyan*, 31a.
78. *FR*, II, p. 115. Cf. *Histoire de l'expédition chrétienne*, p. 450.
79. Cf. among others, the letter from Mgr Foucquet, Nanchang (1701), *LEC*, V, pp. 147–8; and the letter from Father de Chavagnac, Fuzhou (1703), *LEC*, IX, pp. 344–5; for the nineteenth century, see, for example, Louis Wei, p. 44.
80. This work, about which nothing else is known, contained a description of Macao in the early seventeenth century.
81. *ZP*, 26b. This passage from *The Aid to Refutation* points out that, according to the missionaries, man is not made for this earthly world and his true land is in Heaven.
82. Letter from Father d'Entrecolles, Raozhou, Jiangxi (1715), *LEC*, XIII, p. 362.
83. Cf. *FR*, I, p. 107, note 1. Qu Rukui was baptised Ignatius in 1605.

84. Letter from Father d'Entrecolles, Raozhou (1715), *LEC*, XIII, pp. 363–5.
85. *Ershi shenkai, PXJ*, VI, 13a–b.
86. *Pixie zhaiyao lueyi, PXJ*, V, 30b.
87. Le Comte, II, letter to Cardinal de Janson, p. 380.
88. *Tianzhu shiyi shasheng bian (Critique on the Right to Kill Living Creatures, as proclaimed by the True Meaning of the Master of Heaven), PXJ*, V, 15a. Yu Chunxi had obtained his doctorate in 1583 and he died in 1621.
89. *ZP*, 18b.
90. *PXJ*, I, 11b and II, 23b.
91. 'An account of a general movement of persecution in 1746', by Father Chanseaume, *LEC*, XXVII, pp. 283–4.
92. *Aomen xingshi lun*, p. 7331 in the *Yudi congchao* collection, vol. XII.
93. Luis Frois, *Die Geschichte Japans*, translated from the Portuguese (Leipzig, 1926), p. 463. Cited by George Elison, *Deus Destroyed*, p. 37.
94. *ZP*, 19a.
95. *PXJ*, II, 6a. João da Rocha arrived in Macao in 1591 and died in Hangzhou in 1623. Between 1609 and 1619, at the time of the lawsuit, he was living in Nanchang, which was on the route between Macao and Nanking, and he was consequently in a good position to act as an intermediary.
96. The *hetu* is a magic picture which, according to a number of late traditions, had been brought to Yu the Great by a god of the Yellow River.
97. *Zhuxie xianju lu, PXJ*, VI, 18a.
98. An apocryphal work composed during the Han period but which Xu Dashou believes to be authentic. The same expression appears in the *Liezi*, chapter IV. Cf. L. Wieger, *Les Pères du système taoïste*, p. 118, C.
99. *ZP*, 3a.
100. Cf. *Shiji*, chapter 48, biography of Chen She.
101. *Pixie lun*, pp. 1112–13.
102. *Pixie lun*, pp. 1113–14; Matthew 27: 37.
103. This is the aberration deplored by the philosopher, Yan Yuan, in *Curen bian*, *Haun mitu*, 'The recall of the strayed ones', 5th paragraph.
104. Letter from Huang Zhen to the censor, Yan Maoyou, *PXJ*, III, 11a.
105. Sects of Buddhist and Taoist inspiration of the late Ming and the Manchu periods.
106. *Pingshu ding*, chapter 1.
107. *Zuiyan (The Charge), PXJ*, III, 27a.
108. Letter to Yan Maoyou (1638?), *PXJ*, III, 12a.
109. *Ibid.*, 13b.
110. The words used are *xuemai* or *xueshu*.
111. *Shi'er shenkai (Twelve Reasons for Profound Grief), PXJ*, VI, 16a.
112. *PXJ*, VI, 13b–14a. It is impossible to render the style of this quite literary text with any accuracy in translation.
113. Letter from Father de Chavagnac, Fuzhou, Fujian (1703), *LEC*, IX, p. 330.
114. Letter from Father François Dollières (d'Ollières), Peking (8 October 1769), *LEC*, XXX, pp. 172–3.

115. A reference to the books of all kinds brought back to China by Father Nicolas Trigault following his tour of the courts of Europe.
116. This figure is relatively accurate for the date when this text was composed, that is, 1638 or 1639.
117. One of the provinces where the efforts of the missionaries met with the most success during the first half of the seventeenth century.
118. Letter from Huang Zhen to the censor, Yan Maoyou, *PXJ*, III, 11a–b.
119. The Society of Jesus.
120. Namely, the provinces of Nanking and Peking.
121. This list shows that Huang Zhen, who was writing in about 1639, was relatively well informed.
122. Letter from Huang Zhen to Yan Maoyou, *PXJ*, III, 10a–b.
123. To the Chinese, it seemed equally nonsensical that Jesus should be positioned on the right hand of God while the left, the position of honour in China, should be reserved for those who are 'cursed' and condemned to the 'everlasting fire, prepared for the devil and his angels' (Matthew 25:41). Cf. A. F. Wright, 'The Chinese language and foreign ideas', pp. 300–1.
124. *PXJ*, VI, 17a–b.
125. An allusion to an incident in the life of Confucius recorded in the *Lunyu, Shu'er* and the *Mencius, Wanzhang, shang*.
126. Letter from Huang Zhen to Yan Maoyou, *PXJ*, III, 13a.
127. This seems to be yet another instance of the missionaries' prohibition against ancestor worship.
128. *Xiedu shiju* (1638), *PXJ*, III, 33b.
129. Le Comte, I, p. 257.
130. Li Zubai died in 1665. He was employed in the calendar office and was consequently in constant contact with the Jesuit Fathers – a fact which may explain his conversion. He had written a preface for a work by Giacomo Rho, the *Aiqin xingquan*, published in 1633. Cf. Xu Zongze, pp. 70–1.
131. The *Pixie lun* appears in the *Budeyi*, Yang Guangxian's collection of anti-Christian works, but the *Juxi ji* appears to have been lost.
132. The expression, *shaqing*, more precisely denotes the operation which, before the invention of paper, consisted in drying over a fire the little sheets of wood or bamboo which had been used for writing upon.
133. Letter to the censor, Xu, *Budeyi*, I, 2nd text, pp. 1091–6.
134. *PXJ*, I, 16a.
135. *Quyi zhiyan*, *PXJ*, III, 30b, 31b. Jilong and Danshui are two ports in northern Taiwan, which the Spaniards from Manila had occupied but were evicted from by the Dutch, who had been installed in Tainan on the eastern coast since 1624.
136. Jiang Dejing was a native of Jinjiang (in the Quanzhou region in the south of Fujian province), who had received his doctorate in 1622 and had become the minister of the Board of Rites, and an academician during the Chongzhen period (1628–43). He died in 1646. Initially a supporter of the missionaries, he turned against them when he became better informed about their doctrine. Cf. p. 44.

137. *Rangyi baoguo gongjie*, *PXJ*, VI, 10a–b.
138. Literally, 'their claws and their teeth'.
139. Letter to the censor, Xu Zhijiang (1664), *Budeyi*, I, p. 1102.
140. *LEC*, XIV, letter from Father de Mailla, Peking (1717), who cites the request made by the mandarin, 'Tchin-mao', in the same year.
141. As in the letter from Yang Guangxian to the censor, Xu Zhijian, p. 1098.
142. A reference to the missionaries. As from 1595, when Ricci had obtained permission to dress as a member of the Chinese literate elite, all the Jesuit missionaries had adopted this costume.
143. *ZP*, 40b.
144. *Poxie ji xu*, *PXJ*, III, 6a–b.
145. *Xiedu shiju*, *PXJ*, III, 33a, text dated 1638.
146. *Daiyusu* in Japanese.
147. *Deus Destroyed*, pp. 283–4.
148. *Rangyi baoguo gongjie*, *PXJ*, VI, 10a. Addressed to the academician, Jian Dejing, winter 1638–9.
149. *Pixie zhaiyao lueyi*, *PXJ*, V, 30b.
150. Cf. p. 122.
151. Le Comte, II, letter to Cardinal de Janson on the Edict of Tolerance, p. 380.
152. *PXJ*, V, 30b.
153. Adam Schall von Bell was born in Cologne in 1592 and arrived in Macao in 1619. At the end of the Ming period he became president of the astronomical office in Peking and managed to reobtain that post after the arrival of the Manchus. He died in Peking in 1666 when, following the attacks of Yang Guangxian, he was on the point of being condemned to death for treason.
154. We may perhaps see this as a reflection of a traditional saying, identifying whatever is wild with what is barbarian.
155. *Pixie lun*, pp. 1130–2.
156. 'The state of religion in the empire of China in the year 1738', *LEC*, XXV, pp. 267–8.
157. *PXJ*, I, 6b.
158. See Louis Wei, *La Politique missionaire*; and Paul. A. Cohen, *China and Christianity: The Missionary Movement and the Growth of Anti-foreignism, 1860–1870* (Cambridge, Mass., Harvard University Press, 1963).
159. P. Pelliot, *L'Origine des relations de la France avec la Chine. Le premier voyage de 'l'Amphitrite'* (Paris, Geuthner, 1930), p. 22.
160. This message was given to the Europeans in Suzhou. The text is included in a collection of archive documents discovered in the imperial palace of Peking in 1925, 1928, and 1930 and published by Ch'en Yuan, the rector of the Catholic university of Peking, in *Kangxi yu Loma shijie guanxi wenshu* (Peking, 1932). Cf. Pang Ching-jen, 'Documents chinois sur l'histoire des missions catholiques au XVIIe siècle', *Neue Zeitschrift für Missionswissenschaft* (1945), 1st year, no. 1, pp. 39–43.
161. The minister of the Board of Rites intervened in this affair not because it

was a matter of religion, but because foreigners were concerned.

162. Le Comte, II, letter to Cardinal de Janson, p. 407.

163. Le Gobien, 'Histoire de l'édit de l'empereur de la Chine en faveur de la Religion chrétienne', in vol. II of *Nouveaux mémoires sur la Chine de P. Louis Le Comte*, p. 173.

164. Le Comte, I, p. 107.

165. The expression comes from the *Shuduan* chapter of the *Shujing*.

166. The funerary stele of his tomb was discovered in 1956 in the suburbs of Nanking.

167. *PXJ*, I, 15a–16a.

168. *ZP*, 4a–b.

169. *PXJ*, VII, 37b. On the Buddhist critique of Christianity, cf. pp. 214–21.

170. Preface by Jiang Dejing to the *Poxie ji*, *PXJ*, III, 1b–2a.

171. This inscription, which was hung in many churches in China founded by the Jesuits, was to be the subject of many polemics as some people regarded it as evidence of an abominable idolatry, namely, worship of the material sky.

172. See Joseph Dehergne and Donald Leslie, *Juifs de Chine*, plate VII, and p. 155.

173. Le Comte, II, letter to Cardinal de Bouillon, p. 186.

174. This, at least, was the theoretical position. In practice, it was permissible to intervene in affairs of state whenever the superior interests of religion were involved.

175. Reply to the 'Requête présentée à l'empereur par le mandarin Tchinmao', in 1717, *LEC*, XIV, p. 160.

4. Chinese morality and Christian morality

1. Cf. p. 8.

2. *Lunyu*, XII, 1: *keji fuli wei ren* (Humanity consists in conquering oneself in order to return to propriety).

3. In the first version of the catechism in Chinese, dated 1584, and in the original in Latin produced in 1581, the *Vera et brevis divinarum rerum expositio*, chapter 7, presents a pagan who rejoices at finding in the Christian precept, *nihil alteri inferat quod sibi non pateretur*, the equivalent of the expression to be found in the *Lunyu*, XII, 2, *ji suo buyu wu shi yu ren*. The Chinese wood-cut or xylograph is preserved in the Roman Archives of the Society of Jesus, Jap. Sin. section, I, 189, 190.

4. Letter of 10 December 1593, *TV*, II, p. 117.

5. Letter of 14 August 1599, *TV*, II, p. 248.

6. *TV*, I, p. 459: *'Era già stato ristampato questo libro in diverse provincie quattro volte, e le due non per via de' christiani, ma degli gentili, parendogli utile per il ben vivere.'*

7. *FR*, II, p. 181.

8. Prefaces were written for the *Qike* by Yang Tingyun, Cao Yubian (1558–

1634), who received his doctorate in 1592 and was a high-ranking civil servant whose sympathies were with the Donglin, Zheng Yiwei and Chen Liangcai; an introduction for it was written by Xiong Mingyu, who received his doctorate in 1601; a postface was written by Wang Ruchun and introductory notes to each chapter by a certain Cui Chang.

9. Cf. p. 23.
10. *Mencius*, VII A, 1.
11. Cf. Christofer A. Spolatin, *Matteo Ricci's Use of Epictetus* (Waegan, Korea, 1975).
12. *Mencius*, VII A, 3.
13. *Gaozi yishu*, 3, 17b.
14. Letter of February (?) 1605, *TV*, II, p. 257.
15. *Ibid.*
16. In his *TZSY* p. 581, Ricci explains what an examination of conscience means for Christians.
17. The expression comes from the *Zhongyong* and the *Daxue*: 'The worthy man takes stock of himself in solitude' (*junzi shen qi du*).
18. The term *zixing* is the one used by Gao Panlong (cf. *DMB*, p. 701); that of *shendu* appears in Liu Zongzhou (cf. Hummel, p. 531).
19. Fang Hao, I, note on Yang Tingyun.
20. The biography of Wang Yuan (1648–1710) in the *Yanshi xueji* by Dai Wang (Preface dated 1869), chapter 8, notes that Wang Yuan was cured of his drunken habits by Li Gong and thereafter kept a 'Register of personal examination' (*Xingshen lu*) after the manner of Yan Yuan, in which he kept a record of his actions and thoughts with a view to improving himself.
21. Cf. Wu Pei-i, 'Self-examination and confession of sins in traditional China', *Harvard Journal of Asiatic Studies*, XXXIX, 1 (June 1979), pp. 5–38. In this article, Wu Pei-i notes the antiquity of oral and written confession in techniques of healing in Taoist sects. These confessions were made to deities and were accompanied by a commitment to no backsliding. Wu Pei-i's opinion is that the examination of conscience and the practice of self-accusation were used in particular in literate circles between 1570–1670. Now, it was during this very period that the missionaries obtained their greatest successes in these circles. The same author points to the feeling of culpability that is conveyed by the confessions made at the end of the Ming period. Those making confession would seek out their hidden faults and the inadmissible motives behind their most secret thoughts. Wu Pei-i considers this type of confession to be not very different from Christian confession but to stand in clear opposition to the optimism of the Sung period: Cheng Yi in the eleventh century and Zhu Xi in the twelfth were in agreement in that both held that it was good to accuse oneself of one's faults, but that one should not remain submerged in remorse for too long; what mattered was 'not to fall into the same errors again' (*bu er guo*), as the *Lunyu* puts it. The increasingly marked tendency towards introspection at the end of the Ming period is probably attributable to the influence of Wang Yangming (1472–1529) and the currents of thought that he initiated. On

the *Books of Morality* (*Shanshu*) and the *Registers for Self-knowledge*, cf. Chün-fang Yü, *The Renewal of Buddhism in China: Chu-hung and the Late Ming Synthesis*, pp. 101–37.

22. Cf. p. 72, note 34.
23. Cf. Wu Pei-i, *art. cit.* According to Wu Pei-i, counting up one's faults and merits originated from the Taoists, but it would appear that the idea of weighing positive *karma* against negative *karma* stemmed from Buddhism.

    One of the most ancient works on counting up one's faults and merits was the *Taishang ganying pian* by Li Changling (937–1008); it was a very popular work and was often republished.
24. On this opposition, cf. pp. 153–4, 173.
25. This method of notation was not peculiar to Huang Wan. A certain Lin Chun (1498–1541) was also making use of red and black inks to record his good and his bad actions. Since the Han period, at least, the colour red had been used to note the positive numbers, black to note the negative ones.

    The first to have reintroduced this practice during the Ming period was Wu Jiang (end of the fifteenth to the beginning of the sixteenth centuries) and Yuan Huang (1533–1606), according to Wang Fuzhi (*Du tongjian lun*, chapter 3, Peking edn (1975), pp. 80–1). The system was revised and corrected by the great Buddhist master, Zhuhong (1535–1615), who entitled his handbook *Register for Self-knowledge* (*Zizhi lu*). Cf. *DMB*, p. 324.
26. *Mingdao bian* by Huang Wan, chapter 2, cited by Hou Wailu, *Zhongguo sixiang tongshi*, IV B, p. 930.
27. *Ibid.*
28. *Songyuan xue'an*, I, p. 25; and p. 44 of the Guoxue jiben congshu edn.
29. *Zuiyan*, *PXJ*, III, 27a.
30. The *Baopuzi* by Ge Hong (about 317 AD) mentions three *hun* and seven *po* when referring to the ancient Taoist traditions.
31. Literally, 'correct' (*zheng*) as opposed to 'partial or incomplete' (*pian*).
32. *TZSY*, p. 463. A commentary by Huang Baijia, the son of the philosopher, Huang Zongxi, on the subject of a passage in the works of Zhu Xi concerned with whether plants have sensation, cites the Western theory of the three souls as a proof supporting, not a radical distinction between man and other beings, but – on the contrary – a continuity between the various living species. Cf. *Songyuan xue'an*, Guoxue jiben edn, II, chapter 12, p. 32. The passage in question from Zhu Xi runs as follows: 'Every time that I look at the trees blossoming with different kinds of flowers lit up by the morning sun, with all the flowers blooming joyously, they seem to me to have a sense of life (*shengyi*). There is an explosion, a general surge of corollas opening to the sunshine. On the other hand, the dried-up branch with its dead leaves is experiencing a feeling of sadness: that is because its vital energy has gone.'
33. *TZSY*, p. 463.
34. Longobardo, Foreword.
35. This expression usually has an unfavourable meaning in Chinese, denoting duplicity; but that is clearly not the case here.

36. *TZSY*, pp. 434–5.
37. As the 'Chinese man of letters' observes in the *TZSY*, p. 458.
38. *Mencius*, IV B, 19.
39. *TXZZ*, pp. 934–5.
40. These expressions are used by the author to refer to Buddhist ideas on transmigration, for the 'other life' of the Christians was still being likened to Buddhist rebirth. Cf. p. 230, for the interpretation of the life of Jesus, suggesting that he passed in succession through the destinies of god, man, infernal being, man and god.
41. On the Taiji, cf. p. 210.
42. *ZP*, 9a–10a.
43. *Ibid.*, 25a.
44. *Mencius*, VII A, 39. The translation 'making use of his body' for *jian xing* is employed simply for want of a better one. The word *xing* implies not just the body but the entire sensible world.
45. *Yuandao pixie shuo*, *PXJ*, VIII, 16b.
46. These two points are further developed on pp. 170–1.
47. The traditional way of referring to the *xin* (spirit–heart) in Chinese.
48. Cited by R. L. Taylor, *The Cultivation of Sagehood as a Religious Goal in Neo-Confucianism: A Study of Selected Writings of Kao P'an-lung (1562–1626)* (Ann Arbor, Scholars Press, 1978), pp. 122–3.
49. *FR*, II, p. 77.
50. Cf. p. 154.
51. Literally, 'the beginnings' (*duan*).
52. *Mencius*, II A, 6.
53. D. Diderot, *Correspondance*, novembre 1760, ed. Georges Roth (Paris, 1957), p. 226.
54. *Gaozi yishu*, III, 42b.
55. *Mencius*, VI A, 8.
56. Cf. the fine article by Marcel Granet, 'Le langage de la douleur d'après le rituel funéraire de la Chine classique', *Journal de psychologie normale et pathologique*, 19th year, no. 2, February 1922, pp. 97–118, reprinted in M. Granet, *Etudes sociologiques sur la Chine* (Paris, PUF, 1953), pp. 221–42.
57. A. G. Haudricourt, 'Domestication des animaux, culture des plantes et traitement d'autrui', *L'Homme*, II, 1 (January–April 1962), pp. 40–50.
58. We shall be returning to this question in connection with the Chinese ideas of Heaven and the differences between it and the Christian concept of God.
59. Zhongyong, I, 1: *shuai xing zhi wei dao*.
60. *Du sishudaquan shuo*, chapter 7, p. 466 in the Peking edn (1975).
61. *Zhangzi zhengmeng zhu*, chapter 3, Dongwu pian, 5th paragraph.
62. *Lunyu*, XVII, 2.
63. *Lunyu*, VI, 19.
64. *Rizhi lu*, VII, 21st paragraph.
65. Cf. p. 145. Cf. J. Gernet, 'Techniques de recueillement, religion et philosophie: à propos du *jingzuo* néo-confucéen'.
66. The expression is a combination of the Christian and the Chinese terms.

67. *TZSY*, pp. 468–9.
68. *Ibid.*, pp. 469–70.
69. *Ibid.*, pp. 474–5.
70. Preface by Wang Jiazhi in the *Jiren shipian*, Zu Zongze, p. 151. As has been noted on p. 148, the Chinese term *xin*, which is translated as 'spirit', in fact has a much wider meaning. It signifies at the same time heart and reason, intelligence and moral sense.
71. *Pixie shuo*, *PXJ*, V, 24a–25b.
72. *TZSY*, p. 527.
73. *Ibid.*, p. 569.
74. *Ibid.* Cf. *Mencius*, VII A, 15: 'What man is capable of without having learned it is a spontaneous capacity (*liangneng*). What he knows without having learned it is spontaneous knowledge (*liangzhi*). Little children all know how to love their parents.' This notion of *liangzhi*, spontaneous knowledge (literally 'genuine knowledge'), occupies a place of central importance in the intuitionist philosophy of Wang Yangming (Wang Shouren, 1472–1529), whose influence was still considerable at the beginning of the seventeenth century.
75. These are the opening words of *The Invariable Middle* (*Zhongyong*), one of the Four Books.
76. *Lunyu*, XVII, 2.
77. *Pixie jie*, *PXJ*, V, 17a–b. The author is giving a Chinese interpretation to the Christian thesis: goodness is within us. If it is necessary to overcome nature in order to reach the Dao, that means that the Dao is within us whilst our nature is external to us.
78. Cf. p. 163.
79. *Yijing, Xici, shang*, 4.
80. *Zhongyong*, II, 22. Cf. *ibid.*, II, 30: 'Whoever is able to bring his nature to full realisation can associate himself with [the work of] Heaven and Earth.'
81. *ZP*, 7b.
82. These are clearly translations from the Chinese expressions *tianming* and *tianli*.
83. Sainte-Marie, pp. 77–8.
84. This is the title of chapter VII of the *Mencius*. A. C. Graham has shown that the Chinese concept of nature did not refer to stable characteristics but instead to the idea of development in conformity with innate tendencies. Cf. 'The background of the Mencian theory of nature', *Ts'ing-hua Journal of Chinese Studies*, NS, VI, 1–2 (December 1967), pp. 215–71.
85. The spirit, that is to say at the same time both mind and heart (*xin*). Cf. p. 148.
86. The epitaph for Liu Xianting (1648–95) by Wang Yuan in *Guangyang zaji*, Shanghai edn (1957).
87. *TZSY*, pp. 470–1.
88. *TZSY*, p. 629.
89. This, precisely, is the thesis of the *Mencius*: any man may become another Yao or another Shun if he fully develops all the naturally good dispositions that are within him.

90. *TZSY*, p. 630.
91. *Pixie lun*, p. 1116.
92. *Ibid.*, p. 1127.
93. *Lunyu*, XIV, 35.
94. *TZSY*, pp. 577, 578.
95. See p. 106.
96. This testimony shows, as do many others, that in order to convert the Chinese, the missionaries would frequently appeal to the two great virtues of filial piety (*xiao*) and loyalty (*zhong*).
97. To apply loyalty and filial piety first to the Master of Heaven necessarily entails ruining them as expressions of a universal order at once social and cosmic.
98. Different contexts make it necessary to translate *ren* first as 'charity', then as 'humanity'.
99. Literally, 'are external to us compared with the Master of Heaven'. *TZSY*, p. 578.
100. Human nature is a reflection of the principle of universal order (*tianli*), sometimes also called 'heavenly nature' (*tianxing*).
101. All these quotations are taken from chapter VII of the *TZSY*.
102. On the political consequences of the Christian concepts, cf. p. 119.
103. *PXJ*, V, 3a–4a.
104. Quotation from the *Liji, Zhongni yanjiu*, 3. The words *quan shan* mean, more precisely, 'to preserve and perfect goodness within oneself'.
105. *Quli*, chapter 1 of the *Liji*.
106. *ZP*, 33b.
107. *Pixie jie, PXJ*, V. 20b.
108. *TZSY*, p. 575.
109. In one of his notes to the *Zizhi tongjian (Du tongjian lun*, chapter 11, pp. 351–2 in the Peking edn (1975), Wang Fuzhi criticises Du Yu (222–84) for having said that, in the matter of rituals, all that mattered were one's feelings; and he develops the theme of the effect of external conditions and attitudes upon feelings, citing in support of his remarks a passage from the *Liji, Tangong, xia*: 'Feelings expressed without control ['directly'] and action which proceeds along the most direct course – that is the way of Barbarians.'
110. *Zhongyong*, 8: 'The worthy man behaves in conformity with his position.'
111. *Yijing, Xici*, 4.
112. *Zhongyong*, 30.
113. *Esprit des lois*, XIX, 17.
114. This concern for the maintenance of public order was much more marked under the Manchus, who ruled in China from 1644 to 1911 and who, as foreigners themselves, were particularly sensitive to any demonstrations of independence on the part of the Chinese.
115. *Ibid.*, XIX, 19.
116. Cf. pp. 105–6.
117. *Du tongjian lun*, chapter 3, pp. 81–2.

118. *Zhongyong*, I, 39, 36.
119. Longobardo, p. 99.
120. *Rizhi lu*, XIII, 27th paragraph.
121. *Biantian shuo* (1635 or 1636), VII, 25b–26a. The same expression appears in *ZP*, 10b–11a. Ricci, for his part, accused the Buddhists of having stolen the theory of transmigration from Pythagoras and of using it for the purpose of frightening people.
122. Sainte-Marie, p. 77.
123. Longobardo, p. 89. We should also remember the astonishment of the emperor, Kangxi, at the missionaries' constant preoccupation with the Beyond. Cf. p. 71.
124. *Sibian lu jiyao*, chapter 25, 9a.
125. *ZP*, 7a. The expression appears in the *Chuijian lu* by Yu Wenbao of the Sung dynasty.
126. *TZSY*, p. 555.
127. 'In what form shall we give the Bible?', *Chinese Recorder* (1890), p. 454, cited by A. F. Wright, 'The Chinese language and foreign ideas', p. 291.
128. Pierre Nicole, *Essais de morale* (1671–8), cited by Emile Bréhier, *Histoire de la philosophie* (Paris, Alcan, 1929), II, p. 9.
129. Le Comte, II, letter to Father de la Chaize, p. 311.
130. *Shuzuo ji yuanqi*, *PXJ*, VIII, 24b. Cf. also *TXCZ*, 19th absurdity, p. 919: 'Since the Master of Heaven can, in his compassion, redeem sins, everybody can do evil as he feels inclined, knowing that his crimes will be redeemed one day by the Master of Heaven.'
131. *Zhuyi lunlue*, *PXJ*, VI, 2a.
132. Literally, 'founded upon a search for happiness and avoidance of misfortune'.
133. Allusions to the Classics: *fanwei*, 'to conform' with the action of Heaven and Earth, is borrowed from the *Yijing*; *canpei*, 'to collaborate' in the action of Heaven and Earth, is borrowed from the *Zhongyong*. Cf. p. 157, notes 79, 80.
134. *ZP*, 7a–b.
135. *ZP*, 17a.
136. *ZP*, 11a.
137. These differences are also noted by the monk, Total Enlightenment, in his *Biantian shuo*, *PXJ*, VII, pp. 23b–24a.
138. An elegant way of saying that the Barbarians stole the idea of paradise and hell from Buddhism.
139. *Pixie lun*, pp. 1111–12.
140. George Elison, *Deus Destroyed*, p. 283.
141. A memorandum dated the 1st year of the Yongzheng period (1723) which is cited in 'The state of religion in the Empire of China in the year 1738' (*LEC*, XXV, p. 263), remarks that the effect of the missionaries' teaching is to upset the common people: 'the stupid and ignorant people listened to their doctrine and followed their religion, filling their minds and hearts with anxiety and all for no useful purpose'.

142. *TZSY*, pp. 424–5.
143. *Yuandao pixie shuo*, *PXJ*, VIII, 14b–15b.
144. A similar line of reasoning is to be found in Nietzsche: 'If one shifts the centre of gravity of life *out* of life into the "Beyond" – into *Nothingness* – one has deprived life as such of its centre of gravity.' Nietzsche, *The Anti-Christ*, translated by R. J. Hollingdale (Harmondsworth, Penguin, 1968), p. 155.
145. *Zunru jijing*, *PXJ*, III, 16a–17a.
146. *ZP*, 31a–b.
147. Cf. the short work by the monk, Purun, of Hangzhou (1634), the *Zhuzuo ji yuanqi* (1634), *PXJ*, VIII, 23a: 'They teach their followers to avoid what is propitious and seek out what is unpropitious. They train them to run towards misfortune with a light heart, to lament births and offer congratulations when deaths occur.' The same remark is to be found in the *Pi tianzhujiao xi* (1637) by the monk, Chengyong, *PXJ*, VIII, 24a.
148. *TZSY*, pp. 426–7.
149. One owes gratitude to one's parents, to Heaven and to Earth.
150. *ZP*, 25b–26a.
151. In contrast to the Buddhist view.
152. On the infernal regions, cf. p. 176. The purificatory hell (*lianqing*) corresponds to the limbo of the patriarchs, although the translation does not make very clear the distinction between it and purgatory proper (*qingzui*): '[the hell] where crimes are purged'.
153. *Chu shi* (to leave the world) implies the idea of deliverance. The author is transposing Christian ideas into Buddhist concepts.
154. *ZP*, 26a–b.
155. Literally, 'in things and affairs'.
156. There is one omission: the body, the organ of touching.
157. Yan Yuan, *Cunren bian*, *On the Saving of Man*, chapter 1, 2nd paragraph, 'Appeal to the strayed ones' (*Huan mitu*) (1982). Yan Yuan's argument does not stand up since every death is followed by rebirth until such time as one is delivered from the cycle of transmigrations.
158. Cf. *Lankâvatara*, chapter 4.
159. This rigorism should no doubt also be connected with the socio-political changes which took place in the eleventh and twelfth centuries.
160. However, these thinkers did have predecessors in the sixteenth century and can even be connected with a whole current of thought which went back as far as the eleventh century.
161. *Du sishudaquan shuo*, 8, p. 519 of the Peking edn (1975).
162. *Ibid.*, 10, p. 694.
163. Cf. Ian McMorran, 'Wang Fuzhi and neo-Confucian tradition', in *The Unfolding of Neo-Confucianism*, ed. W. T. de Bary (New York, Columbia University Press, 1975), p. 445 and, more generally, pp. 443–6.
164. *Juyetang wenji*, chapter 9, 8a–b, *Fofa lun*.
165. In the twentieth century, the philosopher, Liang Shuming, was to contrast

the Chinese tradition of adapting desires to social and economic necessities not only with the exaltation of the individual and the exacerbation of desires in the modern Western world but also with the annihilation of the self and the renunciation of the world of the Indian tradition.

166. *Lunyu*, XV, 29.
167. These terms, which occur in the *Mencius*, refer to the seeds of goodness which are to be found in man, whose moral duty is to develop them. The 'innate knowledge' of good and evil becomes the cardinal notion in the philosophy of Wang Shouren (Wang Yangming, 1472–1529).
168. Cf. p. 244.
169. Ricci's entire line of reasoning is based upon the opposition between substance and accident. In Chinese reasoning, in contrast, the emphasis is placed upon a hierarchy of values.
170. Letter to Yan Maoyou, *PXJ*, III, 20a–21a.
171. In a similar fashion, the Protestant pastors of the nineteenth century also considered Confucius as the greatest enemy in the conversion of China. Cf. Paul A. Cohen, 'Christian missions and their impact to 1900', in *The Cambridge History of China*, vol. 10, part I (Cambridge University Press, 1978), pp. 564–5.
172. *FR*, I, p. 109. Cf. *TV*, II, p. 386, letter from Ricci to Francesco Pasio (1609): 'We may hope that divine mercy has allowed many of their ancestors to be saved in accordance with natural law and with the aid that God, in his great goodness, granted them.'
173. Letter from Ricci dated 15 February 1609, *TV*, II, p. 387.
174. In the eyes of the Chinese, this may well have appeared to present some analogy with the six ways of rebirth of Buddhism.
175. The original version of this catechism is preserved in the Roman Archives of the Society of Jesus (ARSI), Jap. Sin. section, I, 189, 190. There are several copies of the second version in the Bibliothèque Nationale in Paris, Chinese section, nos. 6815 to 6819.

   The four infernal regions of the second version are, starting with the lowest and moving upwards:
   - the hell of eternal suffering, *yongku diyu*
   - the hell where crimes are purged, *qingzui diyu*
   - the hell for children, *ertong diyu*
   - the purificatory hell, *lianqing diyu*
176. The first duty of filial piety was to ensure a male descendance for the family so that the ancestor cult, which could only be perpetuated through the males, could be continued for ever.
177. Letter from Huang Zhen to the censor, Yan Maoyou, *PXJ*, III, 9a–b.
178. *Zhuzuo ji yuanqi* (1634), *PXJ*, VIII, 22a.
179. *ZP*, 15b.
180. Letter from Huang Zhen to Yan Maoyou, *PXJ*, III, 8b–9a.
181. *Zhuzuo ji yuanqi* (1634), *PXJ*, VIII, 22a.
182. *TV*, II, p. 71.
183. This is one of the lay Buddhists amongst whom the missionaries initially

made a number of conversions, these being favoured by the apparent analogies between Buddhism and Christianity.

184. This catechism is the *Tianzhu shilu* (Truthful Exposition on the Master of Heaven), published the previous year in Zhaoqing.

185. In contrast to what its name might suggest, Chinese geomancy was in no sense a method of divination but a very complicated art for determining what sites were propitious for tombs and temples.

186. *FR*, II, p. 262.

187. Li Yingshi was born in 1559 in Peking and probably died in 1620. He had taken part in the Korean war against Japan, between 1592 and 1597, as a general attached to the general staff. Cf. *FR*, II, p. 261, note 1.

188. This represents a very interesting testimony to a little-known Chinese practice: the promotion of the eldest son to be head of the family even in the lifetime of his father would appear contrary to the usual mores and appears to be connected with the transmission of official duties. As the rest of the text indicates, the son was to be faced with some conflict between his authority as head of the family on the one hand and his duties of filial piety on the other.

189. On this utilitarian and practical view of religion, cf. pp. 82–3, 99.

190. *FR*, II, pp. 247–9.

191. General of Liu Bei of the Shu-Han at the beginning of the third century, who became the god of war.

192. The Taoist god of individual destiny.

193. The chief star of the Great Bear.

194. A Taoist god, an important figure in the Tang period.

195. Letter from Huang Zhen to Yan Maoyou, *PXJ*, III, 9b.

196. *Buren buyan*, *PXJ*, VII, 9a.

197. *TXCZ*, 14th absurdity, p. 920.

198. Examples are to be found in certain heterodox sects. A more theoretical form of iconoclasm is the subject of Paul Demiéville's 'L'iconoclasme anti-bouddhique en Chine', in *Mélanges d'histoire des religions offerts à Henri-Charles Puech* (Ecole Pratique des Hautes Etudes, Vth section, Paris, 1974), pp. 17–25.

199. *ZP*, 20a–b.

200. *Pixie zhaiyao lueyi*, *PXJ*, V, 29a–b.

201. Sainte-Marie, p. 47, who cites Father Barthelemi de Roberedo. Cf. also *DMB*, article on Caballero. This change in policy had not escaped the notice of the Chinese. Cf. *ZP*, 19b, text cited on p. 186.

202. Vincent Cronin, *A Pearl to India*, p. 249.

203. Sainte-Marie, p. 50. The allusion to the 'direction of intention' suggests that Martini and some of the other Jesuits in China had certain Molinist tendencies. A number of them had studied at Coimbra or Evora, where the famous Molina (1536–1600) had once taught.

204. Louis Wei, pp. 33–4. In the early seventeenth century, converts were allowed to maintain the ancestor cult provided that it was limited to a simple act of gratitude towards them, in conformity with the dispositions of

Pope Alexander VII. Cf. the letter from Father de Fontaney written in London in 1740 and included in *LEC*, VIII, p. 168.

205. *Pixie zhaiyao lueyi*, *PXJ*, V, 29a.
206. *ZP*, 20a.
207. *PXJ*, II, 36b–37a.
208. First edn, Peking, 1642, reprinted in 1659, 1738 and 1798, according to Xu Zongze, p. 361.
209. The gift of prophecy was not one of the essential characteristics of the Chinese Saints. On the Chinese concept of *shengren* (Saint), cf. p. 158.
210. Cited by Sainte-Marie, p. 124.
211. *PXJ*, I, 8b.
212. Cf. J. Dehergne, *Répertoire*, p. 354. When the Franciscan, Antonio de Caballero, arrived from Taiwan in 1633, it was the Dominicans of Fu'an who greeted him. Cf. *DMB*, p. 24.
213. *PXJ*, II, 31b, 33b.
214. This was in fact an argument often put forward by the missionaries to encourage the Chinese to follow them: Ricci, for example, wrote: 'From the East to the West, the whole world, with the exception of China, is converted to the doctrine of the Master of Heaven' (*TZSY*, p. 378).
215. This is an echo of an expression from the *Mencius*, III B, 9: 'To have neither father nor sovereign is to resemble the animals.'
216. *Pixie lun*, p. 1125.
217. Letter from Yang Guangxian to the censor, Xu Zhixian, 21 April 1664, *Budeyi*, p. 1091.
218. It is worth noting in passing that the fourth commandment had been given a very wide interpretation by the Chinese and Manchu Christians, to judge from a letter from Father Parennin dated 1727 (*LEC*, XIX, p. 83), which records the Manchu prince, Ourtchen (Urcen), as saying that 'the fourth [commandment] commands one to honour the king, fathers and mothers, the ancients, the Great and all those who have authority over us'.
219. On the practice of burning money and other paper objects for the dead and on contemporary forms of the practice in Taiwan, cf. Hou Ching-lang, *Monnaies d'offrande et la notion de trésorerie dans la religion chinoise* (Mémoires de l'Institut des Hautes Etudes Chinoises, Paris, 1975).
220. Sainte- Marie, pp. 139–40.
221. Cf. p. 95.
222. *Kangxi yu luoma shijie guanxi wenshu yingyin ben*, document no. 14.
223. *Picxie zhaiyao lueyi*, *PXJ*, V, 29b.
224. *ZP*, 19b–20a.
225. *Qike* by Diego de Pantoja (1604).
226. *Tianzhu shiyi* by Ricci (1601).
227. *Jiren shipian*, or *Ten Chapters of an Uncommon Man* by Ricci (1608).
228. *Xixue fan* by Giulio Aleni (1623).
229. *Jiaoyou lun* by Ricci (1595).
230. *Jihe yuanben* by Ricci and Xu Guangqi (a translation of the first six chapters of *The Elements of Euclid* by Clavius) (1605).

231. Ricci explains in his *TZSY* (pp. 568–70) that there is no merit in loving one's parents but that one must love others. Cf. *ZP*, 34a.
232. George Elison, *Deus Destroyed*, p. 282.
233. *Pixie shuo*, *PXJ*, V, 26b.
234. These two passages are cited by Gotô Motomi, 'Evolution of the Decalogue in China', p. 11.
235. *Zhengwang houshuo* (Supplement to the Proof of Their Lies), *PXJ*, VII, 38a.
236. *ZP*, 30b. Cf. *ibid.*, 19a–b: 'they forbid homicide, yet they make cannons'.
237. *ZP*, 10b.
238. *Yuandao pixie shuo*, *PXJ*, VIII, 16b.
239. *ZP*, 30a.
240. Le Comte, I, p. 293. This horror of nudity persists even today.
241. *PXJ*, II, 3b, text dated 1617. But Vagnone did not himself administer the sacraments to women; he delegated the task to a convert from Macao.
242. *ZP*, 18a.
243. *Esprit des lois*, XIX, 18. Louis Wei (p. 44) notes, in the nineteenth century, the same mistrust on the part of the Chinese regarding the relations between the missionaries and their female converts: 'When the priests would listen to the female converts in the confessional box, the public suspected that it was in order to seduce these women, for in Chinese society it was not permitted for men and women ever to meet and speak together either in secret or in public.' The missionaries found themselves obliged to set up separate churches for men and for women. We have proof that they did so as early as the seventeenth century, but this does not appear to have invariably been the rule.
244. Le Comte, II, letter to Father de la Chaize, p. 321. Ricci's first student in mathematics, Qu Rukui, baptised Ignatius in 1605, thus entered upon a second marriage with one of his concubines, on the encouragement of the brother from Macao, Francisco Martins (Huang Mingsha, by his Chinese name). Cf. Fang Hao, I, p. 92.
245. *ZP*, 30b.
246. This claim is often repeated in the missionaries' works in Chinese. Cf. p. 184, note 214.
247. Cf. p. 176.
248. *ZP*, 17b–18a.
249. *Pixie zhaiyao lueyi*, *PXJ*, V, 29a.
250. *ZP*, 35a.
251. 'An account of a general movement of persecution in 1746' by Father Jean Chanseaume, *LEC*, XXVIII, p. 284.
252. George Elison, *Deus Destroyed*, p. 279.
253. *Pi tianzhujiao xi*, *PXJ*, VIII, 24a.

5 Chinese Heaven, Christian God

1. According to H. Maspero (*La Chine antique*, p. 134), Houtu is a masculine deity. On the mythology relating to the Shangdi, cf. *ibid.*, pp. 134–9.

2. Cf. p. 151.

3. *Zhuangzi*, chapter 22. Cf. Léon Wieger, *Les Pères du système taoïste*, p. 391.

4. *Shujing, Wucheng*. Cf. *Yijing, Xici, xia*, 2: 'The Yellow Sovereign, Yao and Shun allowed their long robes to trail and order reigned beneath Heaven.'

5. *Pixie lun*, p. 1109.

6. As has already been noted in chapter 3.

7. *Tianxue shuo* (*Explanations concerning the Heavenly Studies*) *TDXB*, I, pp. 3–18.

8. *TZSY*, pp. 417–18. The quotation is given in shortened form.

9. A quotation often made in connection with Cheng Hao. But the missionaries retained only his second phrase, namely: 'As a regulating power, he is called the Sovereign on High.'

10. My italics.

11. *Pixie lun*, pp. 1121–4.

12. Commentary by Wang Fuzhi to the *Zhengmeng* by Zhang Zai, chapter 1, *Taihe pian*, 11th paragraph.

13. My italics. The principle of heavenly order (*tianli*) manifests itself in the cosmos and nature as well as in human order and morality.

14. *Lianxue geji*, chapter 2, cited by Ch'en Shou-i (1935). Li Suiqiu was a painter and a poet, who died during the siege of Ganzhou when the Manchu armies were advancing into the south of Jiangxi province.

15. *TXZZ*, pp. 930–4.

16. The suggestion here is that, having first likened his Master of Heaven to the Chinese Shangdi, he then sought to eliminate the Chinese idea.

17. *Pixie guanjian lu*, *PXJ*, VI, 8a–b. The author is a certain Zou Weilian, who obtained his doctorate in 1607 and at the end of his life for two years held the post of censor in Fujian province. In all likelihood, he wrote his work during his stay in Fujian province, for the *Poxie ji* is a collection chiefly of works which appeared in Fujian between 1630 and 1640.

18. *Qingshu jingtan*, chapter XV, p.45, cited by Ch'en Shou-i (1935).

19. *Lunyu*, XVII, 16: 'I hate to see violet [an intermediary colour] preferred to vermilion [a primary colour].

20. Probably an oblique reference to the last tale of the *Liezi*.

21. *Lunyu*, II, 4.

22. Literally, 'its sincerity'.

23. On these notions of morality, cf. p. 163.

24. *Lunyu*, VI, 35. Zhu Xi's commentary explains that to pray is simply to advance along the right path and correct one's faults in order to win the help of the spirits. Confucius said: 'Given that my prayer is continuous, why should I have waited until today?'

25. Whereas Ricci claims that sacrifices to Earth were later additions to the cult of Heaven, that is to say the God of the Bible.

26. *Zunru jijing*, *PXJ*, III, 14a–15b.

27. *Zhuyi lunlue*, *PXJ*, VI, 2a–b.

28. Longobardo, p. 86. The italicised words are underlined in the 1701 edition.

The word that Longobardo translated as 'heart' is *xin*, which means both heart and spirit.

29. *Zhuyi lunlue*, *PXJ*, VI, 2a–b.
30. *Gaozi yishu*, III, *Zhitian shuo* (*Comments on the Knowledge of Heaven*), 16b–17b. On the automatic nature of retributions, cf. p. 166.
31. Quotations made by Alfred Forke, *Geschichte der neueren chinesischen Philosophie* (Hamburg, 1938), p. 77, note 5; p. 112, note 3; p. 353, notes 5, 6.
32. Longobardo, pp. 86, 79.
33. *Ibid.*, p. 72.
34. *TZSY*, p. 417.
35. Cited by Ch'en Shou-i (1935).
36. This is one of the translations for the word 'soul' adopted by Aleni.
37. This is an interpretation of the ideas of Wang Yangming (Wang Shouren, 1472–1529). The *liangzhi*, the moral sense inherent in the spirit in its most completely calm state, is likened to the Buddhist absolute.
38. Letter from the 'retired man of letters who rejects illusions', Huang Zhen of Xiazhang (Zhangzhou, in the south of Fujian province), requesting the master, Yan Zhuangji (Yan Maoyou, awarded a doctorate by special favour of the emperor under the Chongzhen dynasty (1628–44) and author of an anthology of the Six Classics), to refute the doctrine of the Master of Heaven (*PXJ*, III, 8b). Huang Zhen, or Huang Tianxiang, is the author of a preface to the *Poxie ji* dated the second moon of the spring of 1639, of another preface to a text in the *Poxie ji* dated 1638, and of two other short works as well as of this letter.
39. Le Comte, II, letter to Cardinal de Bouillon, p. 181.
40. *Ibid.*, p. 183.
41. Longobardo, p. 58.
42. *Ibid.*, Foreword.
43. Passage cited by Sainte-Marie, p. 76.
44. Sainte-Marie, p. 61.
45. *Pixie jie*, *PXJ*, V, 20b.
46. *Lunyu*, XVII, 17.
47. *Pixie lun*, p. 1106.
48. It is probably the case that in the Italian Platonism of the Renaissance, and particularly in Campanella (1568–1639), trends of thought reminiscent of the Chinese ideas could be detected. However, these trends run contrary to the dominant currents of thought, whereas in the Chinese traditions, they predominate.
49. *TZSY*, pp. 411–12.
50. *Zunru jijing*, *PXJ*, III, 17b.
51. *Ibid.*, 18a–19a. On hells, cf. p. 176.
52. Longobardo, p. 74.
53. *Ibid.*, p. 78. Cf. Ricci's letter cited on p. 27. Similarly, in *TZSY*, p. 413: 'If you were to say that the *li* contains the intelligences (*ling*) of the Ten Thousand Beings and that it produces the Ten Thousand Beings, it would then

be [the equivalent of] the Master of Heaven.'
54. Leibniz, letter to M. de Rémond on Chinese philosophy in *Oeuvres complètes*, ed. Dutens, vol. IV, p. 12.
55. Longobardo, p. 77.
56. Cf. Paul Demiéville, *Choix d'études sinologiques* (Leiden, E. J. Brill, 1973).
57. Cf. *DMB*, pp. 1408–9.
58. As is suggested by Yamaguchi Hisakazu in an article in the *Tôhôgaku*, LVII (January, 1979), p. 49.
59. These are the theses expounded in the *Zhengmeng* (*The Correct Initiation*) by Zhang Zai (1020–77).
60. Longobardo, p. 48.
61. *Ibid.*, p. 47.
62. An allusion to the phases of inactivity and activity of the *yin* and the *yang*.
63. Le Comte, III, Preface to the second edn.
64. *Wei Yuan ji*, Peking, Zhonghua shuju (1976), I, p. 10. The Chinese often orientated themselves by reference to the south rather than to the north.
65. The expression appears in the *Yijing, Xici, shang*, and denotes the unceasing production of the *yin* and the *yang*.
66. The two words *chang* (long) and *chang* (constant, eternal) are homophones.
67. *ZP*, 25a. The distinction between the words *qi* (energy) and *qi* (to rise up) is one of tone.
68. Two of the titles that appear in the Table of contents of the *Wanwu zhenyuan*. Cf. Xu Zongze, p. 173. The separation of Heaven and Earth is a traditional way of expressing the formation of the universe.
69. *TZSY*, p. 384.
70. Longobardo, p. 20.
71. *TXZZ*, pp. 926–7.
72. *Ibid.*, 6b.
73. *TZSY*, p. 390.
74. Approximate quotation from the *Yijing, Xici, xia*, 4.
75. Literally, 'that it was dependent (*yilai*) and could not be independent (*zili*)' (*TZSY*, p. 413).
76. *TZSY*, p. 408.
77. *Ibid.*, p. 409.
78. *Bianxue chuyan*, *PXJ*, V, 6a–7a.
79. *Pixie jie*, *PXJ*, V, 19a–20b.
80. Letter from Ricci, cited on p. 27.
81. Longobardo, p. 77.
82. *TZSY*, p. 404.
83. Namely, the combinations 00, 01, 10 and 11.
84. The combinations 000, 001, 010, 011, 100, 101, 110 and 111.
85. *ZP*, 14a–b.
86. *TZSY*, p. 405.
87. The word *yi* denotes change.

88. *TXZZ*, pp. 945–6. On the topic of the failures in natural functioning, cf. p. 153: monsters and natural calamities do happen.
89. *ZP*, 14a.
90. *ZP*, 23a–24a.
91. *ZP*, 24b.
92. *Ibid.*, 37b–38a.
93. J. Needham, *Science and Civilisation in China*, III, pp. 119–20.
94. Letter from Huang Zhen to Yan Maoyou, *PXJ*, III, 9a–10b. However, the eschatological traditions of Buddhist/Taoist origins do present distant analogies with the theme of the Last Judgement. Cf. E. Zürcher, '"Prince Moonlight", Messianism and eschatology in early medieval Buddhism', *T'oung Pao*, LXVIII (1982).
95. *Bianxue chuyan*, *PXJ*, V, 6a.
96. *Bianxue yidu*, cited by Ch'en Shou-i (1936).
97. *Histoire de l'expédition chrétienne*, p. 489. On the refusal of the missionaries to enter into discussion with the Buddhist monks, cf. p. 79.
98. A similar opinion is to be found in Hegel, who writes that 'a consciousness of moral abjection [on the part of the Chinese] is manifested by the fact that the religion of Fo [Buddhism] is very widespread and this considers Nothingness as all that is most sublime and absolute, like God, and proposes scorn for the individual as the highest perfection' (Hegel, *The Philosophy of History*, translated by J. Sibree (New York, Dover, 1956)).
99. *TZSY*, p. 401.
100. This is more or less the substance of the refutation of the monk, Ruchun, that appears in his *Tianxue chupi* (*First Refutation of the Heavenly Studies*), *PXJ*, VIII, 28a–b.
101. Masao Abe, 'Reply to the debate on Christianity and Buddhism', *Japanese Religion*, IV, 2 (1966), p. 56. This reference and those that follow are given by Heinrich Dumoulin in *Christianity meets Buddhism* (La Salle, Illinois, 1974).
102. It is, indeed, really a manner of speaking.
103. Buddhadâsa, *Christianity and Buddhism* (Bangkok, 1967), p. 80.
104. *Ibid.*, p. 83.
105. C. G. Chang, *The Buddhist Teaching of Totality: The Philosophy of Hua Yen Buddhism* (Pasadena and London, University Park, 1981), p. xiv.
106. *Yuandao pixie shuo*, *PXJ*, VIII, 6a–7b.
107. On this belief that the missionaries 'invented' Christianity, cf. pp. 50, 66, 109.
108. The Sanskrit word *deva* (God) was translated as *tian* (heaven) in Chinese. Zhuhong understands the expression *tianzhu* to mean Master of gods, a title already given to Sakra Devendra.
     The world of desire, or *kâmadhâtu*, is the abode of men, animals and certain gods. It comprises, set one on top of another, eight hells, earth and six heavens.
109. *Zhuchuang suibi*, III, *Tianshuo* (*Explanations on Heaven*), reproduced in *PXJ*, VII, 1a–2a.

110. Total Enlightenment, Yuanwu, was a famous Buddhist master from the Tiantong monastery of Ningbo in Zhejiang province. His *Biantian shuo* (*Explanation of the Distinction between the Meanings of the Word Heaven*) contains a preface dating from early in 1636.
111. *Biantian shuo*, *PXJ*, VII, 12a–b.
112. The world of desire (*kâmadhâtu*), the world of appearances (*rûpadhâtu*) and the world of an absence of appearances (*arûpyadhâtu*).
113. *Biantian shuo*, *PXJ*, VII, 20a–21b, 24a–25b.
114. *Yuandao pixie shuo*, *PXJ*, VIII, 4b–5a.
115. *Zhuzuo ji yuanqi*, *PXJ*, VIII, 21a.
116. On the three souls, cf. p. 147.
117. *ZP*, 10a–b.
118. George Elison, *Deus Destroyed*, pp. 265–6.
119. The Jesuits of Japan had resorted to a transcription of this Latin word to translate the name of God.
120. *Daode jing*, 42.
121. Paul Demiéville shows how the word *li*, which originally expressed the idea of an ordering and allotment of land, acquired new meanings under the influence of first Taoism and then Buddhism, where it was used to express the notion of 'thusness' or the nature of Buddha (*buddhatâ*). He writes that Zhu Xi turns the *li* into a 'principle of natural order which is at the same time cosmic, social and moral; but he also retains the Buddhist meaning of a metaphysical absolute which is immanent in each one of us'. See P. Demiéville, *Choix d'études sinologiques* (Leiden, E. J. Brill, 1973), pp. 49–54.
122. *TXCZ*, 1st and 7th absurdities, pp. 914–15, 917–18.
123. He debases it by turning it into brute matter.
124. Cf. p. 118.
125. The missionaries mingle men and women together in their assemblies.
126. An allusion to the criticisms of Ricci and his condemnation of the Saints of Confucianism.
127. *ZP*, 22a–b.
128. *ZP*, 24a.
129. *ZP*, 3a.
130. *ZP*, 7a–b.
131. George Elison, *Deus Destroyed*, p. 284.
132. *Lunyu*, XVII, 17.
133. *Mencius*, V A, 5.
134. *TXCZ*, 7th absurdity, p. 917.
135. Roger Bastide, 'La causalité externe et la causalité interne', *Cahiers internationaux de sociologie*, XXI, 3rd year (1956), p. 98.
136. But, equally, the Chinese rejected the Jewish notion of a personal God endowed with feelings.
137. Le Comte, II, letter to Father de la Chaize, p. 294.
138. The implication is that among the common people the tactics adopted were quite different. Cf. p. 82.

139. Letter from Father Parennin dated 28 September 1735, from Peking, *LEC*, XXIV, pp. 22–3.
140. It seems unlikely that Sunu was envisaging a creation *ex nihilo*. Cf. p. 207. Father Parennin makes Sunu speak as though he were a European.
141. Letter from Father Parennin, Peking, 20 August 1724, *LEC*, XVII, p. 15.
142. A reference to the great maritime expeditions of the early fifteenth century, between 1405 and 1433, which ranged as far as the Red Sea and the eastern coast of Africa.
143. Unlike the missionaries who preached of the existence of 'a Heaven beyond Heaven'.
144. *Lifa lun, PXJ*, VI, 22a–b.
145. That is to say, visible and endowed with particular characteristics, or invisible and entirely indeterminate. On the meaning of the terms, *you* and *wu*, cf. p. 206.
146. *ZP*, 23a.
147. *Pixie lun*, pp. 1108–9.
148. *Pixie jie, PXJ*, V, 20a.
149. The same argument is developed by Yang Guangxian. Cf. p. 265.
150. The rest of the text is not clear. Perhaps the sense is that 'by undergoing sufferings, the Master of Heaven taught others who undergo them to bear them with a light heart. In this way, he was able to save men, emerge from hell and ascend to Heaven.'
151. Literally, 'that is not true'.
152. *Tianxue pouyi, PXJ*, V, 10a–11a. 'The wrong man' is clearly Judas.
153. *TXCZ*, 9th, 10th and 11th absurdities, pp. 918–19.
154. A reference to the Sovereign of Jade, a Taoist deity who was given the official title of Sovereign on High during the Han period.
155. *Humble Remarks on the Distinction between the Doctrines, PXJ*, V, 2b.
156. Preface by Jiang Dejing to the *Poxie ji, PXJ*, III, 1b.
157. Cf. p. 56.
158. Yang Guangxian's remark is quite correct. Cf. *TZSY*, p. 678.
159. *Pixie lun*, pp. 1126–7.
160. *Ibid.*, p. 1117.
161. An allusion to the accusations brought against Jesus of having attempted to usurp the royal power.
162. *Pixie lun*, p. 1117.
163. The *Qixie*, a work mentioned in the *Zhuangzi* in the third century BC.
164. Quotation from the *Yijing, Xici, xia*, 4.
165. An Indian and Buddhist classification. Cf. *Abhidharmakosa*, chapter 8. The four types of births are (1) birth by an egg (*anda-ja*), (2) birth by an embryo (*jarârju-ja*), (3) birth by humidity (*samsveda-ja*) and (4) birth by transformation or metamorphosis (*upapâduka*).
166. Quotations from the *Liji, Neize*, I, 12 and *Quli, xia*, 5.
167. *Pixie lun*, pp. 1110–12.
168. Vincent Cronin, *A Pearl to India*, p. 142. Roberto de Nobili, from a noble Italian family, began preaching in Madurai, in southern India, and develop-

ing methods of adaptation to the Indian milieu which, *mutatis mutandis*, are reminiscent of Ricci's methods in China.

169. *TXCZ*, 8th absurdity, p. 918.
170. *Tianxue chupi, PXJ*, VIII, 30a–31b, 34b.
171. Longobardo, pp. 87–8.
172. *Ibid.*, p. 97. A biography of Ye Xianggao is to be found in *DMB*, pp. 1567–70.
173. Cf. E. P. Boardman, *Christian Influence upon the Ideology of the Taiping Rebellion, 1851–1864* (Madison, University of Wisconsin Press, 1952).

   The Caodist religion, founded in 1919 in Vietnam, is a synthesis of elements borrowed from Christianity, Taoism and Buddhism that follows a similar schema. According to its founder, Caodai, or the Supreme Being, had already manifested himself in the forms of Jesus and Buddha. In the Caodist cathedral of Tay-Ninh, to the north-west of Saigon, Confucius, Laozi, Buddha and Jesus Christ were all revered as were a Chinese general who had become the god of war (Guandi), a Chinese eighth-century poet (Li Bai), and the Bodhisattva, Guanyin. In the course of the mediumistic seances, the following figures were also evoked: Joan of Arc, Victor Hugo, Camille Flammarion, Allen Kardec and Sun Yat-sen.
174. Translated by R. J. Hollingdale (Harmondsworth, Penguin, 1961), p. 274.
175. *Lunyu*, XV, 29 (*ren neng hong dao*) and XII, 1 (*wei ren you ji*).
176. *TXCZ*, 2nd and 5th absurdities, pp. 915–16, 916–17.
177. *TXZZ*, p. 947.
178. The earliest ancestor of mankind, according to some legends.
179. *Bianxue chuyan, PXJ*, V, 5b–6a.
180. The king of hell in the Buddhist tradition and in popular Chinese mythology.
181. A similar remark is to be found in the author of the *TXCZ*, 4th absurdity, p. 916: 'Lucifer has been condemned to hell and yet at the same time he is in this world and leads men astray here.'
182. *ZP*, 13a–b.
183. *Tianxue chupi, PXJ*, VIII, 26a–b.
184. *TZSY*, p. 508.
185. *Hua* means to transform, to civilise or to convert.
186. *Shasheng bian, PXJ*, V, 13b.
187. George Elison, *Deus Destroyed*, p. 275.
188. *Tianxue chupi*, VIII, 26b–27a.
189. An allusion to a passage in the *Mencius* on laws made so that ignorant people are bound to transgress them (*Mencius*, I A, 7).
190. *PXJ*, VIII, 27a.
191. George Elison, *Deus Destroyed*, p. 273.
192. *TXCZ*, 3rd absurdity, p. 916.
193. *ZP*, 12b–13a.
194. *ZP*, 27b.
195. Cf. *Houhanshu, Xiyu, Tianzhu guo*, the section devoted to India. Tradition had it that this golden man was a Buddha.

196. The missionaries opposed the contemporary period, during which the Chinese had, thanks to them, received the revelation of the true God, to all earlier periods, during which they had been steeped in ignorance and error.

197. *ZP*, 27b–28a.

198. George Elison, *Deus Destroyed*, p. 275.

199. *ZP*, 12a–b.

200. *TZSY*, p. 546: 'According to the laws of the ancient kings [of China] and even of the hegemons [seventh century BC], the punishment should not affect the descendants [of the guilty party].'

201. *Bianxue chuyan*, *PXJ*, V, 5b.

202. *ZP*, 12a. Cf. *TZSY*, p. 545.

203. Literally, 'have some detestable things'.

204. Literally, 'on transformations of the universal energy' (*qihua*).

205. *ZP*, 11a–b.

206. *Bianxue chuyan*, *PXJ*, V, 4b–5a.

207. Translated by H. Zimmern (Edinburgh and London, T. N. Foulis, 1907), p. 29.

208. 'In what form shall we give the Bible?' *Chinese Recorder* (1890), p. 454, cited by Arthur F. Wright, 'The Chinese language and foreign ideas'.

209. S. Wells William, *The Middle Kingdom* (New York, 1888), II, p. 370; A. F. Wright, *art. cit.*, p. 302, note 4.

210. Emile Benveniste, 'Catégories de pensée et catégories de langue', *Etudes philosophiques*, IV (October–December 1958), reprinted in *Problèmes de linguistique générale* (Paris, Gallimard, 1966), pp. 63–74.

   In line with Benveniste's remarks, but rather less penetrating, cf. also S. Ullmann, *Précis de sémantique française* (Berne, A. Francke, 1952), p. 300: 'Every linguistic system contains an analysis of the external world which is its own and differs from the analyses of other languages'; and Cassirer, 'Pathologie de la conscience symbolique', *Journal de psychologie* (1929), p. 29: 'The world is not (only) understood and conceived by man by means of language: his vision of the world and his way of life within that vision are already determined by language.' See also Georges Mounin, *Les Problèmes théoriques de la traduction* (Paris, Gallimard, 1963), pp. 43–58, from which these quotations are taken.

211. Emile Benveniste, *ibid.*, p. 71.

212. Emile Benveniste, 'Tendances récentes en linguistique générale', *Journal de psychologie* (1954), nos. 1–2, reprinted in *Problèmes de linguistique générale*, p. 6.

213. Liang Shuming, *Dongxi wenhua ji qi zhexue*, *The Civilisations of the East and the West and Their Philosophies* (Shanghai Commercial Press, 1929), p. 112, passage cited by W. T. de Bary, *Sources of Chinese Tradition* (New York, Columbia University Press, 1960), p. 851.

214. The principle of classification and interpretation used by historians of Chinese thought in the People's Republic in effect derives its inspiration from a thesis expressed by Marx and Lenin: 'there are only two philosophies – materialism and idealism – the one serves the revolution, the other serves reac-

tion, the one is objective and collective, the other falls into subjectivism and individualism'.

215. With the exception, in the spoken language, of a few differences of intonation and the use of certain nominal suffixes, which are attested from the eleventh century. But we are concerned here only with the written language.

216. This relativism was particularly developed among the Taoist thinkers and sophists of the fourth to third centuries BC. Note also the influence of the Buddhist Mâdhyamika school as from the fifth century AD. However, the dialectic of the Mâdhyamika, which sets in opposition series of affirmations and negations, is different from that of the Chinese tradition, in which contraries are not mutually exclusive.

217. In the layout of the equations of the Chinese thirteenth-century mathematicians, the position of the figures alone is enough to indicate the unknown that is involved, whether there are several unknowns, what their powers are, and whether they are positive or negative.

218. Nietzsche, *Beyond Good and Evil* (Edinburgh and London, T. N. Foulis, 1907), p. 29.

219. *FR*, II, p. 77.

220. Letter from Father Foucquet, from Nanchang (1701), *LEC*, V, p. 165.

221. *ZP*, 9a.

222. *TZSY*, p. 462.

223. *Ibid.*, p. 390

224. *Ibid.*, p. 430.

225. *Ibid.*, pp. 411–12. Cf. also pp. 481–2, where Ricci explains four other types of inclusion.

226. *Ibid.*, p. 483.

227. *TZSY*, p. 406, lines 6 to 9.

228. *Gongsun Longzi*, chapter 1. Cf. Ignace Kou Pao-koh, *Deux sophistes chinois: Houei Che et Kong-souen Long* (Paris, PUF, 1953), pp. 20–4, 30–6.

229. *TZSY*, p. 437.

230. The comparison between China and India should be regarded with caution.

231. Marcel Detienne and Jean-Pierre Vernant, *Cunning Intelligence in Greek Culture and Society*, translated by J. Lloyd (Harvester Press, Sussex, 1978), p. 5.

232. *Phaedo*, translated by R. Hackforth (Cambridge University Press, 1955), p. 84.

233. The five phases (*wuxing*) are symbolised by wood, fire, metal, water and earth.

234. *TZSY*, p. 409. Feng Youlan, probably overinfluenced by Western philosophy, makes a similar mistake when, in his *History of Chinese Philosophy*, translated by D. Bodde (Princeton, 1953), II, p. 547, he suggests comparing the *li/qi* pair to the Aristotelian pair constituted by form and matter.

235. Cf. p. 208.

Select bibliography

Sources

Aleni, Giulo. *Xixue fan* (1623), in *Tianxue chuhan*, vol.1

Bartoli, Daniello. *Dell'historia della Compagnia di Giseu, La Cina*, Rome, 1663, reprinted Turin, 1825, vols. XV-XVIII

Budeyi by Yang Guangxian (1597–1669) in *Tianzhu jiao dongchuan wenxian xubian*, vol. 3, pp. 1071–1306

Buglio, Magalhaes, Verbiest. *Xifang yaoji* (*Essential Ideas about the Countries of the West*), Peking, 1669

Ch'en Yuan (ed.). *Kangxi yu Loma shijie guanxi wenshu yingyin ben*, facsimile collection concerning the legations from Rome to Emperor Kangxi, Peking Former Palace edn, 1932

FR D'Elia, Pasquale, M. *Fonti Ricciane*, 3 vols., Rome, Libreria dello Stato, 1942–9

Gaubil, Antoine. *Correspondance de Pékin, 1722–1759*, published by Renée Simon, Geneva, Droz, 1970

Le Comte, Louis. *Nouveau mémoires sur l'état présent de la Chine*, 3 vols., the last of which contains a preface by Le Comte to the 2nd edn of his *Nouveaux mémoires* and the *Histoire de l'édit de l'empereur de la Chine en faveur de la Religion chrétienne*, Paris, 1696–1700

LEC *Lettres édifiantes et curieuses écrites des missions étrangères par quelques missionaires de la Compagnie de Jésus*, 31 vols., Paris, 1717–74

Longobardo, Niccolò. *Traité sur quelques points de la religion des Chinois*, Paris, 1701

Pixie ji (*c.* 1643) in *Tianzhu jiao dongchuan wenxian xubian*, vol. 2, pp. 905–60

Pixie lun (1659) in *Budeyi*

PXJ *Poxie ji* (1639), 8 vols., Japanese reprint, 1855

Poxie lun by Huang Zongxi (1610–1685) in *Zhaodai congshu, ji*, vol. 9, chapter 15

Qingshu jingtan by Wang Qiyuan, 16 chapters, Peking, 1623

TZSY Ricci, Matteo. *Tianzhu shiyi* in *Tianxue chuhan*, vol. 1, French translation in Ch. Jacques, *Choix de lettres édifiantes*, Brussels, 1838, vol. II, pp. 1–179

Jiaoyou lun (*On Friendly Relations*) (1595), *Ershiwu yan* (*The Twenty-five Utterances*) (1604), *Jiren shipian* (*Ten Chapters of an Uncommon Man*) (1608) in *Tianxue chuhan*, vol. 1

298

Ricci, M. and Trigault, N. *Histoire de l'expédition chrétienne au royaume de la Chine*, Desclée de Brouwer, 1978, translated into English by L. Gallagher in *China in the Sixteenth Century: The Journal of Matthew Ricci*, 1953

Ruggieri, Michele. *Shengjiao Tianzhu sjilu*, Roman Archives of the Society of Jesus, Jap. Sin. section, I, 189 and 190, 1584 (adapted version *c.* 1648), Paris, Bibliothèque Nationale, Chinese archives, nos. 6815–19

Sainte-Marie (Antonio Caballero). *Traité sur quelques points importants de la mission de la Chine*, Paris, 1701

TV Tacchi Venturi. *Opere storiche del P. Matteo Ricci*, 2 vols., Macerata, 1911–13

Tianxue chuhan (1628), Zhongguo shixue congshu edn, Taipei, 1965

TXCZ *Tianxue chuzheng* in *Pixie ji*

TXZZ *Tianxue zaizheng* in *Pixie ji*

TDXB *Tizanzhu jiao dongchuang wenxian xubian*, Zhongguo shixue congshu edn, Taipei, 1965

Tianzhu shenpan mingzheng, wood-cut, Paris, Bibliothèque Nationale, Chinese archives, no. 6881

Weitian airen jilun (*Treatise on the Supreme Principle of Fear of Heaven and Love of Men*) by Wang Zheng (1571–1644), Preface by Zheng Man (1594–1638), Paris, Bibliothèque Nationale, Chinese archives, no. 6868, 1628

Xiaoluan bu bringming suo (*The Owl and the Phoenix do not Sing Together*) in *Tianzhu dongchuan wenxian xubian*, vol. 1

ZP *Zuopi* by Xu Dashou, 10 chapters, in *Poxie ji*, vol. 4

Secondary literature

de Bary, W. T. (ed.). *The Unfolding of Neo-Confucianism*, New York, Columbia University Press, 1975

Bernard, Henri. *Sagesse chinoise et philosophie chrétienne*, Tientsin, 1935

Le P. Matteo Ricci et la société chinoise de son temps (*1552–1610*), Tientsin, 1937

'Adaptations chinoises d'ouvrages européens', *Monumenta Serica*, X, 1945, pp. 1–57, 309–88

Boardman, Eugene P. *Christian Influence upon the Ideology of the Taiping Rebellion, 1851–1864*, Madison, Wisconsin University Press, 1952

Ch'en Shou-i. 'Mingmo Qingchu Yesu huishi de rujiao guan ji qi fanying', *Guoli Beijing Daxue guoxue jikan*, V, 2, 1935, pp. 1–64

'Sanbainian qian de jianli kongjiao lun', *Zhongyang yanjiuyuan lishi yuyan yanjiusuo jikan*, VI, 2, 1936, pp. 136–62

Cohen, Paul A. 'The anti-Christian Tradition in China', *Journal of Asian Studies*, XX, 2, 1961, pp. 169–80

China and Christianity: The Missionary Movement and the Growth of Anti-foreignism, 1860–1870, Cambridge, Mass., Harvard University Press, 1963

'Christian missions and their impact to 1900', in *The Cambridge History of China*, vol. 10, Cambridge University Press, 1978

Cronin, Vincent. *A Pearl to India: The Life of Roberto de Nobili*, London, Rupert Hart-Davis, 1959

Dehergne, Joseph. 'Les chrétientés de la Chine de la période Ming (1581–1650)', *Monumenta Serica*, XVI, 1, 1957, pp. 1–136

Répertoire des jésuites en Chine de 1552 à 1800, Bibliothèque de l'Institut Historique de la Société de Jésus, vol. XXXVI, Rome–Paris, 1973

Dehergne, J. and Leslie, D. D. *Juifs de Chine à travers la correspondance inédite des Jésuites du XVIIIᵉ siècle*, Rome, Institut Historique de la Société de Jésus, and Paris, Les Belles Lettres, 1980

Demiéville, Paul. 'Premiers contacts philosophiques entre la Chine et l'Europe', *Diogène*, LVIII, Montreal, 1967, pp. 81–110

Dumoulin, Heinrich. *Christianity meets Buddhism*, La Salle, Illinois, 1974

Elison, George. *Deus Destroyed: The Image of Christianity in Early Modern Japan*, Cambridge, Mass., Harvard University Press, 1973

Etiemble. *Les Jésuites en Chine*, Paris, Julliard, 1966

Fang Hao. *Zhongguo tianzhu jiao shi renwu zhuan*, 2 vols., Hong Kong, Gongjiao zhenli xuehui, 1970

Gernet Jacques. 'La politique de conversion de Matteo Ricci et l'évolution de la vie politique et intellectuelle en Chine aux environs de 1600', in *Sviluppi scientifici, prospettive religiose, movimenti rivoluzionari in Cina*, Florence, Olschki, 1975, pp. 115–44

'Sur les différentes versions du premier catéchisme en chinois de 1584', *Studia Sino-Mongolica*, Wiesbaden, F. Steiner, 1979, pp. 407–16

'Christian and Chinese visions of the world in the seventeeth century', *Chinese Science*, 4, 1980, pp. 1–17

'Techniques de recueillement, religion et philosophie: à propos du *jingzuo* néo-confucéen', *Bulletin de l'Ecole Française d'Extrême-Orient*, LXIX, Paris, 1981, pp. 290–305

DMB Goodrich, L. C. and Fang Chaoying. *Dictionary of Ming Biography, 1368–1644*, 2 vols., New York–London, Columbia University Press, 1976

Gotô, Motomi. 'Evolution of the Decalogue in China – a study on the history of Chinese Christian ideologies', *Memoirs of the Research Department of the Tôyô Bunkô*, XXXVII, Tokyo, 1979, pp. 1–31

Minshin shisô to kirisuto kyô, Tokyo, Kenkyû shuppan, 1979 de Groot, J. J. M. *Sectarianism and Religious Persecution in China*, 2 vols., Amsterdam, 1903, 1904, republished Peking, 1940

Hummel, Arthur W. *Eminent Chinese of the Ch'ing Period (1644–1912)*, 2 vols., Washington, Government Printing Office, 1943

Jennes, Joseph. *A History of the Catholic Church in Japan*, Tokyo, Orient Institute for Religious Research, 1973

Lancashire, D. 'Buddhist reaction to Christianity in late Ming China', *Journal of the Oriental Society of Australia*, VI, 1–2, 1968–9

Mish, John. 'Creating an image of Europe for China: Aleni's *Hsi-fang wen-ta*', *Monumenta Serica*, XXIII, 1964, pp. 1–87

Ochô, Enichi. 'Minmatsu Bukkyô to Kirisutokyô no sôgo hihan', *Otani gakuhô*, XXIX, 2, 1949, and 3–4, 1950

Pang Ching-jen. 'Documents chinois sur l'histoire des missions catholiques au XVIIe siècle', *Neue Zeitschrift für Missionswissenschaft*, 1st year, no. 1, 1945

Pelliot, Paul. *L'Origine des relations de la France avec la Chine: Le premier voyage de l' 'Amphitrite'*, Paris, P. Geuthner, 1930

Pfister, Louis. *Notices biographiques et bibliographiques sur les jésuites de l'ancienne mission de Chine, 1552–1773*, 2 vols., Shanghai, 1932–4

Spolatin, Christofer A. *Matteo Ricci's Use of Epictetus*, Waegan, Korea, 1975

Taylor, R. L. *The Cultivation of Sagehood as a Religious Goal in Neo-Confucianism: A Study of Selected Writings of Kao P'an-lung (1562–1626)*, Ann Arbor, Scholars Press, 1978

Wei, Louis, Tsing-sing. *La Politique missionnaire de la France en Chine, 1842–1856*, Paris, Nouvelles éditions latines, 1960

Wills, J. E. and Spence, J. D. (eds.). *From Ming to Ch'ing: Conquest, Region and Continuity in Seventeenth Century China*, New Haven, Yale University Press, 1979

Wright, Arthur F., 'The Chinese language and foreign ideas', in *Studies in Chinese Thought*, ed. A. F. Wright, Chicago University Press, 1953, pp. 286–303

Wu Pei-i. 'Self-examination and confession of sins in traditional China', *Harvard Journal of Asiatic Studies*, XXXIX, 1, 1979, pp. 5–38

Xu Zongze. *Ming-Qing jian Yesu huishi yizhu tiyao*, Taipei, Zhonghua shuju, 1958

Yamaguchi, Hisakazu. 'Sonrai kara rinri e: O Fushi *Shôsho ingi* no tetsugaku', *Tôhôgaku*, LVII, 1979, pp. 48–61

Yü Chün-fang. *The Renewal of Buddhism in China: Chu-hung and the Late Ming Synthesis*, New York, Columbia University Press, 1981

Zürcher, Erik. 'The first anti-Christian movement in China (Nanking, 1616–1621)', in *Acta Orientalia Neerlandica*, ed. P. W. Pestman, Leiden, 1971, pp. 188–95

Index